A Researcher's
Glossary

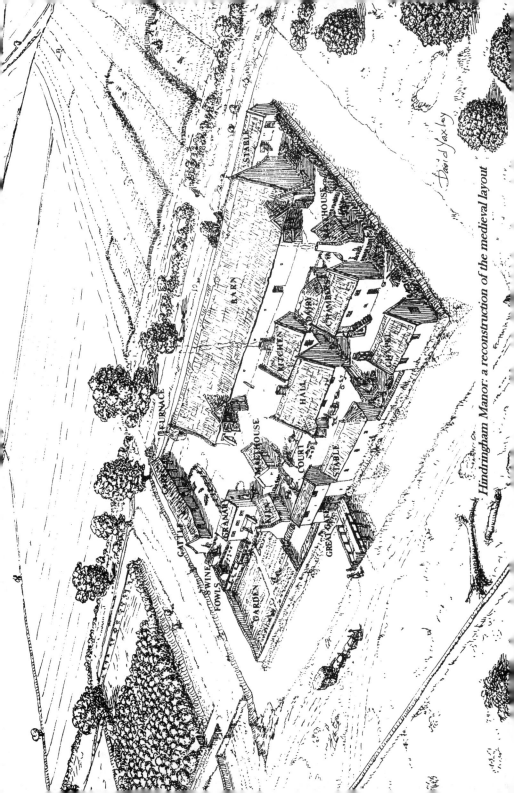

Hindringham Manor: a reconstruction of the medieval layout

A Researcher's
Glossary

of words found in historical documents
of East Anglia

Compiled by
David Yaxley

The Larks Press

Published at the Larks Press
Ordnance Farmhouse, Guist Bottom
Dereham NR20 5PF
Tel/Fax 01328 829207

Printed at the Lanceni Press
Garrood Drive, Fakenham

July 2003

British Library Cataloguing-in-Publication Data
A catalogue record for this book is available
from the British Library

The author is grateful for the facilities for study provided at
the Norfolk Record Office, the Suffolk Record Office (Ipswich branch),
the Public Record Office, Cambridge University Library, Houghton Hall,
and Elveden Estate.
He also acknowledges the great assistance given by the publications of the
Norfolk Record Society and the Norfolk and Norwich Archaeological Society.

ISBN 1 904006 13 2

INTRODUCTION

The material for this glossary has been collected in the course of reading many thousands of documents, most of them from Norfolk but some from north Suffolk. They include documents of the medieval manor; household, estate, and trade accounts; letters; probate records, particularly inventories and executors' accounts; lists; and memoranda. All save a few are from before *c.*1800. Many of the words in the glossary continued in use long after 1800, but the new trade, industrial, and technical terms coined in the 19th century and after have not been included, partly for reasons of space and partly because they can readily be found in modern or fairly modern dictionaries. It is a glossary of English words only; it includes vernacular words occurring in Latin documents, but it is *not* a dictionary of Latin terms. Neither is it a dialect dictionary, although many of the words contained in the glossary were part of the Norfolk 'dialect' or used in a dialectal way, and it is largely a glossary of material objects - buildings, furniture, utensils, implements, tools, and the terms connected with them - rather than the elements of everyday speech that are the stuff of most dialect dictionaries.

The intention of the glossary is to provide a handy reference-book for students of history who come across words like titters-rake and vambrace and would like to know their meaning. It does not pretend to be inclusive, and every reader will discover omissions. Many words that are apparently missing, however, may well be variant spellings of words that are in the glossary. Before the 19th century - and indeed during and after it - almost every written word could be spelt in a variety of ways, and it has not been possible to include even all the variations I have found. Words were sometimes spelt phonetically (see chair, pair, scales), but before the 19th century most of those who could write had had some sort of formal education and usually wrote a word as they thought it *ought* to be spelt rather than how it was pronounced. One way of identifying a word that at first appears unfamiliar is to say it out loud, or at least under the breath. Similarly, a handwritten word that appears at first glance to be un- readable or even nonsensical can often be understood by copying it exactly. Even if the word is correctly transcribed, however, its meaning may not be immediately clear, and one of the functions of this glossary is to provide a meaning, or a range of meanings, for obscure or obsolete words.

The glossary is not an encyclopaedia. The substantial entries for chairs and bedsteads, for example, are concerned with identifying the different types of those items as recorded in documents up to the end of the 17th century. Fine furniture is well beyond the scope of this modest book, and the reader will have to consult standard histories such as Ralph Edwards' *Shorter Dictionary of English Furniture* for the terminology of designs and materials after 1700. The enormous number and confusing nature of the terms used in the cloth trade has also posed problems; I have limited the entries to those words I have found in largely non-specialist inventories and accounts, and would not claim to have covered more than a

i

fraction of the almost infinite number of terms for cloths recorded from the Middle Ages onwards. Words such as barn, bell, or duck that have a clear, modern meaning, have not been included, neither has the 'normal' meaning of words such as catch, charger, or cheek, but there are entries under e.g. plough, where the parts of the implement need explanation, or tanning, where the materials and methods often have unusual or obsolete names. Legal terms in general use have not been included, but an explanation of a few types of conveyancing documents will be found in the Appendix at p. 243.

The quotations are illustrative of varying forms, spellings, usages, and descriptions. It is neither claimed nor implied that they are the earliest or latest known use of the word, but they give an idea of its chronological range. It is regretted that considerations of space and clarity of presentation do not permit references to be given.

Conventions

The head word or words of an entry are in **bold** type and in some entries include variant spellings. Words in SMALL CAPITALS within the entry are cross-references. All words in the quotations that may require explanation or elucidation will be found as head words. Sub-headings within the entry are underlined.

Alternative or multiple meanings

(a) When the meanings are close or related, or the meaning in the illustrative quotations is not clear, alternatives are either given together and separated by commas or semi-colons, or numbered within the entry.

(b) When the meanings are very disparate, separate entries are made.

Quotations

The quotations are in *italics* and are preceded by the year, corrected to the New Style (see entry under DATE). The quotations give the exact words and figures of the original, whether printed or manuscript. A line of three close dots ... means that a word or a phrase has been omitted for the sake of space or clarity. The spaced-out dots . . . mean that the subsequent part of the quotation comes from the same document but with a wider interval than ... Italic words in italic brackets *[italic]* are either

(a) a translation from the Latin. Roman numerals within *[ ]* have been translated to arabic numerals,

(b) a summary of e.g. the contents of a room, using the words of the original, or (c) the name of a room, the status or occupation of a person, etc.

Words in normal type in square brackets [normal] are editorial comment or explanation, or summaries not using the words of the original.

Words with a line through them e.g. ~~one chayer~~ are struck out in the original document.

Quotations in inverted commas are from printed authorities e.g. Sir Thomas Browne or the *Promptorium Parvulorum*. See bibliography.

ii

Abbreviations

Anglo-Fr.	Anglo-French
d.	pence; see entry under d. in text
Du.	Dutch
Fr.	French
Gr.	Greek
It.	Italian
L.	Latin
lb., lbs.	pound, pounds
li.	see entry under li. in text
M.	medieval
MDu.	middle Dutch
ME.	middle English
ML.	medieval Latin
MLG.	middle low German
MLWL	*Medieval Latin Word-List* (see Bibliography)
N.A.	*Norfolk Archaeology*
OE	old English
OED	*Oxford English Dictionary* (see Bibliography)
OFr.	old French
OFris.	old Frisian
OHG.	old high German
ON	old Norse
OSw.	old Swedish
OT.	old Teutonic
Prompt. Parv.	*Promptorium Parvulorum* (see Bibliography)
s.	shillings; see entry under s. in text
Sir Thomas Browne	See Bibliography
Sp.	Spanish
′	foot/feet
″	inch/inches

Bibliography

I have relied heavily on the *Oxford English Dictionary* for derivations and range of meanings. Far too many specialist books have been consulted to list, and this bibliography is largely confined to dictionaries and glossaries of varying date, scope, and usefulness.

Blount, T.	*Glossographia: or a Dictionary, Interpreting all such Hard Words... as are now used in our refined English Tongue* (1656).
Browne, Sir T.	'Notes on certain Birds found in Norfolk' and 'Notes on certain Fishes and Marine Animals found in Norfolk' in *Works* (1912) III, 513-39.
Coles, E.	*An English Dictionary* (1676).
Connor, R.D.	*The Weights and Measures of England* (1987).
Cotgrave, P	*Dictionnaire of the French and English Tongues* (1611).
Davies, T.L.O.	*A Supplementary English Glossary* (1881).
Forby, R.	*The Vocabulary of East Anglia* (1830, reprinted 1970).
Gee, E.	*A Glossary of Building Terms... from the Conquest to c. 1550* (1984).
Grigson, G.	*The Englishman's Flora* (1975).
Halliwell, J.O.	*Dictionary of Archaic Words* (1850, repr. 1989).
Halliwell, J.O. & Wright, T. (eds)	*A Glossary... by Robert Nares* (1888).
Kerridge, E.	*Textile Manufactures in Early Modern England* (1985).
Latham, R.E.	*Revised Medieval Latin Word-List* (1965).
Mayhew, A.L. & Skeat, W.W.	*Concise Dictionary of Middle English* (1888).
Nall, J.G.	*An Etymological and Comparative Glossary of the Dialect and Provincialisms of East Anglia* (1866).
Onions, C.T.	*A Shakespeare Glossary* (1953).
OED	*The Oxford English Dictionary* (1933, second edn. 1989).
Palsgrave, J.	*Les clarissement de la langue Francoyse* (1530).
Salzman, L.F.	*Building in England down to 1540* (1967).
Tweney, C.P. & Hughes, L.E.C.	*Chambers's Technical Dictionary* (1958).
Way, A. (ed.)	*Promptorium Parvulorum sive Clericorum (c.1440,* Camden Soc. 1843).
Wright, J.	*English Dialect Dictionary* (1896-1905).
Wright, T.	*Dictionary of Obsolete and Provincial English* (1886).
Yaxley, D.	*The Prior's Manor-Houses* (1988).

A

A botkin see BODKIN

abate to deduct, especially as discount for quantity. *1664: for 960 [cuttings] abating xvjd. for 200 Mr Morse had afterward vs. vjd.*

abel, abele, able the white poplar, *Populus alba*, yielding strong, light timber that takes nails without splitting. *1319: [carpenter felling] j abel [& riving it and mending the posterns]. 1581: aboute xl^tie years since there was an abell or a pople tree wch was Felled upon the greene. 1591: certayne bords of able xs. . . . xxxv^ty peeces of able sawen for ioystes xs...two bord stockes of the same tymber 1618: one abel tree iiijs.*

a bridges see SATIN

abyte habit (monk's). *1499-1500: [for] iij abytes [& 1 piece of stamin 25s.].*

achates, acat, acates, cates OFr. *achat* purchase: things bought, as against things taken from household stock. *1482: for fresh a cates bout into the howsold.*

acker see ACRE

acre OE *aecer, acer.* A piece of arable land; as much as an oxteam could plough in a day. Defined by statutes 5 Edw I, 31 Edw III, 24 Hen VIII as 40 poles x 4 poles = 4840 square yards, or four ROODS.

acre-staff stick, normally with iron point, used to clear weeds and soil from the coulter of a plough. *1306: j akerstaf jd.*

admiral formerly the commander-in-chief of the navy, with power of hearing all causes and matters to do with the sea. The jurisdiction of the admiralty court was extended by Henry VIII to deal with salvage, fishing, prizes, and general shipping disputes, and this was administered locally by a vice-admiral, usually a member of the gentry, in vice admiralty courts, before a judge rather than a jury. *1537: my lord Amberall.*

agaric, agrick a tree-fungus. 'Female agaric' (OED *Polyporus officinalis*), chiefly found on larch, is cathartic, and together with 'male agric' *Fomes fomentarius*, formerly *Polyporus fomentarius* and *Phellitis igniarius*, formerly *Polyporus igniarius*, used to stanch blood, as tinder, and in dyeing. *1605: A good Purge. Take two ounces of syrrup of Damask roses, two ounces of syrrup of Ruberbe, and one ounce of syrrup Agrick mixt together, and a third part taken in possit ale will serve for a good purge.*

agistment OFr. *agister* to lodge; ML. *adgistere.* Taking in livestock to feed at a rate per head; the rate for doing so. *1700: Estrayes & Egistments.*

ailestole see ALESTOOL

airey an area, enclosed or sunken court, giving access to the basement. *1732-3: Carring stone from ye lower yard to ye Airey in ye west front wher ye fire was & Cleaning ye steps.*

air gun air-guns, using the force of compressed air, were known by the middle of the 18th century. *1792: a curious Air Gun.*

aker, akerstaff see ACRE-STAFF

alb white linen garment with narrow sleeves covering the whole figure of a priest.

aldcopole see ALDER

alder *Alnus glutinosa*; the wood resists decay in wet conditions. Used for scaffolding poles. *1619: 4er lod Aldcopoles to the Building. 1620: for Felling Alders for the Scaffolds 9s. 6d.*

alembic Fr. *alambic*, cap of STILL; called LIMBECK till 17th century.

ale stool, ale stage trestle or X-stand for barrels. *1606: A tuner wth an alle stolle.*

allegants reysons, alligants raisins imported from Alicante, Spain; see RAISINS. *1647: 1 li. Alligants 3d. . . for 18 li. Allegants Reysons 5s. 3d.*

1

allom see ALMONDS; ALUM

almain rivett(t) OFr. *aleman*, German. Light armour made flexible by overlapping plates sliding on rivets. *1591: one almayne ryvett wth the hedpeice vjs viijd. 1597: Olde Almayne Ryvetts 33 & brestplats of olde Almayn Ryvets 4 div's splents for Almayn Ryvets.*

almanack annual table, calendar, with astronomical information. *1671: an almanack & Comb 1s.*

almary, almery see AMBRY

almayn OFr. *aleman* German. *1522: payer of hose of the Almayn facon. 1588: Almayne collar.*

almonds the kernel of the drupe or fruit of the almond tree, *Prunus dulcis* syn. *P. amygdalus.* Eaten after meat to aid digestion; used whole; ground to make thickening agency; ground and mixed with various liquids to make almond-milk; ground with sugar to make MARCHPANE or marzipan. Vallans: of Valencia, Spain, a well-known source of almonds and raisins. *1483: for xij li. of almonds Valans vs. 1587: ij li & a halfe of vallans almons xvijd. 1664: 6 ounces of armon given him fearing he bredd the pestilent fever. 1593: di' li alloms .*

almsman man in receipt of charity; living in almshouse.

altar, alter in church, a table or stand on which to place the consecrated elements of bread and wine, at the east end of the church or aisles. In pre-Reformation times often of stone and therefore rejected by the Protestants as redundant because Christ had made the supreme sacrifice; replaced in Church of England use by a wooden and movable communion table. *1513: a newe awtyr cloth. . . j kyrtell of Chamlett for an Awt' cloth. 1516: autyer.*

altar table, step, or lid; table on which food for doves was placed. *1584: a graven cupbord with an alter. 1665: made a new aulter for the dovehouse...the old one being decayed. . . made a table about the aulter in the dovehouse. . . two punches for the dovehouse aulter xijd.* [punch: supporting post, e.g in mine].

alum, allom hydrated double sulphate of aluminium and potassium, $KAl(SO_4)_2.H_2O$. Used in dyeing, tawing leather, and medicine. Roach alum: rock alum, probably unground. *1589: j qzter of allom. 1647: 1 li of Allum 4d. 1648: halfe a pound of Roach Allum 2d.*

amberall see ADMIRAL

amberie see AMBRY

ambling horse riding horse. See GELDING; NAG. *1588: amblinge nagge.*

ambry L. *armarium*, OFr. *ar'marie, al'marie*, CUPBOARD with door, safe, locker, for food, books, etc. 1602 quote suggests that an ambry hung on the wall, but see 1487. *1487: ij almaryes like a chayer. 1507: cupbord wt an almary in it. 1513: j oold almery. 1595: an ambrye Cubbard. 1597: j ould coulde & j standing ould amery xvjd. 1602: an amery or hanging hutche. 1603: for an amberie a tabell a chare chiste ixs.*

amercement arbitrary fine left to 'mercy' of lord or jury in manor court.

amery, amrye see AMBRY

amice piece of white linen worn over priest's head like hood; cloth for wrapping, scarf.

ampletree see HAMPLETREE

amyste amethyst. See OUCH.

ancares see ANCHORESS

anchor see also ANKER. 1. Ship's anchor. *1584: two Ancres. . . twoo ferrie botes with ancres & cables & ores viij li.* 2. Double pothook. *1592: the angers in the chemny with the haks* 3. End of tie-rod in a house. *1410: [two] ankers [in the east end of the Guildhall weighing 38 lb price of each lb 2d.] 1432-3: les Ankeres. 1576-9: a Barr of yron for the Ancore. 1612: for xx li. of small anchers att iijd. quarter pound xvjs. ixd...for vj anchers and two bolts wayinge v stone ix cwt and a half at iijd. per pound xixs. xd. 1665: puting up the anker at the barnes gabeles end.* 4. Heavy timber acting as support, foundation etc. for e.g. bridge or dam. *1576: iiij peces of ix fote longe for anckors of*

2

Dammyng ijs. xv loades of claye to dam with vs.

anchoress, ancares, ankares female hermit, religious recluse. *1484: to the ankeres in Conesford I bewueth iijs. iiijd.*

anchorite, anker male hermit, recluse. *1484: to the anker at the White Freres in Norwich I bequeth iijs. iiijd.*

ancient, ancyent corruption of ensign; standard, flag; also the bearer of an ensign. *1588: hanging out the ancyents and dryeng the powder. . . iij hedds for the ancyent staves. 1637: an auncient of redd & white taffety sarcenet & a drumm.*

ancre see ANCHOR

andirons, anderns, anders, andieryrnese firedogs, in pairs, distinguished from the simple DOGIRONS by the ornamental front end, standing on either side of the hearth to support logs; often decorated and part of a set. See pp. 61, 117, 241. *1352: aundiron. 1459: aunderis for Lecchen. 1588: one great payer of Andeyerns of Flemmyngs work. 1588: a paire of Andyrons of Copper wth Antiks ov' the Toppes xvs. 1590: arndon. 1591: iron anders 1592: andieryrnese. 1593: 1 paire of Andirons of brasse & wood. 1597: a payer of Aundyrons garnyshed wth Latten. . . a payer of tongs lykewise garnished. . . one payer of latten Aundyrons wth their cases: one payer of Doggeyrons. 1620: one paier of Andyrons tipped with brasse with their fier shovell and tonges suteable.*

angel a gold coin, first minted 1465, the angel was a new issue of the NOBLE, and had the archangel Michael on the reverse; it was first called the angel-noble, and had a value of 6s. 8d. In 1526 the new issue had a value of 7s. 6d., which in 1550-3 rose to 10s. The half-angel of 1604 had a value of 5s. 6d.

angel gold standard or 'guinea' gold. *1588: cheane of Angell golde.*

anker from Dutch or German measure of wine or spirits: the cask in which it was held, being 10 old wine GALLONS or 8⅓ imperial gallons. *1738: Three Half Ancors 1s.*

anker see ANCHOR; ANCHORITE

ankeres see ANCHORESS

antigugle small siphon inserted into mouths of vessels to admit air without gurgling, used for liquids liable to sediment. *1738: silver Antigugle.*

antik, antick It. *antico* grotesque animal or human figure; classical-type head, figure. *1588: a paire of Andyrons of Copper wth Antiks ov' the Toppes xvs. 1619: For the porch dore in the First court entering into the Hall enlarged with stone workmanship and carving with ppoint Jaume and a vause and over ech palester an antick head.*

antiphonal, antiphoner, antyfener book of music for antiphons or anthems, and other portions of service music in the unreformed church.

apentis see PENTICE

aperne, aporne see APRON

apice apprentice, learner

aplate a piece of armour, possibly shoulder-piece or pauldron, perhaps from same derivation as epaulet. *1444: [j sword, 2 irons called] aplates.*

apparitor, apparator an official messenger and summoner for the ecclesiastical courts.

apparel apart from the usual meaning of clothing, it was a strip of coloured material on the front edge of the AMICE, bottom of the ALB, etc.

appropriation the medieval practice of monasteries receiving from laymen TITHES and other property and endowments for parish use. See RECTOR.

approwement OFr. *aproer, approuer* to profit; turning something to profit. *1450: approwement of my londes.*

apres cloth of Ypres? See ARRAS. *1459: j cover of apres, lynyd with lynen clothe. j tester and j seler*

3

of the same.

apron cloth or leather garment worn down the front for work and to protect other clothing; ornamental apron. *1592: on aperne. 1595: two lytle apornes one stuffe aporne. 1598: small Lynnen & one napern. 1647: 2 yards of Canvas to make Gageinge* [boy servant] *Aprons 2s. 4d.*

apron platform or beam at bottom of sluice to intercept fall of water and prevent erosion. *1595: one beame aperne and a beame.*

aqua composit L.*composita* compound, synthesis; medicinal compound. *1593 a pinte of aqua composit xvjd.*

aqua vitae ardent spirits, unrectified alcohol; brandy. *1595: an aquavite glasse.*

archer chest see CHEST

architrave main beam resting on abacus, on capital of column; elements of door or window surround; moulding round exterior of arch.

ark OE *arc*, L. *arca*, chest; CHEST, box, closed basket; meal-chest. *1592: a arke standinge in the hale. 1595: an old arkt.*

arm ? candleholder. *1751: two Oval Sconces in carved & Gilt Frames, Ribbands Ditto & double Branches, six brass Arms.*

arming forming part of arms or armour. See ARROW; BOW; DAGGER; SWORD.

arming nail rivets for joining pieces of armour. *1483: for ij^c of armyngnayle of one sorte ijd...for iij^c of armyngnayle of a nother sorte xijd.*

armon see ALMONDS

armour generally refers to full or part body-armour. White armour: perhaps painted white; polished steel. Bright armour: polished. Black armour: unpolished or blackened. Gilt: gilded, see GILT, PARCEL GILT. Proof: of tried strength, quality; proof against weapons. Plate armour: armour consisting of wrought metal plates joined together to form a continuous protection. Scale armour: armour consisting of small overlapping plates of iron or steel. *1588: one blake Armore of Proofe. 1593: 2 horsemans Armor 1 blacke 1 white. 1597: 2 Launce Armors black complet 2 Launce Armors whyte complet Rem. at Wrights of Norwch Armorer. . . one bright Armor complete rybbed, a launce Armor whyte without the gorgett, a bright Armor pcell guylt complete. . . Coats of plate:10, shirts of male 3 olde & 36 pecs of male small & great. 1608: 10 spurketts of woodworke to hange armor one. 1620: 2 Daies Di' makeinge a frame to hange the Armor uppon.* See also: ALMAYN RIVETT; APLATE; AVENTAIL; BASINET; BRIGANDINE; BURGANETT; CHAMFRAIN; CORSLETT; CUERET; CUISSE; GAMBESON; GARBRASSE; GORGET; GUSSET; HABERGEON; HAKETON; HEADPIECE; JACK; LANCE ARMOUR; MAIL; MILAN; MORRION; PALLET; PARVIS; PAUNCE; PEITREL; PLACARD; PLATE; POLAYN; POLLESON; POLLET; PROOF; SALLET; SLEEVE; SPLENT; VAMBRACE.

arndorn see ANDIRON

arquebus see HARQUEBUS

arras errands

arras, arrys cloth from Arras in Artois; rich TAPESTRY with figures and scenes. *1459: banker of arras. . . j clothe of arras, of the Schiperds. . . j hangyd bedd of arras. . . j clothe of arras, of the Morysh daunce. 1467: serten hokes fore to holde the aras hover a schemeny xijd. 1588: two cusshens of Arras, wth the Armes of the Godsalves, & Townesend. 1597: 6 pieces of Arrys sylk & gold wherof 2 are wyndowe pieces being in depth j yard di' qrter: & thone in length iij yards: thother ij yards 3 qrters: the great piecs bene in depth iij yards di': & in length the first 5 yards 3 qrters the second 8 yards j qrter: the third 2 yards: & the iiijth: 7 yards 3 qrters. . . A Counterpoynt of Imagery Arras.* See HANGING.

arrow a projectile with sharp iron/steel tip and feathered for flight, usually for the long bow, but also applied to missiles from firearms. The standard arrow seems to have been 36 inches long (see YARD), and differed from bearing arrows and FLIGHT arrows. *1592: Syxe*

shefe of Callyver arrowes...fyve shefe of Arminge arrowes...Two shefe of musket arrowes ijs. viijd.
arsenic, arsnicke used for rat-poison etc., and for medicine in small doses.
arstellawe, astellabe, astrolabe an instrument to take altitude; arrangement of armillary circles, circles of the heavens. *1459: j arstellawe* [possible misreading of astellabe].
artichoke usually the globe artichoke, *Cynara scolamus*, probably a cultivated version of the cardoon, and brought to England from Italy in the early 16th cent. The leaves or scales of the flower, and its base, are eaten. The Jerusalem artichoke *Helianthus tuberosus* is a sunflower from S. America. 'Jerusalem' is a corruption of It. *girasole*, sunflower. The tubers are edible. *1648: 12 Hartichokes 1s. 6d.*
ash the common ash, *Fraxinus excelsior*, provides a hard timber, easily split or riven, much used for tool handles and boards, etc. *1538-9: a pece of asche for sple'tur. . . a man ryvyng the same sple'tur for the gyant. 1592: Eashe borde. 1620: Felling & Carying ashes to make ladders & hooks. 1655: 2^C of ashen stuffe for Poles & axells for Coaches.* See HURRE.
ash wood ash was the main constituent of LYE, used for washing clothes etc. *1654: 2 Bushells of ashes to wash with 16d. 1714: a Butter Baskett an ashkettle and ashes 4s. 6d... a letch a wash Baskett.*
ashbing bin for ash to make LYE.
ashlar OFr. *aiseler, aisselier, esselier*, from L. *axis, assis* axle, board, plank; squared, hewn stone. *1465-6: every asheler is xij ynche thykke and xviij ynches longe, wiche multiplied to gedere make ij C xvj ynches. 1620: hewinge 1720 fotte of fresestone vizt Ashlees att iijd ye fotte. 1621: p point Ashler.*
aspen the wood of the aspen, *Populus tremula*, was used for light baskets or 'chips'. *1579: for xxij Espes xvjs.*
assize standard of quality or measurement of e.g. bread, ale, according to the ordinances.
astell OFr. *astelle, astele*, from late L. *hastella*, dim. of *hasta*; splint, thin board. *1410: [1 cartful of] astell [bought in the market 41d.].*
astellabe see ARSTELLAWE
audit ale ale of special strength brewed for use at the annual audit, rent-day etc.
audit chamber chamber in which to keep and audit household, estate, manorial accounts. *1597: The Audit Chamber.*
aulter, autyer, awtry see ALTAR
aumbry see AMBRY
auncient see ANCIENT
aunderis, aundiron see ANDIRON
austrige board see ESTRICH
avaylle profit. *1450: the avaylle of my Conyes.*
aventail OFr. *esventail* air-hole; movable front or mouthpiece of helmet. *1352: ij bacenets cum aventails. 1459: v ventayletts for bassenetts.*
axe there were many types of axes for different purposes. The butcher's axe was used to fell or kill animals, and may be the same as the pole-axe, which had a hammer at the back. The chip-axe was a small axe used with one hand for shaping timber. See also ADZE; BELTE; TWYBILL; p. 242. *1593: in the slaughter howse ij butchers exses. 1588: one chipp Axe.*
axe short for axe-tree, beam. *1323: j axe [for the well 11d.].*
axez ague. *1459: I was falle seek with an axez.*
axle to put an axle into a cart etc. *1417: for exelying of ye carte viijd.*
axletree axle beam of cart, well etc. *1417: an exeltre & ye clavis jd. ob. 1631: ye Axelltree rope Chaine and buckett for ye Drawe well vs.*

5

B

Baaschaumbre, le base chamber i.e. lower chamber or cellar. *1386: [1 lock with nails for the door of the chamber called] le baaschaumbre.*

babin bobbin

back(e)house the house or room at the back of the main house; outshot, leanto, single room used as adjunct to kitchen. Can mean the BAKEHOUSE.

baby doll. *1695: For a Baby for young Miss by my mr his appointmt 1s. 6d.*

backbond, -band, -rope broad leather strap or rope passing over cart-saddle on back of horse and supporting shafts of cart. *1417: iiij bakropys.*

back chair, stool see CHAIR

backiron see BICKERN

back pan baking pan. *1590: ij scommers, a back panne, ij fryinge pannes.*

backrope, bakrope see BACKBOND

baderycke, badryke see BALDRIC

baestyn basting, as wooden spoon/ladle for basting. *1588: one saese of latyn one ladull & a baestyn sticke.*

baffle board or beam that restricts flow e.g. in sluice. *1595: ij elmynge Baffles.*

bag bags came in all shapes and sizes, often for specialised use. *1327: j bagg [for the court rolls 2d.]. 1593: 1 Chesse borde chesse men & chesse bagg iiijd.*

baggs badges. *1588: a testure imbrodred wth Baggs.*

bagnio bath. *1751: a Copper for the use of the Bagnio with Lead Iron Work &c.*

bail see BILE

baize see BAYES

bakehouse room or detaching building with OVEN for baking. See BACKHOUSE.

balas OFr. *balais,* ML *balascus,* from Arabic *balakhsh,* an area near Samarkand where they were found. A rose-coloured ruby. *1467: a nowche of goolde set with a fyne safyre, a grete balyse and v perles.*

balaster see BALUSTER

bald(e) see BALLED

baldric, baderycke, badrycke, ballderk, bawedreck leather strap running diagonally across chest to support sword etc.; strap to support shield; leather strap from which clapper of bell hung. *1545: A syde of lether for ye bawedrecks of ye bells.*

balenger, balinger OFr. *baleinier,* whale-ship. The balinger was a small, light, single-masted sea-going ship of the 15th and 16th centuries. *1466: ij c of oken borde for the new balynger. 1467: my mastyr solde his parte of the balenger to Hew Candy for viij marc.*

balkes, le large baulks or timbers. *1357: viij balkes [for malt-kiln]. 1371: [repairing the kiln with] le balkes [removing and raising].*

ball (archit.) ornamental ball of brick or stone to surmount wall, pillar, turret etc. *1665: great neckes collers & balls. . . two moulds [wooden] for great & small bowles for tirrets.*

ballderk see BALDRIC

balled, bald (horse) uncut horse, a stallion, with balls i.e. testicles. *1562: great balde horse. 1590: one bayed balde truncke horse iij li. vjs. viijd. 1665: the browne bald horse colt.* See STONED.

ballester see BALUSTER

ballhous, bellhouse bellows

ballimong see BULLIMONG

balm wine medicinal drink prepared from various herbs including balm *Melissa officinalis*

6

and field balm or lesser calamint *Clinopodium calamintha*; wine flavoured with oil of balsam. *1738: [10 gallon cask of] Balm Wine 6s.*

baluster, balaster, balester   It. *balausta, balaustra*, from *balausto*, flower of wild pomegranate, the double-curving calyx-tube of which resembles the shape of the baluster. Fr. *balustre.* Corrupted to barrester, bannister by 17th cent. Short pillar or post of stone or wood supporting rail. *1655: [breaking* CARFE *with dimensions] for Railes and Ballesters. . . for turning 68 Ballesters at 5d. & 2 Heads upon ye long walkes gate 4s. a peece. 1665: flitch for balusters. . . baluster stock. . . overwhart cutts for balasters.*

baly bailiff

balyse see BALAS

banbury vat see VAT

band, shirt neck band or collar of shirt to make it fit closely. *1590: three Shirte Bandes.*

bandoleer, bandeleire, bandileare   Fr. *bandouillere*, It. *bandoliera*, Sp. *bandolera*, dim. of *banda*, band; broad belt worn over shoulder and across breast to support musket, with a number of pouches for charges. *1592: Ten bandeleires vs.*

banker, bankar   Anglo-Fr. *banquer*, banker, covering for bench; extended to long narrow piece of cloth or tapestry. *1444: ij bankar. 1459: j banker of arras with a man schetyng at j blode hownde. . . j banker hangyng tapestry worke. . . j nothir of tapestry worke newe, in the hall wendowe. 1481: xvj yerdes of banker viijs.*

bankettinge trencher see TRENCHER

banquetting house detached, ornamental building in garden for special meals; room for formal meals. *1654: thatchinge ye Banquettinge House.*

banyan   Arabic *banyan*, trader; garment worn by same; loose gown or shirt. *1763: banyan of Norwich toy* [cloth].

bar earth bank. *1311 [making] barres[& hedges in Le Laund].*

bar(re) iron strengthening band on gate, window etc. *1298: ix barres [of iron and nails for the church window]. 1312: [making 7 staples and] ij barres [for the great gate and the gate on the bridge] ijd. ob. 1315: j barre & j stapel [for the south gate 2d.]. 1321: barres [of iron] & snecks iijd.*

barber's block round block on which wigs were made and displayed. *1763: 4 Barbers Blocks & 1 stand 7s. 6 Wigg stands 4s. 6d.*

barberry, bareberry   ML. *barbaris.* The once common barberry, *Berberis vulgaris*, supplied acid berries, used as fruit and flavouring, and the bark yielded a yellow dye. It was also used for curing jaundice. The bushes were eradicated by farmers in the 18th and 19th centuries as they were supposed to act as host to cereal rust. *1647: gathering the Bareburies Tho: Campe fecht 6d.*

barde barred. See CHEST.

bare threshed. *1654: for 8 Coome Fetches bare.*

bare to prune, take out branches. *1647: bareinge & bushinge of the younge trees.*

barffehowes shed, shelter of rough materials. See BARFREY. *1590: fishous & barffehowes.*

barfrey 1. The medieval meaning was tower, shelter, shed, penthouse; the word from which 'belfry' was corrupted. *1310: [carpenter for two days making] j berfrey [in the carthouse]. 1326: [making] j barfrey [on the long house].* 2. Specific building timber, neither stud, spar, rafter, joist, brace, nor groundsill. The 1662 quote gives a barfrey of 18 feet, which at 2d. a foot is cheaper than studs in the same account (3d. a foot), more expensive than a pair of spars (1s. 8d. the couple), and the same price as joists. *1298: j roftre iiij stuch ij borfreyis ij Byer & iij Wyndbeams. 1593: [carpenter] one dorman one payre of silles one payre of barfraies. 1597: ij Sparrs a Barfrie pees & ij braces xviijd. 1608-9: fower peces...for barferies & wyndbeames. 1662: a bocke & sprendles & 2 peeces of barphew & short sparres...barphew 18 foot long at 2d. the foot.*

barg tool, ? chisel or cold-chisel. *1590: j barg. . . j old bardg* [among carpenter's tools].
bargain and sale see p.243
bargeboards boards, often ornamental, fixed on to the gable-ends of a roof, originally to protect the edge of the thatch.
barleyseal, -siel, -sele season for sowing barley.
barn, tithe barn in which TITHE corn etc. was stacked and threshed, not any large barn.
barphew see BARFREY
barras, barus, barrus coarse linen, originally imported from Holland. *1718: [coach] new Crimson Caffey Seat Cloth...Lined with a Striped Barus...a new Striped Barrus lining.*
barrator OFr. *barateor*, fraudulent dealer, cheat; buyer and seller of ecclesiastical offices, simonist. *1603: indyted for a comon barrator.*
barrel a unit of capacity. In the 15th century a barrel of beer was 36 GALLONS, a barrel of ale 32 gallons; this carried on until 1688 when a barrel of beer or ale was to be 34 gallons, which also was the capacity for vinegar from 1699. In 1803 the capacity for ale and beer was raised to 36 gallons, and in 1824 it became 36 Imperial gallons. The wine barrel was 31½ wine gallons, which were smaller than ale gallons. The barrel of herrings and eels seems to have varied from 30 gallons to 32 gallons, and should have contained 1440 fish. Soap and honey were generally 32 gallons to the barrel, oil 31½ gallons. See R.D. Connor, *The Weights and Measures of England*, pp.172-5, for this extremely complicated matter. Barrels and casks were used not just for liquids but also to carry harness, armour, clothes etc. on board ship. See also LAST; PIPE; TUN.
barrel, tin for containing spring blinds. *1751: two tin spring Barrels. 1792: 3 blind barrells & sundry pulls.*
barrel churn see CHURN   bearing barrow 13th cent.
barrow, bearing a stretcher-type handbarrow, without wheel. See CRUDBARROW; WHEELBARROW. *1576: for a bearing Barrowe xvjd. for ij Whele Barrowes vijs. viijd.*
barrow hog a castrated boar. *1603: A sowe two barrowe hogs and two piggs xxxs.*
barsreleive, basareleave see BAS-RELIEF.
bartlement see BATTLEMENTS
barwe a barrow. See CRUDBARROW; WHEELBARROW
basan, bazan see BASIL
base base or plinth for a main post. *1344: [making] bases [placing the said] bases. 1423: bases & powayles.*
basil, bassell sheepskin tanned in bark. See TANNING. *1602: xj bassell skines iijs. viijd.*
basinet, bascenet, bassinet OFr. *bacinet, bassinet*, dim. of *bacin*, basin. Small light round headpiece of armour, closed at the front with AVENTAIL or visor. *1352: ij bacents [with aventails]. 1459: ventayletts for bassentts.*
bas-relief ornamental low relief in stone or wood. *1733: Takeing down ye Chimney peice in ye Dining room to putt in a new mantle & ye Basareleave. . . puting the Barsreleive and Chimney peice.*
bast OE *bæst*, inner bark of lime tree, plaited to make Russia matting; rope made of bast. *1340: vij cord de Bast [for horses and cows]. 1361: [7 pairs of] bastes [for tethering cows in summer 2s. 4d.]. 1410: basten ropes.*
bastard musket see MUSKET
baste plover see PLOVER
bastell OFr. *bastille*, late L. *bastilia* from *bastire*, to build; tower, bastion of castle. *1459: salt saler like a bastell.*
bat fowling *Prompt. Parv.:* 'Batfowlyn (or go to take birdes in the nyght, P.)'. Catching

8

birds by night when roosting. A bat fowling net had two forms: either shaped like a large tennis-racket with a head approx. 5 feet long by 3 feet wide, on a handle (17th century), or a semicircle of wood, hinged in the middle and held at either end of the semicircle, with a loose net forming a pouch. *1603: a bat fowling nett. 1673: a batt fowling nett 5s.*

Bath stove 18th-century hob grate, with a plate just above the fire to produce a draught, which was often excessive. *1779: A Handsome Bath stove.*

bathing In the Middle Ages bathing in the higher ranks of society was often a communal activity, with a board across the large tub to hold food and drink. The bath-tub itself was wooden, padded inside with linen or other cloth to avoid splinters. Bathing probably became more frequent in the 18th century, although there is little evidence either way - there are some references to personal washing or bathing utensils in inventories before then, but the ordinary basins, KEELERS and tubs would have been used. *1709: bathing tub.*

batter basket possibly battel from *battle*, to feed, nourish; or basket with batter, i.e. sides sloping inward to top. *1713: batter basket.*

battering axe masons' axe or hammer for rough shaping of stone. 'Battering' also meant reworking, sharpening. *1733: pd the Smith for battering Axes shuting Saws &c.*

battledore, batleder, batteldor flat wooden bat or BEETLE used in washing clothes, also for smoothing linen; hence also applied to similarly-shaped tools, e.g. baker's peel; small wooden bat used in game of battledore and shuttlecock. *1583: one maunde & a batleder. 1591: one battledore & one rowlinge pynn iiijd. 1595: a flaskett for clothes a rowling pynne & a battledore. 1612: batledore to smoth clothes. 1685: shittle cocks & battledores.*

battle-door barley a species of cultivated barley, *Hordeum zeocriton*, with short broad ears, nearly extinct in 1848; also called sprat barley. *1654: for 3 Coom of seed - battle-door Barly 1 li. 4s.*

battlements vertically-indented parapet, originally for defence. The higher parts were cops or merlons, the lower spaces between them embrasures or crenelles. By the 16th century battlements were largely ornamental, and in Norfolk were often quite small in scale and made of moulded brick. In the 17th century battlements or bartlements were sometimes flat roofs over e.g. bay windows or porches, and the walls fronting them. 'Battlementing' can also mean DENTILATION. *1600-2: The barlments decayed & rotten for want of covering with lath & mortar & leade...ij great wyndaws next the gardyn...the barllments over them being of timber for want of being covered with leade lathe &c rotten. 1620: Battlemts xvij*[XX] *xviij Att jd. ob. A peice. 1686: for 20 Battlements from Burneham 10s. 1665: lowning the wall both sides the porters lodge setting ramping battlements upon the same & round about the porters lodges, battlementing the eaves on both sides the said court yard.* See RAMPING.

baudkin, bawdkyn see BODKIN

bauk balk of timber. *1647: a new Bauke for ye Iron Harrow 1s. 6d.*

bawdreck see BALDRIC

bay mill dam, embankment, retaining wall. *1274: xxx bord ad bayam vs. in carp' baye viijd. ob. 1279: j bord ad baya' [boat bay]. 1288: [carpenter making] j Baye [at the eastern head of the pond with putting it in position and ramming it]. 1320: bord de Wakefeld [for the repair] del bay [of the great bridge].*

bay the bay-tree, *Laurus nobilis*, bore berries that were supposed to be effective against poisons of venomous creatures, and would help in childbirth, consumption, coughs etc. *1589: iij li. of bayes ixd.*

bayle, bayling see BILE

bayes, baize Fr. *baies* from L. *badius* chestnut-coloured; thickish woollen cloth with short nap, originally with a linen warp. The manufactury was introduced into England 1561. It was produced in many colours.

bayne bath, BAGNIO. *1482: paid at the bayne for you vs. iiijd*

bead see BED

beads string of 165 beads divided into 15 sets, for devotional purposes in the Roman Catholic church; rosary. Usually referred to as a pair. *1474: a box with bedys, qwere of ij payre of jett, with Paternosterys of corall xld...v payre of box xd...a payre of beddes of segamore iiijd...a payre of bedys of ambre, xxd...a payre of beydys of jette with Patter nosteris of corall, pris xxd. 1513: J peyir Corall bedes iij tymez l[s] Gawdeez sylv' and Gylt. J peyir beedez of blake Gette Gawdees of sylv' and gylt.*

beake, beaker see BICKERN

beam, beam knife, beam nail see PLOUGH

beamfill, bemefill to fill in the space between the WALLPLATE and the rafters, or between the rafters themselves or vertical studs of a wall. *1467: made a comenaunt with Saunson the tylere that he schalle pergete and whighte and bemefille alle the new byldynge, and he schall have for his labore, xiijs. iiijd., and ij M[le] of bryke.*

bearing blanket, cloth, sheet child's christening-robe; burying cloth. *1513: a lytyl beryngshete wt a opeyn red seme. 1592: Beryng blanket ijs. 1595: one bearing cloth & a fac clothe viijs.*

bearing skep large skep with 2 upright handles through which a pole was thrust for carrying by 2 persons. See p. 242; CORBELL. *1352: v Beringskippes. 1444: j beryngsceppes. 1504-5: ij beryng skeppes vd.*

beat to dress stone; dressing i.e. recutting mill-stones. *1536: betyng of the mill. 1647: beatinge on the stones of the horse mill. 1733: Beating Tarris & pointing Do &c [masons].*

beaufat buffet. *1771: Beaufat £2 6s.*

beaver felted cloth. *1417: v yerdis of bever for horse hansis.*

beaver hat made of beaver-fur. *1459: j hatte of bever, lynyd with damaske gilt* [misreading of silk?]. *c.1626: as for a beaver hate, if you cowld fitt your selfe with a spetiall good on...I send 50s. to bye on if it coms to a littell more I will allow it.*

bech, beech the common beech, *Fagus sylvatica.* See BOARD.

beck large shallow vessel, tub. See LIMBECK; UNDERBECK. *1745: beck over the Copper...beck under the marsh tub.*

beck, bek ON *bekkr*, OE *bece*, brook, stream.

beckharne see BICKERN

bed loosely-woven worsted or serge cloth for bed hangings. *1602: iiij mydell beads of darnocks at j li. vs. iij Elbrod darnocke beads at j li. vijs.*

bed often refers to the furniture of a bed, e.g. MATTRESS etc., bedlinen, curtains and canopy. See BEDSTEAD. *1597: cunnyfer bedd* [coney or rabbit fur]. *1745: white work'd India bed.* Feather bed: mattress stuffed with feathers. Flock bed: mattress stuffed with tufts and refuse of wool and cotton. Other materials for the mattress were chaff (flights) and straw (palliasse). *1584: A canvice flock bed. 1589: a strawe bedde wth a bolster of strawe a payer of sheets an empty matterys & a cou'let. 1591: a chaffebedde. 1597: a cunnyfer bedd. 1716: a flight bed.*

beddes, bedys see BEADS

bedell see BEETLE

bedscrews possibly cramps. *1751: One old Jack, two setts of Bedscrews, a Table, a Bench.*

bedstead the different types of bedstead and furniture of the bed have been grouped for convenience under this heading.

bedcord cord for trussing between holes in the bedframe to support the bed or mattress. See bedlines. *1708: 128 Bed Cords at 3 li. 4s.*

bedhead: vertical head, often carved, of the bed; see tester. *1591: a bedsheade & Featt.*

bedlines: cords trussed across the bedframe to support mat, mattress, and bed; occur in

10

pairs (for cross-trussing?). *1464: lyne to the same bed vjd. 1595: a payer of bedd leynes. 1665: Two bed lynes waying 8¾ pound 3s. 6d.*

bedmat: thin strong mat laid over bedlines and under mattress or featherbed. *1620: a canvas mattresse and a Bedmatt.*

bedpan: warming pan. The excretory sense was probably not in use till 19th century. *1584: A bedd panne xvjd.*

bedsettle: 1. SETTLE convertible to a bed. 2. Settle en suite with bed, or at foot. *1592: Bedsettle. 1604: ij bedsettells.*

bedsides: boarded or pannelled sides that were joined at head and foot to make a bed. See below, boarded. *1589: j playne bedstead & iij sydes for a bed xijd. 1590: ij payer of bedsides. 1593: one old pair of bedboards. 1597: the head foote & one syde of a bedstead.*

bedstaff: 1. A staff for smoothing down linen on bed. 2. A staff for putting across bed-frame to support bedding; the common number seems to have been six. *1595: halfe a doz' bedde staves. . . vj bedstaves. 1620: a long Bedstaff and sixe short.*

bellknops: ornamental knobs at each corner of a bedstead with canopy or ceiling.

boarded: 1. Bed with boarded or panelled sides; usual implication of the term is of a second or third-rate bed. 2. With boards rather than bedlines to support bed. Boarded bedsteads do not usually have testers or canopies mentioned and should be seen as unenclosed beds. *1588: j borded bedsteade, wth a testor xvjs. 1589: 3 sydes for a bed. 1591: bourden beds. 1591: three payre of borded Bedsteedes. . . bording bed fastened to the plancher wth nailes. 1591: old bourthersbedsteads.*

canopy: roof of a bed, either of cloth or of wood, when it is called the ceiling. *1597: A Cannopie paned wth tufftaffeta white & black: & cloth of bawdkyn wch is lyned wth redd buckerhm: the head gylt & the bellknops lykewise.* See below, sparver.

ceiled: 1. Posted bedstead with wooden canopy or ceiling. 2. 'Ceiled' in sense of panelled (as in ceiled chamber) would mean a panelled bedstead, with or without tester or canopy. See CEIL. *1467: a bede, a cyle, a counterpeynt and a testor of Aras with out goolde. 1592: a bedstede wth a seelinge of waynescott vs. 1595: one seeled bedstead. 1597: a selyng bedstead.*

couch bedstead: bed with dual use as couch or daybed. *1590: Cooch bedd. 1636: one couch bedsteade. 1637: one old Cowch wth a bed twilted of blewe lynen cloth the cou'inge of braunched stuff figured wth greene & oring tawney pt silke.*

dower: part of the wife's dowry. *1637: one dowere bed.*

fabrics: used for head, curtains, canopy, tester, valence, bed coverings. *1593: [posted bed with wainscot head] with tester & vallence of redd cloth...5 curtains of redd & yellowe saye. 1597: 2 trayne Curtains of sarsenet in 8 panes redd & grene. 1637: one guilt bedstead the valines of cloath of gould & taffety curtines 6 li. 13s. 4d.*

field: bed that could be dismantled for portability, often used by officers of the musters in the field. *1588: one filde bedde of yron, wth a tester of black Buckeram wth Godsalves armes. . . one filde bedsteade wth a tester of saye and Curtens of Mockadowe. 1593: feild bedstede corded 1 matt the tester 4 Curtins of painted fustein 3 Curtine Rodds 1 fetherbedd 1 boulster 2 blanketts 1 cou'inge of pullm worke wth birds eyes & 1 longe ioyned forme iij li. 1792: a field Bedstead.* See below, standing.

Flanders: of Flemish or Dutch fashion i.e. a panelled bedstead with curtains and tester. *1592: Flaunders seled bedstead.*

folding: portable bed folding into a box. *1592: a lytle fowldinge bedsted of waynscote vjs. viijd.*

French: bed with simple wooden frame covered with material and curtains to form plain rectangular box. *1636: one frenche bedsteade wth the furniture.*

gilt: exposed posts and headboard gilded. *1637: [Great Parlour Chamber] one guilt bedstead the valines of cloath of gould & taffety curtines 6 li. 13s. 4d.*

11

<u>half-headed</u>: bed with canopy covering only top half of bed, supported only by the posts of the bedhead. See <u>tester</u> below. *1591: half headed bed. 1792: half teaster Bedstead.*

<u>hanging bed</u> see <u>trussing</u>

<u>irons</u>: *[smith] 4 irons to a bedstead 8d.*

<u>joined</u>: joined work as opposed to boarded or panelled bed. *1592: joyned bed.*

<u>livery</u>: 'livery' has the connotation of service, servants etc., e.g. allowance of food, drink, clothing etc. (see CUPBOARD; LIVERY). Many livery beds were undoubtedly for servants of varying status. However, some were sophisticated and of considerable value; the two most valuable beds at Thornage Hall in 1593 were livery beds. In this and other large inventories they are differentiated from <u>posted</u> bedsteads; heads, canopies, and curtains are listed with the more valuable livery bedsteads. One possibility is that the livery bed was a postless bed of the medieval form, with canopies and curtains suspended from the ceiling of the room, but there was certainly a good deal of woodwork about many livery beds. *1573: wax, rosell & turpentine to gome the livery beddes. 1593: 1 liverye bedstead wth a tester and valence of red & yellowe saye xxxvjs. . . 1 liverye bedstede corded xls. . . 1 liverye bedstede corded 1 matt 1 Canopie of brode clothe redd, ymbrodered wth black vellett & guilt bells, 1 downe bedd 1 downe boulster 2 downe pillowes [blankets, rug, covering] 3 Curtins of Crimsine duble sarcenett & 1 matteris xxj li. . . .[my lady's chamber] 1 liverye bedstede corded 1 matt a Canapie of black vellett pincked 2 Curtins of grene cloth [and furnishings] vj li. xvjs. viijd. . . 1 other liverye bedsteede corded 1 matt 1 Canapie of black vellett wth Copper lace 2 Curtins of blewe & yellowe damaske 2 downe beds [and furnishings] xiiij li. vjs. viijd. . . [maids' chamber] 2 liverye bedsteads corded 2 matts 1 old Canapie of grene cloth wth grene & redd fringe [and furnishings] iiij li. 1620: [carpenter] 5 Daies makeinge a Lyverie Bedsteade 6s. 8d.* See <u>sparver</u> below.

<u>low bedstead</u>: without full posts and ceiling. *1588: one lowe bedsteade wth halfe postes turned wth acornes the bedd of Joyned Worke iiij li.*

<u>pair</u>: perhaps identical small bedsteads; but see VIRGINALS. *1587: j pair of bedsteads.*

<u>pallet</u>: Fr. *paille*, straw, giving ME *paillet*; straw bed. *1591: [Great Chamber] a pallet. 1688: one Pallett Bedstead.*

<u>posted</u>: general name for the bed with either four posts or two foot-posts and a high bedhead, with a canopy or ceiling, the sides of which were sometimes trimmed with a valence. The <u>canopy</u>, often confusingly called the <u>tester</u>, was of wood e.g. wainscot, or cloth. The grander beds had 5 curtains - one at the foot and two at each side - hung on rods. The wooden bedhead or tester could be heavily carved, but some were of fabric. The head posts were sometimes detachable from the bedhead. The posted bed arrived early in the 16th century; the medieval bed had curtains and canopy suspended from the ceiling of the room. *1588: one bedsteade wth turned posts, the tester vallence & curtens of redde and yellow saie...iiij li. . . one posted bedsteade wth a fayer hedde of ioyners Worke, the tester & vallence paned wth blacke and tawnye satten, the vallence frynged abowte wth blacke and crymsen silke, v curtens of crymsen taffeta...x li. 1593: 1 great posted beddstede varnished wth tester & vallence ymbroydered uppon redd cloth wth 5 Curtins of silke & 3 Curtin rodds...xij li. . . 1 posted beddsteede wth a tester of wainscott & vallence of purple vellett & tissue wth 3 Curtins of damaske blewe & yellowe, 3 Curtin Rodds...iiij li. xs. . . 1 posted bedstede carved corded...wth tester & vallence of blacke figured vellett & russett satten ymbroydred wth yellowe 5 Curtins of blacke & yellowe sarcenet & 3 Curtin rodds...xij li. . . 1 close posted beddsteade wth a heade of wainscott ingraven wth tester & vallence of redd cloth wth armes of Butts & Buers at the heade, 5 Curtins of red & yellowe saye & 3 Curtin rodds...liijs. iiijd. 1595: one posted bedstead seeled. 1597: 2 longe posts for the feete & 2 short for the head of a bedde being walnuttree: & 4 Lathes or rayles therto for the valleyns above to hange on.* See <u>sparver</u> below.

<u>running</u>: see <u>trendle</u> below.

settee: 18th-century bedstead capable of being used as a settee. *1787: a settee Bedstead wth Bed.*

slope: bedstead with canopy sloping down from the head, possibly to fit under a sloping ceiling or roof. *1637: One slope bedstead with one old matt & cord Curtaines and valance much moth eaten 1 li.*

Spanish: possibly of Spanish walnut.

sparver: canopy, sometimes with curtains mentioned separately, sometimes including curtains; OED quotes 1519 'some have curteyns; some sparvers aboute the bedde to kepe away gnattis', and 1641 'a great Sparver round about over the Bed'. The sparver was the medieval form of bed canopy, suspended by cords from the ceiling. See COSTER, and posted above. *1464: sylke to henge wyth a bed iij li. xs. . . makynge off a speruer off sarsynett vs. 1597: an fayr sparver of gren satten imbrodered wt golde the trayn of grene tafyta. . . A Spver imbrydered wth yellow satten upon grene sylke: & the Q: armes thereupon at the head & in the mydds imbrodered rich . . . one Large Sparver of stytched sylk: wth the trayne of redd sarcenet. . . a sparver of 7 panes: russett velvet poudred wth golde, & Crimson velvet imbrodered wth golden gards flory 3 together thwart: wth the trayne of doble sarcenet in 20 panes Crimson & yellowe. . . one square sparver of brode clothe tawney imbrodered wth yellowe wth the head & 5 Curteyns of the same. 1601: a paynted sparver of Canvas.*

standing: general term for a bed of the posted type. *1546: a standing bedstede made for the Warres couvered wth Clothe and Therle of Srie his Armes and the garters upon the same. 1594: stonding bedstead wth a trickle bedstead under it.* See also field; trendle.

stock: the outer rail of the unposted bedstead. *1591: iij stockbedsteeds.*

stump: without posts; possibly posts have been sawn off. *1792: a stump bedstead.*

table: bedstead convertible into table. *1751: an old Table Bedstead.*

tent: 1. No posts but tent-like canopy stretched from the headboard or suspended from the ceiling. 2. Light posts and tent-like canopy. *1779: a Tent bedstead with Check'd furniture.*

tester: 1.Up to the 16th century and the development of the posted bedstead the tester seems usually to have meant the headboard or bedhead, usually wooden but sometimes of cloth. 2. The canopy or ceiling. A half-tester had the canopy extending half the length of the bed. See ceiled, half-headed, posted, sparver above. *1459: j fetherbedde j bolster j seler j tester, withe one gentlewoman in grene, taking a mallard in her hondes. 1513: Celer & tester wt iij curteyns of whyt Lenen cloth. 1588: one filde bedde of yron, with a tester of blacke Buckeram wth Godsalves armes . . . j borded bedsteade, wth a testor. 1597: one teaster of a bedde wth the Q: armes rich imbroydered wth red & yellowe twist lace & gold...One teaster of murrey velvet paned wth clothe of golde rich & wth the tres HR in golde. 1792: half teaster Bedstead.*

trendle, trickle, truckle etc: low bed on wheels or castors that could be stowed under the main bed; usually for children or servants. *1459: rynnyng bedde. 1591: trindle bedd. 1591: trickell bedde. 1592: joyned trundle bed. . . plain trundle bed. 1603: A Trukle bed a fether bed uppon it a Mattres a bolster two blanketts and a coverlett xxxs. . . a trundle bed. 1617: bedsteade wt a tryndle bedstead goinge under it.*

trussing: OFr. *trousser, trusser,* to pack, bind up; travelling bedstead, hammock-type bed. *1484: a litel white bedde that hangeth over the gressyngs [stairs] for a trussinge bed. 1588: a trussinge bedsteade of Waynscot.*

turn up: convertible to chest or press; folding. *1751: a Turn up Bedstead & Sacking with Crimson Damask Curtains.*

wainscot: oak imported from France, Germany, Holland and the Baltic, used for panelling and furniture. See WAINSCOT, and folding, posted, and trussing above.

walnut: made of walnut, possibly Spanish walnut. *1597: one bedstead of wallnut tree.*

bedstool stool for getting on to the bed.

beed, beedstead bed, BEDSTEAD
beef fork long-handled 2 or 3 pronged fork for handling meat on spit or in pot. *1593: 1 befe fork. 1740: beefork.*
beer see PILLOWBEER
beer the word beer was common only from the 16th century, and denoted ale with hops added to enhance the taste and keeping properties. See BREWING.
beer bowl large bowl for beer *1637: 2 beere boules [silver].*
beer cart see CART
beereger, bereger, bereegre, beregood beer + aigre from Fr. *aigre*, sour; sour beer, vinegar, formed by fermentation of beer. *1484: a runlett halfful of good bereegre. 1593: 1 hoggshead wth bereger. 1637-9: he the sayd Thomas did fuck Jeremy Botterets wife agaynst a Barrells head until he made the Beregood fly out at the Bunge hoole. . . did occupie mother Botteret agaynst a Barrels head until he made all the Beere turne to Beeregood.*
beerstool alestool, two Xs of wood joined by longitudinal timbers to form a stand for barrels.
beeskep Up to the 19th century beehives were usually skeps of plaited straw or sedge, of conical shape, with a small hole in the side of the bottom or larger end. They could be enlarged with an EKE, HAVER, or IMP, a round of similar material placed under the skep. See p. 28. *1597: vj emptie beeskepps and ij eekes xiiijd. 1603: iiij [new] beeskepes xijd.*
beest, beestings first milk drawn from cow, sheep etc. after giving birth.
beetle OE *bietel, betel*, beating tool, large wooden hammer, for 1. Beating flax, hemp etc. on a BUNCHING STOCK. *1592: iiij stamping betells & c'ten towe. 1593: bushing stoke & betelles.* 2. Beating clothes in the wash. *1589: ij washing betles.* 3. General use as a mallet. *1598: ij bedelles. 1731: 2 Hop beetels & Iorn Wedges. 1736: one beattle and three wedges one huke and hatchard 5s. 1738: Riving bettle.* 4. Head of a pile-driver. *1579: iiij greate Betelles xvjd. A Ram viijd. 1583: [Sheringham pier] unto three men, two of them goinge in the crane and the thirde to guyde the pyles and unlose the bettles. . . for iron wourke occupied aboute the crane, beetels and peeres. 1621: iron worke done Aboute ye Beetle of ye Crane to Drive downe Piles.* Cf. 'beetle-brain', blockhead.
beidings see BERDINGS
bell garden cloche, large bell-shaped cover, usually of earthenware, to bring on plants e.g. rhubarb, sea-kale. *1738: Eight Bells 8s.*
bellknop knob or finial on bedposts. See BEDSTEAD.
bell metal alloy of copper and tin in proportion $3\frac{1}{4}$-4 copper: 1 tin. Formerly used for large bells.
belouse, bellous bellows. *1507-8: a peyr of bellous ijd. ob.*
belsoller ringing chamber in church. See SOLAR. *1547: the wyndow upon ye belsoller.*
belt bellyband of a carthorse. *1592: Two saddles two belts a Spanyshe staffe.*
belt large axe for splitting wood. See p. 242. *1352: [1 worn] belte. 1584: one belte one pyche fork. 1617: one old Belt and one hatchet xviijd. 1648: 1 new belt to Rive wood wthall.*
belwes bellows. *1444: j par. de belwes.*
bench OE *benc*, ON *benkr*, L. *bancum*. Horizontal board providing seating for more than one person; by the 16th century 'bench' may imply having a back. See p. 242; CEIL; FORM. *1388: Benchez ad le Dees [dais]. 1593: Benche-Bourd. 1593: one sceled bench & ij formes.*
bend half of the back skin of an ox divided longitudinally, providing the stoutest and thickest leather for shoe soles etc. See BUTT; TANNING. *1649: halfe a bende of Leather to mende the pumpe 3s. 4d. 1655: a Bend of Leather for my mr his Chariott 13s.*
bend bowls perhaps bowls made of leather. *1592: certain bend bowelles [in fishhouse].*
benne bees. *1507: the kepyng of my hyves wt benne both of the v that long to the church and of myn*

awn...wt the wax of the seyd benne.

bercher ML. *bercaria, bercheria*, sheepfold. *1277: [thatching] dom' Bercher [and other places in the court].*

berdings possibly ON *bard*, brim, beak, prow; pointed ends of palings, which by the references appear to be cut when in position or even attached; possibly = bindings. *1326: [making 225 perches of palings & placing them with] berdings [to the same pales 9s. 4½d.]. 1328: [50 perches of palings placed iiijs. ijd.] In berdings [for 50 perches of pales 2s. 1d.]. 1330: [64 perches of palings placed 5s. 4jd.] In berdings [120 perches of palings 3s. 5d.].*

bere cloth bier cloth. *1552: a bere cloth of blewe Saye. . . one bere cloth of blak worsted.*

bereger, beregood, bereeger see BEEREGER

berfrey see BARFREY

berise beer. *1484: xj barellys berise.*

bern barn

beryng see BEARINGSKEP; BEARING-CLOTH

besom a broom made of birch twigs bound round a wooden shaft; most entries in accounts for BROOMS are this type. *1483: for besomys jd.*

best summer see BRESSUMER

betel, betille, bettle see BEETLE

betyng baiting, lodging in a temporary fashion e.g. at an inn.

betore ME *betor*, OFr. *butor*, bittern *Botaurus stelaris.*

bever ML. *biber, bibera*, OFr. *beivre*, drink, drinking; snack between meals, especially in afternoon. *1451: as for bever, ther is promysid me somme, but I myt not gete it yette.*

bever see BEAVER

bewewelenen see LINEN

bewroe see BUREAU

bezor julup see JULUP

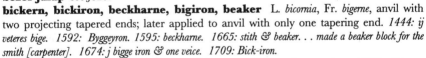

13th-cent. bickern

bickern, bickiron, beckharne, bigiron, beaker L. *bicornia*, Fr. *bigerne*, anvil with two projecting tapered ends; later applied to anvil with only one tapering end. *1444: ij veteres bige. 1592: Byggeyron. 1595: beckharne. 1665: stith & beaker. . . made a beaker block for the smith [carpenter]. 1674: j bigge iron & one veice. 1709: Bick-iron.*

biggin, biggen F. *béguin*, child's cap; night-cap; coif for serjeant-at-law. *1604: viij crosse clouts and ij biggens.*

bile, byle OTeut. *beugan*, to bend, ME *beyl*, hoop or ring, Scottish *boul, bool*; curved or semicircular handle, usually of iron. *1354: [dairy 21 plates 23 dishes 12 saucers 3 cups] iiij Bilerins [1 bowl]. 1509: a cawdern wt a byle. 1593: a payle wth a wooden bayle. 1594: iiij payles wth yron byles. 1597: ij greate hanging keatles wth biles & iiij smale hanging keatles with biles. 1617: five Kettles whereof one wtout band or byle. 1648: small payles bayleinge & cleatinge.*

bill OE *bil, billes* sword; iron or steel blade about a foot long with one sharp edge, slightly curved and mounted on a long handle. See p. 242. *1313: j byl ixd. 1463: vj Normandy byllys xvjs. vjd. 1464: a Walshe bylle. 1584: one Brusshe byll. 1588: iij forest bills, wherof one a blacke staffe.* The weapon form was more concave, with the back continuing as a spike. The black bill, which is usually mentioned in the context of weaponry, may have differed from the brown bill only in the colour of its shaft. *1584: Two swords, one staffe, one black bill, on brushe hooke xxs. 1588: one black byll & one watchinge stafe xijd. 1592: Three browne bylls iijs. 1592: one black byll vjd. 1593: 12 blacke bills 6 boore speeres & 1 pece of old male.*

billament habiliments or ornaments, particularly those worn about the head, such as jewels, earrings etc. *1537: ij Frenche hoods wt the byllymts. 1601: a flannell petticote wth two billament laces xvjs.*

15

billet OFr. *billete*, dim. of *bille*, trunk, length of timber; thick piece of wood cut to length and split for fuel. *1467: for di' a M^{le} belettes ijs. iiijd. 1535: a hundred billets. . . j lode of byllet. 1595: in ye byllett howse. 1654: som decayed Billett in ye wood yard about 300. . . 5m Billett...att 27s. 6d. p̱ m. 1655: To Tilney 6 ds riving of Billett 6s. 1738: The Round Stack of Billet and the other Firing that lay in the corner near it £4.*

billet work derivation as BILLET. In heraldry, a billet is an upright rectangle, and in furnishing fabrics billet work meant strips of alternate colours. *1593: 2 Cushins of billett worke xiijs iiijd.*

binding rope, often made of straw, to bind thatch to the rafters. See SWAY. *1353: sweth & Byndyngs. 1381: bonds & byndyngges. 1662: 3 bunches of pricwood & a bunce of binding.*

bing OE *binn*, manger, crib, hutch, bin. 1. Wooden hutch or tub for bread etc. *1318: bynge [for bread]. 1593: a bread binge. 1595: one boultinge bynge vs. [for BOLTING or sifting flour]. 1637: one greate binge a chipping binge [for parings or crusts of bread]. 1745: a Bing for Dryed Bacon, and a Bing for Oatemeal, Pease &c.* 2. For wine. *1738: In the Wine cellar: In the two Bings thirty-five dozen Bottles of Red Port.* 3. Manger, crib. *1322: binges [for horses under the barn].* 4. Corn storage. *1392: [repairing] les bynges [in the granary with carpentering, board bought, and nails 3s. 6½d.].*

birding piece gun for fowling. *1681: a birding peese.*

birdlime sticky substance smeared on branches to catch birds. *1587: i boxe and birdlyme ijs. iiijd.*

birdnet net, often of considerable length, dragged across heath or stubble to catch small birds such as larks for eating. *1591: 1 byrdnet ij ould flues.* See HAY.

birds' eyes, bird work cloth with pattern resembling birds' eyes, particularly that called PULHAM WORK. See COVERING. *1588: coveringe of birdes Eyes. 1593: pullhm worke with birds eyes. 1625: ij Coverletts one of Birde Worke. 1637: j old dornix Carpet of Birdwork* [table carpet].

bird spit small SPIT for roasting birds. *1513: Byrddespete.*

bird work see BIRDS' EYES

bishop to confirm, to be confirmed. Confirmation was carried out at the age of 7 in the late-medieval Church and 12-14 after the Reformation, and was the final form of acceptance into the Church. *1530: child was bushopped.*

bisket, bisketbread OFr. *bescoit, bescuit*, from L. *biscoctum*, twice baked; crisp, thin, dry bread. *1601: oringes lemans & bisketbread.* See MAPLE BISK.

bit the part of the horse's bridle that fits in the mouth, with reins attached for guiding the horse. Many varieties of bit occur in documents. *1599: x great bytts. ij small bitts wt bosses. v small bytts wthout bosses. iij olde bytts. one trenche [a plain bit]. xj loose mouthes. v snaffles... j Common bytte for the Jenete... x halfe checke bitts.*

bit, bitt strong post, in pairs on ship's deck or cart for fastening ropes. *1664: made a new cart ladder & a new bitt for the cart. . . one new bitt putt into the cart.*

bitter possibly 'botter', buttery, storeroom. See BUTTERY. *1350: [a partition made] dil bitter.*

black, bone black pigment made from burnt and ground bone, synonymous with ivory black. *1819: 3 st. best bone black.*

black bill, staff see BILL

blacking for blacking leather or metal. *1620: for 9 li. blacking 1s. 6d.*

black jack large leather jug, tarred on the outside. *1597: 2 black Jacks.*

black soap SOAP prepared by boiling seaweed with fat, giving a high iodine content. *1415-6: [12d. received for sifting one barrel of] Blaksope.*

blakalyere Black-a-lyre: from Lire or Liere in Brabant; velvety cloth of various colours.

1459: rydyng hoode of blakalyere. 1465: iiij yerdes and di' of blak a lyr, prise the yerde vs.

blanket OFr. *blanquette*, dim. of *blanc*, white; undyed woollen cloth, afterwards of various colours. *1459: ij jacketts of russet felwet, the one lynyd wth blanket, t'other with lynen clothe. 1537: [25½ yards] of blankett. 1597: ij yardes iij quarters of white blanckett iiij yardes and a quarter of redd blankett iij yardes and a quarter of black puke blankett and v yardes and a quarter of white Frezed blanckett. 1649: for the weavinge & fullinge of 83 yards of Blanckettinge at 6d. p yard.*

bleaching yard yard for laying out cloth, especially linen, to whiten.

blewing, blewen see BLUE

block logs or stumps. *1654: [sawyers] riving Blockes.*

blome bar of raw iron for working, square and with a knob at each end. *1595: A blome A Stythe & A beckharne xxs.* 18th-cent. blome

bloodstick short stick with lead at one end used to drive the FLEAM into the vein for bleeding. *1788: bloodstick and flames.*

blower mechanical bellows. *1751: A Blower Fire Shovel Tongs Poker & Fender.*

blowing iron, yerne bellows. *1588: one blowing yerne typped with silv'.*

blue powder with mild bleaching property made of ultramarine, bicarbonate of soda, and glucose. *1647: 1 qtr of poudr blew 4d.*

boak see BOOCK

boar male uncastrated swine.

board a basic material for building construction and furniture-making etc., before the 18th century board can be roughly classified as 1. English in origin - oak, ash, elm, beech, and various other woods from deciduous trees, and 2. Foreign in origin - oak and other hardwoods e.g. walnut from Europe, and softwoods from northern Europe and Scandinavia. These, being imported, were often more expensive than the native timber, and were accordingly used in expensive ways e.g. for chests or doors, or in places where the comparative lightness and resistance to weather e.g. of fir was desirable. The term 'board' seems to have been imprecise, but generally meant a sawn piece of wood, about 10 feet long, with a thickness of not more than about two inches and a breadth several times its thickness. A few particular boards are:

estrich, d'estrich: east + OE *rice*, kingdom, boards from the Baltic area, usually oak. *1335: bord de Estrich [for boat] ij iijd. 1335: x bord de Estrys [for well].*

riggeholt: from the area of Riga on the Baltic, but although this was the centre for exporting fir boards the actual use of Riggeholt boards often points to them being oak. *1327: [half a quarter] bord de riggeholt iiijs. ijd.*

wainscot: oak from the Baltic; differentiated from Riggeholt boards by the 14th century. See WAINSCOT. *1390: xvj bordes de Wayneskot [repairing chancel] iijs.*

Wakefield see WAKEFIELD

board a table.

board, tailor's table for tailor to sit on while working.

board cloth table cloth. *1597: iiij oulde bordeclothes.*

boarspear wild boar were to be found in many of the deer-parks in Norfolk, e.g. at Thornage in the late 16th century. Gaston Phoebus' *Book of Hunting* of the 14th cent. shows the boarspear having a long, narrow leaf-shaped blade with a wooden cross-piece bound at right angles to the shaft 12-18 inches from the point to limit penetration. The boarspear of the 16th cent. often had the cross-piece forged with the spearhead. The hunting boarspear probably evolved into the military weapon known as the PARTIZAN. *1593: 2 boore speeres.*

boat see SKEFE; TROUCKE   14th-cent. boarspears

boat boat-shaped vessel for sauce, gravy etc. *1637: 5 silv' boats*.

bocke see BOOCKE

boche buck, the male of the fallow deer. *1464: ij boche scynnys viijd*.

bochell see BUSHELL

boclayng bocking, coarse woollen cloth originating in Bocking in Essex. *1592: in boclayng vs*.

bocrame see BUCKRAM

bodkin ML. *baldikinus*, OFr. *baudekin*, from It. *Baldacco*, Baghdad; rich cloth with warp of gold and weft of silk, originally from Baghdad; rich embroidered cloth, brocade, shot silk. Another meaning and derivation might be from BODKIN, a dagger, etc. leading to dagger-shaped pieces of cloth sewn sardine-wise (see quot. 1588); this sense was used as early as 1638 for two or more people wedged together on a seat. *1442: j vest' de rubi Bawdekyn*. *1588: a Wyndowe Cushhinge of olde peces of Clothe bodkyn iijs. iiijd*. *1593: a little Chayre of cloth a Botkin*. *1597: Cannopie paned wth tufftaffeta white & black & cloth of bawdkyn*.

bodkin a small dagger; long pin for pinning up women's hair; a large two-eyed blunt needle for drawing thread or tape. *1546-7: for ij bodkynes jd. ob*.

bofot, bofytt buffet. See STOOL.

boil, boyle see BILE

boiler hanging pot or cauldron for boiling. *1636: two boylers*. *1723: boyler as it hangs*.

bokerame see BUCKRAM

bole, boll measure of 6 BUSHELS; place where lead miners smelted ore. See POUND.

boll(e), bollis see BOWL

bollance bowline: rope from the weather side of square sails to keep them steady. *1584: ij bollances for the wynterfare*.

bollekyn dim. of bowl, small bowl. *1335: [8 plates] j bollekyn & vj [Saucers]*.

boller possibly a bowlmaker, turner; 1593 quot. has house-timbers in yard. *1593: Thomas Wright, boller*. *1656: Of Smith a Boller in Hevingham for an oke root*.

bollock see BULLOCK

bollock, bollok testicle; shaped like testicles with ball-knobs or cullions. *1459: j bollok haftyd dager, harnesyd wyth sylver*.

bollyd 1. With bowl. 2. Balled, that is with ball or knob on stem etc. *1513: ix good bollydcandelstykks*. See BULLIONED.

boliounded see BULLIONED

bolster long stuffed pillow, usually the width of the bed and placed under the individual pillows. See BED; BEDSTEAD.

bolster wide cold chisel of steel for cutting brick, stone etc. *1620: [smith] iij forelocks and a boulster*. *1665: two bolsters and one round mandrel*.

bolt, bolting OFr. *buleter*, from It. *burattare*, to sift; to pass through bolting-cloth. A bolting-hutch, tun etc. was a chest fitted with a sieve for sifting flour; a POKE was a sack. See HUTCH. *1312: j bultepoke vd*. *1352: [cowl for] bulting*. *1444: bultingpoke*. *1513: j bultyngtonne*. *1536: iiij yards of bultyll for to make bultipooks upon*. *1587: Bultin poocke*. *1590: Boulting house*. *c.1600: One Large boultinge hutch with three particions*. *1615: Boultinge huch*. *1647: 2 yards of Bulter 1s. 4d*. *1649: [smith] mending the frame to thre bulter 6d*. *1709: bolting mill*.

bolter, bolster one who bolts flour etc. *1415-6: [wage] Willelmi Brown Bulster [for the whole year 12s.]*

bolus from Gr. βωλος, lump, clod; large, round pill. 1681: 'Medicine made up to be swallowed, taken on a knives point'. *1680: a purging Bolus 10s. . . The Ague Bolus 10s.* [for

18

one person]. *The Bolus against the Ague for the young Gentlemen 10s.*

bolyond, bolyons see BULLIONED

bomb 1. Bombard, leather jug or bottle, black jack. 2. Round mould in two parts for a bomb pudding. *1709: 1 Copper bomb.*

bond 1. Simple bond or obligation to pay named sum of money fully and unconditionally. 2. Penal bond or obligation: deed etc. shall be made void by payment of money, rent by a certain date, the sum named being the penalty for not paying. See DEBT.

bond binding for thatch. *1370: bondyngs [about the bridge]. 1382: bondes & byndyngges.*

bone black, bone lace see BLACK; LACE

bont hammer Possibly from 'bont', a swelling, convexity i.e. a ball-pein hammer, one side of the head being rounded. *1674: 2 bont hammers 1 hand hammer.*

boocke, boak, bock balk, tie-beam, lintel, bressumer. See SPRENDLE. *1648: for cuttinge out the boaks & sills & layinge them in the malthouse. 1662: Groundseele & stoods & boockes & sparres & dogs...a bocke & sprendles & 2 peeces of barphew.*

book, cart OE *buc*, belly, body, trunk; CART body, buck. *1537: ij carpenters...makyng of a newe cart booke. 1593: one cart Booke and one Currye Booke. 1752: 2 old Book carts.*

book as well as the normal sense, was a newsheet, ephemeral publication. *1647: the Fryday Booke 2d.*

book box when books were expensive care was taken to keep them safe. *1584: A hanginge box to putt in Bookes wth locke and kye ijs. vjd.*

booking see BUCKING

boorder boarder in house

boore see BOAR

boot boat. *1597: ij ould bootes with ther Ores xiijs. iiijd.*

boothose overstockings to protect finer stockings from contact with boot; tops or fringes with decorative borders turned down over boot tops. *1589: j peece of playne botehose fringe xviijd. . . x yards of botehose fringe xvd.*

borcher, borther see BERCHER

bord destrissh see BOARD

borde Alisandre striped silk originating from Alexandria. *1484: bedde of borde Alisandre.*

border braid of hair worn round female forehead, sometimes ornamented with jewels. *1603: one trunck & therin one Carkanett one border with other Jewells.*

border frame. *1663: the borders & pillers of the said windows.*

borderer one who lives on the border of a park of estate.

bordings see BERDING

bordnail large NAIL for nailing boards. *1328: cc bordnail iiijd. ob.*

bordwales horizontal timbers running round top of boat, gunwales. *1318: j pare de bordwales.*

borfrey see BARFREY

Borgoyne, burgoyne glass 1. Glass from Burgundy. 2. Glass with burgeons, that is buds or knops. *1621: Glayser All the windowes to be glaysed with good Borgoyne glasse well set and simend with a good quary defending the wether.*

borner burner (brick)

borrsspere see BOARSPEAR

borther see BERCHER

bosart buzzard, *Buteo buteo. c.1490: wesellis, lobsters [stoats], polkattys, bosarts.*

boteler butler. *1466: To the Priors boteler for bred ijs. xd.*

botewryte boatwright, boat-builder. *1500-1: to the botewryte...ijs. jd.*

19

botkin see BODKIN

botman boatman. *1300: [wages 8 servants in family] j Botman [1 shepherd].*

botme bottom, low-lying land. *1342: [making 15 rods of ditch] apud le botme.*

botmel poss. same word as 'bottemholt, botmeholt boards'; perhaps Baltic boards, not wainscot, riggeholt, or estrich. See BOARD. *1433: in botmels & plankes.*

botmynng bottoming, providing a bottom. *1318: botmynggj syve.*

botorre, botry see BUTTERY

botthose see BOOTHOSE

bottle slyder slider or coaster for sending bottles along table.

bottom fie clean the bottom. *1664: hope* [helped] *to emptie & bottome fie the well in the stone cortyard.*

bottom, fish fish kettle. *1779: Two fish bottoms.*

bouket see BUCKET

boulting see BOLT

bounk bunk. *1636: [Falconer's chamber] one bounke & a hawkes pearke.*

bourther boarded. See BEDSTEAD.

bow usually means a long-bow, still in general use at the beginning of the 17th century. Ewe, ewing, ewghe, iwyn etc.: bow of YEW. Elm was also used. *1590: one bowe of elme vj shaftes and one pytchforke xvd. 1591: one bagg wth yugh bowes xxxs. one bagg wth elme bowes xvs. c'teine yugh bowstaves iij li. c'ten other elme bowstaves vjs. 1602: Artylery: 2 longe bowes of ewe wth 24 shefe Arowes.* Arming bow: military, forming part of arms and armour, particularly for the musters. *1590: An Arming Bowe & 21 Arrowes in an old Case iijs 4d. 1592: one arminge bowe wth a ware brasse & shooting glove.* Standard bow: seems to be better than an ordinary bow in the 15th century. *1467: And I gaffe take home a standard bowe that Melson gafe me; it is worthe in mony vjs. viijd. And I moste gaffe to Melson ther fore as good a bowe as he kane schese in a boweres schope...a schetenge glove koste iiijd. . . . a bowe for Wady ijs...for a quyvere vs...for iij flytes, ij bottebolts and ij byres xvijd...for xiij strynges vjd. . . paid for a bowcase xxd...for a bowcase for Danyelle viijd.* See STANDARD. Stone bow: CROSSBOW or catapult used for shooting stones. *1603: stone bowe.*

bowgett Fr. *bougette*, dim. of *bouge*, leather bag, wallet, budget. *1463: a bowgett xijd...a payre bowgetts iijs. iiijd.*

bowl, bowel, boll etc. there were many varieties of bowl, distinguished by material, size, or purpose, e.g. *1373: j bolle [for use in harvest] iiijd. 1481: a waching bollis xd..j dosen drynking bolles vjd. 1597: thre litell bowels & one great bowell. 1620: a great Boule to washe dishes in.*

bowling, bolling ON *bol-r*, trunk of tree; pollarded trees. *c.1580: wee finde 140 small Bowlings upon the said Lands which we value upon the place as they stand to be worth in grosso vj li.*

bowl see BALL

bow net 1. Lobster or crab pot. 2. NET attached to bow or arc of wood or metal. *1752: 14 Fishing Netts 1 Sea Nett 13 Bow Netts.*

boxiron shield-shaped or oblong clothes-iron with hollow base, into which a cast-iron heater of same shape would be inserted when red-hot. *1788: Two Boxirons and Heaters.*

boy OFr. *boye, boie*, halter, fetter. *1718: slade & a boy to ye Cart.*

bracket a support, often ᒋ shaped or with a T section; a corbel, support for a statue, etc. *1621: the sawing & carpenters worke For the bracketting of the gallery round about.*

brad thin flat tapering NAIL with lip on one side of head. *1612: for v hundred of Bradds vjs. iijd.* See BROD.

brain plate plate for sheeps' brains, etc. *1709: 1 steel braine plate.*

branch holder for more than one candle, chandelier, candlabrum. *1589: ij branches to set candeles in xvjd. 1590: a branch of latten to put in candles xs. 1709: A Black branch on each side of the*

Chimney. *1792: 1 pair of branches & 6 hooks.*

branched ornamented with foliage pattern. *1552: oon vestiment of braunched silke. 1637: [bed] cou'inge of braunched stuff figured with greene & oring tawney pt silke.*

brand Iron tool heated to burn identification mark on cattle, men etc.; similar tool using dye instead of heat. *1593: 1 marking pann of brasse & 4 brands wherof 2 be W.B. & the other be I.B.* [William and Jane Butts].

brandlet ON *brand-reid*, brand + carriage, OE *brandrod*, gridiron, tripod, trivet; but sometimes occurs with TRIVET. In 16th-17th cent. probably a hoop on 3 or 4 legs, with a long handle, for standing pots in. *1376: brandelet xd ob. 1513: ij smale brantledez oold brandeledez & pothokes weying xxxj li. 1584: Brandlidd. 1591: Bryndlet.*

brandy wheat smutty, affected with blight, burnt. *1603: 10 bushilles of Brandie wheate 1 li. 1721: a parsell of brandy wheat in the straw.*

brank buckwheat, *Fagopyrum esculentum*, introduced to Europe in the 13th century by the Turks; the seed was used as fodder for animals. *1597: j govestead of Branck at neles berne estemed at xx combes iij li. vjs. viijd.*

brankeredge furnishing fabric, possibly a version of 'branched' cloth. *1597: one pece of hanging of brankeredge. . . one Counterpoint of brankeredge lyned.*

brasen made of brass or bronze. *1625: iiij brasen kettells j brasse pott. 1649: a braseen fryinge pann & Cullinder 9s.*

brass modern brass is an alloy of copper and zinc in the proportion 2:1. However, as the word 'bronze' only came into use *c.*1730 for the alloy of copper and tin in the proportion 9:1, many references to 'brass' before then must mean 'bronze', particularly if the object is a cooking pot, etc. See BRONZE. *1731:* [Sir Thomas Robinson on Houghton] *a fine Lacoon in brass...upon the staircase he has several other fine bronzes. 1745 [Houghton inventory]: a large Gladiator of Brass.* [Horace Walpole, *Aedes Walpolianae*, 1747 has bronze for all statues at Houghton].

brattle to lop branches of trees after felling; lop standing trees. *1663: bratled timber tops...& fagotted some of the small wood there. 1663: they carryed the pruninges of the trees in the Little orchard out of the same after they had bratled & fagotted them, and sett them up in the woodyard. 1664: stubbed up a crabtree & white thorne...bratled & fagotted the same. 1665: bratled wood...made little faggots to be burnt in chamber chimneys.*

brattlings products of brattling. *1319: Bretlants.*

brayden, brayding ME *brayen*, from OFr. *breier*, to beat small, crush, pulverise. *1590: one brayding stock* [block of wood]. *1597: a brayden table & a payer of cannhookes.* See HEMP.

bread The Stiffkey household accounts for 1593 distinguish 4 types of bread (17-24 Dec. 1593 example):-

Mancheat:	119 loaves consumed @ 0.64d. each
cheat:	16 loaves consumed @ 1.75d. each
yeomans:	181 loaves consumed @ 0.92d. each
household:	9 loaves consumed @ 4d. each

William Harrison, writing in 1577-87, (*Elizabethan England*, ed. Lothrop Withington) gives a contemporary account of English bread, on which the following is based. *Manchet or mancheat* was the finest wheaten bread, small loaves of finely sifted or bolted flour; weight, 6 oz. *Cheat* was more coarsely sifted, resulting in 'whole wheat' bread; large loaves 16 oz. *Yeomans* was probably what Harrison called 'brown bread', baked from flour as it came from the mill, with no sifting; Harrison gives no weight, but probably about 16 oz. per loaf. *Household* was the coarsest bread, in very large loaves, for consumption by the lowest servants and animals. Coarse bread was made from a mixture of barley, peas, and malt, in the proportion 2:2:1, or barley, wheat or rye, and malt in the proportion 2:1:1. See C. Anne Wilson, *Food and Drink in Britain*, p.259.

The names of types of bread could vary between households; for instance, Costessey Hall in the week 6-13 April 1583 had mancheat (75 loaves baked), cheat (214), seconde (72) and corse (61) using in all 5 bushels of wheat and 3 bushels of rye. Household expense accounts were often arranged in six columns, e.g.

[1]Mancheat - [2]loaves remaining at beginning of week - [3]loaves baked during week - [4]loaves consumed during week - [5]loaves remaining at end of week - [6]cost.

bread pan large thick earthenware pan, used for making dough and for leaving bread in to rise. *1592: ij oulde brede panese xiijs. iiijd.*

breadgrate see GRATE

breadth the breadth of cloth varied from period to period - see R.D. Connor, *The Weights and Measures of England* 1987, pp 91-5. The Assize of 1196 decreed a breadth of 2 yards, which was reduced by the Statute of Northampton (1328) to 54 or 58½ inches. Late medieval statutes varied the breadth. An act of 1535/6 laid down a broad-cloth breadth of 63 inches, reduced in 1584/5 to 58½ inches. Until the invention of the flying shuttle in 1784 two persons were needed for weaving broadcloth, whereas one could weave narrow cloth, that is about half the width of broadcloth. See WEB. *1513: ij peyr sheets of ij broods & dj...iij peir shets of ij breds. 1597: one fustyan of fower brethes.*

break see BRECK

break in connexion with timber, 'break' would seem to mean split, with wedges; but see quot. 1654. The combination of 'breaking' with 'carfe', which OED derives from OE *ceorfan, cearf*, to cut, and queries if it means the cut end of a piece of timber, would seem to mean, as in quot. 1655, sawing stocks e.g. 1 foot 3 inches in diameter and 13 feet long, to be split for rails and balusters. However, in these instances 'carf' may mean sawn timbers, i.e. squared off, of the dimensions quoted ready for breaking or splitting. *1619: for 39ᵘᵉ Footte in splitting Carff viz iijᶜ Bord or planke For Dressers at jd. the Footte. 1654: splitt worke...& 1 breaking carf. . . [sawing] 1 Breaking carfe of 12 foot. 1655: 3 breaking Carfes 1.3 foot deep and 13 foot long 3s 3d; 3 fo. deep and 9 f. long 2s 3d; 2 f. deep and 9 f. long 18d for Railes and Ballesters. . . Breaking carfe of 16 foot...for sawing 600 & a halfe of splitt for Oxnet use and 1C½ more for the fulling mill at 2s 6d & 1 Breaking carfe of 12 foot 2s.* See BOARD; DRESSER; PLANK; SPLITTING.

breast see PLOUGH; CART

breat see BRET

breck often spelt 'break' before the 20th century: light land broken by the plough after lying fallow, usually on a regular cycle of e.g. 2-3 years of cultivation and 20 years in fallow. *1712: To have sixty Acres in a Breck, & what turnips they sow to be part of the Brecks.*

breck breach, gap; small ditch. *1306: [digging one] breck [at hallecroft].*

breek see BRICK

breed see CHEESE BREAD

breekgirdle a belt or girdle worn round the loins. *1502-3: [for] breekgyrdyll [and knife 10d.].*

bregandine, breggandire see BRIGANDINE

breketyle see BRICK; BRICK TILE

bremestone see BRIMSTONE

bren bran; burn.

brennyng burning

brenyngwode wood for burning. *1314: [cutting down] brenyngwode [and making faggots].*

bressumer Fr. *sommier*, beam; breast-summer, horizontal main beam, typically along the front and back of a timber-framed house between ground and first floor. *c.1720: 8 Best Summer of Firr 17 ft Long for the Towers.*

brestyron see WRESTIRON

bret(t) Ray 1672 says the bret is the turbot, but Sir Thomas Browne distinguishes the turbot from the bret, and it seems to have been the brill, *Scophthalmus rhombus*, max. length 29½ inches and av. weight 5-8 lbs. The turbot, *Psetta maxima*, is larger, with max. length 39½ inches and av. weight 11-26 lbs. The bretcock is the male. *1593: Breatts & skoles...a greatt breate xxd...Brettcocks.*

brethe breadth

bretherwood brotherhood

bretlants see BRATTLE

brewing traditional brewing was divisible into 9 stages:-
1. barley was put into a vat or vessel with water to steep.
2. after about 3 days taken out and laid in heaps to drain..
3. turned and laid in fresh heaps; when it began to shoot and produce sugar it was spread out on the malt-floor and dried, either as air-dried malt or if in a kiln, kiln-dried.
4. the malt was ground, in a pair of malt QUERNS in domestic brewing.
5. the ground malt was put in a MASH-VAT or mash-tun, hot water was mixed with it and it was agitated with OARS to separate the soluble wort from the insoluble matter. Sometimes it was given 2 or 3 mashings.
6. the clear wort was run off into the boiling copper, mixed with hops, and boiled.
7. after boiling, the whole was cooled in shallow vats or coolers.
8. fermentation took place in tuns, where the liquor was mixed with yeast. The process took between 18 and 48 hours.
9. the beer was then drawn off into barrels.
William Harrison (writing 1577-87) estimated that 100 gallons of beer could be made from 1 COOMB of malt; at Hunstanton in 1526, 40 coomb of malt made 61 barrels (2196 gallons) of beer, which is about 55 gallons per coomb. At Costessey Hall in 1582, 6 coomb of malt was brewed into 6½ hogsheads (341¼ gallons, about 57 gallons per coomb). At Brome in 1665 (the following quotation) either it was very weak beer (89 gallons per coomb) or the 'hoggheads' were barrel-size, which would give 61 gallons per coomb. *1665: for brewing the above mentioned 6 co. j bu. of malt and j bu. form'ly in the house making thereof above xj hogsheads iiijs.*

brewing (house) room where household brewing was done; various spellings e.g. *1588: the Brewome. 1592: bruame.*

brick most brick in Norfolk before the 17th-18th centuries was burnt in a CLAMP rather than a kiln. The bricks were cut out from a brick-floor of clay, or clay and sand mixture, and stacked; when dry they were built into rows with spaces in between for the firing material, usually underwood or brushwood, which was then lit and the whole thing covered over with turf. After a suitable lapse of time the turf was removed and the fired bricks revealed. This method produced many underburnt or overburnt bricks. Kiln-firing involved a conical or rectangular kiln of brick; the unfired bricks were stacked inside, a fire lit in a tunnel which led to the kiln, and the hot air passed into the kiln and burnt the bricks. Place-bricks or plain bricks: laid out on a level 'place' after being made, place bricks often bear the marks of grass or straw on their underside. Stock bricks: made on a table to which was fixed the stock, a solid brick-sized block of wood over which the mould containing the brick was slipped to remove the brick. Stock bricks were thought to be superior to place bricks. *1579: playne brick [at 11s per thousand] stock brick [at 14s per thousand].*

23

Medieval bricks were made from 'strong' clay, with very little sand in them, resulting in an extremely hard brick with much cracking and warping in the firing. By the 16th century sand was being added to the clay to eliminate the cracking and warping; the bricks were cheaper, but not so hard. See SAMEL. *1546-7: For burning a clamp of brick containing xj ^{xx} C & vC at rate of ijs. iiijd. the burning of every C wth xxd. allowed his servants for gloves at the burning...for burning a kill of brick [23s. 4d.] xxvij li. xs. 1619: in full payment for makeinge & Burninge xj ^{xx} & viij M Brick this Sommr in ij Clampes v li. vjd. 1619-20: Payde for 465500 bricks makeing at 4s. 6d. a thowsand 104 li. 10s. 0d. [should be £104 12s. 6d.]...For 8000 raw bricks and setting downe two kylnes 1 li. 13s. 0d. 1621: Carriage of ij mil' plase Brick att 5 lod.*

brickaxe, -exe double-headed axe with chisel-shaped blade.

brickell brick-kiln. *1619: for making 2 brickills 3 li. 10s. For bricks to make the first kill 19s. Strawe for the bricks and bringing it 3 li. 7s. For altering th'old moulds and dressing them 8s. 1665: pulled downe bothe the gulls at the brickell being decayed lengthened and wrought up the same againe to save fireinge.*

brick light ? brick surrounds and mullions etc. of windows. *1621-2: To the bricklayer in pt of lights of windowes 4 li...[bricklayer] in full of 85 bricke lights 2 li. 7s. 6d.*

brickstriker brickmaker. *1665: fetched straw for the brickstrikers.*

brick table table used for making bricks. *1664: they carryed strawe sand Bricketables formes pallad boards &c to the Brickell and covering for the Brickearth.*

brick tile 1. Brick, as in medieval wall-tile. 2. PAMMENTS, flooring brick or tile. 3. Roof-tile. *1509: C & a qrter of Brykk Tyle. 1532: v ^{C} bryckTyle wt the Caryage iijs. iiijd.*

bridges, satin a see SATIN

brigandine OFr. *brigandine*, 'armour for a brigand'. Body armour of steel rings or small plates sewn on a jerkin of cloth or leather and covered with a similar material; originally worn by foot-soldiers and in two halves, front and back, hence 'pair' of brigandines. *1450: arrayed in maner of werre, with curesse, brigaunders, jakks. 1459: j payre bregandines, helyd with rede felwet...ij white payre of brigaundiris. 1464: a payr of breganderys cueryd wth blak ledyr. 1597: a briggandyne cou'd wth tawny sylke one briggandyne wth sleves, cou'd wth crymsyn satten...Briggandynes wthout sleves 5 black and one of whyte fustyan.*

brig, brigge bridge

briggetre main bearer-joist of bridge. OED also gives splinter-bar or swingletree; an adjustable beam supporting spindle of upper stone in mill. *1327: [making] j briggetre [at the bank].*

brimstone sulphur, used in compounds e.g. brimstone and treacle, as medicine.

brine solution of salt for pickling meat, fish etc. *1595: iiij brynne tubbes. 1655: 2 Barrells of Colchester Oysters wth their brininge and a Letter 5s. 6d.* The second quotation might possibly mean 'bringing'.

briste breast. See PLOUGH.

britchends hinder part of horse, etc.; thick end of bolt; transf. bole or stump of tree. *1664: 66 rootes & britchends [of stubbed trees].*

broach ME *broche*, L. *brocca*, pointed thing. 1. A SPIT, see TORNBROCHE. *Prompt. Parv.*: 'broche for spyrlynge or herynge.' *1352: j broche [of iron]. 1459: ij bytyll brocchys rounde.* 2. Small pointed peg of wood. *1310: [repairing stable] In x ^{C} broch & C splents.* 3. Two-foot long flexible rod of sallow, hazel, or any pliant wood, with both ends pointed, used for securing thatch, staple fashion. *1313: in broches & virgis [rods] ijs. iiijd. . . broches & sweyes xxijd. ob.*

broadcloth originally fine black cloth for garments, 54 inches wide. *1505-6: [received] iij dozen brodes [price 4 li 4s.]. 1584: A Clokke of brode clothe xxxs. . . A payer of vynicöns of brode clothe.* See BREADTH.

24

brochette tapers fixed on BROACH or spike.

brod hand-made round-headed NAIL. *1343: viij [great cleats with] iiij^{xx}xvj g'ssis broddes. 1410: Broddys.*

brode knife broad or bread knife. *1597: one payer of brode knyfes wth their case.*

broderer, browderer embroiderer. *1546: James & John Thym browderes Chamber.*

brodkyns Fr. *brodequins*, buskins, half-boots, similar to what were later called start-ups. *1483: for a payer of brodkynes xd.*

broil to grill.

brondlyt see BRANDLET

brood see BREADTH

broom up to the 18th century at least brooms were usually of bound birch twigs, or dried heather, and very cheap. *1562: for xl bromes iiijd. 1587: burching bromes. 1647: 7 brooms 9d. 1687: for sixteen dozen of Broomes 1 li. 10s.*

brothell OE *broðen*, ME *broþel*, ruined; a degenerate, scoundrel. *1450: The Lord Moleyns hathe a cumpany of brothell with hym that rekk not qhat they don.*

browes browse, stored fodder. *1664: rayles stowed for browes for the deere* [railed around].

brown bill see BILL

brown of Spain Spanish brown, earth pigment of brown colour due to iron peroxide, used for paint. *1587: xiiij li. of browne of spayne xvjd. 1589: c'tayne red ocker & browne of spayne. 1648: 1 li. browne of spaine 3d.*

bruarne see BREWING

bruery Fr. *bruyère*, heather; hence heath, common. *1614: meadow pasture & bruery.*

brush ME *brusche*, OFr. *brosse, broce, broche*, brushwood; to trim hedges, cut down small wood, nettles etc. *1665: brushing bushes.*

brush bill, hook hook or BILL for brushing hedges etc. *1584: twoe swords, one staffe, one blackebill, on brushhook. 1625: j brushe hooke.*

brushing chamber chamber where clothes were brushed, cleaned, and stored. *1589: In the Brushing chamber Item a square table to brush one xiijs. iiijd. ij great presses ij li. xs. iij waynscote chystes xxvjs. viijd. a chyst barred with iron xs.*

bruster, bruz tool for cutting holes in the naves and felloes of wooden wheels to receive spokes. See p. 230; BRYSSING. *1592: two brusters and three mandrels.*

brymblesith bramble-SCYTHE, with a shorter and stumpier blade than corn scythe. *1590: one corne sith & one Brymblesith.*

bryndlet see BRANDLET

brynne see BRINE

brysshinge see BRUSHING

bryssing cutting holes with a BRUSTER or bruz in naves and felloes of wooden wheels to receive spokes. See p. 230. *1417: for bryssyng of a payre carte Nawys vjd.*

buck L. *bucare*, to steep, to steep in LYE. Hence bucking tub, or buck; the lye itself. *1654: Whiting of Cloth Bucking and tending it 5 weeks.*

buck, buckwheat *Fagopyrum esculentum*, introduced into Europe by the Turks in 13th cent. The seeds were eaten, and used for animals and poultry. *1587: in the bucke barn. 1654: 21 Coome Buck...thrashing.*

bucket up to the 19th century usually of wood bound with iron bands, but occasionally of metal. See PIGGIN; STOUP. *1312: j buket [for the well 6d.]...[mending 1 iron hoop for the well] buket jd. 1324: ij buketts vjd. 1328: j buket jd. 1350: [two hoops for] le Bouket.*

bucking copper, tub copper or tub for steeping cloth in LYE; a wash-tub. The 1647 quote may refer to a lye-latch, or tub for making lye. *1603: Two stands for bokintubbes. 1647:*

a new Buckinge tubb 14s. for the hoopes & bottome to the flote 6s. for makeing the flote 2s. 6d.
buckler OFr. *boucler*, from L. *bucculdrius*, having a boss; a small round shield. *1592: An oulde Buckler.*
buckram up to mid-late 16th century was a fine cotton or linen fabric; from later 16th century coarse linen or cloth stiffened with gum. *1588: filde bed of yron, wth a testor of blacke Buckeram with Godsalves Arms. 1597: [chair] the Case of yellow Buckram.*
bud young, immature. *1592: j bud bollock of a year old. 1746: Ten Budds come two Years Old very small 12£ and Eleven Budds come 1 Year Old 7£.*
budd God's beard, an oath; sometimes shortened to 'sbud. *1637-9: by gods budd.*
buff Fr. *buffe*, buffalo; stout oxhide leather dressed with oil, one face rough, whitish-yellow in colour, used for jerkins, soldiers' coats and equipment. *1592: Eleven porteflask of seales skynne & ij of Buffe.*
buffet *Prompt. Parv.*: 'Bofet, thre fotyd stole (boffet stole, P.) *Tripes...*Buffett stole. *Scabellum, tripos, trisilis.*' Possibly related to Fr. *buffet*, cupboard or credence. Forby: 'a four-legged stool set on a frame like a table. It is the poor man's sideboard, table, or stool'. A very common item of furniture in inventories. A buffet form must obviously have four legs. *1588: one old buffet forme viijd. 1594: a shorte buffette forme iij smalle buffette stoles.*See STOOL.
buffin narrow (half an ell wide, i.e. 22½ inches) camblets of worsted, going out of fashion *c.*1620; also grosgrain camblets, made by the Norwich Strangers *c.* 1575-1625. *1593: 1 peticote of crimsine buffin lyned wth Crimsine bayes. 1604: one gowne of buffyn faced with black cunny and lyned with white cotton xls.*
bulkin bull-calf. *1654: a Bulkin taken up as Stray...the Guilder...for guildinge him 1s.*
bull Oxen do not seem to have been used as draught animals to any great extent in Norfolk; the normal plough-team in the 13th-15th cent., for instance, was two horses, but occasionally oxen were used for carts. Ungelded bulls must have been difficult to manage. See OXEN. *1654: Paid for a pair of trace for ye Bulls 18d.*
bullimong pease second element OE *gemang, gemong*, mixture; a mixture of grains used for cattle feed.
bullioned Fr. *boulon, boule*, ball, knob, boss, swelling ornament. *1459: Saltseller boliouned inwarde. . .[vessel] with flatt pieces bolyond in the botham. . . basyn, one is bolyond. 1463-4: to Martyn Goldsmythe, for bolyons gyldynge ijd.* See BOLLYD.
bulster see BOLTER
bulter 1. Sieve for sifting flour. See BOLT; TEMS. *1649: [smith] mendinge the frame of the bulter 6d.* 2. Cloth used for sifting or bolting flour, and flour bags. *1647: 2 yards of Bulter 1s. 4d.*
bultepoke, bultipook, bultinpook bag or sack (see POKE) for holding flour. *1313: j bultepoke. 1536: iiij yards of bultyll for to make bultipooks upon. 1587: i bultin poocke vjd. . . i little bulting tubbe iiijd.*
bulting mill hand machine for sifting flour. See BOLT.
bultyngtonne see BOLT
bunching from bunch, to strike, thump; pounding hemp or flax to bruise the flesh prior to retting. See BRAYDEN; HEMP. Bunching block or stock: heavy wooden stock or table for bunching. *1584: a bunchinge blocke. iij stampinge beetles. 1593: bushing stocke & betelles. 1649: for the bunchinge of 6 stone of hempe 2s.*
burdey, burdet, burdit. Fr. *bordat*, cotton fabric possibly from Egypt. *1764: Burdey napkins.*
bureau, buroe, burroe, bewroe OFr. *burel*, F. *bureau*, coarse woollen cloth or baise for covering writing desks. A writing desk with drawers, in various types, from late 17th century. *1756: One Mahogany Buroe & bookCase wth folding doors & looking Glasses.*

26

burgamot pears Fr. *bergamotte*, corruption of Turkish *beg-armudi*, 'prince's pear'. Shown as round, knobbly pears in 17th-century illustrations. *1655: 2 Barrells of Burgamot Pears.*

burganett, burgonet light steel hat for pikemen; helmet with visor. *1588: x Burganetts & x gorgetts* [neck-piece].

burling yearling heifer. *1593: two of one yeare old burlinge hefferds xxs. 1595: iij burlings, & ij weanlings xxxs.*

burn treating with hot iron. *1665: burning the grey mare of the lampas ijd.*

burrock ML. *burrochius*, OFr. *bourroiche*, wicker eel-pot or fish-trap. *1587: certen Burrocks.*

bush to trim to shape; to protect with bushes or brushwood. *1648: bareinge & bushinge of the younge trees. 1664: bushed the haystack.*

bush knife long knife for pruning. *1592: bush knife iiijd.*

bushel a measure of volume containing 4 pecks or 8 gallons, used for corn etc., containing (1826) 2218.192 cu. inches. There were local variations: see quot. 1592. Also the tub-shaped wood or metal vessel itself. A straight length of wood or metal, the strike, was used to strike across the top of the vessel if a level, rather than heaped, measure was specified. The volume is often abbreviated *bz. 1314: [j measure of wood containing] j bussell iiijd. ob. 1592: [hayward of Wells] who hath alwaies a x gallon bushell appointed hym for his tyme to measure coalles and salt by.* See p. 242.

bushing see BUNCHING

bushop see BISHOP

busk Cotgr. 1611: 'Bus, a buske, plated bodie, or other quilted thing, worne to make, or keepe, the bodie straight.' A strip of whalebone, wood etc. for stiffening the front of a corset; the corset itself. *1633: j hollow busk 6d...j hollow buske for the stumacher 6d.*

buskins covering, usually leather, for the ankle and calf, buttoned or strapped on. *1537: a payer of white buskens.*

bussell see BUSHEL

bustian, busthen, bustyon imported cotton fabric used for church vestments. *1552: one blacke vestment of bustyon. . . whight vestiment of Busthen.*

butkin small fish, possibly diminutive of BUTT.

butler in early-medieval use the servant in charge of the wine-cellar; cup-bearer. The family of D'Albini of Castle Rising and Buckenham held the office of chief butler to the sovereign.

butt the back part of a tanned hide, making the thickest leather, used for shoe soles etc. See TANNING.

butt large wooden tub.

butt end or short piece of land.

butt flatfish, possibly young turbot; Nall has 'Flounder', quoting Yarrell, *British Fishes*. Sir Thomas Browne has simply 'Butts of various kinds'. *1593: on Munday for butts xd...for sandlins & butts viijd...butts satt iiijd. 1647: 6 payer of sole fish and 6 Butts 2s. 4d.*

butter fresh i.e unsalted butter was always reckoned by volume (pint), salt butter by weight (pound). *1498-9: xij galouns and a quarte of butter, the price of a galoun xd.*

butterhand butterpat, the flat bat which, in pairs, was used to shape and firm the butter.

butteris, butteres farrier's tool for paring horse-hoofs, a paring-knife. *1584: one butteris for a smithe.*

buttery OFr. *boterie*, from L. *butta, bota*, cask. Originally a room for storing drink, but from the early Middle Ages was a room for the storage of food, kitchen utensils, and tableware. A buttery is a common room in inventories from the 15th century, and often has a chamber above it, e.g. the chamber over the buttery, the buttery chamber. *1459: The*

Bottre. 1513: In le botry. 1592: in the botorre. 1595: ye plor buttery ...ye Hall buttery.

byecoket, bicocket   OFr. *bicoquet*, cap, with a peak in front and behind; cap of state, often heavily ornamented. *1463-4: makynge clene off a byecoket. 1464: to the goldsmythe that made the bokelys pendawntes and barrys to my masters salat and his byecockit xs. iiijd.*

bygerne   ME *biker*, ON *bikarr*, beaker. Beakers. *1374: [6 dishes 6 plates with certain] bygerne & [cups against harvest].*

byggeyron   see BICKERN

byl   see BILL

byle   see BILE

byler   boiler; and see BILE. *1710: three kittels 2 bylers and 4 skillets.*

byndyngges, byndyngs   see BINDING

byndyngtwyggs   short lengths of forked wood used to secure the bindings of a thatched roof. See BINDING, BROACH.

byrddespete   birdspit, see SPIT

byshell   see BUSHEL

Beeskeps 1760s

28

C

C L. *centum*, one hundred. The Saxon and the old Norse hundred was six score or 120, the long hundred. In Domesday Book the hundred = 120, and many other medieval and post-medieval documents use the long hundred for some items. *Fleta* (1290) has 'a last of herrings consists of 10 thousands and each thousand of 10 hundreds and each hundred of six score...But a hundred of canvas, cloth, and the like is reckoned as six score ells, while the hundred of iron is reckoned as five score.' Even as late as 1820 no fewer than 13 different items were still sold or measured by the hundred of 120 in some parts of the country, while for 26 items 100 lb. = one HUNDREDWEIGHT. J. Chamberlayne 1708 has 'Codfish, Haberdine, Ling &c have 124 to the C'. The value of C can often only be determined by calculation, e.g. by the number shown against the cost or valuation:-

Ewes Tenn Hundred and Twenty att Cclxiiij li. vjs. viijd
Lambes there seven hundred fower score & twelve Cxxxix li. xvjs.

Using the long hundred of 120 for the animals but not for the value, we get 1220 ewes valued at 52d. each and 932 lambs at 36d. each. Any other combination of 100 and 120 value for 'hundred' or C does not result in a whole number of pence per animal. In another example, a corn account of 1663 lists eight separate amounts of corn in Roman numerals, with the greatest as iiij^{xx} xv coombs ij bushels and the smallest iij coombs; when added together they come to 316 coombs 1 bu. 2 pecks, which is totalled CCCxvj co. j bu. ij pec., giving a value for C of 100. In some cases, even when an arabic numeral is used, it may be used in the Roman sense:- *1655: for sawing 600 & a halfe of splitt for Oxnet use and 1* ^{C} *½ more for the fulling mill at 2s. 6d.*, where both the '600' and the 'C' may mean the long hundred. In other instances the value of the 'hundred' is stated: *1665: for planing 240 score and 5 deal planke for planchering in uch by square Measure 6800 feet at six score to the hundred.* Valid tests are when arabic and Roman numerals are used in the same phrase and can be checked against each other as in the example of corn above, or when, as in the sheep, the cost or value can be worked out against the numbers involved.

The capital C is often written Ꜿ, that is a capital C with a stroke through it; C; or even Ꝺ.

Sawyers' and carpenters' measures also used the long hundred e.g. in 1664 the sawyers at Brome Hall, Suffolk, recorded the amount of timber sawn in the following notation:-

Ꝺ =	120	e.g. ꝺꝺꜾ+++++⌐ = 355
Ꜿ =	60	ꝺꝺ+++ⅠⅠⅠⅠ = 274
+ =	10	ꝺ++⌐ = <u>141</u>
⌐ =	5	770
Ⅰ =	1	

The total given is '650 feet' but here the hundred is the long hundred, i.e. 6 x 120 = 720, + 50 = 770. See also BRICK; D; I; J; L; M; V; X.

C, c. a HUNDREDWEIGHT.

C, c. a COOMB.

cabinet originally a case or closed cupboard for housing and displaying works of art, letters etc. As a room, it is the diminutive of cabin, that is a little room; often, in large houses, the room in which smaller pictures, rare objects etc. were hung and displayed. At Houghton in 1745 the Cabinet contained a table, two settees, 15 chairs, 2 sconces, a fireplace, and 51 pictures. *1603: two mapps two carpitts six cushens One Cabenet.*

cacer see SAUCER

caddow, caddaw a jackdaw, *Corvus monedula*. *1333: in stoppyng of cadowis Holys. 1702: Kyling the cardews in the church.*

caderne see CAULDRON

cade L. *cadus*, Fr. *cade*, cask. Used mainly for HERRINGS, a cade had the capacity of half a barrel and held 6 long hundreds, that is 6 x 120 = 720; later 500. There were 20 cades to the last. *1352: iiij cades. 1468-9: ij laste of shotyn heryng, price the cade iijs. viijd. xj marc. 1560: iij Cads of Read heryngs at viijs vjd the cade xxvjs vjd*[should be xxvs. vjd.].

cadgett round wooden frame on which the cadgers, or sellers of hawks, carried their birds. *1592: on cadgett & cadgett Clothe.*

cadarne, cadiorn see CAULDRON

caffa, caffoy a furnishing material. E. Kerridge, *Textile Manufactures in Early Modern England*, 1985, 70 says 'a figured satin with a ferret silk warp and a linen weft. A variety of satin of Bridges, it was originally called *satin caphari, satin caffard*, or simply *caffard*. Over here the Flemings used the forms *caffa* and *capha*.' Peter Thornton, *Seventeenth-Century Interior Decoration in England, France, and Holland*, 1983, 112, 355, describes caffa as a woollen velvet, e.g. worsted pile on linen ground. Versions made in silk were called Genoa velvet, although they were made in several other places e.g. Lyon (ibid. 115). The misleading term 'Utrecht velvet' or *velours d'Utrecht* has been used for this fabric, although it was never made in Utrecht; the term may have derived from its being woven on a draw-loom, and was thus *velours de trek*. It was first made in Norwich *c.*1577. *1597: sparver of Damask Caffa changeable greene & orange tawney wth the trayne of sarcenet changeable grene & yellowe. 1730: blue Caffoy curtains lined with Shalloon. . . 164 yds of fine Crimson Caffoy for the Salloon @ 14s 6d ꝑ yd. 1745: the hangings were all of genoa damask, or figured velvet.* See also COFER.

caffern dish see CHAFINGDISH

cag(g) ON *kaggi*, cask. Not an accurate measure. See KEG. *1530: a cagge of elis. 1595: A cagge wth some sope. 1647: 1 cagg of Sturgeon.*

calabar, calabur, calabyr Fr. *Calabre*, Calabria (reason unknown). Squirrel fur. Perhaps the grey fur of the Siberian squirrel *Pteromys volans*. See VAIR. *1466: for a furre and di' of Calabre xxviijs. vjd. 1513: J gowne furyd wt calabyr and myn. 1590: One short grograyne Cloake lyned wth Squirrell and Calaber xls.*

calamanco, calimanco Flemish woollen cloth with glossy surface, woven with a satin twill and chequered on one side. *1603: iiij pieces of Callomynkes the wch was pawned...iiij li.*

calath L. *calathus*, tall basket or wicker container for vessels.

calcidenys see CHALCEDONY

cale L. *kalium*, potash obtained from the prickly saltwort *Salcola kali* or glasswort *Salicornia stricta* by calcination, and used in the manufacture of glass. *1700: 1 box Glas cale.*

caleis a chalice

calewise calves. *1592: iij Wenelyn calewise xxs.*

caliver light musket or HARQUEBUS, fired without a rest. It could fire ball shot or short arrows. *1588: j Calyver wth flaske & toucheboxe xiijs iiijd. 1592: Syxe shefe of Caleyver arrowes vs. 1595: a fowling peece caliv' a petronell. 1597: 2 Calyvers & 2 graven peces...Calyvers one sett wth bone 2 graven & gylt. 1599: his part and moyetie of one Caliv' Furnyshed.*

calk chalk. *1619: for ij daies worke in Digginge the Calkepitt neare ye Churche xviijd.*

callico from Calicut, India, the original place of the manufacture of light cotton fabrics. *1681: 1 callicoe shirt 6s. 1709: colour'd Callico curtains. . . black & white Callico bed lined with red & white Callico*

callomynkes see CALAMANCO

30

calyon round stone, pebble; fieldstone flints or beach pebbles. *1410-11: [11 cartfuls of] Calyon [price of each cartful 9d.]...[1 load of] Calyon [from] Mussholt ixd. 1541-2: carying ij loods of calyon from the late abbey to the chapell . . . dyggyng of Freston & calyon in the seid late abbey.*

camaka costly, strong oriental fabric originally of camel hair and silk.

camblet, camlet, chamlett fine cloth, made in the 16th and 17th centuries from the long hair of the angora goat. *1459: ij jakkett of chamletts. 1593: vallence of blacke & yellowe chamlytt. . . vallence of blewe chamlett.*

cambric fine white linen, originally from Cambrai.

camping OE *camp*, to fight. On a field some 150-200 yards in length two sides of between 10 and 15 men faced each other and their own goal, which was 10-15 yards wide. A ball the size of a cricket ball was thrown between the two sides, and the object was to carry it through their own goal. If tackled, the player in possession had to throw the ball to another player. If it was played with a large football it was called 'kicking camp' and if with shoes on 'savage camp'. The Camping land, ground, or close can be found in many Norfolk places, including Swaffham, N. Elmham, and E. Bilney.

can OE *canne*, ON *kanna*, vessel for holding liquid, drinking pot. *1578-9: a gylte canne with a cover. 1602: a drinking cann of wood one of lether. 1588: ij cannes wth covers xxvij ounces iij quarters. 1636: one silver Cann. 1637: 2 barrell Canns. . . iij silv' Canns. 1649: a great Woodinge Cann 1s. 8d.*

can hook short rope or chain with a flat hook at each end, with slinging or lifting tackle fastened to the middle of the rope, for lifting barrels - the tension when the lift is applied holds the hooks on to the barrel. *1591: one pair of can hooks.*

canded L. *candidus*, white, clear, purified. *1649: 1 pinte & 3 quarters of Canded oyle 2s. 4d. . . 2 pints of Candie oyl 2s. 8d.*

candle candles were made of wax (the best) or tallow, rendered down from animal fat. They were made by several different processes. 1. Dipping the wick (the pith of rushes, the stalk or leaves of the great mullein, *Verbascum thapsus*, cotton, or other textiles) in melted wax or tallow. 2. Building up by hand. 3. Pouring melted wax on the wick, and repeating when the first pouring was hard. 4. Drawing the wick with fat or wax applied through a cylinder. 5. In moulds. Towards the end of the 18th century spermaceti candles, using refined spermaceti from the sperm whale with a small admixture of wax, were made. About 1820 stearine (tallow from which the glycerine has been extracted) with plaited wicks came into use, and in 1850 candles began to be made from paraffin wax, now the universal material for common candles. The candlemoulds that appear in inventories etc. were usually of pewter or tin, and were not used for wax candles. In a large establishment there would be a special place for making candles. *1321: x li. de candelweycks [bought and sent to the lord's chamber 12d.]. 1513: j candelmowld. 1592: a small talow kellere iij gret talow kelleres xxd. a candell skopet ijd... a breasen wayte belonging to the candell ho. . . xij li. candell iijs. viijd. . . tried tallow xxviij stonne v li. iiijs. iiijd. a bagge to try withall ijd. a candell mould xxd. a candell traye xijd. the steale to depe the cottones iijd. 1608: the Candell howse.* See CANDLESTICK.

candlerish, - rush the pith of the soft rush *Juncus effusus*, used for wicks in rushlights. *1587: ij bunches of Candlerisshes.*

candlescot Candle-rent, rent on deteriorating house-property. *1312: in candelscot jd.*

candlestick the earliest medieval candlesticks were of the spike or pricket type, a flat base supporting a spike on which the candle was stuck. This type lasted into the 17th century, but was superseded by the socket type, which was used in the Roman period and was reintroduced into England in the 14th-15th centuries. Wood, pottery, and metal were used. There were many different types - see F.W. Robins, *Story of the Lamp* (1970), 28. Wire candlesticks had a coil or spiral of wire as the socket, up which the platform or lift rose with a knob in the slot. Plate candlesticks were mounted on a flat plate, bowled candlesticks on a dish. A chimney candlestick was a cylinder with a small platform which could be raised as the candle burnt. A BRANCH was a standing or hanging candelabrum. Watch: nightlight for watching at sick-bed. *1459: hangyng candylstyk. 1513: ix good bollydcandelstykks ij oold candellstykks. 1589: iij bell candlesticks. 1591: a hanging plate candelstick. 1593: 4 brasen Candlestickes 6 pewter candlestickes. 1595: too cannsticks of pewter. 1625: ij Candlestickes of fine brass engraven. 1637: [silver] 2 candlesticks. . . twoe silv' wyer Candlesticks. . . one braunch of brasse for Candles 10s. 1664: fitting of a screene into a pewter Candlesticke being broken ixd. 1692: chimney candlestick. 1751: Twelve Tin Watch Candlesticks.* See ARM; PLATE.

cannabye canopy. See BEDSTEAD.

cannon bit cylindrical metal horse-bit, slightly curved. *1597: j Cannon bytte for the Jenete.*

canopy ceiling of a curtain or posted bed. *1591: one lynnynge cannabye. 1597: A Cannopie paned with tufftaffeta white & black.* See BEDSTEAD.

cansey see CAUSEY

canstick see CANDLESTICK

cantilever, cantilabor cantilever, BRACKET to support ceiling, balcony, etc. *1620: The architrave freese and cornish round about the gallery conteineth in length alowing 20 inches For every cantilabor 312 foote.*

cant shaft cant is angled, see CANT WINDOW. Cant shafts had the corners cut off, giving e.g. a square shaft an octagonal section. *1620: More there is sett up and Finished 35 shaftes of chimms being 8 cant shaftes wch at 1 li. 4s. the shafte comes to 42 li.*

cant window bay window, the angles of which are bevelled. *1483: for ij panchons at the garden gate, with the kant ther above viijd. 1620: The principall muniall in the cant square and carrell windows. 1665: three cant windows.*

canvas, canevas Originally made from HEMP, *Cannabis sativa*. Strong unbleached cloth of hemp or flax, of various thicknesses, used for sheets, bags, aprons, tablecloths, etc. *1300: [4 ells] de canevez [for the table 6d.]. 1319: [12 ells] de canevas p iiij saccs xvd. 1537: grey canves for shets. 1584: A canvice flock bed. 1647: 2 yards of canvas to make Aprons 2s. 4d. 1648: canvas to make baggs on & Inkle for strings.*

capcase L. *capsa*, travelling case, bag, wallet, box. *1589: one old capkas. 1592: on capcase vjd. 1612: j capkes & the toles that ware in it.*

caper flowerbud of caper *Capparis spinosa*, or seed pods of nasturtium *Tropaeolum majus*, or caper spurge *Euphorbia lathyris*; used for pickling. *1530: a lityll barell of caps weyng vj lb & di.*

capital pledge see FRANKPLEDGE

capmill windmill with movable upper storey. *1288: [making head irons of] Le Loftmill & Capmill.*

capon, caponet cock castrated to improve its size. *1649: a woodinge platter for to make Capons meate in 3d.*

cap pan 1. Possibly from OE *copp*, cup, vessel, or ON *kopp-r*, cup, small dairy vessel. 2. Possibly to cook cap-puddings, pudding with plums or currants forming a black top. 3. Possibly with domed or cap-like lid. *1593: A Cappe pann of brasse vs.*

cap paper wrapping or brown paper, possibly from being folded into dunce's-cap shape to hold powders etc. *1648: 1 quirr of strong Cappap vd.*

car, carre small carriage, cart. *1444: j carectula, Anglice, a carre.*

caraway, carroway the seeds of the umbelliferous plant *Carum carvi*, aromatic with carminative and purgative properties. Sweetmeats were flavoured with caraway seeds. *1647: 4 oz Carroway Cumfitts Red & White. 1648: halfe a pound of Caroway Cumfitts 1s. 2d. 1654: Caraway water.*

carbine short musket, carried by the carabin, a mounted musketeer, from the early17th century.

carcanet ornamental neckpiece or collar, set with jewels. *1603: one trunck & therein one Carkanett.*

card It. or Sp. *carda*, thistle. 1. Frame set with teasels for raising knap on cloth; iron implement with fine teeth for same purpose. 2. Pair of cards: frame set with fine iron teeth, fastened to a stock or table, with hand-held similar, for combing out wool, hemp, flax fibres.

carde coarse silk of linen material for vestments.

cardrin see CAULDRON

cardus Probably L. *cardus*, thistle; blessed thistle *Cardus benedictus*, (now *Cnicus benedictus),* and milk thistle *Silybum marianum* have white veins and were held to increase the flow of mother's milk, and were used to treat fevers, worms, and poisons. *1649: for spinage seede & Cardus seede 4d.*

carell, carall see CARROLL

carf see BREAK; SPLIT

carpet ML. *carpeta, carpita,* OFr. *capite,* coarse cloth. Up to the 17th century 'carpet' usually meant a covering for a table or similar furniture. TAPESTRY and TURKEYWORK, which also might be hung for ornament, birdwork (see BIRDSEYES), silk, needlework, and cotton were used. *1588: a Table wth a frame ioyned vjs. Two Carpetts of Tappestrie uppon the same, the one lyned wth canvas, thother unlyned xxvjs. . . a carpet for the square table of grene Cotton xijd a carpet for the Cupborde of grene Cotton vjd. one lyverie Cupborde wth a Carpet of divers colors vs. 1597: one Carpet nedleworke j yarde 3 qrters longe: a ell brode. . . one Carpet turkyworke ij yards j qrter longe: an ell brode. . . 2 old turkye Carpetts hanging in the Chamber. 1637: j old dornix Carpit of Birdwork. . . one large carpet of silke orres & a side board cloath of the same six silke orres quishiones* [ORRIS is lace in gold, silver etc. here presumably on a silk ground, or perhaps in golden or silvery silk]*. . . one great drawing table one livery table one livery cubbard wth carpets belonging to them 4 li. 1709: litle table & tapestry Carpet over it.* Floor carpets were uncommon before the 17th century, and even by the middle of the 18th century usually occur only in large houses. See SCOTCH. *1597: one old turkye worke Carpet to spreade on the floore to tread upon. 1745: Ten Large Carpetts to the Rooms Fiveteen Small D⁰.*

carpet frame loom for weaving tapestry or other carpets. *1593: [gallery] 1 Carpett frame wth the furniture.*

carpet work woven wool material for table carpets. *1593: 6 Cushins of carpett work ixs.*

carrel(l) a dress velour cloth of Flemish origin, with a squared surface resembling tiles, hence the name from *carrelé.* From 1574 it was copied in worsted. *1588: Testure of Taunie velvet & silke whitecharrell. 1593: canopy of carrell. . . blanket of carrell. 1597: sparver of Crymsyn sylke Carrell. . . twylte of crimson carrell sylke.*

carrel(l) wooden cubicle in monastic cloister, for private study or storage.

carroll window bay window projecting squarely from the wall. See CANT. *1525: le makyng of the Carall in the cloystir. . . for le sawyng for le caroll. . . to the loksmyth for le makyng of the Engylls for le carillys. 1621: principall muniall in the cant square and caroll windows.*

carsye see KERSEY

cart the English medieval farm cart was usually of the two-wheeled TUMBREL type: a flat body, to which hurdles or sides could be added, drawn by a pair of horses or oxen, one on either side of the thiller or central shaft, with trace animals if necessary. Before the 18th century, when four-wheeled farm carts came into general use, the difference between a cart and a tumbril may have been that the latter had permanent sides and front. In the

18th century a great variety of specialised carts developed. See p.242; HERMAPHRODITE.

axe: the axle of the cart.

bare (beer) cart: cart without iron tyres.

bitt: ML *bitus*, post, whipping post; upright posts to which the hurdles or sides were fixed.

book/bock/buck: the body of the cart.

breast-cart: light cart pulled by horse wearing a breast-collar instead of a cart-saddle or neck-collar.

broadwheel cart: from 1662 a lower limit of 6 inches was imposed on the wheels of wagons on public highways. The Act of 1753 prohibited the use on turnpike roads of wagons with tyres less than 9 inches wide, unless drawn by oxen or fewer than five horses. Broadwheel wagons could be drawn by up to 8 horses without extra charge. See A. Cossons, 'The Turnpike Roads of Norfolk', *N.A. xxx*, 193-4.

bryssing: cutting holes in nave to receive spokes.

clate: cart-hurdle, to provide sides for flat carts.

clout: iron plate to protect axletree from wear.

curry: small flat two-wheeled cart with no sides. See CURRY.

fellows/felloes: rim of a wooden wheel, made in sections.

gong: gang, set.

hurdles: removable sides of cart, made of wattle hurdling.

hurt: the shoulder of an axle, against which the nave of the wheel rubs.

hurtiron: iron plate to protect the hurt from wear.

ladder: the ladder-like framework projecting forward from the front side of the cart.

lynpin: linchpin, pin passing through end of axle to keep wheel on.

nave: the hub of the wooden wheel.

net: net to spread over the cartload.

rail: wooden rails fixed on cart to hold load.

seel/seal/sill: the framing-piece of the cart body.

shack cart: for carting SHACK - fallen corn or mown stubble.

shod cart: cart with iron-tyred wheels.

soap: used for greasing the cartwheels.

taxed cart two-wheeled one-horse cart charged, under Act 35 Geo. III c.109, a reduced duty of 10s., later abolished. The cart had to have the words 'a taxed cart' and the owner's name and place of abode painted on it.

unshod: cart without iron tyres.

weriron: iron plate to protect axle; poss. same as clout above.

winding bands: bands of iron to bind broken wheels.

1306: [making] ij clats [of rods for the carts 1d]. . . xij cluts [boughts with nails 13½d.]. . . In j wereyren empt' jd. . . flokez [bought for greasing the carts 8¼d. and 4 li. wax for the carts 5d. and 7 li. grease 8¾d.] . . . j sella [bought for cart 9¼d.]. 1310: xxj clutis [bought for axles 19d.]. . . [1 pair of wheels 2s with] iij spokes & vj felghes [felloes]. 1312: j axe [bought 4d. Fitting axle to cart and making 3 pair] de seles iijd. . . j hurtyrin jd. . . viij cluts ij lynpinnes & ij hurthyrynes viijd. 1417: Item ye carte exelyng viijd. Item for Bryssyng of a payre carte Nawys vjd. Item in posting & stavyng ijd. a payre of carte hyrdlyys iiijd. ob. 1537: ij carpenters... makyng of a newe cart booke. 1591: a Load cart, a dung cart. 1593: 1 beere Carte iijs. iiijd. 3 shodd Carts v li. 1 Curry & 1 old carte unshodd xiijs. iiijd. 1593: ij shacke Cartes wth ij payre of shodde wheles one tumbrell. 1597: j shodd carte & too ould tumbrells xxs. 1636: 8 gonge of Carte Fellows for wheles 4s. 6d. 1 li. 16s.; one payer of Carte whelles 20s.; 25 spokes for Carte wheels 3s. 6d.; One Carte Navse 10d.; 10 gonge of Coch Fellows at 2s. 6d.; 3 gonge of Carte spookes at 3s.; One rune of Carte whelles 1 li. 6s. 8d.; 2 payer of small naves 2s.; 8 gonge small Fellows

34

8s.; One payer small Curye whells 17s. 6d. 1647: plateing of broken Carteseale 4d. Carte brads 2d. 1648: 12 Cart Cloutes wayinge 23 li. 7s. 8d. 1649: 2 windeing bands for the Cart wheeles 1s. 8d. 1663: four cart cloughts and cloughting xiiijd. 1664: Sope for the carts by George Page xijd. 1721: for a Dragg Nett & carting Nett £3 9s. 1741: A Road Cart 5£ a Turnip Cart 10s. a Waggon 6 li. 1752: 3 old Waggons 5 old Tumblers 2 old Breast carts 2 old Book carts. 1788: One Waggon, Two Broadwheel Carts, Two other D⁰, a Milk D⁰, Market D⁰. 1813: Taxed cart and Harness.

case travelling writing box. *1589: a case of bords for wrightinge xs.*

case covering, curtain covers to protect fine furniture, removed when it was in use; curtains hung outside bedcurtains to protect them from sunlight and dirt. See COVER. *1745: One Bed, Bedstead & wrought Hangings, Green Case curtain to the bed...One Bed, Bedstead and Green Velvett Hangings...Green Silk Case Curtains to the Bed. 1792: Twelve walnut tree Chairs stuffed & cov'd with green velvet gilt frames & blue tammy Cases...Six chairs & 2 Elbow ditto stuffed and covered with rich green velvet trimmed with gold lace carved & gilt frames & green serge cases.*

case of drawers small table-top CHEST OF DRAWERS for toilet things; see PEWTER. *1674: a case of Drawers. 1707: One case of Drawers & one looking glass £3 10s...small case of drawers.*

cask nail see NAIL

casket small box or chest for items of value. *1593: 1 little old Caskett wth Barres of yron.*

cassia 1. Inferior kind of cinnamon from bark of *Cinnamomum cassia.* 2. Leaves of the Pudding Pipe tree, *Cassia fistula,* known as senna leaves and used as laxative. 3. Pulp of the pods of *Cassia fistula,* laxative.

cassock loose long coat, originally worn by soldiers etc. The ecclesiastical use came in the 17th cent.

cast a cast of falcons was the number, usually two, thrown off at one time. *1603: One Cast of Faukens iij li.*

cast to dig, throw up with spade; fye out, dredge. *1621: casting sand. . .casting the sluces. 1665: casting the moat.*

castilian Spanish gold coin worth about 5s. *1507: another payr beds gawded wt Casteltyns* [pair of beads decorated with castilians]

casting net possibly casting in sense of dredging, i.e. taking fish out of pond before cleaning, or net to catch birds. *1771: A casting net 7s. a gun screw, dogs garlands, hawking net 1s. 6d. pair crutches 6d. Parcel of shot 3s.* [in closet under staircase].

casting sheet 1. Cast in sense of giving birth. 2. Cast in sense of reckon up, that is on squared cloth. *1591: vj pillowberes j diap table cloth j castinge shete & one fine table cloth. 1592: one Castinge sheete xxd.*

castor, carster Fr. and L. *castor,* beaver. A hat of the 17th and early 18th century, originally of BEAVER fur but later of other hairs, felted. *1708: 21 Carsters 3 li. 3s. 45 Carsters at 2s. 6d. per peece.*

catch an indefinite, medium-sized quantity of corn, hay etc. *1584: cauche of haye. 1594: on Cauche of peas. 1594: j cauche of wheat. 1594: a small cauch of haye. 1606: one Cautche of Rye iiij li... one Catche of Barlye v li...one Cautche of Pease xxs.*

catche(r)s, pair of possibly 'cats', a trivet formed by three iron bars that interlock at their centres to give a three-footed and three-pronged support for pots or kettles. See TRISTRAM. *1743: one pair of Cheeks one pair of Catchers one Poker. 1779: a Stove Grate with Dutch Tile & Chimney Board, Fire shovel, Tongs, Poker, Fender & steel Catches.*

caterer, cater, cator one who caters or supplies provisions, mainly food, for household. *1464: my mastre toke the catore. 1525: Itm for the Caturs costys vd.*

cator basket basket for provisions. *1619: A Cator basket & iiij windles.*

cauch, caucht see CATCH

caude cord. *1589: iij qzters of browne caude xijd.*

caudring, caudron see CAULDRON

cauldron large boiler, pot with handle or ears. See p. 117. *1509: a cawdern wt a byle* [see BYLE]. *1592: one brasse potte & one Cadiorn xvijs. iiijd. 1597: ij bras potts one Cadarne one kettell. 1597: a copper cawldron with ij eares. 1599: one great Cawdron unbound* [that is, without strengthening iron bands].

causey, cansey causeway, raised road or track; the spelling 'causey' is older than 'causeway'. *1540: gravell for ye Causye.*

cave to winnow, separate bits of ears etc. from corn; a sieve for caving. *1583: twoe Caves iiijs. viijd. 1603: a bunching block a Cave two trevets. 1664: straw chaff & caving.*

cave coop, small shelter. *1589: a hen cave.*

cawdern see CAULDRON

caudle gruel mixed with wine or ale and sweetened and spiced, chiefly as medicine. *1637: j Cawdell cup wth a cov'* [silver].

ceatel see KETTLE

cechin see KITCHEN

ceil, ceiled, ceiling to line walls with wooden panelling, WAINSCOT; the panelling; furniture made of wooden panels; occasionally to plaster, plasterwork. *1572/3: I have perused the schambers and there is but one seled, the rest are too be hanged. 1584: a pece of waynscott selyng for the chimney. 1589: a seeled chayer...a seeled chist. 1591: of wainskotte seelinge A pece in ye next chamber & ells wher. 1593: one seeled bench. 1595: one seeled bedstead. 1608: the hall in sceled... two windowes sceled belowe...one side of the Chimney newe sceled & the other partly sceled. . . the Parlour seeled rounde aboute except ij paynes. . . j seeled dore wth latche & snatche. 1647: The Hall Chamber Clossett. Seeled all ovirrownd about with particions for writinge. 1665: riving 64 hundred larth (whereof 38 of hart larth for the frett worke seeler)...riving three score hundred larth whereof 39 for the frett worke seelings. 1709: 1 Indian picture upon the cieling.*

ceiling canopy of a BEDSTEAD.

cellar room, usually below, but occasionally at, ground level, for storage, particularly drink. *1597: The great Cellar. 1608: the seller by the parler.*

celure canopy of BEDSTEAD, usually of cloth and suspended from ceiling or rafters. *1513: Celer & tester wth iij curteyns of whyt Lenen cloth. Celor and testor wth iij Coteyne of Grene saye.*

cempt see KEMPT

cendal, sendell cloth similar to SARCENET but coarser.

cersnett see SARCENET

cettchen see KITCHEN

chafe-cool see CHAFER

chafer by the 16th cent., usually a brazier burning charcoal, for heating rooms; some 15th-century references show that 'chafer' was equivalent to the later CHAFING-DISH. *1459: chaufer to sette upon a table for hote water. . . j grete chafron of brasse ij chafernes of a lase sorte iiij chafernes of the French gyse for sewers* [servers]. *1465: a chaffer of sylver weyinge xviij unnces and a quarter, and my master payd hym therfor of old grots ls. And in new grotez ijs. vjd. 1484: a bras Chafour to sett by the fyre, and a Chafour for Coles. 1595: one olde brasen chaffer...a chafyng dyshe.*

chaff leap OE *léap*, basket; basket for chaff. See LEAP. *1595: a chaffe leape.*

chafhous building in which chaff was kept. *1312: [hooks and bands bought] ad le chafhous iijd.*

chafing-dish small table-top brazier, using charcoal, for keeping food warm or heating up small vessels. Later versions used a small spirit or oil lamp. *1594: a latten Chaffingedishe. 1595: one olde brasen chaffer...a chafynge dyshe. 1637: [silver] one Chaffindish wth a handle. 1734: Three Chaffering Dishes and two Lamps 12s.*

chair It is impossible in this glossary to describe or identify all the varieties of chair met with in historical documents, especially after 1700. Up to the 17th century chairs were mainly of oak, elm, or ash with some walnut, and of heavy joined or boarded construction. Chairs were unusual in houses below the middle class before the reign of Elizabeth, and even in the second half of the 16th century they were outnumbered by stools, forms, benches etc. even in large houses; but from 1600 onwards chairs became much more common, and by the end of the 17th century were the normal form of domestic seating except in the smallest and poorest houses. The following are the main types of chair found in Norfolk documents before about 1700.

back: chair with a back but no arms; having an upholstered or covered back. *1588: a little chayer for a woman wth a backe. 1593: 2 backe chaires of wainscott xs. 1637: 3 backe Chayers covered wth silke damaske & 2 lowe stooles covered wth the same 3 li. . . . 2 old backchayers Cou'd wth needleworke heigh ons 5s. . . one greate back chayer 2 lowe backchayers...& cotten Cou's ou' yem. 1688: Eighteen Backe Chaires covered with Russia Leather at five shillings p̄ peice...fower smale Backe chaires covered wth serge. 1751: Eight Walnutt Tree Back Stools cover'd with Yellow Damask & serge Cases.*

bone-set: inlaid with bone or ivory.

cane: popular from the late 17th cent. Split woven cane in a wooden frame. Often made in sets. *1685: 3 dozen cane chairs. 1713: 8 cane Chairs 2 large Ditto 10 Cushings.*

child: usually small versions of adult chairs for child's use. *1637: 2 turned chayers for children. 1719: To a Chair for Ma̅ Horatio 2s* [Horace Walpole, aged 2].

close: chair with a hole in the seat and a receptacle underneath, used for sanitary purposes. See CLOSE STOOL. *1513: j Close chayer. 1588: [gallery] closse chayre of strawe ijs. 1597: one Close Chayer cou'ed wth black clothe.*

Dutch: marquetry or inlaid chairs; perhaps with cabriole legs. The low price of some examples, however, suggests that they were not of high quality. *1589: ij dutche chayers. 1685: Pd Mr Levett for 6 dutch chairs by my selfe in earnest 0 - 11s - 0d by Mr Man 1 li - 10s - 0d in all 02: 01: 0.*

embroidered see upholstered

foult, folded: folding chairs, possibly for travelling or stowing away. Usually of two X-frames joined by stretchers. Some were elaborate and costly. *1588: [chamber] one foulte chayer of black & redd Mockadow vijs. 1597: an auncyent costly Chayer folding Carved & tharmes of Fraunce lymmed...one folding chayer layed wth bone: backe & seat of russet velvet...a lowe folding Chayer, the seat & backe of redd velvet...2 foldinge Chayers the backe & seate of Crymsyn satten damask imbrodered. Md the feete of one syde of one of them are broken.*

framed: constructed with a frame i.e. not wainscot or ceiled. *1588: one olde framed chayer, the backe and seate covered with olde grene fygured silke one other framed Chayer sometyme sett wth bone. . . one framed chayer, the backe & seate of chaungeable taffeta imbrodered wth blacke vellet xiijs iiijd.*

gout: chair with extendable and movable footrest. *1745: 1 Gout Chair.*

great: large, important. See back chair, upholstered, wicker.

long: long in the seat, perhaps to rest legs. *1459:* [Sir John Fastolf's chamber] *j longe chayre j grene chayre.*

low: with shorter legs than usual. *1597: one lowe chayer covered wth black velvet. . . A lowe chayer wt a seat of redd clothe before ye window. . . one Lowe chayer maple.*

seeled: CEILED, that is of panelled construction, usually contained within a heavy frame.

state: main chair for the head of an aristocratic household. *1459: j rede curtayne of saye for the chayre* [no chair mentioned, so perhaps was fixed to the floor].

turned: legs and backposts turned on lathe as opposed to square form. Often had turned balusters between the frame. *1534: a new torned chayer xjd ob. 1588: ij chayers, j waynscott, j turned ijs. 1592: turned chayers of ashewoode.*

upholstered: chairs were upholstered from at least the 16th century, and the profuse descriptions illustrate the variety of materials and patterns as well as the value of the better chairs of a household. *1588: two fayer Imbroydered chayers the one of satten the other of skarlet. . . one fayer Chayer of greene clothe Imbroydered. 1593: 1 Chaire of nedleworke wth redd & grene fringe vs. . . . 1 newe chaire of Crimsin vellett ymbroydered wth gould xxs...1 other old Chaire of Crimsine wellett imbroydered wth gould vjs viijd. . . 1 Chayre wth a backe of nedleworke & a seate of grene cloth & 1 little chayre of cloth a Botkin. . . 1 Chaire wth a lether backe. 1597: one great Chayer cou'ed wth watchet blewe velvet wth armes & fringed wth changeable...one great Chayer wth seat & back of clothe of golde...a gret chayer of grene cloth imbrudered wth golde one lytell stolle of the same...one Chayer couered wth Crymsyn velvet layed wth bone lase of golde a longe Cusshion suteable to the same. . . an old fashond Chayer of ~~Walnuttree cou'd wth scottish nedleworke~~ with snapdragons.*

wainscot: constructed of oak panels. See WAINSCOT.

walnut: an alternative to oak, walnut chairs are found in some big houses from the late 16th century. See WALNUTTREE. *1597: a Chayer of Walnuttree.*

wicker: basketwork. *1589: a great wicker chayre ijs. 1597: one wycker Chayer.*

woman's: 1. Low nursing chair. 2. Either a wide chair, or without arms, to accommodate wide dresses. *1588: a little chayer for a woman wth a backe, the seate of tuffed mockadoe ijs. 1589: j womans chayre of waynscote.*

chaise 18th-century light pleasure or travelling carriage, open or with closed top, of two or four wheels, drawn by a pair or two pairs of horses. *1748: One old Chaize and Harness 15s. 1771: Chaise House and stable: A one horse chaise on springs wth cushion & harness £10 10s. A grey chaise gelding £5 5s.* See CHARIOT.

chalcedony a transparent or translucent semi-precious stone, a sub-variety of quartz, with a wax-like polish, identifiable only from the 15th century onwards. *1484: peir bedys of calcidenys, gaudied wth silver and gilt.*

chalder, chaldron. a measure of capacity, originally of 32 bushels, but 36 bushels from 1664/5. In 1695 a chaldron of coal = 53 cwt = 3 wagon loads = 6 cart loads. This is the official weight in the Act of Parliament, but probably it was considerably less in practice. Earlier chalders may have had regional variations. See R.D. Connor, *The Weights and Meaures of England*, pp 181-2. *1482-3: pro ij chalder lyme vjs. 1518-9: a schaldr of lyme. 1533: ix chalders off coll after vs. a chaldre xlvs. 1647: for 2 Chalder of Coles 1 li. 8s. . . Paid for 10 Chalder of Coles 6 li. 5s.*

chale L. *calla, caula*, hurdle. *1352: ij chale.*

chamaphilis ? Gr. μήλοντρίλος, loving apple, i.e. tomato (unlikely). A medicine. *1648: oz.iij of Chamaphilis 1s. 6d.*

chamber L. *camera*, room. Up to the 14th century most chambers in rural Norfolk houses for which there is documentary evidence were ground-level rooms not attached to other parts of the house, that is they were free-standing buildings. In towns, and with the development of upper floors in rural housing in the late Middle Ages, the word chamber denoted an upper room, usually a sleeping room, apart from (a) the great chamber in a large house, which was an upper-floor room but used as a living and reception room, and (b) a chamber devoted to a particular purpose in the household e.g. the cheese chamber. By the late 16th century, inventories and other documents employ an enormous variety of names for chambers:- 1. Named after the occupant: *1459: The Coke is Chambour...Thomas Fastolf Chamboure.* 2. Named after the dominant colour: *1513: le Whytchambre.* 3. Named by its position relative to other rooms: e.g. chamber over the hall, hall chamber; middle chamber; chamber over the parlour chamber; chamber by the dairy; inner chamber (often the subsidiary to a main bedchamber). 4. Named according to function: fish chamber, brushing chamber, drying chamber. 5. Named because of its importance e.g. Great chamber. 6. Status of occupants: maids' chamber for either serving maids or unmarried members of the family; men's chamber; husbandmen's chamber. 7. Time of construction: new chamber.

chamber pot   small metal or earthenware pot for night-time urination. Standard equipment of many houses without inside privies until the 20th century. Of the 44 chambers in Costessey Hall in 1597, 5 had only a chamber pot, 6 had only a close-stool, and 5 had both pot and stool. Chamber pots are often found listed together in one place, e.g. the kitchen or buttery. *1595: ij Chamber potts of pewter.* See CHAIR; CLOSE STOOL.

chamfrain, shamfron   armour for the face of a war-horse. *1465: to hym that made the shawfron iiijs. ijd...For a shamfron of stele vjs. viijd.*

chamlytt, chamlett   see CAMBLET

chamfrett   chamfered, with one or more edges shaved away. *1612: half a thowsand of Chamfrett bricks vs.*

champerty   bargain made with litigants for share in what may be granted by the court. *1450: mayntenaunces, champerties, embraceries.*

champian   Fr. *champ*, field; open-field country, corn-growing. *1631: The parte of it [Norfolk] toward the Sea & mutch of the rest Westwarde is Champian: the other parte toward Suffolk, Woodland & Pasture grounde. . .The Champian parte is of an other nature consisting wholy in effect of Corne & sheepe.*

chandler   properly a candlemaker or candle-supplier. Occasionally means a candlestick.

change   the change or exchange of pewter and silver, both recyclable materials, was done regularly at larger houses, new vessels being received in place of the old, with a cash adjustment. See PEWTER. *1530: to a pewterer for exchangyng of xl pounds of pewter er'y Ld jd. ob for ye exchange vjs. To ye said Pewterer for A Bason and ij newe Ewers for ye exchangyng of them iiijs. viijd. 1648: for the changeinge of a Bason 2s. . . changeinge of Fortie pound of Pewter 6s. 8d.*

changeable   cloth displaying different colours or patterns under different aspects. *1588: one framed chayer, the backe & seate of Chaungeable taffeta imbrodered wth blacke vellet xiijs. iiijd. 1597: One great Chayer...fringed with changeable.*

chapel, domestic   the domestic chapel, licensed by the bishop, was a prestigious feature of the large house from the Middle Ages to the 19th Century. After the Reformation domestic chapels were used on occasion for non-religious purposes. *1597: The Chappell nowe the folding house. 1603: In the Chappell Itm tenne Combes of wheate* [and scales, fans, and agricultural implements].

charcoal   often written 'cole, coles', charcoal was an important fuel for braziers, chafers, chafing-dishes, and cooking generally until 'sea-coal' became universally available in the 18th century. *1465: a cartfolle of charcolle vjs. 1466: for xxiiij quarters of charcoles, prise the quarter vd. qu'. 1654: To John Brett of Sparham for cutting wood and coaling it amountinge to 3 Load 10 sacks & 3 Bushells att 11s. p Load 1 li. 18s. 6d.*

charger   Large plate or flat dish for meat. *1584: one charger of pewter xviijd.*

chariot   Before 17th cent. *charet*, English version of Fr. *charette*, dim. of OFr. *charre*, carriage, cart. A chariot was a private carriage, originally 4-wheeled, but in 18th century 2-wheeled with back seats only. *1654: Robin Rumball goeing towards London wth my Mr his wheeld chariott. 1718: For a new Crimson Silk Curtain & fixing it up to the back of the Chariot. 1738: In the Coach House A Chariot £24 A Chaise £4 10s.*

charn   see CHURN

39

chasuble large conical clerical garment reaching from the neck to below the knees; seams covered with ORPHREYS.

chatching see KITCHEN

chatts young shoots or suckers, particularly of blackthorn. *1664: stubbed up chatts in the little orchard.*

chayer, chayeare see CHAIR. The spelling seems to support the theory that before the 18th century all dipthongs were pronounced, so that 'chair' became a two-syllable word, although it must be noted that phonetic spelling was certainly not the rule in the 16th and 17th centuries.

cheat see BREAD

cheek side of window-frame, door; side-piece, of brick or iron, to contain a coal fire. *1647: one large fire Cradle a gallowbalk and twoo Cheeks. 1692: cole cradle with ye cheeks. 1743: One pair of Cheeks.*

cheel ME *chele*, throat. Leather made from the throat region. *1591:* [tanner] *xxj whole soales & vij heades & ij cheeles.*

cheese cheese was made in Norfolk from cow's and sheep's milk, and was often quite hard when made from skimmed milk. Bang, or Suffolk cheese, was made from milk skimmed several times, and was said to be of extreme toughness and fit to be cut up into gate latches or used as wheels for wheelbarrows, and the ships sailing against the Armada were said to have used Suffolk cheese when they ran out of iron shot. Cheese is one of the few items of food sometimes found in inventories. Cheeses in medieval Norfolk were quite small, averaging on some manors in the 13-14th century between 1¼ and 3¾ lbs each; later the average was about 7-8 lbs. *1734: In the Garrett forty Cheeses 20 Stone 2 li. 6s. 8d.* The names of the individual vessels vary, but the basic cheese-making process was as follows:-
1. Slightly warmed milk was curdled by adding <u>rennet</u>.
2. When the curd was firmly settled at the bottom of the tub the whey was drawn off, leaving the curd.
3. The curd was cut into slabs and placed on the cheese-<u>tongs</u> over the tub to drain and ripen.
4. The firmed curd was then put in a cheese-mould or <u>vat</u> with muslin lining and the cheese-<u>bread</u> or cover put in place.
5. if necessary and available, a cheese-<u>press</u> was used to compress and harden the cheese.
6. the cheese was removed from the vat and stored in a cheese chamber.
<u>board</u>: table for standing cheese on, or for making cheese. *1636: two cheeseboards upon trusselles. 1665: made & sett up cheese boards.*
<u>bread</u>: the cover to the cheese-vat or mould, of sufficient weight to act as a press. *1513: ij Chesfatts j Chesebrede...j chesetubbe j chese Rakke. 1584: one cheesepresse twoo cheesefatts with cheesebreeds. 1588: v chees fatts & iij breades [and press, tub]. 1595: iij cheese breeds being rowghe & unskored. 1595: vij Cheesefatts wth there breeds. 1709: 8 fats, 4 breads.*
<u>chamber</u>: the hardened or ripened cheese was stored in a chamber apart from the new, soft cheese. *1699: wyer Lattice for the Cheese Chamber window.*
<u>fat</u>: see <u>vat</u>, under.
<u>hard</u>: hard cheese was made from skimmed milk, and though it kept well was not very palatable. *1602: in harde cheese vjs.*
<u>house</u>: earlier name for the cheese chamber. *1351: dil Cheshus. 1361: le Chesehous.*
<u>plank</u>: probably synonymous with cheese-table.
<u>press</u>: contrivance for pressing cheese to expel moisture when firmer cheese than that produced by the cheese-bread was needed. Early presses were weighted, later ones

40

operated by a screw. *1322: ij presuras [bought 3d.].*

rennet: true rennet was extracted from the 4th stomach of a suckling calf. However, various alternatives were used. Leonard Mascall (d. 1589) lists: 'runnet, of a lambe, kidde, or hare, or the flowers of wild thistle, or the seede of blessed thistle, or the juice of the figge tree... or the leaves and hoarines which groweth at the small end of the artichokes, or ginger, or the inner skin of a house hens stomacke, or the spawne egges of a pike... or the blacke mutable thistle.'

table: table on which the cheese was made.

tongs: a contrivance in the form of a Jacob's-ladder XXXX placed across the tub or vat; freshly made cheeses would be put on the tongs to dry. *1595: A payer of Cheese tonges. 1764: cheese breed & tongs.*

tub: flattish wooden tub in which curds and whey were separated by curdling with rennet.

two-meal cheese: made of both 'meals', that is morning new milk and evening cream-milk. *1654: a qu. of old 2 meal Cheese 1 li. 15s. 1655: 79 li. of 2 meale Cheese 9s. 6d.*

vat: strong wooden tub with a cheese-cloth or muslin lining in which the curds were put, with the heavy cheese-bread or cover to apply pressure. *1318: ij stomach [bought 2d] ij chesefates [bought 7d].* See cheese-bread.

wey, weigh: normally = 224 lbs., but sometimes 336 lbs. *1593: in the Chamber Lxiiij^r Cheses beinge in weight a Waye and a quarter.* [about 3 lbs. 5 oz., or just over 6½ lbs. per cheese, depending on the size of the WAY]. See also p. 72.

cheese toaster small trivet-like contrivance with a pan for toasting cheese in front of fire; a toasting-fork. *1709: Cheese toster.*

chefe sheaf. *1513: j chefe arowez.*

cheling keeling or codfish. *1455-6: half hundred chelyng & j qr of drycheling.*

chemer see CHIMERE

cheney see CHINA

chenez chains.

cherevehischott sheriff's scot, tax paid to meet sheriff's expenses.

chesen cheeses. *1594: xj lytle chesen iijs.*

chest L. *cista*, chest. The domestic chest reached its heyday in the latter half of the 16th and the first half of the 17th century. Chests were used in the Middle Ages, but they may appear under other names such as COFFER and STANDARD. No chests are recorded in Fastolf's inventory of 1459. By the 1590s chests and coffers were very common as storage furniture. For example, in 39 Shipdham inventories 1584-1614, 20 households had chests, 34 had coffers, and only 2 had neither, averaging 2¾ chests or coffers per household. By the early 18th century the CHEST-OF-DRAWERS and the PRESS were replacing the chest except in the poorer households, although a sample of inventories 1700-30 shows that over 40% of households still had one or more chests. The traditional chest vanished almost completely from larger houses in the 18th century - the 45-room Stow Hall had no chests in 1709. 'Chest' in the 16th and 17th centuries implies joined construction, with a flat lid, whereas 'coffer' implies a smaller chest with a curved or coffered lid. Chests were often used as containers of clothes, linen etc. when travelling. The material was generally wood, mainly oak, although leather was sometimes used either as the main material or to cover the wood. See p. 241.

bound/barred: chests for travelling use were often reinforced and protected with iron bands and bars. *1588: ij blacke plated chests viijs. . . j greate chest bounde wth yron ijs. 1590: Chyste bownden with barrs iijs. iiijd. 1591: One barde chest wth a locke ijs. 1593: chest bound with Iron* [held 28 pair of sheets and 3 pillowbeers]. *1597: an old blacke leather chest wth yron barres...2 great*

41

Chests cou'ed wth black leather bounde & barred wth yron.
carved: chests were often carved with abstract or architectural patterns, or with scenes in low relief. *1584: a chest carved wth a draer in the bottom. 1588: a great graven Chest of waynscot xs. 1637: one great Carved chest 1 li.*
chair chest: chair with a chest underneath the seat.
clothes: chests were the main item of furniture for the storage of clothes before the advent of the standing WARDROBE. *1591: great gowne chest.*
cyprus/cypress: of cypress wood. *1597: one fayer large Chest of Sypres. 1688: one Sipris Chest.*
Danske: of Baltic oak or pine; Danish. *1588: j great Danske Chest vs. . . one olde Danske chest xijd. 1590: danske chest of setworke viijs. 1592: a danske chest wth ten payer of corse hemping sheetes therin vj table clothes vj table clothes vj pyllowe beeres vj table napkyns.*
evidence: chest for documents. *1593 [chapel] 1 great Evidence chest.*
furrendeal: softwood, fir, or deal. *1592: furrindeale chest. 1620: a fruite chest of Furrendeale.*
great: of the largest size.
japanned: lacquered. *1751: a large Japan'd India Chest with Drawers & Leather Cover.*
iron: iron-bound, or made completely of iron. *1637: one furrindell chest & an iron chest.*
ship: for travelling aboard ship. *1591: one shippe chest.*
spruce: chest made of imported deal from the Norway spruce, and therefore more expensive than native hardwood. But see SPRUCE. *1513: [parlour] J oold spruce chest. 1593: j little spruce chest.*
stone: small box made of stone; CASKET. *1589: j littell chest of Jasper stone gilte.*
wainscot: of Baltic oak - see WAINSCOT; panels set in a frame or of boarded construction.
chest-of-drawers drawers had been included in some CHESTS and CUPBOARDS from the 16th century, but complete chests of drawers, sometimes called nests, cases, or - confusingly - pairs of drawers, only become common pieces of furniture in inventories from about 1670. Early chest-of-drawers were often small, of table-top size, or for a specific purpose. See PEWTER. *1613: j joined frame wth three drawers prised att xiijs iiijd. 1616: one frame wth ptitions for boxes. 1674: one chest of drawers.*
chetel, chetyll, chetylse see KETTLE
chetis sheets
chevron, cheverun couple of rafters, ∧. *1256: x cheveruns [for mending the barn]. 1274: iij cheveruns iiijd ob. 1274: iiij* ^{xx}*xiiij cheverune [bought 14s. 4d.].*
chimbnie, chimbrie, chimlye, chimine see CHIMNEY
chimere, chymere, chemer loose upper robe or cloak; that worn by bishop had lawn sleeves attached. *1459: j chemer of blak, lynyd with blak bokerame. . . j chymere cloke of blewe satatne, lynyd with blake silke.*
chimney OFr. *cheminée*, fireplace, chimney, from L. *caminata*, furnace, forge, oven. Fireplace, flue, or vent. Chimneys in many houses up to the 15th century were in the form of smoke-hoods, suspended over an open, central hearth, or attached to the walls of the room, or self-supporting on corner pillars. Some early chimneys were of timber-frame and plaster construction. *1264: [making furnace] cu' Chimine vjs iiijd ob. qu. 1380: [repairing] Le gottuer dil chymne [of the chamber]. 1386: [stone and lime for repairing] dil chymene [and partition wall]...j pol ad le Chymene...[making the scaffolding for] le Chymene. 1544: makyng of a newe schymney. 1589: one stayned clorth & one hale in ye chimbrie. 1637: one Crosbarr of yron in the Chimny. 1647: for the sweeping of 10 chimlyes 3s. 4d.* See FIREPLACE; FLUE; HEARTH.
chimney back cast-iron plate, often with a raised design, forming the back to the fireplace or hearth. *1709: iron back to the chimney.*
chimney board painted or ornamental board to set in front of a fireplace when not in

42

use. *1742: Grate poker chimney board.*
chimney candlestick see CANDLESTICK
chimney cloth cloth to hang in front of unused fireplace. *1590: iij chimney cloths.*
chimneyman collector of HEARTH TAX. *1679: 3 Mar. ye chimneyman to Mich last 1 li. 1s.*
China, cheney chinese, or in that style. *1751: a Bedstead, and Yellow Cheney Furniture.*
chintz Hindi *chint*, pl. *chints*, wrongly assumed to be singular. Originally painted or stained calico from India, in use as furnishing fabric from mid-17th century; new chintzes were cottons printed in floral designs and multiple colours. *1745: One Bed, Bedstead, and work't Chint's hanging. 1764: The Chints Chamber: One bed as it stand...Chints Hangings...Seven Chints chairs...Two Chints Window Curtains.*
chip, kyp share-beam of plough. See PLOUGH.
chipaxe small one-handed axe; adze. See AXE.
chipyren see PLOUGH
chires cherries. *1709: 16 moraley Chires.*
chisel the carpenter's tool for paring wood, cutting joints etc. *1353: j chisell jd ob. 1622: a Settinge Chysell xviijd.*
chitchin see KITCHEN
choys shoes. *1481: For Rychard the fole is choys iiijd.*
chrismatory metal box for holding the chrism or holy oil in the unreformed church. *1552: crismatorie of pewter.*
church reeve churchwarden. *1556: for the chyrchreves & the queste menes Costs whan they wer before the Vyseters at Walssynghme.*
church work religious cloth, acquired at the Dissolution of the monasteries or chantries. *1537: to Mr Robt Southwell & to doct' Leyton the Kyng's comyssiõs by the hands of my son Nycholas, for an old hangyng xs. of the Hey Hall at Westacre, & for an old cope xxs. 1589: a bedstead with a tester and valence of church worke and curtaynes ij li. . . a litle cubbord & a clothe of churchworke iijs.*
churn two basic types were used for churning cream to make butter. 1. Hand churn or plunge churn, which was a truncated cone, 30 inches or so high, and of wooden stave construction; a pole or dash with a perforated disc (the lead) attached to the end was inserted through the top or head and worked up and down with a plunging motion to agitate the cream and form the butter. See p. 72. *1300: emend' j chyrne. 1313: j chyrne viijd. 1649: a leede & dash for a hand Churcn 1s. 8d. 1688: one Barrell Chirne and one hande Chirne 10s. 1709: 2 hand chirns, a barrel chirn. 1742: one churn & staff.* 2. Barrel churn: a small wooden barrel mounted on gimbals on a stand was swung to and fro, or end over end, or had internal paddles operated by a cranked handle. Both types were in use until the 20th century, although the barrel churn was perhaps commoner by the 18th century. *1647: Barrel Charne 18s. the frame 3s. 6d.. . .mendinge Cranke to the Barrell Churne 10d.*
chushing see CUSHION   Barrel churn 1760s
chymne see CHIMNEY
chynne OE *cinn*, fissure, crack. To crack open. *1425: [to enquire whether stone] wille chippe or chynne or affraye with frost or weder or water.*
cichen see KITCHEN
ciller see KEELER
cinell kennel. *1672: ye dogs cinell.*
cinnamon the inner bark of an East Indies tree, *Cinnamomum zeylanicum*, dried and used as spice; as medicine, used as mild purge. <u>Large cinnamon</u>: unpowdered bark in a roll. <u>White cinnamon</u>: inner bark of *Canella alba*. <u>Black cinnamon</u>: from W. Indian tree *Pimenta acris*. <u>Bastard cinnamon</u>: see CASSIA. *1482: in synamon styckes j li. 1520: a pound of cynmyn*

43

iijd. 1587: vj oz of large synnamon at 8d. iiijs. 1647: oz4 of L: sinomon 2s. See CASSIA.

cipher ring ring with a monogram. *1738: A Cypher Ring 10s. 6d.*

cipris, ciprus see CYPRESS, CYPRUS

cistern 1. Reservoir, tank, or pond. *1312: [digging] cisterne xijs. jd.* [representing at the contemporary cost of labour between 96 and 140 man-days]. 2. A large container for liquid or other things, of wood, pewter, lead, or other materials. *1352: [lead for] j cisterne. 1371: trestall ad sistnam. 1377: [solder] ad le systne. 1396: [plumber digging] j pype p̱ le cist'ne cu' sood* [solder]. *[carpenter making pale fence by] le pipe [leading from the] cist'ne. 1590: ye susterne of leade. 1595: v coom barley in the sisterne. 1620: a greate Cesterne of leade. 1637: a still a sistorne of pewter. 1647: a sisterne to sett beare in, in the plor 4s. 6d. 1688: one Pewter cisterne and one Bason 8s. 6d. 1709: [Great Hall] a marble fountain & cistern; [pantry] a Japan cistern; [wash house] 3 leaden Cisterns.*

citron fruit of the tree *Citrus medica*; juicy, acid, larger than a lemon. Used as medicine. *1647: halfe a pound of Canded Citron 2s. 1648: Rinde of Cytron Dryd. 1654: 1 qr green Citron 12d.*

cittern wire-stringed musical instrument similar to lute but with pear-shaped flat back and played with a plectrum; popular in 16th-17th centuries. *1630: Two old Sytherns & an old Viall.*

cive see SIEVE

clamp see BRICK. *1619: makeinge & Burninge xjˣˣ & viij M Brick in ij Clampes 5 li. 6s.*

clapboard 1. Small thin boards of split oak or deal, imported from N. Germany and used for barrel staves or wainscot. *1572: Twoe hundred Clapborde. 1613: xx clapbords at iiijd apece vjs. viijd. 1620: for 100 Clapbord 3 li. 10s. 1622: for Clappbord deale... for the model of the buildinge* [Raynham Hall]. 2. Weatherboard, thin boards with wedge-shaped section for cladding buildings. See BOARD. *1592: xiij clobarde wth endes & peeces of other wodde xs.*

clapgate small self-closing gate. *1664: freestone rubish... laid at the street gate & clapgate in the park.*

clapper contrivance in a mill to shake the hopper to cause grain to move down to the millstone. *1335: [carpenter making] les clapers.*

clapper tongue of a bell.

clapper-board device for scaring birds, consisting of a bat-shaped piece of wood on which two smaller bats are hinged, which when shaken rattled alarmingly.

clapping board, table chopping or moulding board, table. *1692: Cheese chamber: All ye Cheese a Chirne full of hopps & a Clapping table. 1727: [pantry] one Clapinge Board one bowl one Seive.*

clasp hook, with eye, for fastening clothes; often elaborate or jewelled. *1587: xxij claspes & eyes ijs. ijd.* [in shop; retail price about 1½d. each]

clate hurdle, often for temporary or removable sides of the flat medieval CART. See CLAY. *1305: [carts section] ij clats jd. 1312: in clats [for] Le plauncher [of house above the gate]. 1343: viij [large] cletis [with 80 large broddes].*

clavel, claver OFr. *clavel*, keystone, lintel. *1622: 2 Clavers in the kitchen, the springer stone in the middle to be 3 foote and 4 inches broade in the foote, and 2 foote at the top, and 2 foote & ½ hye. 6 stones in the great claver to be 2 foot & 4 inches broad every of them and 10 inches belowe & 13 inches thicke above. 6 stones in the little Claver to be 20 inches broad a peece and the 7 stones to be 2 foote broad at the same highth & thicknes as before.*

claver part of the drawing mechanism of the PLOUGH, HARROW, etc. A hook fixed to the end of the chain or rope, or a U-shaped iron for bolting on end of plough etc. to form loop to attach tackle. See HAMBLETREE. *1746: old iron hamble trees & clavers.*

clay, cley wattle hurdle for herding sheep etc. See CLATE. *1255: Cxxij Cleys & xiij*

44

lothurdles. 1265: xxvj cleys ad fald' ijs. ijd. 1317: iiij^{xx} clays vs jd. ob.
clay crome a CROME for working clay for clay lump, daubing etc. *1593: j flaggspade j clay crome j dawbinge forke.*
clay lump a method of building construction peculiar to East Anglia. Clay or a mixture of clay, soil, and sand was dug, spread out, and watered; chopped straw was spread over the clay and trodden in by horses to provide a binding agent, and the mixture was then pressed into moulds to give large blocks, usually about 15 by 9 by 6 inches, which were then dried. On a foundation of brick or flint the blocks were built rapidly into a wall using mortar made of a strong clay, and the whole was rendered inside and out either with a lime plaster or some waterproofing material like tar or bitumen. Houses of clay lump have the reputation of being warm in winter and cool in summer.
cleanser, clenser fine SIEVE, hair sieve for brewery or dairy. *1595: [brewing equipment] one Clenser. 1649: a Clenser for the Dayry maid 9d.*
cleat 1. A small thin metal plate nailed to sole of shoe. *1647: a payer of shoes soleing & Cleatinge.* 2. to patch. *1648: [smith] payles bayleinge & cleatinge.* See BILE.
cleat, cleet a wooden wedge to make firm and solid the cord-bound joints of scaffolding. *1620: 18 doz Clettes making 9s. . . for Cutting out of Cleets for scaffolding 15s.*
cleaver hook or broad knife for cleaving meat or small wood. *1649: a new Cleyver 1s. 2d.*
clenesingsewe sive see CLEANSER; SIEVE
clerestory range of windows above the aisles to light the nave of a church.
clerk of the kitchen in a great household, the official, often of gentry origin, in charge of the provision of food. *1620: The Clarke of the Kitchens chamber.*
clete see CLATE
clewe see CLUE
cley see CLAY
cleyman worker in clay in building trade; dauber of clay on wattle-and-daub walls. *1410: ij cleymen [for making 2 floors] behynden ye dees ijs.*
clicket small CLAPPER-BOARD or rattle used by lepers.
cliff cleft wood. *1664: to cutt cliff for pale. . . fetched cliff for pale & larth.*
cloakbag bag, sometimes heavily ornamented, for carrying cloaks and other garments. *1649: 1 new Cloake bagg 2s. 6d.*
clobarde see CLAPBOARD
clock In the 16th and 17th centuries clocks were uncommon, even in the largest houses, which might rely on an institutional clock in a special room or tower. In 1709 the inventory of Stow Bardolph Hall, a mansion furnished in the latest taste, mentions no clock, but by 1819 a man was specially employed to wind the clocks. Even the 1745 inventory of a grand house such as Houghton, built 1722-35, besides the clock on the roof of the South Office, includes only one clock, in the Little Parlour on the ground floor; no clocks are mentioned in the staterooms of the Grand Storey. In 1764 Raynham Hall had a 'clock room' with a clock, but the other four clocks were all in the kitchen and servants' rooms. In smaller houses clocks were uncommon, and there were few watches or even hour-glasses. By the late 17th century, however, clocks were appearing in inventories of the rural middle classes. *1530-1: [Thetford Priory] [for mending] le clokk [in the dormitory 2s. 6d.]. 1588: [Parlour] one little clock. 1593: In the Clockhouse Itm one Clock furnished unprised. 1597: At the stayers heade Itm nere by a Clock & Chymes wth 5 bells. . . 2 great plumbes & 2 small plumbes of lead for the Clock. 1619: for ij Ropes for [taking down] ye Clock vjs viijd. [from Coxford Priory to transport to Raynham]. 1674: [blacksmith] 1 houreglasse. 1692: [yeoman, parlour] a ballance Clock as it stand. 1705: [carpenter] A Clocke & Weights. 1709: [blacksmith] a clock 2 li. 1779: [kitchen]*

Eight Day Clock in a Wainscot Case.

clockline originally cord for suspending clock weights; this type of cord. *1655: For 12 li. white lead 4s. 6d. 3 li. Red 1s. 2 peeces of twine 14d. 12 yds of Clock line 2s.*

clockreel device used by spinners to clock up the number of turns made by the reel as yarn was wound on to it. In use in Norwich by 1584. *1588: A Lynnen wheele a ijs. vjd. a Clocke reele viijd. 1593: a newe maunde & j olde Clocke reele.*

clokke cloak. *1584: A Clokke of brode Cloth xxxs.*

close closed, with lid or door, e.g. close MAUND.

close-stool, -chair stool, chair or receptacle for defecation in the private chamber. Usually in the form of an oblong box, sometimes complete with a case for travelling. The seat was often covered with padded cloth or leather, with a lid. The pan was pewter or earthenware. *1591: j close stoole wth a Cushin. 1597: one close stoole wth the pot of pew[ter]. . . one Close stoole of Furrendeale covered wth yellowe. . . one Close stolle wth a Cover covered wth yellowe 2 erthen potts for them. 1631: close stoole covered with lether. 1649: the Close stoole 7s. . . 2 Close stools 17s. 3 new Panns wayeinge 14 li. 1 li.. 1688: for close stoole case & Pan 7s. 6d.*

closet originally a private place, but by the 16th century almost always a small room used for storage or even a closed cupboard. See CEIL. *1532: for ij dayes worke & di' in makyng a Closett in my chamber xd. 1593: In the Closett by the Chimny in my La: Chamber [desk, casket, runlet with wine, glasses, gallypots, bottles, vinegar and grate]. 1595: ye clossett by ye parlour. 1684: for the hanging of Malls closett 1 li. 19s. 1709: closet to Kitchen Chamber* [silk hangings, 3 stools, curtains, cane squob, glass on door, picture over door]. *1764: closet adjoining Saloon Eight bell glasses Eight Sconces and Two Carpets.*

cloth, cupboard cloth to lie on top of a CUPBOARD. See CARPET. *1588: j cupboarde Clothe of diaper xs. xij playne cupboarde Clothes xiijs. iiijd. 1637: 2 green livery cubboard cloaths wrought wth silke fringes.*

cloth, table Medieval table-cloths were of flax or HEMP. 13th-14th century manorial accounts use *canevas*, from the L. *canabaceus*, CANVAS, hempen, for the cloth for the hall table, and this was used even on servants' tables for the meals during harvest. By the 16th century LINEN table-cloths were common. *1588: iij longe diaper table clothes xls. ij square diaper table clothes xxs. ij longe fyne Table clothes xxs. xxij fyne and corse Table clothes xxxs. vij ordynarie playne Table clothes xiiijs. vj corse Table Clothes for the Hall vjs. 1593: 3 damaske worke Table clothes...2 longe Tableclothes of Holland & 2 square clothes of Holland. 10 Tableclothes for the hall.*

cloth, window curtains, or cloths for window-seat. *1588: [parlour] two wyndowe clothes of Fustyan of Naples striped vjd. one other wyndowe Clothe of grene Cotton iiijd.*

cloth see HANGING; PAINTED CLOTH; TAPESTRY; TYER.

cloth of Cologne tightly-woven strips of ribbon textile from Cologne.

clothesake clothes-sack, bag, often of leather, for clothes. *1466: ij keyies for the tronke and the clothesake vjd.*

clothes cart wheeled clothes-basket. *1734: One Cloathes Cart.*

clouffs see CLOVES

clout see CART

clout nail with short stem and large flat head used to reinforce soles of shoes and boots; patch. *1482: for clowtyng of Andrewes schoys jd. ob. 1537: peyer of shois...& for the clowghtyng.*

clout piece of cloth, rag; kerchief. Cross-clout: linen kerchief worn across forehead. *1604: viij cross clouts and ij biggens.*

clove-gillyflower clove-scented species of pink, *Dianthus* sp.

cloves dried flowerbud of *Carophyllus aromaticus*, used as spice. In 1647-9 the steward of Houghton bought 4 oz a month. *1533: a qrte of clouffs. 1587: i box of beaten clowes iiij oz & a* *halfe ijs. iiijd. 1589: j qzter & di' of Cloues iijs. ixd. 1648: oz4 of cloves 2s. 4d.*

clowght see CLOUT

cloys see CLOVES

clue ball of yarn or thread; 'clew' is the usual form up to the 17th century. *1588: xxxvj clewes of lynnen yarne & one coffer xxvjs. viijd. 1711: [worsted weaver] 23 Narrow clews.*

clyster pipe clyster: medicine, enema injected into the rectum to cleanse the bowels; the pipe used to inject the same. The apparatus was the size of a small garden syringe. *1562: to Gibs of Norwch the poticarie for ij glisters vd. 1636: one glister pipe. 1680: A Clyster pipe prepared 6d. 1719: A glister-pipe & bladder 5d.* [for gardener, as syringe]

coach private coaches became more common for the gentry in the 17th century. They were an expensive item: Robert Walpole's coach cost £35 8s. 3d. to renovate in 1718, and in 1746 his son, the 2nd Earl of Orford, owed a total of £374 5s. 1d. to 3 coachmakers. *1593: In the Cotchhouse. 1 Cotch wth the furniture £13 6s. 8d. 1673: one tree for ye courch 1s. 6d.*

coal, coal, cole, coles can mean 1. Charcoal, usually burnt in a brazier, chafer, or chafing-dish. 2. SEA-COAL, imported into Norfolk from Northumberland from the late Middle Ages, and increasingly in use in large houses by 1600. A coal-burning fireplace in an inventory can be distinguished from a wood-burning fireplace by the presence of a COAL-CRADLE and/or a PUR or poker. Coal was bought in the 16th and 17th centuries by the CHALDER. See BUSHEL. In 1647-9 Houghton Hall bought coal in quantity, imported through Wells, from March to June. For the sea-coal trade through the Glaven ports, see J. Hooton, *The Glaven Ports*, pp 187-93. *1498-9: le chalder of colys iijs. viijd. 1535: ij bolls of colis. . . j Chaldron Coolis. 1583: a crayer called the Jone of Clay, lately arryved laden wyth Newcastel coles at the port of Clay. 1603: one coole rake One fyer panne for seacole. 1603: one Iron grate for Coale. 1647: Paid for 10 Chalder of Coles 6 li. 5s.*

coal cradle fire-basket or iron grate specifically to burn sea-coal, or possibly charcoal, and movable from place to place. Wood fires did not need cradles or grates. *1572-3 a cradell for a cole fyer vijs. 1593: 1 paire of yron Andirons 1 paire of cole creadles in the chimnye. 1597: on yron Cole cradle. 1602: an iron cradle for to burne sea coales xiijs. iiijd. 1608: a cradell for a cole fier imployed about the house. 1637: j iron cradle to burne coales in xiijs. iiijd.*

coal irons the ANDIRONS and DOGIRONS of a wood-burning hearth could be adapted for coal by fixing horizontal bars, provided the coal came in large lumps. *1593: 1 paire of Cole irons. 1595: A payer of irons wth barres for A coale fyer. 1620: a large payer of yron Andirons with three Barrs of Iron to support the coale fire.*

coal fork unusual, as the normal implements for a coal fire were poker and tongs. *1637: a peel a cole rake a coale forke an iron grate.*

coal rake for raking over the remains of an old or dead fire and salvaging the unburnt lumps. *1593: 1 old colerake. 1649: a Colrake mendinge 4d.*

coal shoe coal-skuttle.

coat of plate see ARMOUR

coaule see COWL

cob possibly transferred from the meaning of cob as large, round, lumpish: nails with large round heads. *1647: staves pallett nayles cobs & shews.*

cobble fieldstones, flints. *1679: pd my Cousin Cobb for A ld of Cobble 3s.*

cobert see CUPBOARD

côbe abbreviated form of COOMB. *1595: in wheat Ten côbes.*

cobirons, cobierns, cobiorns, coboornes from the knob or cob at the top end. Pair of upright iron bars, either free-standing or leaning against the back of the hearth, with hooks at intervals to support spits across the open fire. Usually found in kitchen or buttery. Distinct from the ANDIRONS and DOGIRONS which supported the logs of the open fire. See p. 61. *1588: one payre of Brasenn Cobiernes. 1606: ij payer of cobiornes.*

cock small ∩-shaped stack, sometimes supported on a wooden frame, in which the hay is dried in the field before stacking.

cockel, cockle small shallow dish or saucer. *1539: they bought that yere newe cokelys & many other thyngs yt war in dekaye.*

cock boat rowing boat, used to reach ships or for fishing. Could be of considerable size. *1593: j cocke boote called the goosear with xij flues j cocke boote called the Spanton with spurling nets j cocke boote called the eyght oare boat with vj dooles of lines.*

cocker, cokere person who put the hay into cocks. *1392: [74 mowers working for one day, at the lord's table for all repasts in the same day with the expenses of] Cxx cokeres [for one day etc. paid 3d. a day].*

cocker coarse half-boot, buskin, gaiter, often of untanned leather.

cod husk, outer skin, pod. *1530: a topenett of fyggs cods. 1594: Fytches [vetches] in the Coddes.*

codge swelles see COGSWILL

codmoppe a young cod. *1466: xxix codmoppes xd.*

cofer possibly CAFFA, although the use of a silk fabric to make blankets seems unlikely. *1513: x zards of Cofer to make a payr blanketts.*

coffer storage box, often found in inventories alongside CHESTS and therefore considered distinct from them. A writer of 1649 says the coffer had a curved lid, the chest a flat lid; perhaps the difference was in the use or contents, the coffer being for travelling or for valuables. See R. Edwardes, *Shorter Dict. of Eng. Furniture,* 1977, pp 183-4. *1391: j [new] Cofer. 1451: your trussing cofer [for travelling]. 1453: cofors and countewery. 1513: J long Cofyr J lytyl stondyng Cofyr J long cofyr. 1584: one cloth presse with two chests & thre Coffers xxxs. 1588: Colfer bounde wth yron. 1591: j great Cheist wth the locke vjs. j Cofer wth the locke xviijd. 1595: an old candell cofer wth candelles therein. 1602: the conveiances and the evidencies...be put into a colfer under the lockes and keys...and the same colfer to be kept in the common towne cheste remaininge in the church.*

coffin a piedish, mould. *1595: a Custer [custard] coffing.*

cofter Fr. *couverture,* coveter or COVERLET. *1484: a Fetherbedde and a traunsom...and the Cofters of Worsted.*

cog the medieval cog was the standard merchant ship, single-masted with one large square sail. By the end of the 15th century the word meant a smaller vessel, used for coastal trade and fishing.

cogswill a swill was a large, shallow basket, and a cogswill was probably for use in a COG or COCK-BOAT. *1584: [fisherman] eyghtene cogswylles ixs. 1593: [stored in tower of Eccles church] xxxx codge swelles.*

cogwheel toothed wheel in mechanism of mill, often with fruitwood teeth. *1367: dil Cogwhel & comyngs.*

coif close-fitting cap covering top, back and sides of head; nightcap; lawyer's cap; cap of iron or steel, later leather, worn under helmet. *1588: night coife wrought xxd. 1599: Eight Coyfes iijs. iiijd.*

colander, cullinder perforated bowl for draining food. *1599: one earthin Cullenner. 1649: a braseen fryinge pann & Cullinder 9s.*

Colchester oysters Colchester was a celebrated source of first-class oysters, although oysters were available all round the Norfolk coast until the end of the 19th century. *1655: for double Barrells of Colchestr oystrs 1 li. 13s. 8d.*

cold see COWL

colder according to Forby, colder in Norfolk was 'broken ears of corn mixed with fragments of straw, beaten off by the flail', and in Suffolk 'light ears and chaff left in the caving sieve, after dressing corn'. In the early 20th century a farm-boy noted that it was barley beards and rubbish of no food value. The refuse of wheat was used as a binding medium for mortar. Chaff, particularly of barley, was often put under the floorboards to insulate and to discourage mice, which don't like the serrated beards. *1579: ij bz of colder xd. 1612: for carting of stone sand silt Clay and Colder...for carrynge Colder out of the howse. 1743: one Colder skep. 1781: Colder skep, Windell, Colder Riddle, wheat Riddle.*

cole, colle, cool see COWL

colfer see COFFER

colk a core, a mass or pig of iron. *1466: v colkes of yren; item, v boltes [which weigh 10 li.].*

college pot probably a pot with the arms of a college; OED gives '? some kind of tankard or drinking-vessel', citing *Three Silver College-pots, of different sizes* 1689. *1637: 1 great Colledge pott of silv'.*

collering cloth collow, colly = to blacken with soot or coal-dust; could these be cloths for black-leading? *1709: 15 Rubbers 13 Collering cloaths 7 Deer cloaths.*

colme see COOMB

columbine dove-grey. *1552: on Cope of Colübyn satten of bridges.*

colyere collar. *1482-3: pro iiij colyeres xijd.*

colys coals

comb 16th-17th century combs were often double-sided, with different fineness of teeth to each side. *1587: viij dozin penny combes at ixd. the dozin vjs. 5 Ivery Combes ijs. vjd. xiiij boxes for Combes xiiijd.*

comb see COOMB

coming, comyng coaming, that is topping, cresting a wall. *1370: daub' & comyng [said wall].*

coming, comyng ML. *comba*, part of mill-wheel. See COGWHEEL.

commode 1. Article of furniture, dating from the early 18th century, with drawers or close cupboard; chest-of drawers; chiffonier; sideboard. 2. Small chest or chair enclosing and hiding chamber utensil. See CHAIR; CLOSE STOOL. *1764: comode table with cover.*

compas(s) compost, muck, sewage.

compaskart muckcart, two-wheeled tumbril. *1584: one shodd carte & one compasscarte. 1591: One compaskart xs.*

compass to make, complete. *1537: [shoemaker] for compassing of a peyer of boots.*

compass circular, curved. *c.1730: 12...Wallnuttree Chair Frames with Compass Seates...a fine Compass India back vener'd with the finest Grenople Wallnuttree.*

compass rafters, roof arched, curved braces to rafters. *1620: with compasse rafters and vineals on the top. 1621-2: 10 foote of Compassed head for the same Dore.*

compost prepared manure or mould; muck. *1595: compasse in the yard.*

comyn, coomyn see CUMMIN

coney, cony OFr. *conil*, pl. *conis*, rabbit. The rabbit was introduced into England in early Norman times. Coney/cony was the normal medieval name for the animal, but later, by the 16th century, 'coney' was used for the mature animal and 'rabbit' for the young. By the middle of the 17th century 'rabbit' was coming to be used for any age. In the Stiffkey account for 1593, conies were bought between Sept. and Dec. for an average of 4¼d. each and Dec. - end Jan. at 5¾d. each; none were recorded between 22 Jan. and 24 Sept. Rabbits were bought between 29 Apr. and 9 July at 2¼d. each, and between Sept. and the end of Dec. at 4¼d. each. At Oxnead in 1654-6 only rabbits are mentioned in the accounts, averaging 6d. each in August and Sept. and 9d.-10d. each in Oct. and Nov. No conies or rabbits occur as purchases in the Houghton Hall account of 1647-9 - presumably they were caught on the estate. The fur was used for clothes and bedclothes. *1459: j rede pane furryd with connynge. . . redde panne of kinyng skynnys. c. 1490: vj coupyll blake conyes or rennyng rabbettys, or some blake and some whyght...to store with a newe ground...at Oxenhed, more lyeke a pynnefold than a parke. 1560: to the warryners wyffe of Methold for brynge of iiij cupell connyes iijd. c.1600: his warren of Conies & Rabbits called Cossie Warren.* See COUNTERPOINT; HAY; MUELL RABBIT

confidante name given by George Hepplewhite to settee of two chairs coupled on S-plan, or three made like spokes of wheel. *1792: 2 Confidantes covered with chintz.*

conger, counger conger EEL, *Conger conger.* Can be up to 9 feet long and weigh up to 140 lbs. *1593: a counger xiiijd.*

conserve, consarve preparation, often medicinal, from fruit or herbs. *1680: [apothecary] a consarve 8d.*

constable up to the 19th century constables were appointed in some places by the manorial court leet, and later by the vestry (officially from 1842). Their duties included watch and ward, supervising punishment of offenders against manorial customs and the common law, supervising and carrying out the legal provisions for alehouses, supervising duties connected with the poor, rates, militia etc.

consuetudinary book of liturgical custom and practice in the unreformed church.

contour to shape, especially rounded forms. *1621: rayling, penceling & contoring of walls & stearecases.*

contra point see COUNTERPOINT

cooch see COUCH, COACH

coolhouse a coldhouse was for working with herbs, distilling etc. *1593: In the Coolehowse 1 still uppon a Copper of brasse.*

cookshold, cuckold form of short tongs to enable the cook to hold hot pans and pots. *1764: [kitchen] one pot Hook, Three Cuckolds, two racks & irons. 1779: 3 spits, a Cuckold. 1791: [pantry] 2 spits and cookshold. 1836: [back house] 1 dripping pan 1 Cuckold and Dredging Box.*

cooler wide shallow pan or bowl for cooling liquid, used in the dairy and brewhouse. See KEELER. *1298: [dairy] j Cular ob. 1300: j cular ad Lac [milk]. 1637: one copper j cooler and other brewing vessels 7 li. 1649: a new Cooler 1 li. 9s. 1662: hanging of the Cooler & a Coper leed. 1664: the Cooler in the brewhouse. 1745: coolers with shoots [spouts].*

coolis, colis coals.

coomb, come, coom, comb measure of capacity for grain etc. equal to 4 BUSHELS. 2 coombs = 1 SEAM or quarter. As the density varies from grain to grain, the actual weight of a coomb also varies - roughly 14 stone for oats, 16 for barley, and 18 for wheat.

coop basket placed over sitting hens; small low wooden hut for the same purpose. *1562: lytle henn cope for the daerie woman.*

cope short ecclesiastical cloak, semicircular in shape, with hood.

coperosse see COPPERAS

copeys 1. Hasp, shackle. 2. A piece of wood or metal fixed on an oar with a hole for the thole pin. *1320: j corda & j copeys [for the boat].*

copher stool coffer stool. See STOOL.

cophine L. *coffinus, cophinus,* basket. *1273: ij cophines [for carrying loaves to Norwich 1d.] 1306: emend' iiij Cophines viij wyndel.*

copper large vessel, of copper or bronze, hanging on chains over a fire or fixed in a masonry stand with a grate under it, used for heating water, boiling clothes, brewing etc.

50

1591: a Copp hanged in a furnace. 1647: One Copper hunged with the Fier irons. 1709: [wash-house] one Copper & leads. 1723: A Copper as it hangs 1 li. 10s. a boyler as it hangs. 1742: one small copper as it hangs 15s.

copperas blue copperas: sulphate of copper; green copperas: sulphate of iron; white copperas: sulphate of zinc. Green copperas or green vitriol was used in dyeing, TANNING, and making INK. *1464: For medesen for yen, take a lytell whyte coperosse and bray it and put it in a lytell rennynge watyr, and put it to the yhen. 1562: verdegreace...grene copres turpentine bremestone to dresse the balde colts fots xijd. . . for coprosse & galles vjd.*

copyhold manorial tenure of property with, originally, the obligation to perform services for the lord as well as pay rent. The title to the property was a copy of the entry in the manor court roll recording the transfer of the title to the tenant. Abolished 1926.

corbell L. *corbellum*, Englished corbell, corbele, a large baskett with two upright handles to take a pole between two men. A BEARING-SKEP for carrying grain, malt. *1311: j maltskeppe & j corbell vjd.*

cordwainer, cordener originally a worker in cordwain or Cordovan leather; a shoemaker.

corlew see CURLEW

cornscreen sieve for screening or sifting grain. *1584: one corneskreene vjs viijd.*

cornice, cornish horizontal moulded projection around the eaves of a building. *1621-2: the great Cornishe on the Front to be covered wth lead. 1664: reared up the peeres to the cornish.*

cornschowele cornshovel. See SHOVEL. *1352: j cornschowele.*

corporal double linen cloth on altar, the back half brought over to cover the elements of the mass in the unreformed church. Kept in a corporal-case.

corslet from double diminutive of Fr. *cors*, body. Defensive armour covering the body. In 16th and 17th centuries often meant a set comprising light helmet, breast-plate and back-plate (light cavalry), or open helmet, collar, breast- and back-plates, gorgets, tassets, arm plates, and gauntlets. See ALMAIN RIVETT. *1597: A Corslett furnysched...but no pyke. . . 4 black Corsletts: whereof 2 want their gorgetts. the brestplate & back of one Corslett. 1606: one Cosslytt xijs. iiijd.*

cosscheneys, cosschinse, cosshines, cosyngese see CUSHION

cosset a lamb or wether brought up by hand. *1593: one cosset wether vs.*

cosslytt see CORSLET

coster OFr. *costier*, side. Side curtain, particularly of a bed; riddels, or side curtains of altar. See BEDSTEAD. *1464-5: a coster of tapstery werke, conteyynge in lengthe xij zerdez; and in depthe iiij yerdez, and it is lyned, and it drawyth in yerdez lvij, the price of the yerde is xvjd. . . makenge of a bed wyth v costres to the same xxs.*

costhouse ? guesthouse. *1528: [repairing] le costhouse.*

cotar coulter of PLOUGH. *1320: j cotar [of iron].*

cotch see COACH

cote OE *cote*, small building; small detached house, cottage. *1386: [repairing] dil millecote. 1595: one calves coate buylded wth timber & borded xiijs. iiijd.*

coteyard yard in which COTE situated. *1414: [making hedges around] le coteyard [of the sheep].*

coteyne see CURTAIN

cott, cout variant of CLOUT. *1647: Carte Couts & brads. . . for Cotts wayenge 1 li. 4d.*

cotton true cotton, from several varieties of the plant *gossypium*, has been used in England since the Middle Ages for clothes and fabrics. It was originally imported from north Africa, and later from America. In the 16th-17th centuries it was used mainly for clothing, although Indian painted cottons (callico, chintz, pintado) were imitated by European

51

printed cottons from the late 17th century and were used for furnishing fabrics. Some coarse wool cloths were 'cottoned' by raising a soft, fluffy nap and then shearing it to leave an even surface, and these were known as 'cottons' - see E. Kerridge, *Textile Manufactures in Early Modern England*, 1985, pp.18-19. Cotton was also used for candlewicks. *1562: spun coten for candles. 1649: deyinge & fressinge of 22 yards & halfe of Red Cotton & 22 yards & halfe of yellow Cotton at 9d. ℔ yard.*

cottoning board board or table on which cloth was put for raising a nap. *1601: nine cottninge boordes xviijd.*

couch a couch-bedstead was a simple form of bed without a great head or canopy. A couch could also be a sumptuous piece of furniture or day-bed, a seat of state. In the 17th century and after it could also be a settee or sofa, sometimes with hinged ends or arm-rests. *1637: an old Cowch wth a bed twilted of blewe lynen cloth.*

coulde see COWL

counter Roman numerals were used for inventories and accounts from the Middle Ages to the 18th century, although by the 16th century arabic numerals were in use, sometimes combined with Roman. From the middle of the 17th century arabic replaced Roman numerals in most documents. As it was impossible to add up Roman numerals by placing them in columns, counting was done either on an abacus, or a counter or counter-table. The counter was a squared-off board, with counters or jettons placed to represent various numbers. Addition or subtraction was carried out by transferring the jettons to the next column. Counters were common in all classes of house except the smallest up to the end of the 17th century. The counter/counter table could be any size from a foot square to a large board, and in the Middle Ages the counter might take the form of a chequered cloth. Some counters were folded and portable, some extendable, some covered and lidded, and some in the form of a table. The counter was often located in the PARLOUR.

100 li	20 li	1 li	s	d	½ ¼d
10 5	10 5	10 5	10 5	6	
1 1 1	1 1 1	1 1 1	1 1 1	1 1 1	
1 1 1	1 1 1	1 1 1	1 1 1	1 1 1	
x *v*	*x* *v*	*x* *v*	*x* *v*	*vj*	
j j j	*j j j*	*j j j*	*j j j*	*j j j*	
j j j	*j j j*	*j j j*	*j j j*	*j j j*	
examples		⊙ ⊙	⊙ ⊙	⊙	is
⊙ ⊙	⊙ ⊙ ⊙	⊙ ⊙ ⊙	⊙ ⊙ ⊙	⊙ ⊙ ⊙	£279
		⊙	⊙		19s. 9d.
⊙				⊙ ⊙	£543
	⊙ ⊙	⊙ ⊙ ⊙	⊙ ⊙ ⊙	⊙ ⊙ ⊙	8s. 11d.
				⊙ ⊙	

Counting and running totals could be carried out without a counter by using a notation of dots in the margin of a document on the same system as the counter itself:-

1589 inventory
Heydon Hall

xl   v li   viijs.   viijd.   xj li   viijs.   xd.

xx   iiij li.   iiijs.   iiijd   viij li.   xjs.   viijd   ix li.   iiijs.   vjd.

total: iiij^XX xviij li. xviijs. [£98 18s.]

1453: cofors and countewery. 1459: j pece of rede say for accomptyng borde. 1588: Counter foulte. 1590: Counter without a cover. 1591: one Kounter vs. 1592: counter bord with stools. 1593: 1 ould counter table wth three loose leaves. 1593: counter without a lid. 1595: one Counter wth an olde darnex carpyt.

counterfeit made to a pattern. See PEWTER; TAPESTRY; also PARTISAN.

counterpoint, counterpane, contrapoint L. *culcita puncta,* OFr. *cuilte-pointe, coulte-pointe, coute-pointe*; 'Counterpane' uses L. *pannus,* cloth. Punctured quilt, stitched through. In the Costessey Hall inventory of 1597 the counterpoints are of lighter but more sumptuous material than the much more numerous COVERLETS. See also CONEY; COVERING. *1459: j redde panne of kinyng* [coney] *skynnys. 1467: a bed of cremysen damaske embrowdered with Cyle* [ceil] *counterpoynte and testour all after one. 1482: a contrepoint of verdyrs, conteyning in breede iiij yerds and di', and in length v yerdes and di'...a contrepoint with ymagery, of iiij yerds and a quarter broode, and v yerdes and a quarter long. 1513: a kovyrpayn of Fyn dyap. 1597: one Counterpoint of figured velvet taunye blewe & yellow. A Counterpoynt of Imagery Arras: for the bedd. . . one Counterpoint of brankeredge lyned* [this is crossed out and may be the same as *an old Coverlet of brankeredge lyned*] *. . . a Counterpoynt of yellow satten fygured in panes redd & blewe. 1745: one Green Velvett Counter Pane. 1764: A Quilt & Counterpin.1751: a tufted Contrapoint.*

country cattle the native Norfolk dun cattle. William Marshall, *Rural Economy of Norfolk* (1795) i. p.8: 'small boned, short-legged, round barrelled, well loined, thin thighed, clean chapped; the head in general fine, and the horns clean, middle-sized, and bent upwards: the favourite colour, a blood red, with a white or mottled face... no better flesh'd beasts are sent to Smithfield.' A. Young, *General View of the Agriculture of the County of Norfolk* (1804), 445: 'they [Norfolk] have a breed of their own which possesses no qualities sufficient to make it an object of particular attention.' *1590: x contry yearlings. 1594: one Countrey Heyffer xxvjs. viijd.*

course, corse a corpse. *1591: the shirts wch they did were ware burnte the residue the wynders had them & the fetherbed wch they did laye one was burnte because the course lay xxiiijth howers upon it & ther was noe body wold have it.*

courser up to the 17th century a large, strong horse used to carry armoured men in tournament and battle. *1464: costys for the cowseries...to tarye behynd wyth the couser.*

court baron manorial court, dealing only with the business of the manor.

court cupboard see CUPBOARD

court leet possibly from OE *læte,* connected with *læten,* let. The court leet was a manorial court which, in addition to dealing with manorial affairs, had jurisdiction over certain criminal and civil offences such as assault, highways, the breaking of ASSIZES, view of FRANKPLEDGE, and election of CONSTABLES, and had the means to punish offenders - PILLORY, stocks, CUCKING-STOOL, and gallows.

courtezan a person attached to a court, either of a great personage or a court of law. *1426: a courtezane of the Court of Rome...a weel lerned man holden, and a suffisant courtezan of the seyd court.*

cove the concave arch of a vault; quadrant curve joining the ceiling to the cornice. See COVING. *1732-3: pulling down the nosings & slips & coves.*

covell see COWL

cover temporary covers were used on furniture from at least the early 17th century. See CASE COVER. *1637: One large backchayer twoe heigh stooles one lowe stoole one footestool Cou'd wth greene velvet & Cotten Cou's ov' ym 2 li.*

coveracle, coverecle, covercle OFr. *covercle,* cover, lid. *1459: vj bolles, with oon coveracle gilt... j stondyng cuppe, all gilt, with a coveracle.*

53

covering, cover for bed. Early references seem to distinguish between covering and coverlet. Possibly the COVERLET was for use at night and the covering for protection when the bed was not in use. See COUNTERPOINT. *1459: j coveryng of grene saye. j coverlet of other warke . . . j coverlet of grene warke. ij coveryngs of white grene and blewe. 1513: J Covylyght Whyt & grene J Coveryng of Whytsaye. 1588: Coveringe of birdes Eyes. 1592: iij owld cowerynse iijs. 1593: 1 large cov'inge of Stammell. . . 1 Cov'inge of pullm worke wth birds eyes.*

coverlet, coverlight OFr. *covre-lit*, bed-cover. Coverlets in larger houses were often rich and highly decorative. Of the 34 coverlets in the inventory of Costessey Hall in 1597, 11 were tapestry including two VERDURE and one IMAGERY, nine were ARRAS, and the rest included one 'with the Kingstones armes' and at least three makeshift coverlets. See COUNTERPOINT; COVERING. *1459: Coke is Chambour...j redde coverlyte of rosys and blood houndys hedys. . . j coverlet of white rosys, at every corner iiij and one in the myddell. 1597: one blewe sumpter Clothe for the Coverlet. . . one coverlet of an old tapestry verdure hanging. . . one Coverlet of verdure Arras, lyned wth Canvas. . . one Coverlett of old turkye Carpet work. 1764: One Quilt, and coverlid.*

coving curved moulding of brick, plaster etc. at junction of wall and ceiling; curved iron plates at top of fireback to direct smoke into flue. *1709: iron back to the chimney & coveings in the chimney.*

covyn act of conspiring between two or more to defraud. *1450: he...is of covyn with the seid misdoers.*

cowcumber see CUCUMBER

cowdron see CAULDRON

cowel possibly from ML. *cupella*, ME. *cowl*, cup: to bleed or cup for medicinal purposes. *1665: cowelling the grey mare for a blowe upon the styfle bone. . . cowelling the browne bald horse colt for a straine in the chest.*

cowerynse see COVERING

cowl ML. *cupella*, OFr. *cuvele*, ME *cuvel*, cask, tub. 1. A large tub with two upstanding ears through which a cowl-staff was passed for carriage by two men. Cf. CORBELL. *1352: covell' [for bolting flour]. 1357: ij cowles xxd. 1591: ij bread grates iiij traies ij tubs & j Cowell* [but see 2]. 2. By the 16th century a cowl was a kind of cupboard (a) to stand brass, pewter etc. on. *1591: one cowld wt ye brass thereon standinge xvjs. 1592: a coole wth wooden dysshes on yt. 1594: one cowle wth brasse viz. potts of all sorts. 1595: one brasscoull. 1595: one cowle wth certaine dishes trenchers and spoons. 1666: [hall] one cold for pewter. 1722: A pewter Cold as it stand 1 li. 10s. 1746: a pair of spice drawers, a tea-kettle, & one pewter-cold, all very ordinary.* (b) Mention of the 'back' or 'DRESSER' suggests that sometimes a raised back or worktop was part of the cowl. *1585: one Cowle without a backe. 1589: cowle wth ye dresser. 1593: a Cowle and a Backe of wodd xvjd.* (c) A cowl is different from a CUPBOARD. *1584: a cubberd made cowle fation. 1603: 1 litle borded cubberd wth a colde adioyninge. 1637: one Couberd and one Coulde.* 3. hutch or COOP. *1592: one coule for Fowles. 1595: a hennes cowle.*

cow leech cow doctor. *1655: Cow leech. Bullockes. To Powlett of Cawson for drinching & blouding 38 Bullockes for ye Murrain and Gargett and 12d. to ye sawers helping 18s. 6d.*

cowntewery a COUNTER. *1453: cofors and cowntewery.*

coyne, coynestone see QUOIN

crab crab-apples, apples for cider or VERJUICE. Crushed in a press or with a heavy balk, and strained through a cradle or sieve. *1414: de iiijd. de Crabbes [sold this year]. 1465: for a presse to presse crabbes in and to make syther. 1499-1500: for stampyng of crabb xxjd. 1592: cradle to straine crabbs. 1593: stamping of crabbes. 1595: stampeles for crabbes.*

cracche L. *craccha*, CRIB; rack for animal fodder. *1330: [2 carpenters making] xj cracches [for sheep for 3 days 15d.. 1 carpenter for the said] cracch [for 3½ days 8¾d.].*

54

cradle grate, usually for coal fire. *1595: yron cradle. 1692: cole cradle with ye Cheeks.*

cradle wooden tub, with perforated bottom or a tap, in which unripe fruit was converted into VERJUICE. See CRAB.

cragg a basket. *1593: 2 Craggs 1 baskett.*

cramp, crampit iron bar with end bent to form hook; small iron bar with bent ends to hold two pieces of stone together. *1585-6: for iiij score pownde and seven of Irone Crampettes xviijs. for newe workyng of thirtye pownde of ye ould Crampetes ijs. vjd. 1592: one workinge yron thre crampyts and one moulde. 1738: 72 [foot] run of Cramps to Portland stone.*

cranage, cranedge dues paid for the use of a crane. *1481: crainage vjd. 1621-2: For Cranedge of the Lead at Norwch & bringinge it to the blackfryers 10s.*

crane coloured ash-grey, the colour of the common European crane, *Grus grus*. *1552: ij dekons of Crane Culler. 1588: crane colored fustyan.*

cranewery probably crane-coloured. Unlikely to be cranberry, as this name for the native British shrub *Vaccinium oxycoccos* was imported from America in the 17th century. *1513: vj zerds of Cranewery russet.*

crate L. *crata*, hurdle. *1328: [making] Rackes cribbes Crates [and other necessities in the court].* See CLATE; CLAY.

crater L. *cratera*, a bowl. Large bowl. *1459: iij crateras [of silver, of which 1 given to Margaret Hoddesone].*

cravice see CRAYFISH

crayer small sailing vessel of two or three masts and of 30-50 tons, principally for trading rather than fishing. *1481: his crayer laden with wete. 1583: a crayer called the Jone of Clay, lately arryved laden wyth Newcastel coles at the port of Clay. 1595: the forth pte of a Crayer xx li.*

crayfish, crafish, cravice crayfish or crawfish is a general term for crustaceans other than crabs, but it was specially applied to the freshwater crustacean *Astarchus fluviatilis*, now *Austropotamobius pallipes*. Sir Thomas Browne: 'the Gammarus or crawfish butt scarce in our rivers butt frequently taken in the Bure or north river and in the severall branches thereof, and very remarkable large crawfishes to bee found in the river which runnes by Castleaker and Nerford'. The price in accounts varies widely, but very few were purchased. One hundred were bought for 18d. at Oxnead in 1654, which suggests they were very small, while at Stiffkey in 1593 one crayfish cost 6d., suggesting that the latter may have been the spiny lobster *Palinurus vulgaris*. *1481: v crevys ijd. 1583: small cravices xiiij. 1593: [2-9 April] a Creafishe vjd. . . [14-21 May] ij creafishes & viij Crabbes xijd. 1654: 100 Crafishes 18d.*

cream cupboard cold cupboard to keep cream in; table or board to stand cream-pots on. *1685: Dayry...two tubbes two keelers one Creame Cupbord six cheese Fatts.*

cream stick flat ladle or scummer for skimming cream. *1709: 2 Cream ferkins, a Cream pot, a cream stick.*

crease crest, curved ridge-tile. See CREST. *1665: pulled downe the creases from about the top of the great dyning roome.*

credill cradle. *1597: ij payer of wooding stooles and a childes credill xviijd.*

creeper(s) 1. Small grapnels for retrieving buckets from the bottom of a well. 2. Small iron firedog, a pair of which were placed in the hearth between the andirons. *1310: [mending] j crepar jd. 1584: payer Crepers & two iron Wegis. 1587: One payer of crepers vjd.*

creeper(s) Forby: PATTEN with iron stumps instead of rings.

creeping of(to) the Cross before the Reformation, creeping on all fours to kiss a processional or ceremonial cross. *1504: and to offyr at the Crepynge of ye Crosse on Good Friday jd.*

cresset iron basket holding combustibles for lighting, fixed to pole or building. *1538-9: xvj li. of talow to the Cresset light. for piche and rosin to the same light. 1589: one cresset of iron.*

crest, creast, cresting the top of the ridge of a roof, composed of sedge on thatched roofs and curved or ridge-tiles on tiled roofs; also coping-stones. *1618-20: There is 860 foote of straight and tracery creast For the gable ends at 16d. the foote 57 - 7 - 6. For part of the creast for the gable ends on the west side of new stone.*

crewel worsted yarn of two threads for tapestry and embroidery; the cloth made of this yarn; the balls or bobbins. *1537: di' li. of blacke cruell for the javelyns xijd. 1552: altar cloth of diaper crewel. 1593: 1 Canapie of grene cloth ymbroydered wth yellowe wth a Cruell fringe of blacke & yelowe. 1711: 41 Grosse & a half of greasy yarn £20. 35 gross of Cruell £19 10s.*

crewse see CRUSE

crib rack or trough in which fodder for horses or cattle is placed. *1313: [carpentering] crybbes in novo stabl' xd. 1328: [daubing] cribbes [for horses].*

crockstone shallow drum of stone or brick on which a TIPE or cupola stands. *1618-20: For sawing framing and rearing 4 hollow tipes upon the stearecases in the little court with their vauses & crockstones: and boarding and fully finishing them.. c.1620: Foure hollow Tipes within the little court...Wch Tipes the curbs are made of timber:..in the mannor of Vauses with crockstones in the sayd curbs carved For the [illeg.] of the Freise and architrave wch is to be made of stone.* See CURB; VAUSE.

crome hook, crook. A long-shafted tool with 3 or 4 tines bent at 90°, for pulling about muck, clay, soil, hay etc. A fire crome was used for pulling burning thatch off houses. See DAUB; MUCK CROME; DRAFT HOOK. *1584: iij taynd crom. . . a claye crome. 1592: hay crome. 1592: iij drawing cromes. 1617: dawbing fork & crome. 1712: muck crome. 1746: turnip crome.*

crome the hook of a simple hook-and-eye HINGE. *1310: in cromynge de ij gates jd... cromes ad ij gates jd. ob.*

cronix probably CORNICE. *c.1619: [over gate at entrance to house] 2 pillosters of Ionicke with there basis pedistalls cronix and subbase and the body of the pillosters cutt in rusticke.*

crossbow bow to shoot short feathered bolts or short arrows (quarrels). The lath was the wooden or steel spring or bow, fixed at right angles to the tiller or stock of wood, which was grooved for the reception of the bolt. The crossbow was loaded or wound by an apparatus, the rack, winder, or WYNDAC, operated by a crank that drew back the cord. *1459: iij grete crosbowes of stele, with one grete dowble wyndas ther too. j coffyre, full of quarrellys of a smale sorte. xij quarrellis of grete sorte, feddered with brasse. . . xi crosbowes wherof iij stele, and v wyndas. 1592: iij win of crosbow thred jd. ob. 1595: In Box & rowghe tymber for the makynge of Crosebow tyllers ijs. iiij new Crosebow lathes roughe and untempered viijs. ij Crosse bowes and a Racke.*

cross clout see CLOUT

cross cut sawn as opposed to split timber. See OVERWHART. *1655: 2 deales splitting 8d. and for d' a peece in cross cutts*

crossgarnet ⊢ shaped hinge, with the horizontal part of the ⊢ attached to the moving part of the door or window. *c.1623: [smith] One Iron Bar in a light with hookes and hinges Crossgarnets and Cassements. . . Crossegarnets Hookes and hinges for pound.*

cross to brush clothes frame † to hang clothes on to brush: *1751: Cross to brush Cloaths*

crotch eye crotchet, small hook for fastening gates etc. *1819: crotch eyes and brads to gates.*

crouchmass festival of the Invention of the Cross, 3rd May.

crow crowbar, iron bar with bent and beaked end used as lever.

crowdbarrow, crowdingbarrow see CRUDBARROW

crown glass glass of silica, potash, and lime, without lead or iron, made in thin circular sheets by blowing. Windows of crown glass often show a slight curvature. Bull's-eye: the centre of the sheet. *1737: 8 squ of plate Glass put in & 15 squ of Crown glass at ye house. 1819: One Crown Square in Harness Room 9d.*

crudbarrow wheelbarrow with one front wheel and two rear handles, pushed or 'crowded', with perhaps a secondary association with crud/curd in the sense of earth, clay, muck. The wheelbarrow was in use by the 13th century, but the early illustrations show it without the legs. The wheels were often bought separately from the body. The phrase 'crowding a barrow' was still in use in the 20th century. See also BARROW. *1477: sche sent my modyr word be Kate, that sche zuld come bedyr wanne God sent tyme, thoow sche xuld be crod in a barwe. 1584: one Crudyng barrow xijd. 1591: one crowdinge barrowe. 1663-4: Two strakes for a crudbarrow wheele xijd. 1665: virrells gudirons & plates for a crudbarrowe xviijd. . . sawing 6 paire of crudbarrowe stringes & feet to them xijd. 1710: for making 2 Crowd-Barrows 2s.*

cruell see CREWEL

crues see CRUSE

cruet metal vessel with lid for the mingled wine and water for the pre-Reformation mass. *1459: j haly water stop, with j sprenkell and ij cruettes.*

crupper leather strap buckled to the back of the saddle and passing under the horse's tail to stop the saddle sliding forward. *1779: a sadle Bridle & crupper.*

cruse small vessel, either of pot or metal, usually for drinking. The earthenware cruse was often rimmed with silver. *1483: for drynkyng crewses for howsold viijd. 1584: one crewse typped wth sylver vjs. viijd. one old crewse typped wth sylver defacyd ijs. 1587: one pewter cruse. 1590: Three stoninge potts & a drinckinge crues.*

cubbad, cubberd, cubert see CUPBOARD

cucking stool, cuckstool from cuck, to shit. An apparatus for the punishment of women, in the form of a CLOSE-STOOL or chair, in which scolds, loose women etc. were bound and exposed to the scorn of the populace, or sometimes, with the cucking stool on the end of a counterbalanced beam, ducked in a pond or river. From its form it was often called a TREBUCHET. *1335: [carpentered] dil Cucstol & dil thewe. 1389: [repairing] dil Cuckestool.*

cuckold see COOK'S HOLD

cucumber *Cucumis sativus* was known in Anglo-Saxon England and grown here by the early 14th century. The spelling cowcumber in the 17th and 18th centuries was associated with the pronunciation, and was out-of-date by the early 19th century. *1719: two hundred Asparygrass two cowcumbers 2s. 6d.*

cuearne, cuerne see QUERN

cueret, cuerat, curet, curat, cuirass, from Fr. *cuir*, leather; body armour, originally of leather, consisting of breast-plate and back-plate, buckled together. Current in the 16th-17th centuries. The cueret was sometimes seen as a complete set of upper-body armour. *1588: for vj curatts, old and evill, at xvijs. . . iij curats wthout hedpiecys xxxs. 1593: 8 Corseletts 1 Cueret iijs. iiijd. 1597: 4 Curetts: 4 headpecs: 4 gorgetts. Curetts rybbed 2 the bodies only. 1603: one foulinge peece, a Curate furnyshed, one staffe.*

cuisse thigh-piece in a suit of armour.

cular see COOLER

culle, cullis, cullit the quantities in the quotations suggest that a culle was a rough or estimated quantity, often quite large. Coll, cole is Scottish for haystack, and perhaps a culle should be seen as a stack. *1584: 1 Culles of wheate in the west ende in shofes estemed at iiij Combe xxvjs. viijd. in the same end 1 Culles of blye in shofe estemed at xl Combe viij li. 1592: one cullis of hey. 1593: one little culles of buck. one little culles of otes. 1595: j cullit of fetches.* See GOAF.

cullener see COLANDER

cullesent variant of cognizance, heraldic bearing, badge, mark or token. Hentzner 1591: 'The English are serious, like the Germans - lovers of shew; liking to be followed... by whole troops of servants, who wear their masters' arms in silver, fastened to their left arms.' 1618: 'All the cullizans (signs or badges, in the zodiac) except one.' *1612: j cullesent*

& j selfer spon iiijs.

culverin a small hand-gun; from the early 16th century a long piece of artillery was also called a culverin, with variations such as demi-culverin. *1591: A pike and A culver.*

cummin, cumin, comyn OE *cymen.* The seeds of *Cuminum cyminum,* an umbelliferous plant resembling fennel from the Levant, have aromatic and carminative qualities. *1554: One pound of Coomyn & an other of frankencense to ayer the Cofers in the house at Brome, & to gyve to the Doves there. 1587: j li. of Comyn seede viijd.*

cunnyfer coney-fur, the fur of the CONEY or rabbit. *1597: one ould cunnyfer bedd.*

cunstall see CONSTABLE

cupboard originally a board or table on which to set cups for use or display. This sense had more-or-less gone by the 16th century, except for the 'court' cupboard and its variants. Fastolf's inventory of Caister Castle in 1459 has 6 cupboard cloths but no cupboards, suggesting that they were built-in and so not reckoned as furniture. The Houghton inventory of 1513 has 3 cupboards, two of them in chambers and one in 'Le drawt', but with no details. By the end of the 16th century the number and variety of cupboards had grown immensely. Up to 1600 the AMBRY still appears occasionally, and the enclosed cupboard or cupboard with doors, known from the early 16th century, was its successor. In the 17th century and after 'cupboard' nearly always implied that it was enclosed with doors. Some of the varieties often met with are:-

boarded of boarded rather than joined construction. *1593: 1 old borded Cubberde viijd. 1603: j litle borded cubberd with a colde adjoyninge.*

box probably same as boarded. *1595: A box cubborde wth a cubberd Cloath.*

corner made from the end of the 17th century, for display. *1709: Japan corner cupboard.*

court Fr. *court,* short. Tier of 3 display and service shelves, joined and supported at the corners by turned posts; about 4 feet high and 5 feet long, although it may be longer. G. Chapman, *May-Day,* 1611: 'court-cupboards planted with flaggons, cups and beakers'. Later called buffet. The 'court cupboard' of the antique trade is a cupboard in two or three stages, the main one being enclosed and the upper one enclosed, recessed, and often canted. The term court cupboard is not very common in the 16th and 17th centuries. *1620: a Cort Cubbord with his Carpett. . . a Cort Cubbord with his cloth of white Damaske.*

close cupboard with doors. *1546: In the wasshing Hous First two close cobords and a presse. 1593: 1 Close Cubbard.*

drawers the court cupboard could have a drawer or drawers. The quotation of 1608 is an inventory of fittings, which would imply that the articles are fixed to the structure. *1595: a cubbud wth ye drawer wth Leaden wayts. 1608: two Cubberds & 3 drawers under the south window wth 2 lockes.*

fixed see above. Many cupboards must have been made without backs, and the quotations may reflect the uncertainty whether the item should be counted as movable for the purposes of the inventory. *1592: one Cubborde and ij trussells sett in the grounde. 1620: a Cubbard fastened to the Skreine.*

Flanders/Flemish carved oak panels from the Low Countries were popular in the 16th and 17th centuries, and the importation of such panels was revived in the 19th century. *1592: One Flanders cupborde.*

food *1589: a cubbord to keepe flesshe in vjs. viijd.*

glass perhaps a court cupboard, but more likely a closed cupboard. *1591: j Cupbord to set in glasses xijd.*

graven the court cupboard, being mainly shelves, gave little scope for extensive carving, so 'graven' or 'carved' may imply a cupboard with doors. *1584: a graven cupbord with an*

58

alter. 1593: 1 Cubbard carved wth guilt ymages & 1 old redd Cubberd Cloth xs.

<u>livery</u> in some cases the livery cupboard might have been an alternative term for the court cupboard; livery = delivery of food, that is a cupboard from which food was served. Typical livery cupboards of the 16th and 17th centuries had doors either pierced or formed of small turned balusters, and were often quite small. They are sometimes found in bedchambers, which suggests either that they were used as subsidiary food-stores or that they were being used as general storage, perhaps for small items of clothing or toilet. Thomas Hirne's house in St. Simon's. Norwich, in 1637 had livery cupboards in 7 rooms, 5 of which were bedchambers. *1588: one lyverie Cupborde wth turned postes, wth a carpett of grene brode cotten ijs. iiijd. 1589: a cubbord with lock and key xs. a cubbord to keepe flesshe in vjs. viijd. 1597: One Cubbord or lyvery table: wth one Carpet of nedlework. 1637: One old broken presse and j old broken liv'y Cubbord wth posts 1 li. 10s... one old smale livery table one livery Cubbord b[?] square 3s. . . one litle liv'y Cubbord painted greene 4s.*

<u>press</u> implies a closed cupboard, usually shelved, to keep clothes in. *1588: a cubbert presse wt iij locks xs. 1636: j Cobert wth presses xxxvs. 1714: an Iron pott and a press Cupboard 12s.* See PRESS.

<u>standing</u> perhaps taller than a livery cupboard. *1587: one standinge cupbourde wt a liverye cupbourde xxxs.*

<u>table</u> composite furniture was popular in the 16th and 17th centuries. *1592: a lyttle square table wth a Cubbord in ytt. 1620: a Foulding table with Cupbords.*

<u>tester</u> a back to the cupboard, possible with shelves like a welsh dresser. *1588: a cowbard & the testour ov' it.*

cupboard cloth the custom up to the 18th century was to have a cloth, sometimes quite elaborate and costly, to cover the top of the CUPBOARD - which implies that the cupboard-top could not be not much more than about four feet high. *1506-7: ij cubboord clothes xxd. 1513: A Cupburd cloth of dyap. 1593: 1 newe square Cubberd Carpett of nedleworke. 1637: 2 green livery cubboard cloaths wrought with silke fringes.*

curb raised band of stone, brick, or wood, not high enough to be a dwarf wall, to receive lower ends of palisade, column, pilaster etc. See CROCKSTONE.

curball curb; frame, coaming round top of well, copper, trap-door etc. *1729: 4 peices 18' long & a Curball for a well.*

curing covering for bed. See COVERING.

curlew the common curlew, *Numenius arquata*, appears as an occasional item in household accounts. The Stiffkey accounts for 1593 record curlews only in December and January, but at Oxnead in 1655 single curlews appear in September and October, and at Houghton (1647-9) there is only one entry, for three curlews, on 15th November 1647. The comparative rarity in accounts suggests that it was not abundant in the 16th and 17th centuries, although Sir Thomas Browne noted 'The Arcuata or curlewe frequent about the sea coast'. The stone curlew, Norfolk plover, or thicknee, *Burhinus œdicnemus*, is a summer visitor, and does not occur at all in the above accounts. *1593: for a Curlew vjd. . . ij curlewes xxd. 1647: 3 Curlues 4s. 6d. 1655: 1 Corlew and 2 green Pluver 20d.*

currants dried grapes, originally from Corinth and known as RAISINS of Corinth. *1499-1500: iij lib' of reysons of Corens. 1647: for 6 li. Currantts 4s.*

curry a small two-wheeled CART with a flat bottom and no fixed sides. *1584: a payer curry wheles iiijs. 1588: ij little Curryes. 1590: One Carte Booke one Curry Booke. 1636: one payer small Curye whells xvijs. vjd.*

curtain, bed see BEDSTEAD

curtain, picture a small curtain hung in front of a particularly valuable painting to protect it from the light. *1636: [in wardrape in a trunk] one picture curtain.*

curtain, window even in large houses, window curtains were not common before the second half of the 16th century. In smaller houses they probably followed the general adoption of glazing in the 17th and 18th centuries. *1590: ij littell Curteyns for the windowes. 1591: [parlour] j curtayne for the wyndowe & ye iron for it to run upon xvjd. . . [parlour chamber] curtins of chaungeable mockadoe with the curten irons. . . [little parlour] curtens for the windowe and the enterie. 1593: 3 windowe Curtins of blacke & yellowe saye & 3 Curtin Rodds iiijs. . .2 windowe Curtins of yelowe cotton & 2 Curtin rodds vjs. 1597: one payer of wyndow Curteyns satten Abridges old: of 6 panes both yellow & orenge tawney. 1637: One old dornix Curtin about a yarde depe motheaten & ratt eaten & j yron rod 3s.*

curtal, curten nag Fr. *courtault*, shortened. Horse with docked tail; small breed of horse which often had docked tail. *1505: my blacke curten nagge.*

curtle see KIRTLE

curye L. *curia*, court, courtyard. *1310: [2 boards for mending] le Curye fald.*

cushion a word that presented more spelling difficulties than almost any other. To ameliorate the hardness of wooden furniture, largely without upholstery, most medium to large houses had an abundance of cushions, stuffed with feathers or flock and with covers that were often highly ornamental and expensive. Some cushions were quite large and heavy. *1466-7: for makenge of vij coshones of cremysene and grene velvet iijs. fore stuffynge of the said coshones, for vj stone Federis, prise the stone ijs.* Some examples of the different cushions found in inventories and accounts are:-

armorial and figurative *1588: Two Cusshens of Arras, with the Armes of the Godsalves, and Townesendes vjs. viijd. 1593: 1 other old longe Cushin Chequored wth horse heades on yt . . .1 Cushin of nedlework wt the horse heade in the midest. 1597: 3 Cusshions of tapstry wth the pollaxe wthout stuffing &c. 1601: Three other Cushions of tappestry worke wth St George on horsebacke ixs.*

built-in to furniture *1593: 6 Cushin stooles of Tapstry worke wth buckeram covers xxiijs. . . .1 old Cushin stoole of nedleworke chequorwise xxd.*

carpetwork *1593: 6 Carpett worke Cushins xxs. . . 1 other Cushin of Carpett worke white & blacke.*

patterned *1593: 2 other Cushins of billett worke xiijs. iiijd. 1597: one Cusshion of stryped satten.*

plain *1459: iiij cosschonys of rede saye... j cusschen of redde silke.*

rich materials *1593:1 longe yellowe Cushin of Satten a bridges ymbroydered wth black vs. . . 1 other longe Cushin of black vellett ymbroydered with yellowe xxs. . . 2 old square vellet Cushins iiijs. . . 1 old Cushin of Crimsin vellett & yelowe. 1597: one olde Cusshing Case of clothe of tyssewe. . . 2 longe Cusshyns Case of clothe of golde: whereof theone is bothe syds alyke thother having one syde of grene damask: wthout stuffinge. 1637: six silke orries quishenes two large windowe quishiones of the same lined with green taffetye.*

needlework *1593: 1 large Cushin of nedleworke blewe & yelowe vjs. viijd.*

other materials *1588: j longe windowe Cusshinge of grene brode cotten and redde figured ijs. vjd. 1589: six cushyns of Turkey worke stuffed with fethers ij li. 1597: one Cusshion of redd leather.*

window-seat *1588: A Wyndowe Cusshinge of olde peces of clothe bodkyn iijs. iiijd. iij Wyndowe Cusshens, one of changeable Taffata of blacke and redde imbrodered wth Marie golds & Roses, and other flouers, and the other two of grene figured silke xxvs. 1593:1 old windowe Cushin of black vellett with silver bone lace iijs. iiijd.*

cushnet a little cushion, pincushion; PINPILLOW. A night cushnet was either for putting pins in when undressing, or a small cushion for ease in bed. *1593: 2 Cushnetts the 1 ymbroydered the other wrought wth nedleworke. 1595: A lytle box wth gloves pynnes lace A Lookyng glasse, A coome, A night cushnet.*

60

custer custard. *1595: a godderd of pewter a Custer coffing twoe strayners of pewter.*

cut to demolish, spread. *1649: 3 days of Rawlyn to cutt mowle hills 3s.*

cutting saw saw of medium size between the long saw and the handsaw, used for cutting across the grain. See SAW. *1592: A long sawe a belt a Rabbet a cutting saw two hand sawes with other tooles.*

cuwe L. *cuna, cuwa*, tub or vat. Tub perhaps the size of a TUN, but open at the top. See COWL. *1352: [4 great] cuwe & iiij kelers.*

cwt. = HUNDREDWEIGHT

cyetica sciatica. *1444: He hath hadde a cyetica that hath letted hym a gret while to ride.*

cyne chine, a joint consisting of the whole or part of the backbone of the animal. *1649: Cyne of Beefe wayeinge 5 st.9 li. - 1 li. 2s. 6d.*

cynmyn see CINNAMON

cypress the cypress, *Cupressus sempervirens*, native to Persia and the Middle East, produces a hard, durable wood that was used for furniture, particularly chests. *1459: iij payre tablys of cipris. 1597: one fayer large chest of Cypres. 1688: Sipris Chest.*

Cyprus, sipers a term applied to several varieties of cloth, but particularly to a light transparent black cloth originally made in Cyprus but made in England from the late 16th century and used as a kerchief and in mourning; sometimes cloth of gold, or satin. *1467: a kercher of sypres xviijd. 1633: for cipris for 2 hatbands 5s. . . for ij yards of bl. cipris 5s.*

cything see KITCHEN

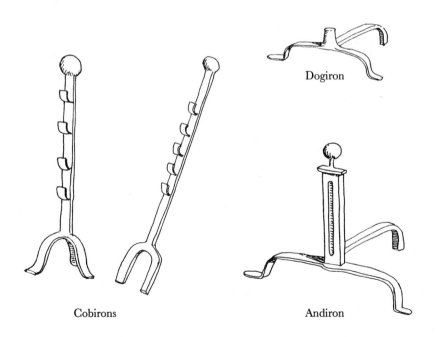

Dogiron

Cobirons

Andiron

61

D

D the Roman numeral for five hundred. See C; I; J; L; M; V; X.

d. L. *denarius*, penny, 12 of which made a shilling. In Roman numeration placed after the figure but before ob. (OBOLUS, halfpenny) e.g. viijd. ob. = 8½d.

dabbing see DAUB

dagg heavy pistol or handgun. *1597: 2 pocket Daggs. 1603: two daggs, one old pistoll...two Scottishe daggers, two swords, two daggers.*

dagger, arming military dagger, part of arms. See ARMING. *1459: little schort armyng dager.*

dairy, diery, deygh the room for processing milk into CHEESE and butter. Most farmhouses, even the smallest, had a dairy, which had to be kept cool, and was usually fitted with a latticed or louvred window. See p. 72; CHURN; DAYE. *1320: [thatching] dayerye...[hooks and bands for the window] of the dayerie jd. ob. 1537: ij payles for the deygh hous vd.*

daïs, dese L. *discus*, OFr. *deis*, disc, dish. The sense moves from dish to table to high table, set on a platform or daïs. The table at the upper end of the hall for family and chief guests was raised on a platform above the general floor level. See p. 241; DESCLOTH. *1388: [repairing] Benches ad le Dees. 1513:[hall] J hangyng at ye dese of Red say wt a borde' a bove.*

dale, dale tree sewer or pit, soakaway (Cotgrave 1611); wooden trough, conduit, pipe for carrying off water, etc. *1591:* [with brewing vessels] *a stocke a dale tree. 1593:[brewing house] 1 dale. 1637: a cooler 2 dales 2 pipes & other brewing vessels. 1692: ye scales weights pedds Dale trees swil tubes & hoggs trows. 1746:[brewhouse] one Cooler, one Dale Tree, and one Cheesepress.*

dalmatic wide-sleeved tunic reaching to below knees, worn in the unreformed church by a deacon at high mass and by the bishop under his chasuble.

damasin, damson small dark-blue plum, *Prunus domestica* or *P. communis* var. *damascena*. The name was derived from Damascus, but the plum comes from the wild bullace, and was one of the principal varieties of plum in the Middle Ages and 16th century. The fruits were gathered ripe, halved, dried, and preserved in syrup. 'Damson' was also applied to other varieties of plum.

damask derived from Damascus. 1. Rich silk fabric, with elaborate designs and figures, often multi-coloured. 2. Twilled linen fabric figured in the weaving. 3. Fabric of linen and worsted. Norwich was the centre of the linen/worsted damask industry. Used for clothing, bed curtains, bed coverings, and upholstery. *1459: j hatte of bever, lynyd with damaske gilt. . .ij yerds and j quarter of white damaske. . . a typpet, halfe damask and halfe felwet. . . j hode of damaske russet. 1513: J pce of Tawny Damaske...J rede Gyrdyll sylv' & Gylt Damaske corde. 1593:[bed] tester and vallance of black & white damaske. . . [bed] wth 3 Curtins of damaske blewe & yellowe. . .[bed] tester & vallance of Crimsin vellett & white damaske ymbroydered wth garters. 1597: sparver of damask caffa...Twylte of Caffa damask changeable grene & orenge tawny. 1637: 3 backe chayers covered wth silke dammaske.*

damask 1. Damascened, that is metal, particularly steel, with incised designs filled with silver or gold. 2. Ornamented with pattern as on damascened blades etc. 3. Colour of damask rose, deep red. *1589: ij damaske potts iiijs.*

damask prunes imported prunes, dried plums. See DAMASIN. *1647: 2 li. of Damaske Prunes 6d.*

damnified from damnify, to injure, damage. Condemned, adulterated, gone off. In the quotation the damnified drink is roughly half the price of that not so described. *1729: five Gall' of damnified Barcelona 6s. 8d. Ten Gall' of damnified Cyder 13s. 4d. four Gall' of damnified Clarett 5s. 4d.*

damsque see DANSKE

dan, danne small buoy of wood or inflated skin, with a flagged pole, for marking fishing lines, etc. *1584: eyght lynes, twelve strings, two dands, two towes. 1591: one boute anker two dannes.*

danckes, dannc see DANSKE

dannock, danhocke possibly Gael. *domag*, gauntlet. Wool or leather mittens, with all fingers in one compartment. *1498-9: pro glovys et dannokes and horskynys and scheepys skynys xs. 1591: j payer of danhocke. 1593: a payer of dannocks. 1619: a payer leather Danock or gloves xiiijd.*

danske Danish; applied particularly to CHESTS, made of Baltic oak or, perhaps, deal; also to pewter and other things. See FAN. *1587: ij eared pottes with covers of pewter called danske pottes. 1588: Danckes cheste. 1590: danske chest wt setworke viijs. 1590: one danske Fan and one hayer vjs. viijd. 1590: a danske fanne 2 fyeing fannes. 1591: one danske chest with a locke iiijs. 1592: a danske pewter pott. 1593: rye. a dansk Fan vjs. 1593: Corse linnen remayning in a danske chest.*

darnex, darnache, darniche see DORNIX

darys dace, *Leuciscus leuciscus*, a freshwater fish attaining 6-10 inches and a weight of 1¼ lbs. *1506-7: eelys, rochys, darys and tenchys.*

dash plunger of the upright CHURN. *1649: a leede & dash for a hand Churn 1s. 8d.*

dashnet see NET

date, dating In England the Julian or Old Style (O.S.) calendar was in use until 1752. In this calendar the year began on 25th March, and ended on 24th March following, although, confusingly, 1st January was often celebrated as the New Year. On 24th February 1582 the Pope, Gregory XIII, issued a bull ordering the reform of the calendar by omitting ten days between 4th and 14th October 1582 to bring it into conformity with the solar year. The year was to begin on 1st January, and every fourth year was to be a leap year. This Gregorian or New Style (N.S.) calendar was not adopted in England until 1752, when by an Act of Parliament, 24 Geo. II, c. 23, (1751) the year was to begin on 1st January and the days between 2nd and 14th September 1752 were to be omitted. This means that up to 1752 any date between 1st January and 24th March was recorded as being in what we would see as the previous year; for example, a document dated '24th February 1545' would be in what we would call 1546. The dates of quotations throughout this glossary have been converted to the New Style. Dating of documents is further complicated by the medieval, and later, practice of establishing the day of the year by reference to a saint's day e.g. 'the day after the feast of St. Peter's chains' (1st August) = 2nd August, and the year by the regnal year, which began on the day of accession, e.g. 'in the 25th year of Queen Elizabeth' (17th Nov. 1582 - 16th Nov. 1583) or the year dating from the accession of some other dignatory who had power over the institution concerned (e.g. 'in the 2nd year of Prior Gilbert'). For establishing the exact date in these instances one has to have recourse to C.R. Cheney, *Handbook of Dates for Students of English History* (1948, and subsequent reprints), and lists of the accession of kings and the appointment or installation of bishops, priors etc.

daub to apply the clay to a wattle-and-daub building; the clay itself. *1665: made clay splented risered & daubed betweene the studds. 1654: dawbing ye howse of office.*

daubing fork, crome, spade implements for mixing and applying the clay to timber-framed buildings. See CROME. *1584: dawbing forks. 1594: a dawben forke & a dawber spade. 1617: dawbing fork & crome.*

daye, dey OE *dæge*, female servant, housekeeper, maker of bread; in Middle Ages the woman (sometimes man) in charge of the DAIRY, a word derived from 'daye'. *1273: [delivered to the] daye [at Gateley vj bushels barley]. 1307: Emme Le deye. 1328: [wage of 6 servants] & j daye [in winter] ijs. iiijd. 1538: the daye wyff.*

63

dayerye see DAIRY

dead-eye, dead man's eye round flat wooden block with one or three holes, through which a lanyard passed to extend the stays or shrouds of a ship. *1466: the closynge of dedemen yen. 1468: xlviij dedmanes eyene viijs.*

dead light skylight made not to open. *1621-2: To Stanyon for 62 dead Lights xs. iiijd.*

dead lime slaked lime. *1482: [for digging] dedlyme [and clay].*

deadnail large NAIL made 'dead' by clinching or bending over the projecting point on the other side of the plank. *1327: dednail [for the granary ½d.].*

deal MLGerm. *dele*, plank, floor. Sawn BOARD not less than 9 inches broad and not more than 3 inches thick, and 6 feet or more in length. Historically, 'deal' was mostly applied to fir or pine imported from N. Germany and the Baltic area. These were distinguished from Eastland or oak boards by 1260, although the term 'deal' does not appear till the 15th century. Furrendeal: deal of fir. Still deals: OED gives quot. 1667 for door lined with slit-deal. *The Country-Builders' Estimates c.* 1727 has 'Boarded Partitions, with rough slit Deal, at 14s. per square...Whole Deal and slit Deal Partitions, groved and planed on both sides, at 2s. per Yard'. 'Still' in the 1728 quote is probably a misspelling of slit, that is sawn thin for the purpose. *1588: table & bench of furendell. 1592: form of Furrendeale joyned. 1597: one close stoll of furindell. c.1620: new bording the Floore strong and substantial with planed deales. 1621: 29 spruce deales 7 li. 19s. 6d...540 deales 28 li. 16s. 1647: 6 large Deals at 1s. 4d. p deale. 1664: hewed severall stockes of deale at the sawing pitt. 1681: when I cast up the charge of felling, sawing, and hewing, I found the charge to be as much as the timber was worth, and the deale boards being now cheape, may be bought for lesse than the workemanship of the others. 1728: 12 Still Deals for Boarding ye well . . . 80 14' yellow deals.*

debt in INVENTORIES, debts owing to the deceased are often classed either as 'sperate', of which there was some hope of payment, or 'desperate', those with little or no hope of being paid. Debts could be money lent with or without BOND, money owed for services rendered, rents owed, goods bought and not paid for, and in the case of clergy money owed for payment of commutated TITHE. Clergy were often owed large sums, e.g. William Clapham, Rector of Runton 1603 was owed 'by handbills' £300 out of an inventory total of £624 5s. 4d.; John Hill, minister of Yarmouth 1602, was owed £85 out of total of £100 19s. 4. The administration accounts, where they survive, often show the discharge of debts. See OBLIGATION; SPECIALITY. *1584: [debts] Robte Becker for j bote & the fearme thereof for iiij yeares xxvjs. viijd. for ev'ye yeare v li. vjs. 8d. 1590: One obligacon of div'se sommes of money for the payment of one hundreth and x pounds Ad ffiñ nat dñi Cx li. 1591: In Bondes owing hym wherof their is desperat xx li iiij^{xx} li. 1594: in desperate debts owing by badd debtors uppon specialtiez CC li. 1611: one bonde Obligatory of Robt Egmores xxvjs. viijd. 1713: Debts sperate 254 li. 2s. 1d. Debts Desperate 39 li. 17s. 1737: Debts Good & Bad about £44 10s. 10d.*

decker work embroidered fabric. *1751: a Decker Work Toilett. . . A Lath Bottom Bedstead with colour'd Decker Work Furniture lined with Pink Lustring...The Decker Work Hangings of the Room* [in 1792 this is the Best Needlework Chamber] *. . . Decker Work Bed Chamber...a Bedstead...Decker Work Furniture...six Walnutt Tree Chairs the Seats covered with Decker Work..*

dedemen yen see DEAD-EYE

deer cloth polishing cloth of soft deerskin. *1709: 15 Rubbers 13 Collering cloaths 7 Deer cloaths.*

deer leather soft leather for clothes. *1459: ij jakketts of derys lether, with j coler of blak felwet*

deer suet solid fat from loins and kidneys, used for cooking and greasing armour to protect from rust. *1593: [with armour] 3 Cakes of deeres suytt*

dees see DAÏS

demesne the state of possession; property, particuarly land, held in one's own hand and not let out to FARM; lordship.

demiceint girdle of two halves. Cotgrave 1611: 'a woman's girdle, whose forepart is of gold or silver, and hinder of silke &c.' *1467: a lytell gerdyll of sylke and goolde called a demysent and the harneys of goolde. 1513: j Demycent of sylv' and gylt.*

demilance lance with a short staff.

demise to transfer property or estate. See p. 243

dentilation ornamental treatment of e.g. a cornice, with alternate blocks or bricks being recessed or projected. ▢▢▢▢▢

deping, deeping section of fishing-net. 1615: 'Each net must be in depth seven deepings. Each deeping must be a fathom, that is two yards, deep.' *1592: xviij newe depings.*

descloth 1. Cloth to hang on DAÏS behind table and chair. 2. Table-cloth. *1587: one holld dese clothe one benche borde viijd. 1595: [hall] paynted cloth called a descloth iijs. iiijd.*

desk sometimes supported on legs, but often in the 16th-17th centuries a box with a sloping top; bookstand. *1592: Tow standinge desks & ij other deskes ijs. 1593: 4 bookes viz Jasor, 1 psalter, Billson, 1 old pchment of diues & pauper & 1 folding desk vs. 1613: his Bookes xiiij li. A Table and the deskes whereon his bookes doe stande xs. 1637: one deske to reede on 1s. 1764:[dressing room] a reading Desk with two Sconces.*

desperate debt see DEBT

deye, deygh see DAYE, DAIRY

deying dyeing. See COTTON.

di' abbrev. of L. *dimidius, dimidiatus*, half. Often put after the word it relates to without 'and' - see quot. 1599. *1538-9: di' Mᵗ of sodellers nayle. 1593: di' linge xijd. 1599: a dosin di' trenchers. . . Tares j acr' di'* [1½ dozen trenchers, 1½ acres].

dial clock, watch, mariner's compass. *1590: one diall and one mapp ijs.*

diaper, dioper, diper linen fabric with pattern formed by the different directions of the threads, typically of lines crossing diamondwise, the spaces filled in with other small patterns. Not woven in England in quantity before the Flemings introduced it in the late 16th cent. *1513: iiij table clothes of dyap. 1530-1: a pece of diaper to lenthe' the clothe of the hey tabyll. 1592: a dioper bordcloth...xxiiijⁱ diop napkins...2 diop towells. 1593: 16 Towells wherof 6 be diap xs...6 longe diap Table clothes xls. 9 Cubberd clothes wherof 2 be diaper xviijs...7 Towells wherof 3 be diap xiiijs. 1 old Canapie & Curtins of diaper wth black spotts. 1764: Two Dozn & two Diaper [napkins] One Dozn & seven Diaper[towels].*

dibble implement with iron shaft just over two feet long with a D or T-handle at one end and a heavy, droplet-shaped plunger at the other, for making holes in which to drop seed. Often used one in each hand, with the seed-dropper following.

didall triangular-shaped spade for cleaning out ditches and water courses; metal scoop on long pole, for the same. *1591: j crome & j dydell. 1597: a didall and iij ladd nettes...iiij dydalls.*

diery, dierie see DAIRY

diet living allowance for servants when master was away from house. When the master was at home the servants lived on the food bought or brought in and recorded in the household accounts. *1655: Mr Bramptons dyett of 158 Meals since Ladyday 3 li. 19s. . . For dyett For Bern: dickinson after 20 li. p ann'. John Griffin 10 li.*

digging staff possibly a DIDALL; or a small spade on a long handle for digging out rabbits. *1595: a Fyrrett a dygginge staffe Twoe nightstaves.*

dight, dite furnishing, adorning, putting in order, attending to, treating, dressing. *1417: schod oure hors and dyzght oure harneys. 1464: the kynggys horseleche, For dytynge of my masterys horsses* *iijs. iiijd. . . for dytynge of a gowne of my ladys xxiijd. 1466: dytenge of his swyrde and his bylle xijd. 1467: my wyffe payd to a schorgon* [surgeon], *for dytenge of heme wane he was horte xijd. 1533: for Furryng of John Walpoles Russet gowne & ditynge of the Fryse xvjd.*

dight to winnow corn. *1537: thresshing & dytyng of xxvj combes & ij buchells of whete.*

dike OE *dic* and Old Saxon, OFris. *dik* can be both a ditch and a bank. The use of dike as a bank goes back at least to the 15th century. In N. Norfolk one spoke of a 'deek' and 'holl', meaning the bank and the ditch. In other parts of the county the 'dike' was the ditch. *1450: brak doun the gardeyn dike...and toke a wey a bullok. 1482-3: pro le dykyng [at Santon 20d.]. 1656: agreeing to throw ye dike downe and Leveling ye ground. 1675: for scouring the Dike by the Church 13s. . . for 25 rod of dikeing and a halfe of dikeing at 7d. p rod.*

dimity L. *dimitum,* Gr. διμιτος, double-thread; It. *dimito,* 'a kind of coarse cotton or flanell' (1598). Stout cloth, with raised stripes and/or figures. Originally of cotton, by the 16th century it was of mixed yarns e.g. cotton and wool. *1709: 2 Pair of white Indian Dimity Curtains with fringe. 1757: 6 fine Dimity Waistcoats £10 10s. 1779: a dimotty Cover to the Drawers with festoon & Ribbons.*

dining room the term for the room in which a gentry family ate most of its principal meals, 'dining room' came into use in the 17th century, replacing the earlier HALL and dining CHAMBER, dining PARLOUR. It might still be on an upper floor - see quot. 1665. Even in 1745 the principal dining-room at Houghton Hall was called the Marble Parlour, and the subsidiary dining-room was the Common Parlour; both were on the Grand Storey or first floor. *1665: three new doorestall to be sett up between the best gallery and dyning roome.*

dioculum, diachylon Gr. διαχυλος, succulent; OFr. *diaculon,* medicine made of juices; now lead plaster (lead oxide, olive oil, water). *1648: White Dioculu' 2d.*

dirt waggon trolley used to collect dirty plates, uneaten food etc. *1764: one dirt waggon.*

discharge relieving beam, timber, or arch in a building. *1620: sawing lintles & discharges with dore cases and dores . . . with all manner of dorecases and dores lintles & discharges.*

dish L. *discus,* disc, dish. By the 13th and 14th centuries 'dish' covered many types of flat plate from the large meat-dish for dressing or basting meat, through the 'family' dish, about 8 inches in diameter with a slightly turned-up rim, to the smallest plates. From the 15th century 'dish' means any type of flat plate with a turned-up rim. See D.C. Yaxley, *The Prior's Manor-houses,* 1988, pp. 49-51. *1625: boxe of banquetting dishes ls.[50s.]*

distrain to seize goods, cattle etc. in order to force a person to appear in court, perform obligation, pay rent or debt. etc. *1522: streynyg.*

dite see DIGHT

diurnal every day; newspaper issued daily. *1648: for a diurnall 2d.*

div^S divers, several.

dizzy probably the same as dotty, dotted, said of sheep that have hydatids - a cyst containing the larva of the tapeworm - on the brain, a condition causing erratic motion and behaviour. *1593: j dizey hogge. . . ij dozey lambes ijs. . . j dizeie lambe xijd.*

dodge eyerns see DOGIRONS

dog grappling-iron for holding and moving timber. *1621: For anckers doggs cramps spickes and bolts. 1661: groundseele & stoods & boockes & sparres & dogs.*

dog garland dog-collar or, transferred from the nautical sense of a garland (provision-net) a net to contain dog-food. *1771: a gun screw, dogs garlands, hawking net 1s. 6d.*

doggesal possibly door-sill. See DOORSTALL. *1392: [carpenter] j nov' Dorestal...[making] Doggesal [for the same 2d.]*

dog horse horse bought as a carcase for feeding dogs. *1676: Pd ould Rogison for his Dog*

Mare 5s... Pd for a dog horse from Bircham 4s. 1720-1: a Dogg Horse 5s. 1748: Paid for Dogg Horses in January £3 1s.

dogirons, dogs, dodgeirons usually in pairs: iron supports for the logs of an open hearth, consisting of a bar with a pair of legs at either end, placed on either side of the centre of the hearth. Occasionally ornamented with brass, but not as decorative as ANDIRONS. See pp. 61, 117. *1593: 1 paire of doggirons ijs. 1597: a payer of Aundyrons...a payer of Doggeyrons. 1603: i p of Cobbirons & i p of doggeirons. 1637: One payer of dogyrons wth brasse pillers one payer of short dogyrons j payer of dogyrons wth brasse knopes 3s. 1709: a brasse harth & dogs of the same. . . a steel hearth & dogs of the same.*

dog wheel treadwheel, inside which a dog ran to turn the spit. *1592: a dogge wheele vjd.*

dole, dool dole or dolestone: marker, boundary marker. Also portions of the heath, common, or open field, marked out. *1445: The vikare of Paston and yowre fadre...wher thorwe and acordidde, and doolis sette howe broode the weye schulde ben, and now he hath pullid uppe the doolis. c.1612: [lord of Horsford] did longe since geve unto everye tenant sartayne ground wch is called their doles from whence they should take ther fyering. 1738: [map] Dole tree. . . dole hole. . . Dole gap & Bush . . . Dole corner. . . Boundary pit. . . Boundary gate. . . Boundary Tree.*

dole, doole portions, bundles, sets. *1593: j cocke boote called the Eyght oare boote wth vj dooles of lynes.*

dominical 1. Belonging to Sunday. 2. Belonging to DEMESNE or domain. *1560: [grant of site of rectory] with the houses edyfyings & buyldings theruppon situate, And all their domynycall of glebe lands.*

donkey conspicuous by their absence from inventories and accounts, donkeys were nevertheless known. They seem to have become more common in the 19th century. *1673: paid for an ass 10s. 1679: Pd my Cousen Cobbe for a shee Asse 1 li.*

dong *Prompt. Parv.* 'donge, matresse, *calcitra*, matricu'; MATTRESS, mattress cover. *1459: donge of parle sylke. . . j fedder bedde Item j donge of fyne blewe. 1584: two donges & fower blankets xxs.*

dooke duck

door-case frame of the door. *1620: all the outside and dore Cases in like maner with a facio of brick to devid the storyes.*

doornail large-headed NAIL, used to construct doors or for ornamentation in patterns. *1328: xl durenayl [for barn daor 1d.] 1345: [carpentering new doors for the passage and kitchen 4d. 8 estrich boards 14d.]. C durnayl [for the same 4d.].*

doorstall doorpost, door-frame. *1374: [fitting] le Durestall [of the barn]. 1392:[making 1] nov' Dorestal. 1616: two new gates two dorestalls one boate. 1662: a dorestall for the Stalles end 3s. 6d. 1665: 1 day and stuf for the outward dorstal. stuf for the closet dorstall 2s. 6d. for a dorstal and a threshel for stares foot 1s. 9d. 1665: cutt out spaces for three doorestalls... hewed four seu'all stockes of timber for doorestalls...began the moulding of the three new doorestall to be sett up betweene the best gallery and dyning roome.*

doosen dozen

dorman, dormant dormant, horizontal beam, sleeper. *1453: iiij dormants for the drawte chamer, and the malthouse, and the browere...they shall be leyd this next weke. 1471: [laying in] Dormaunts. 1521-2: For ye Dormont iijs. iiijd. 1556: for payntyng of the Dormant that the roode stand on iijs. iiijd. payd to thomas farthing for a day woorke in Remouyng of the Dormant. payd for fyve boshells of lyme for that same woork xvjd. 1572: 4 Okes for to make dormans. 1593: one dorman two halfe dormas bords & giests with partition one pile of timber one dorman. 1602: One dorman xvj fott long vs. iiijd. 1665: put up pieces to support the dormanes in the stable.*

dormer a window standing out from the slope of a pitched roof. Dutch dormers have a triangular pediment over the window. See LUCARNE. *1621: the Roufe of the sayd ould Barne to*

67

be taken of, and framed new, by Reson, ther must be windowes mayde into the Court with doores, & dutch dormers in the Roufe... french eaves and dutch dormers and gable ends acording to the plote.

dornix fabric of wool, linen, silk or mixture, originating in Doornijk (Tournai); at first imported, but by the 15th century manufactured in Norwich. Used for hangings, coverlets and table carpets, and occasionally worn by servants and lower classes. *1593: 1 Cov'ing of dornix grene & yellowe. 1 Cov'ing of dornix redd & blewe. . . the hangings there of dornix of blacke & yellowe. 1593: one counter wth an olde darnex carpyt. A great chest wth an olde darnix carpyt. 1597: 4 peecs of Dornix hangings cont. together in length 14 yards di'. 1603: one other Coverlett of dornix of birds eye worke. 1637: the darnicke chamb'. . . j old dornix Carpit of Birdwork. 1753: A Green Darnick Bed as it stands, very old £2 5s.*

dorter dormitory, bedchamber. *1367: [reeder and servant thatched] le Garit & le Dotto'. 1525-6: le makyng of a new payer of dors for ye dortyr.*

dosser, dosse head OFr. *dossier, dozier* from *dos*, back: ornamental cloth to cover the back of seat, chair etc. *1584: a paynted cloth att the dosse head* [of bed]. *1614: for a dosse for Mr Chatteris* [the parson] *to kneel on vjd.*

dotterel, dottril a wading bird, *Eudromias morinellus*. In the 1593 Stiffkey account, 41 were bought between 22 April and 7 May, and none at any other time. A similar pattern of visiting can be observed today. Now uncommon in Norfolk. *1593: a dussen dottrill ijs.*

doublet in use from 14th to 17th century: close-fitting body garment, with or without sleeves, of varying styles. *1596: a doublet of tawnye fustian & a doublet of white fustian xxvjs. viijd.*

douffehouse see DOVEHOUSE

douned fustian see FUSTIAN

dovehouse the Norfolk word for pigeon-house, dovecote. In locative names often corrupted to duffus, duffers, e.g. duffers meadow. See ALTAR; SALT CAT. *1526: dyggyng of xxxij lode of stone at ye olde Douffehouse in Fryng. 1621: a lock and a staple for the doue house. 1664: made cleane the dovehouse. 1665: made a new aulter for the dovehouse... the old one being decayed... made a table about the aulter in the dovehouse... two punches for the dovehouse aulter. 1738: In the Dove house Barn.*

dovetails hinges in shape of two dovetails joined at the narrower ends. *1621: 8 pair of duftayles 6s. 8d. 1663-4: six paire of duftayles xvd.*

dowe dove, pigeon. *1530: in reward the xvij daye of Novembre to Osbert Reds sone, for bryngyng of stockdowes ijd. 1663-4: j Com. iij bu. ij pec. of titters for the Dowes. 1664: Salt for the dowes j pecke xijd.* See DOVEHOUSE.

dower 1. The part of a deceased husband's estate held by his widow. 2. Property or money brought by wife to marriage.

drab thick woollen cloth for winter. *1753: One light Drab coat & Breeches, much worn 15s.*

draf(f) grains that remain after BREWING; refuse, dregs, lees. *1417: a comb draf. 1476: I prey yow aspye some old thryffty draff wyff in London for me.*

draft hook, draught hook 1. A draw-hoe, that is, one drawn towards the user as opposed to the dutch or pushed HOE. 2. Hook on a long pole for pulling down thatch from burning buildings. 3. A CROME. *1588: a sholve a mattocke a drafte hoke a towe comb & a heckell. 1596: ij syes ij pykes iiij sykles on drafte howke on payer Chenes with a Fetterlocke & iiij weedinge howkes.*

draft loom, draff loom see DRAW LOOM

drag a land-survey, listing holdings and tenancies.

drag, drag net fishing net dragged through the water and along the bottom. *1482: a dragge of viij fadom, the fadom xijd. 1590: One dragg to catch fyshe. 1720-1: for a Dragg Nett & Casting Nett £3 9s.*

drag rake up to the 19th century a drag rake was exclusively a hand-tool, a long shaft with a wide head having wooden or iron teeth up to 6 inches long to gather up corn, hay etc. The distinction between kinds of rake in the second 1591 quot. is not altogether clear. See RAKE; RIVE. From the early 19th century a drag-rake was a horse-drawn implement with two wheels 6-10 feet apart, bearing between them a set of long curved tines which could be raised by a lever to release the gathered material. *1585: iiij drag rakes v folowing rakes. 1591: one yron dragge Rake & an other wth tymber teethe xxd. 1591: viij dragg rakes viij followinge rakes ij barne rakes iij hayerakes. 1591: iij drage Ryves. 1597: iij ould dragg rakes vjd. 1621: for 3 drag rakes 3s. 4d.*

dragger one who dragged sheep to the shearers. *1647: to 6 dragers 5s.*

dragon beam, joist beam going diagonally into the corner of a floor, roof etc. to bear the corner-post or hip rafter. *c.1620: making of a floore all the whole bredth For the plasterer to seele to: with dragon Joyce and all other carpentry worke.*

drainer one employed in draining, that is cutting and clearing ditches to drain land. *1655: Drayners. Wickham and Allen together 12 dˢ 11s. levelling ye Comon 1 li. 4s. . . . To ye drayners for 9 dˢ in ye meadow 9s. 9d. . . To Loss and Mayson 8 dˢ together in drayning work 8s. 8d.*

drains in BREWING the dregs from which the wort has been drained. *1621: 7 combes draines 4s. 8d.*

draught animals for drawing or pulling implements or carts rather than for riding. *1597: Draught oxen vj. Draught horses iiij stoned: Geldings iij.*

draught bridge drawbridge. *1459: The Chamber over the Draught Brigge...ij chaynes for the draught brigge.*

draught chamber see DRAWT

draw to take the firing of bricks from the KILN. *1663-4: hope [helped] to drawe a kelled of bricke.*

drawer plank or beam, sometimes of considerable size. *1664: Two drawing planke of the Eavesboards. . .Two oaking drawers taken of stuff cut for the pspect...severall drawers of four post stockes for the said gates. 1664-5: one beame drawing 12 foot long to laye ou' the chimney peeces in the great hall cutt 8 and 11 inch square.* See DRESSER.

drawer drawers were incorporated in chests from the 16th century but only became common as sets or CHESTS OF DRAWERS towards the end of the 17th century. See CHEST. Early sets of drawers were called case, nest, set, and, confusingly, pair of drawers. The 1608 quot. is from an inventory of fittings, so the drawers must have been part of the structure. *1608: two Cubberds & 3 drawers under the South windowe wth 2 lockes. 1634: on neast of drawing boxes. 1674: a Case of Drawers. 1711: 2 beds 4 li. 6 Chairs a table & a pair of Drawers 16s. 1723: a pair of spice Drawers . . . A Nest of drawers. 1753: 1 Sawce Pan & Cover 1 Pewter Dish, 4 Plates Dᴼ & 1 old Sett of Drawers 5s.*

drawer of window shutter, blind. *1572 [part of lease] glass locks keys sealings doores gates benches covers and drawers of windows. 1592: on drawing for a window of Buckeram. 1595: [in larder with oddments] A drawynge wyndowe.*

drawing see DRAWER

drawing crome a CROME for use in the garden. See DRAFT HOOK. *1592: iij drawing cromes.*

drawing room shortened form of WITHDRAWING room, private room to which the family could withdraw from the more public HALL; the term not in use before the 17th century. *1680: to the maid that waited in the drawing room 2s. 1709: Drawing Room to the great Parlour. . . Drawing Room to the dineing room.*

69

drawing window see DRAWER OF WINDOW

draw loom loom for weaving damasks and plain, twill, and satin weaves in fine, bold patterns; it needed skill to set up but little to operate. *1602: a draffe lombe.*

drawt 1. Privy, cesspit. *1459: My Maister is Chambre and the withe draughte withe the Stable. 1508/9: [cleaning out] le drawghte iiijd.* 2. Small chamber, private room, office. *1453: Sir Thomas Howes hath purveyed iiij dormants for the drawte chamer...I have take the mesure in the draute chamer, ther as ye wold yor cofors and countewery shuld be sette for the whyle; and ther is no space besyde the bedd, thow the bedd wer remevyd to the dore, for to sette bothe your bord and your kofors ther, and to have space to go and sytte be syde. Wherfor I have purveyd that ye shall have the same drawte chamer that ye had befor ther, as ye shall ly to your self. 1459: The White [? Withe] Draught Chamber for Lewys and William Worcester* [contained bed with furnishings]. *1513: In le drawt J bedstead J fedyrbedde J bolstr J peir blanketts J oold covyrlyght of Whyt and blak J Cupbord.* See WITH DRAUGHT.

draw well a deep WELL, with water fetched up by bucket on a rope or chain wound round a capstan (AXLETREE). *1631: ye Axelltree rope Chaine and buckett for ye Drawe well vs.*

dredging box box with perforated lid for sprinkling flour, salt, sugar etc. *1647: a dreging box 6d. 1723: a Dredging box a salt. 1762: Pepper Box & Dredging Box.*

dresciourbord, drescourbord, dresscione see DRESSER

dresser in the Middle Ages and later, a board, plank, or bench for dressing and preparing food, particularly meat. The 1300 quot. suggests that the dresser might be a room. By the 17th century the dresser was becoming a standing piece of furniture rather than just a board or working table, and was augmenting or replacing the CUPBOARD as a display unit. *1300: [nails for the partition wall] del Dresur. 1352: dresciour bord. . . drescourbord. . . dresscione. 1593:[larder] 2 dresser bordes 3 tressells. 1597: j little dresser ij dresser knyves. 1608:[kitchen] two dresser bordes One ould chopinge borde One skoringe borde. 1637: One coole & a dresser. 1647: [kitchen] One white dresser under the wyndowe and a shelf underitt and a Rack to lay Speets on...[pantry] Fowere dressers... in the back kitchyn one dresser under the wyndowe. 1709: [kitchen] 4 dressers. 1748:[parlour] A green Bed as it stands A Napkin press a Dresser Oval Table.*

dresser plank or balk of considerable dimensions. *1619: 39 foote in splittinge carff viz iij Bord or planke for Dressers. 1619-20: 4 Breakinge Carff for Dressers of Ashe 2 fotte 3 inches Deepe & 7 fotte Di' longe. 1620: sawinge the great Oke at Coxford into 4 Tables, or Table Peice and ij longe Dressers...the said Dressers 40 fotte 12d.* See BOARD; CARFE; DRAWER.

dressing knife cleaver, knife for dressing or preparing meat. *1513: J dressyng knyf. 1597: j little dresser ij dresser knyves ij other smale knyves & a little ould dagger.*

drift large heavy hammer, mallet. Huloet (1552) 'Drift, betle, or malle, to dryve pyles or stakes'. See BEETLE. *1588: j Drift of Iron. 1665:[smith made] one drift for joyners.*

drift, driftway road or lane for driving cattle or sheep.

drinking up to, and in a few cases slightly beyond, the Reformation a quantity of malt given by one or more of the brethren of a guild was brewed and sold for guild funds to the members of the guild; usually consumed on the premises, this was called a drinking. *1530: rec' vijs. of a dryckyng made by Frances Gedney, Henry Dyman, & Robt Wiseman.*

drinking cloth small tablecloth used after the main tablecloth had been removed. *1591: xj bord cloathes & iij drinckinge clothes xliiijs.*

drinch a drench, draught or dose of medicine for animals; to drench. *1648: drinchinge & blouding the sick Bullock. 1655: drinching & blouding 38 Bullocks ...24 qts March beer to drinch ye Bullockes.[in margin Bullocks drink]. 1664: drinching & dressing the blacke gelding called Symonds supposing he had the yellowes xxd.*

dripping pan, dripper originally the pan standing under the spit to catch the dripping fat. Up to the 20th century a roasting pan for oven use was still called a dripping pan, and

the fat saved from the roast was called dripping. See LATCHPAN. *1459: j droppyng panne.*
1593: dropingpanns. 1688: latting dripping pann. 1751: one Copper Dripper.
drive to undo feather beds and fluff up the feathers before remaking them. *1530: in*
reward to the fetherbedd dryver the xth daye of Novembre, for dryvyng of xx beds vjs. viijd. 1649: 3 days
helping the feather driver 2s.
dromme drum. See TABOR. *1597: A dromme lent by Mr Taylor to a smythe of Norwich.*
droping pan see DRIPPING PAN
dross chaff, dirt of corn. *1663: also recd halfe the drosse there being in all six combe.*
drug, drudge, dudge to pull along, drag. *1732: Helping ye plumber & drudging Stone to ye*
shead... dudging ye Coping stone to ye Garden Walls.
drug low truck, with small, wide, solid wheels, for transporting timber. *1621-2: a drug*
with slug wheles.
drug see TRUG
drycheling see CHELING
dryfatte damp-proof VAT. *1579: for dryefattes & chystes to putte in armor...xxxixs. iijd.*
drying chamber room for drying severally clothes, linen, fish etc. *1588: Dryinge chamber:*
[shop chest, cupboard, table, tailor's board]. 1593: In Fish in the dryinge Chamber [cod, ling]. 1637:
the dryinge chamber [linen]. 1662: the lukums in the drieng chamber [lucums or LUCARNES are
dormer windows, so here the chamber was in the roof-space].
dry larder see LARDER
ducape plain woven stout lustrous fabric. *1730: 12 yds pale pink rich ducape £6.*
duck strong untwilled linen cloth. *1751: about 100ᵈ Yards of Duck on the Floor.*
dudfen, dudfin cart-horse bridle. *1590: dudfen halters. 1593: 8 dudfin halters 3 unwinked*
halters. 1664: old dudfins Dudfin bitts. See HALTER.
duftayles see DOVETAILS
dugg teat, udder of cow. *1655: 2 Duggs 2s.*
dun, dund dull greyish-brown colour; the colour of the native Norfolk cattle. *1592: one*
dunde mare & a foole xiijs. iiijd. 1597: one owld dunnd meare.
durenayl see DOORNAIL
durestall see DOORSTALL
durneth OSw. *dyrni,* doorpost, door-frame. See DOORSTALL. *1368: [putting in one] durneth*
[in cart house].
dussynge dozen. *1595: x dussynge of Trenchers.*
dustall frame, framework. See DOORSTALL. *1637: One little old frame table broken a peecs*
wantinge the ledge & dustall for thende therof 1s.
Dutch cloak wide loose sleeved cloak. *1590: One olde Dutche Cloake of Damask xiijs. iiijd.*
Dutch chair see CHAIR
Dutch tile see PANTILE; TILE
Dutch dormer DORMER window with a Dutch gable. *c.1623: Dutch dormers in the Roufe.*
Dutch gable a triangular pediment crowning a gable with ogee or concave gable-edges.

Dutch horse suspended clothes-airer. *1751: two wet Horses...two Dutch Horses brass Pulleys*
Jacks & Lines compleat.
Dutch oven contrivance in form of semicircular niche of metal, on legs, which stood
with the open front facing the fire and was used for small roasts, plate-warming etc. *1779:*
one Dutch oven.

71

Dutch twine a fine strong twine. *1674: for Dutch twine for my hare Nett 2s.*
dyaper see DIAPER
dyre see DAIRY
dyte see DIGHT
dytyn pan small pan for preparing food, medicine etc. See DIGHT. *1459: j caudron, j dytyn panne of brasse, j droppyng panne.*
dyzght see DIGHT

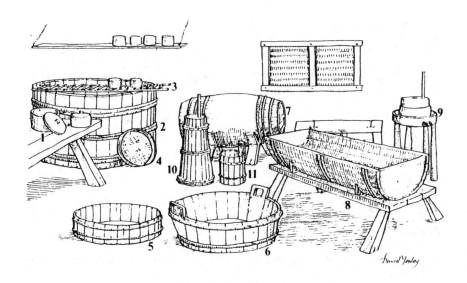

Medieval Dairy

1. Cheese vat   2. Vat   3. Cheese tong   4. Milk-sieve   5. Keeler   6. Soe   7. Tine
8. Trough for dough (kneading trough)   9. Quern   10. Churn   11. Milk-pail or piggin

E

Ear small lug or handle, often unperforated. *1665: 2 eares for a paile* [iron].

earbell small bell to adorn horse head-harness. *1647: 6 dozen Earebells 7s.*

earth to PLOUGH. Fallow land was usually earthed or ploughed 3 or 4 times to prepare it for autumn-sown wheat; spring sowing took place after 1 or 2 earthings. After ploughing the land was harrowed, the seed sown, and harrowed in. *1664: [28 May] They began to plowe the som'land in the parks. [4 & 11 June] made an end of plowing the first earth in the parks. [16-30 July ploughed the second earth; 16 Sept-1 Oct ploughed the third earth] & harrowed the same againe gitting the same in good case to sowe & soe began to plowe some wheat & waterfurrowe there.*

earthing earthenware. *1713: 3 Earthing pans...2 Earthing potts and Suett in them...6 Earthing dishes.*

earwire thin gold or silver wire for pierced ears. *1680: 2 pr eare wyers 6d.*

eashe see ASH

eastland board see BOARD; ESTRICH BOARD

eatage grazing, grazing rights. *1654: for ye grass of Little Harper and the eatage.*

eavesboard long boards placed under the eaves, to tilt the lowest course of tiles or slates the better to throw off water; to protect the under-edge of a thatched roof; to provide a fascia. Guttering could be attached to the eavesboards. *1306: [8 studs] ad evesebord [of the barn 8d]. 1609-10: great nayles for the Eaves boardes iiijd. 30 ᵛ foote of quarters for eaves boardes xiijd. 1664: two drawing planke of the eavesboards. 1728: 1 peice for eaves board 25 feet.*

edder udder

eel the eel *Anguilla anguilla* was an important part of the fish diet in the Middle Ages and after. Eels could be kept in fishponds, but were often caught in rivers. The word 'eel' seems to have led to difficulties in identification. Sir Thomas Browne: 'Mustela fluuiatilis or eele poult to bee had in Norwich riuer and between it and Yarmouth as also in the riuers of marshland resembling an eele and a cod, a very good dish and the Liuer thereof well answers the commendations of the Ancients'. This is possibly the burbot *Lota lota*, a freshwater fish, rather than one of the eelpouts, which are marine, although of course the Yare and other rivers were tidal for some of their length. Browne continues: 'Of eeles the common eele and the glot which hath somewhat a different shape in the bignesse of the head and is affirmed to have yong ones often found within it'. The glot or gloat was described in 1883: 'The "hooking" eel or "gloat", - the blackish medium-sized eel taken by anglers, babbers, and on night-lines.' If Browne was right and the young were carried in the female, the viviparous blenny, *Zoarces viviparus*, an eel-pout, would seem to be a candidate, although this is a marine and estuarine rather than freshwater fish. Isaac Walton (1653) is no more precise: 'there be several sorts or kinds of Eels; as the silver Eel, the green or greenish Eel, with which the river of Thames abounds, and those are called Grigs; and a blackish Eel, whose head is more flat and bigger than ordinary Eels; and also an Eel whose fins are reddish, and but seldom taken in this nation.' The young eel is brown or yellowy-gold, and the silver eel is, in fact, the mature form but has a black back. A 'scutcheon eel' perhaps had a mark or feature resembling an escutcheon, although this trait is not remarked on the common eel species; a scutcheon or scute is a fish-scale. The conger eel *Conger conger* is much larger than the common eel, growing up to 9 feet long. 'Browet' is possibly for making into broth. *1500-01: xxvj stykke of browet eelys price viijs viijd. 1530: a cagge of elis vs. 1655: For 16 Lemmons 1s. 3 Cabbages 6d. Scutcheon Ealls 2s.*

eel pick, spear a long-handled implement to catch and hold eels, having 3 or 4 prongs with serrated edges or barbed tips. See p. 75. *1587: A picke for Eles. 1590: Elepick.*

egistment see AGIST

eke narrow circle of wood or straw on which the beehive or BEESKEP was placed to increase its capacity. See HAVER; IMP. *1597: vj emptie beeskepps and ij eekes xiiijd.*

elbrod an ELL broad. *1602: 3 Elbrod darnocke beads* [beds] *j li. vijs. 2 Elbrod darnocke heavell iijs.*

ele aisle of church. *1484: my body to be beried in the Ele of the Cherch of Mauteby.*

electuary medicinal conserve or paste: powder mixed with honey or syrup. *1680: an electuary 1s.*

elis see EEL

elk strictly *Alces malchis* the largest species of deer, MOOSE in the U.S.A. In Britain, the name has been applied to large deer, bison, wapiti (*Cervus canadensis*), and eland. However, elk was also a name for the wild swan, the whooper *Cygnus cygnus,* or a wild goose. *1601:* [present to the sheriff] *an Elke.*

ell measurement of length, especially for cloth. The English ell was established at the Court of Exchequer in 1474 at 45 inches; the Flemish ell = 27 inches, the French ell 54 inches. *1466: for xxj Flemeshe elles of Hasborow clothe, prise the elle, iiijd. 1513: J very fyn Kerchy of an elle. . . ij eluys of blak sarcenes. 1530: a nelle of canves. 1597: one Carpet nedleworke: j yarde 3 qrters longe: an ell brode.* See STICK.

elm the English elm, *Ulmus procera,* is uncommon in Norfolk; the wych elm, *U. glabra* and the smooth-leafed elm *U. carpinifolia* are common, and provided timber for furniture, floorboards, and, as it stands up to submersion pretty well, waterpipes and piles.

elmes alms

embracery attempt to corrupt jury, against the provisions of 38 Ed. III stat. 11 cap. 12. *1450: all trespasses, extorcions, riottes, forcible entrees, mayntenaunces, champerties, embraceries, offenses, and mesprisions.*

emetarye inventory. *1606: An Emetarye of the Goods.*

engrain, engreyne to dye scarlet - see GRAINS; GREYNED. From the 17th century it came to mean to make dye sink into the texture. *1465: ij yerdes of Fyn crymsen engreyned prise the yerde xiijs. iiijd...iiij yerdes of cremysen owt of greyne for ij yemen, prise the yerde vs.*

engyll see HENGLE

entercoys interclose, screen. *1344:[8 great hurdles with 96 great brads for] viij intercoys [to attach to small posts of the barn ijs. iiijd.]*

entry first or entry room in house; porch; gatehouse. *1593: chamber next Entry. Chamber over Entry. 1608: In the entrie goine up the armerie.*

erber, herber the herb and flower garden of a medieval house. *1288: [1 door towards] Erber ijd.*

erdyng earthen. See EARTHING. *1592: vj Erdyng potse iiijd.*

eringes, eringoes the root of sea holly, *Eryngium maritimum,* candied and eaten as a sweet and an aphrodisiac. *1647: 4 oz of Canded Eringoes 1s. 10d...Sittuorne, Eringes & Maple Biskett..*

errable arable. *1580: In other errable ground about eight score thirtene acres in the errable feildes.*

escheator officer who certified into the Exchequer land or property (escheats) falling to the king e.g. estate of a minor, forfeitures.

eshinge made of ASH. *1613: an eshinge Chayer prayssed at xvjd.*

espe see ASPEN

ess an S-shaped iron for hanging pots; POTHOOK. See HAKE. *1637: 2 haks & 2 esses.*

essche, esshe see ASH

74

estrayes straying animals. *1700-1: Estrayes & Egistments.*

estrich board east + *riche*, from OE *rice*, kingdom. BOARD imported from the Baltic or North Sea ports. Estrich boards of wainscot were German oak, and Rygalds, Righolts etc. were from Riga and its neighbourhood - the differentiation began soon after 1300. The standard length was probably 10 feet. See L.F. Salzman, *Building in England*, pp. 245-7. *1328:[1 quarter[= 30]] de Estrichbord [for doors and other things 3s. 1½d.]. . . [half a quarter] bord de riggeholt iiijs. ijd. 1328: j Estryckbord [for mending casks 1½d.]. 1335: in x bord de Estrys [for the well 13d.]. 1345: [repairing windows] j bordo destrissh iijd. . . viij bord destrissh xiiijd [new doors for the passage to the kitchen].*

euyr see EWER

everlasting in the 16th and 17th centuries, material used for uniforms; same as durance. Later, strong close-woven worsted, also called lasting. *1753: One Plodd Night Gown, lined with Everlasting £1 1s.*

evidence documents, deeds etc. *1610: a Trunke wherin his evydence & Apparell.*

ewe yew

ewer jug or pitcher with wide spout, used to bring water for hand-washing to the table or chamber. Could be valuable. *1459: ij ewers, gilt, pounsed with floures and braunches, weing xxxix unces. . . ij ewers, the oon demi gilt, and the othir the bordures gilt, weiyng lj unces. . . iiij ewers, of the old facion, weiyng lxxvij unces. 1588: Ewer of sylver and psell gilte.*

ewery, ewry chamber where ewers kept, with towels, table linen etc.; more generally, the service wing of a house. *1546: The Nether storie being called thewry courte and pcell of tholde Lodginge. . . The Seconde story of thewrie Courte. 1620: in the seeling of the youery and the timber ptissions on both sides. . . In the youery and passage to the closet.*

ewghe, ewhe, ewing yew. *1588: a yewghe bowe.* See BOW.

exchange, change the changing of silver or pewter vessels for new ones, the difference in value being paid in cash. *1530: to a pewterer for exhangyng of xl pounds of pewter ev'y Ld jd. ob. for ye exchange vjs. vjd. To ye said Pewterer for A Bason and ij newe Ewers for ye exchangyng of them iiijs. viijd.*

excise internal taxation on goods e.g. beer, which in e.g. 1657 was taxed at 2s. 6d. a barrel on strong and 6d. a barrel on small beer. *1647: for Excise of beere to Michaelmas 1647 and for flesh 3s. 7d.*

exe, exse an AXE. *1589: brickexe, hammer exe, hand pickexe.*

exeltre see AXLETREE

exelyng fitting AXLE to CART etc. *1417: for exelyng of ye carte viijd.*

extree AXLETREE. *1664: One whoope for the end of an extree.*

eyes elaborate, often jewelled, clasps were hooked into eyes to fasten the bodice, skirt etc. *1587: xxij claspes & eyes ijs. jd.*

eyorn iron. *1636: one Eyorn harow.*

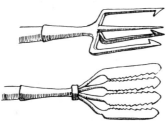

Types of eel-pick or spear

75

F

Fac cloth possibly cloth to cover dead person's face. *1595: one bearing cloth & a fac clothe viijs.*

face chaps, lower half of pig's cheeks. *1738: Seven Hamms and Eleven Faces.*

facines see FARCY

faddom see FATHOM

fadine see FATHOM

faggot bundle of hazel, ash, etc. rods and twigs; bundle of FURZE. *1372: [making] Dc^m fagotts vs [sold for 24s. 6d.]. 1385: [making] mill CCCCLx faggotts [this year xiijs. iijd. ob].*

faggot to bind into faggots. *1664: they carryed the pruninges of the trees in the Little orchard out of the same after they had bratled & fagotted them...for making of...17 loads 16 fagotts of small [wood].*

falchion broad curved sword, with the edge on the convex side. *1597: A fawchyn...the hilt, pomel, locker, & chape guylt.*

fald gate, falgate, folgate, fallgate 1. Gate of the fold. 2. Gate at entrance to field, heath etc. 3. The heath or common itself. 4. Fall-gate or falling-gate, either with rails falling into slots, or the whole gate raised and lowered over a stream. *1327: [digging 73 perches of ditch from] falgate [towards the land of the parson of Thornage 4s. 11½d.]. 1350: falyate [to meadow]. 1537: for a fallgate xijd. 1544: A falde gate to hange at ye Hethe, And for hoks, hengells, wt other yrons for ye seyd gate. 1548: ye fall gat. 1588: ij fall gattes with sartaine pales & rayles. 1663: a folgate 6s. 8d. hanging of the folgate 2s.*

false roof space between ceiling and roof timbers in a pitched roof. Forby glosses it as the space between the ceiling of the garret and the roof. The false roofs in the 17-room house of the 1595 quot. are surely garrets rather than small roof-spaces. See VANCE ROOF. *1588: fauc[or fanc] ruffe. 1588: vij bords in the false Rofe. 1593: on the fausse roffe. 1595: False roofe ov' the halle: one owld Cawdron Certayne owlde Irone syxe saulte Fyshes vjs. viijd. . . in the newe Faulse Roofe [2 bedsteads with their furnishings 26s. 8d., one chest 12d.]. 1616: In the false roofe over ye hall certaine daells [deals] & other things xvs.*

fan, wan, van, L. *vanna* a shallow, oval or scallop-shaped basket about 30 inches long with a rim and 2 handles on one side, for winnowing the threshed corn by oscillation or tossing in a breeze. 'DANSK' or Danish: an expensive variant form. See pp. 86, 242; FEY. *1352: ij wynewskeppes j Fan j cornschowele. 1498-9: for fannyng iiijd. 1590:[malting house] a danske fanne ij fyeing fannes. 1592: one fann xijd. 1593: a dansk Fan vjs. 1664: fanning the tares.*

fanc ruffe see FALSE ROOF, VANCE ROOF

fanon a short stole, originally a kind of napkin, attached to the left wrist of the priest at the medieval mass; a MANIPLE. *1459: j fanon, encheked white & blewe.*

farcy, fassers disease, particularly of horses, allied to glanders: swelling under the horse's belly and chaps. *1453: hese hors hath j farseyn and grete rennyng sorys in hese leggis. 1483: paied for a medesyn for a horse that had the farsy xijd. 1619: Curinge the Blacke Stone horse of Div^s Fassers vjs. 1665: dressing & cureing the sorrold horse of the water facines & stranglings*

farm ML *firma*, fixed payment; a fixed yearly payment of rent for land, property, the right to collect taxes or customs, etc., by the early 16th century extended to the actual land, holding, house etc.

farras possibly misspelling of FORCER. *1620: In the farras ou' the hall skreine.*

farthing four farthings made a penny (d. see D.); a farthing was represented in Roman and arabic figures by the abbreviation q' (see Q') for the latin *quarta, quadrans.*

fassers see FARCY

fastyngong Shrove Tuesday. *1451: he be heste it you not till Fastyngong. 1481: That she hathe occupied seene ester xix yere, unto fastyngong the xx yere of the king.*

fat see VAT

fathoop hoop for vats. *1590: xxvij fathoops iiijs.*

fathom the standard fathom is 6 feet, the average distance from fingertip to fingertip with arms fully outstretched. As a measure of reed, 6 bundles each a foot in diameter. *1415-6: Cxl fadines [of reeds 11s. 10d.]. 1584: vij faddome of Rede and caryage from Norwyche for fleyking iiijs. vjd. 1591: xxx Feadomes of Reede iiijs. 1710: 24 fathom of Reede for flaking the Roofe of the said Barn, at 10d. a fathom.*

faucet originally the peg or spigot to stop the vent hole in a barrel; the tap in a barrel. *1595: platters spoones tapes & Fassetts.*

faucke the forkbeard, *Phycis blennoides,* a seafish growing up to 30-36 inches long. *1593: to Thomson for Whittins on Wed viijd. to him for a faucke vjd.*

faunce roof see FALSE ROOF; VANCE ROOF

fawchyn see FALCHION

feache see VETCH

feadome see FATHOM

fearnothing, fearnought thick woollen cloth, used in rough weather on ships etc. *1708: 3 yards of fearenothing at 1s. per yd.*

feather key, linch-pin. *1665: [smith] two feathers to truss the bell.*

feather-driver the man who drove or fluffed up the feathers of a featherbed. *1534-5: To the fetherbed dryver for le dryvyng 7 bedds & for le makyng of 2 pelues with other things vs. iiijd. 1648: to Richard Frost for 3 dayes worke to helpe the Feather driver 2s.*

feather house room to keep feathers in for making featherbeds, pillows, etc.. *1665: One locke for the feather house.*

felechep fellowship, band, gang. *1452: the seid felechep wold have kelled the seid two servauntes.*

felloe, felghe exterior rim, or part of it, of a wheel; curved parts that make up the wheel. *1310: iij spokes & vj felghes. 1382: [certain] gongs de Folghes [sold]. 1636: 16 gonge of Carte Fellowes at 4s. 6d.* See CART; GONG.

felwett see VELVET

fembell, femelyng fimble, female. See HEMP.

fence wall up to the end of the 17th century 'fence' was used in the sense of 'defence', a barrier, more than just a boundary. *1621: stones...for ye makinge A fence walle. . .For Buildinge a new Fence walle at the halle gats [262 yards at 8d. per yard] . . . building newe Bricke walle f^M iij^C iiij^{xx} xix yards at 9d. the yard.*

fenugreek, fenegreek leguminous plant, *Trigonella fœnum Græcum,* whose seeds were used medicinally as a purge and to clear the lungs. *1673: paid for fenegreek 3d.*

feoffment, enfeoffment see p. 243

ferret, ferrit It. *fioretto, fioretti* little flower. 1. Floss-silk, silk waste, carded like wool and spun on a wheel. 2. Tape, usually of cotton but sometimes silk. *1700: A Box with Buttons and Ferritt 10s. 1711: Ferrits and worsteads 2 li..*

fesand, feson see PHEASANT

fess pale blue; the cloth so coloured. *1465-6: ij fesses and a brod wete clothe of blew vj li. xd.*

fetches, fitches see VETCH

fetterlock, fetyrlock originally consisting of a U-shaped shackle with the ends joined by a barrell-lock, it was used to prevent horses straying. Sometimes a chain was used instead of the shackle. By the beginning of the 14th century it was in use on barns, gates, and boats. *1310: j feterlock [for the barn door 1½d.]. . . vj feterlocks [for the gates of the wood 7½d.].*

1323: feterlock [for the boat]. 1596: on payer Chenes with a Fetterloke.
fey, fie, fye to winnow, winnowing. *1590: ij fyeing fannes. 1655: thrashinge & ye fey of 60 Coom Barly at 6d. a Coom.*
fey, fie, fye cleaning out, clearing, dredging. *1505-6: Willelmo Stapylton for feying of a welle iiijd. 1649: for feyinge the Pitt. 1655: Almshouse Pond feyed. . . feyinge of ye Almes-Pond 2 li. 1s. 6d.*
ff as an initial letter in a word = capital F.
fickle, fickell, fickle, fiddle OE *metefoétels*, CUPBOARD for food, from OE *fetel*, girdle, to make ready. *Prompt. Parv.:* 'Metesytel, to kepe in mete (metfyttel, or almery, K., mete fetyll, or almery, P.) *Cibulum.*' The editor of *Prompt. Parv.* notes that as in Medulla *cibutum* is 'a mete whycche' or hutch, it might be a long chest like a settle. Transcribers sometimes seem to mistake *f* for a long *s* in this word. *1296: j fitell jd. 1343: [2 gates] & j Fycell iijd. q'. 1352: j metefetle. 1444: j metefetell. 1589: iij ferkings & j meatfittle ijs. 1593: an old Meat fiddle. 1595: j meale fiddle. 1637: Fouer bolls and a meate fickele. 1738: one Meat Pickle...one meat fickle.*
field bed see BEDSTEAD
field bird pheasant, possibly partridge. *1665: toped the wall by the feildbird yard with clay.*
field marking stating of boundaries in the open field. *1665-6: allowed Tho. Rayner at the Feildmarkeinge 2s.*
fig figs were grown in England from the 16th century; the great blue fig was reckoned the best variety, but most figs occurring in household accounts were probably dried and imported. A list of fruit trees recommended to Houghton *c.*1720 gives only Early, White, and Black figs, at 1s. each, as against 5 varieties of apricots, 6 nectarines, 10 vines, 12 cherries, 18 peaches, 19 plums, 22 apples, and 41 pears. See FRAIL. *1648: 2 li. of blue Figgs 1s. 1712: for the South walls ther is wanting 10 piches 5 figges 5 Cheres 2 pears 30 vins for the upper part of the walls.*
figure portrait. *1588: One picture being the figure of the late Ladie Godsalve vs.*
fill-bell see THILBELL
filler see THILLER
filleting woven heavy tape for binding. *1692: filletting and Inkle 5s. 6d.*
filleting, filliting (archit.) narrow flat band separating mouldings or bands of tiles. *1819: 60 feet Run filliting to tiling &c. @ 1d. 5s.*
filigree, filligreen It. *filigrana*, from L. *filium*, thread, and *granum*, grain. Delicate jewels, vessels etc. made of silver and gold wires and beads. *1745: silver filligreen cabinett.*
filling wheel wheel to fill spools with yarn. *1604: iiij ould spining wheles and ij ould filling wheles.*
fimble female see HEMP
fin unidentified fish, fairly large, but definitely not the finner or rorqual. *1655: 2 Codfish 2s. 6d. 2 Fins 4s. 100 Sound 1s. 6d.*
fine, fine and recovery see p. 243
fineared veneered. *1745: fineared table of lapis Lazuli. 1751: One large Ebbony finnear'd Table with french brass Ornaments. . . an Oblong Veiner'd Rosewood Table with two additional Flapps.*
fir spruce, larch; whitewood in general. Until the 18th cent. imported, usually as BOARD, from the Baltic and Scandinavia. *1305: Bords de fir. 1309: ccxvij sparres de fir [for making a sheepfold 52s. 2d.]. 1584: one fyrretable wth a payre tressels & thre formes. 1603: A furr chiste.*
fir, firre ? lath; but see FURRMAKER; FURZE; LATH.
fircle boat sea-going boat, type unknown. 'Fercule' is frame, barrow, or bier, or the word might be derived from L. *furcum*, fork, but none of these seems to apply to a boat. *1591: One Fircle boote called the grate [arrested by the admiral].*
fire fork long 2 or 3-pronged fork for manipulating logs on a fire; replaced by poker or

78

PUR for coal fires. *1588: j fierforke vjd. 1593: 1 payre of Andyrons 1 paire of tongs & 1 fireforke xijs.*

firehouse 'house' meaning room, chamber: the room with a fire. The term is generally found in small cottages having up to four rooms. *1553: [cottage surrendered to use of another on condition that person surrendering should have dwelling] in le fyre house.*

fire pan small shovel on long handle for removing ashes; flat pan for carrying fire. *1597: one steale of a broken fyre panne garnyshed.*

fire shovel probably only in use with coal fires. *1620: fier Shovells twoe whereof one to sift the Ashes or cinders from the coales.*

fire stone flint or iron pyrites for striking sparks.

firkin a cask whose capacity varied with its use: ale or beer was 9 GALLONS, wine was 84 gallons, butter 64 lb. gross, 56 lb. nett, but variations existed. *1655: For 42 pintes of fresh Butter at 5d. & a Firking weighinge 70 li.20s. 1 li. 17s. 6d.*

firmer chisel see FORMER

fish, dried fish were dried to preserve them. *1664: dryed the fish in the sun & packed them up againe.* See COD; DRYING CHAMBER; LING; STOCKFISH.

fish bottom fish-kettle, oval pan for cooking fish. *1734: two salvers and two fish bottoms.*

fish house room for storing and preserving fish. *1637: chamber ou' the fish house.*

fish plate oval plate for serving fish. *1745: 8 Pewter Rings, and two fish plates.*

fishing see NET

fissicke physic. *1591: Fissicke Books xxs.*

fitches, fytches see VETCH

fitell, fittle see FICKLE; MEATFICKLE

flag turf cut and dried for fuel or turfing. *1310: In flaggs [nothing]. 1597: di' thousand Flagges xijd. 1613: In haye pease & other Corn with the flages there. 1619: for the Bowlinge Allye...for 5 daies in gravinge Flagg vs.*

flaghouse building in which flags or turfs were stored. *1614: one howse called the Flagghowse.*

flagspade flag or turf cutter, often with a ♠-shaped blade and long handle with a crosspiece to push against. The medieval flagspade was of wood with an iron cutting-edge. *1312: [1 iron for] j flaggesped ijd. 1592: a flagge spade a muck crome iij pitcheforks one old sithe a busshell vs.*

flaget flacket, a flask, bottle or similar vessel. *1459: j flaget of silver, weiying xxxviij unces.*

flail implement for threshing corn, peas etc., consisting of a handle 4-5 feet long joined by a hinge of leather to a beater 2 feet long. Most threshers seem to have had their own flails rather than using flails provided by the master. See p. 86.

flake, fleke 1. Wattle hurdle. 2. Shallow wicker or straw basket. *1306: [making one] fleke [for lead]. 1313: j flake [bought 5d.]. 1341: [mending corbels sports 2 fans] & fleyke ijd. 1387: [reeds bought for mending the house for] flekes [made from them ijs.].* See FLEGHE.

flaking reeds, laid across the rafters and bound on with a small handful of reed and then plastered over, were used for flaking over rafters instead of battens or laths. See FATHOM.

flame see FLEAM

Flanders tick see TICK

flannel introduced in the 16th century by the Flemings, flannel had a tight hard-spun warp and loose-spun weft of wool, with a soft smooth surface. *1592: A Flannell cou'let of nedleworke xiijs. iiijd.*

flask, flasket case of horn, leather, or metal, for carrying liquid or gunpowder. *1592: Two steele flasks wth touchboxes vs. iiijd. Eleven other Flasks of wood wth touchboxes xvjs. One white wroughte flaske wth touchbox ijs. Syxe playne flasketts of horne vs. Eleven porteflasks of seales skynne & ij of buffe iiijs. 1595: one sword ij old daggers a Callyver and ij old flaxkitts viijs. 1618: one brushe one*

79

hande flaske xvjd.
flaskbox box for powderflasks. See FLASK. *1593: 2 cases of pistolls with firelocks 1 flaskebox.*
flasket 1. Large basket, usually tall, particularly for clothes. 2. Powder FLASK. *1562: for a flaskeat to shzve* [serve] *pore folks in at the gates viijd. 1593: one rollinge flasket a mande. 1593: flaskett for clothes. 1595: a hande flaskett, wth Treane dishes...a flaskett wth towe & lynnynge. 1648: 2 flasketts for the washmaids 4s. 4d.*
flathe see FLAY
flat tile peg or pin-tiles, made in Norfolk from at least the 14th century. They were about 10 inches long by 8 inches wide and half-an-inch thick, and latched on to horizontal laths by oak pegs driven through the two or three holes near the top. From *c.*1700 they were largely replaced by PANTILES. See TILE. *1728: 87 pantyles 26 roof tyle 260 flatt tyle.*
flaxen made of flax that is, LINEN. *1592: Tenne Flaxen sheets ls. Eyght Flaxen pilloberes xijs.*
flay, flathe fish of the ray or skate species. *1465: paid for a Flathe xiijd. 1503-4: for flathe and codd xxd. 1545: for Flathe bought at m'kett and Cokels and playce ixd. . . playce bought at Derhm iijd. for a pece of Flathe ther iiijd. 1582: Fleythe one bo. pr' ijs. viijd. 1655: 70 whitins 2 Flayes 3^C oysters wanting 20 - 15s. 8d...3 sides of Flay 2s. 6d...1 Flay 1s. 6d.*
fleam small short blade on handle driven into the vein by the BLOODSTICK for the purpose of bleeding an animal.

fleaspotted, fleabitten horse with tiny spots of grey or sorrel on a light ground. *1588: one stone horse flebitne gray. 1593: 1 white flespotted cart geldinge.*
fleet 1. Water channel, stream, ditch; channel filled by tide. 2. Shallow standing water. 3. A sewer. 4. Adj. meaning shallow. *1317: [digging] del flet [at the meadow]. 1665: abating 6 yards for a fleeter foundation.*
fleet to skim cream from milk, hence fleeter, fleeting; made from skimmed milk. *1592: ½ qtr of flett cheese. 1647: fleeteinge dishes bought for the dayry 5d. 1654: 12 flett Cheese sold @ 2d. a pound 18s. 4d. 1779: Butter pint & Fleeter.*
fleet net drift net paid out by a herring boat. *1591: on fleete nett & a payer of coddnetts.*
fleghe possibly a form of FLAKE. *1396: Le fleghes [of the dovehouse].*
fleke, fleyke see FLAKE
flekis see FLITCH
flesh hook a hook, usually shown with 2 or 3 curved prongs on a two-foot-long handle, for removing meat from the cauldron. See p. 117. *1444: j fleshoke. 1595: a Fleshe hoocke.*
flesh tub wooden tub for pickling meat in brine. *1616: [larder] a Table, a Cubberd, flesh tubbs, and other things xxs.*
flew see FLUE
fleythe see FLAY
flick see FLITCH
flight the husk of oats and other grain, used among other things for stuffing beds. *1701: Two flight beds & bolsters & one old bedstead.*
flight light ARROW for very long and straight shots. *1455: a flyte shot or more from his place. 1467: for iij flytes, ij bottebolts & ij byres xvijd.*
flitch the side of an animal, usually a pig, cured. *1593: a flyck of beefe & a flich of bacon. 1602: Fyve payer of Flyckes of Bacon. 1631: tow bacon flekis.*
flitch slice of timber cut lengthways from trunk, usually having the natural surface i.e. bark as one side. *1665: one flitch 10½ feet by 5 inches by 5 inches.*

float, flote shallow wooden tub. See BUCKING TUB. *1591: ij getts & j flote.*

flock, flockle, flockwork coarse tufts or refuse of cotton and wool, used for stuffing beds, pillows, cushions, and quilted clothing, and for caulking boats. *1256: [for mending boat - board and pitch and nails] & floks iiijd. 1584: A canvice flock bed. 1590: a flockebed ij blanketts ij Coverletts ij flockle bolsters and a strawe case xs. viijd. . . . .a posted bedstede wth a flocke teaster xijs.*

flockard, flokard a flowing veil. *1464-5: ij flokardes ijs. 1481: a peir of flokkardes for my Lady Barneis xijs. viijd.*

floor cloth canvas spread with thick layers of pigment, the predecessor of linoleum. *1745: one Piece of painted floor cloth. 1792: Two lengths of painted floor Cloth ¾ wide about 42 yards.*

florishing in 17-18th-century fat, silky, linen thread used for mending damask, linen etc. *c. 1680: 4 yds florishing 6d.*

flour kid a kid was a small wooden tub, variant spelling of KIT. *1756: a flower Binn...a Flower Kidd.*

flower pot from the Middle Ages many houses, some quite small, had flower pots, often of pewter, for growing flowers. *1592: one lattin pott for flowers. 1647: in the Gardyne Thirtene flower potts. 1709: 5 Wooden flower pots upon the stair case blew & gold.*

flue the medieval flue or smoke-duct was often of board and was probably a fire-hood suspended over the open hearth. It could be plastered with clay inside and out in an attempt to make it fireproof. See p. 241. *1293: [carpentering] Flews [of the hall]. 1310: v bord [bought for] j flewe [for the solar 5d.]. 1319: xiiij bord [for the] flewes [of the kitchen 3s.]. 1416: [1 table of] waynskott ꝑ les Flew [of the chamber]...[wages] William Daghs [throwing clay for 1 day]...[nails bought for the same] flewes iiijd. 1664: priming the five flewe boards towards the'ast in the greene cort yard & striking them over againe.*

flue, flew fishing net, either a dragnet or a fixed NET. *1465: fore knyttynge of a flew xvjd. 1584: fyftene mackerell netts two spyrling netts, also tenne hearring flewes & nyne nynescores hearing netts, with warropes 9 li. xs. 1591: j byrdnet ij ould flues. 1591: j Flew net for ye Sea. 1593: j cocke boote called the goosears with xij flues.*

fly a FAN or fanner, implement to blow chaff from the threshed grain. *1743: one Fly one riddle one Colder skep.*

flyck see FLITCH

fly jack see JACK

fodder, fodyr, fother weight of lead: 20 cwt.(2240 lb.), now usually 19½ cwt. (2184 lb.). See POUND. *1546: ij fudder of lead x li. 1621-2: To March the keeleman for bringing 8 fodder of lead being 67 piggs and Charge of Loding &c. 1 li. 2s.*

foderyngbyng bin for fodder, that is a manger or CRIB. *1391: [pales for making cows'] foderyngbyng.*

foins fur of the foin or beech-marten, *Mustela foina.* The original name of the animal was marter, hence martren, 'of the marter.' The fur was used for trimming robes etc. *1505: furre of foynnez. 1513: iiij coots of fonse. 1637: One black gowne faced wth foyns 3 li.*

foldcote hut or small building belonging to the sheep-fold. See p. 242. *1352: [xlviij clayes and all the pales and j iron and] j Foldecote.*

folding house room for folding and ironing clothes, sheets etc. *1597: The Chappell nowe the folding house...a longe table to folde Clothes on.*

folgate see FALGATE

folghes see FELLOES

folt, foult folded, folding. *1591: one folt table.* See CHAIR; TABLE.

font, fount spring, WELL. *1407: [repairing] dil font [with one weight made new].*

footcloth 1. Large ornamented cloth hanging to the ground on each side of a horse. 2.

Cloth to put feet on; carpet. *1588: footecloth lyned wth bocrame xs.*

footing 1. Making the footings for a wall. *1306: in fotingg stabule.* 2. Making a foot or base for a pot etc. *1320: in foting [1 bronze pot 2d.]*

footlane possibly the same as footstall, the base of a pillar. *1665:[masons] cutt footlanes & skemes for part of the heading of the wall of the bridge.*

footman a stand to support pot or kettle in front of a fire. *1779: One footman, two round D⁰. 1792: a wainscot table, a footman, Three bronzed Tea kitchens.*

footman originally a servant going on foot, particularly a runner going before the carriage; from the late 17th century a servant, often liveried, attendant in the house or when travelling.

footmans inn lodging-chamber for the footmen. *1597: Footemans ynne vizt the Chamber next the lytle plor [with two beds].*

foot-pace a raised floor, platform, DAIS; a step around something like a monument. *1620: a drawing table uppon the footpace.*

foot-plough wheelless plough, swing PLOUGH. *1745: one Foot Plough. 1747: one Wheel-Plow 1 li. 2 foot Plows 12s.*

forcelet, forslet little fort, fortified place. *1452: [gang] kepe a frunture and a forslet at the hows of...Robert Ledeham. . . kept atte his hous in maner of a forcelet.*

forcer OFr. *forcer, forcier*, small chest, coffer, casket. *1448: for the broke sylver...ther is none in your forcer; she supposyd that ye left it at Norwiche in your cofere. 1513: a lytell forcer.* See FARRAS.

fore house building in front of a house; room at front of house. *1591: Foore howse* [contained cupboard, bed, 2 tables, 3 chairs, chest, fire-irons, salt box].

forelock wedge; wedge or cottar driven through the end of a bolt to keep it in place. *1620: [smith] 3 forelocks and a boulster 2s.*

fore iron 1. ? Small spit placed in front of open fire. *1318: tenayl ad le spet & ad Le foreyne vd.* 2. Fender. *1709: a tosting iron, an iron sifter, a fore iron, a fire shovel, a pair of tongs. 1723: An Iron Range Fore iron Fore pann Tongs Purr Toasting Iron.*

forest bill see BILL

forest work tapestry or cloth with sylvan scene. *1593: 5 pcs of hangings tapestry: one of Imagery: 4 of forest work.*

fork basic tool for farm and garden, up to the 19th century often with wooden prongs. A pitchfork, originating from a forked branch, had a straight shaft 5-6 feet long with just two tines or prongs, and was used for pitching sheaves of corn, hay etc. on to the cart or the stack. A topping fork and a gib fork had two tines and shorter shafts and were used for topping off the stack. A muck fork had 3-5 tines and was used for handling muck in the yard and field. The digging fork with 4 tines, short shaft, and ∇- or T-shaped grip can be seen in late-medieval manuscripts. The D-shaped grip was a development of the 18th and 19th century. *1278: iiij furc' [of iron bought 4½d.]. 1292: iij furc' [of iron bought for harvest 3d.]. 1306: ij tindis ad furc' [of iron 1d.] 1313: [1 iron for] j pycforke jd. qu'. 1321: [4 irons for] picforkes vjd. 1325 [4 spades 4 shovels] & iiij furcis firm'[muckforks] xvd. 1593: gibfork. 1746: six pitching Forks one Topping fork five Gibb Forks.*

fork, table uncommon in England until the 17th century. Before *c.*1600 a two-pronged fork might be used for serving or carving. *1515: ij silv' sponys, being in a purse, j yrof being a gemewe spone, and the other a spone wt a fork. 1637: one longe spoone wth a forke [silver]. 1734: Two Dozen Ivory Hafted Knives and forks £6 2s. 6d. One Dozen and halfe of Black helved Ditto 7s. 6d. Eleven Bucks Horn Ditto 7s. 1787: One dozen Knives and Forks, with green Handles and Silver Furrells.*

form backless bench, one of the normal multiple-seating pieces of furniture for most houses up to *c*.1700. *Prompt. Parv.* 'Foorme, longe stole'. *1592: forme of Furrendeale joyned. 1593: one sceled bench & ij formes. 1597: 3 longe formes of Esshe. 1608: fower formes fixed in the grounde.*

former, fourmer OFr. *formoir*, from *former*, to form, subsequently altered to *fermoir.* Firmer chisel, a short chisel for mortices etc. Early examples often had the blade tapering inwards to the handle. Sometimes applied to mason's chisel. *1590: v fourmers xxjd.*

forstage ship's forecastle; ship with forecastle. *1462: there shulde come in to Seyne CC gret forstages owt of Spayne.*

fother see FODDER

fotmel of lead the Assize of Weights and Measures, *c*.1302/3, defines fotmel as 6 stone of 12 lbs a stone, less 2 lbs. = 70 lbs. See POUND.

foullenger fowling-gear.

foulte, fowlte folded, folding. See CHAIR; TABLE.

foumart, fulmer, fitchet the polecat, *Putorius fœtidus* or *Mustela putorius.*

fountain large bowl, cistern. *1459: fountayne of latayne to set in pottys of wine.*

foreyne see FORE IRON

fower, fowre four. The spelling, as in chayer, fayer, payer (chair, fair, pair), almost invariable up to the 18th century, indicates that the dipthong -ou- was pronounced disyllabically.

fower fyer, man who fies out ditch, privy etc. See FEY. *1410: [paid to the Master] Fowere [in the privy 3s. 4d.]*

fowite folded, folding. See CHAIR; TABLE. *1592: on fowite table iijs.*

fowling piece gun used for wildfowling. *1595: a Corselett a fowling peece caliv' a petronell penn.*

foynnez see FOINS

frail, frayle, frayll rush basket, used for packing dried fruit etc. *1498-9: a frayll of fyggs and a frayll of reysons viijs. xd. 1647: a frayle 4d.*

frame a loom. *1592: a fram for silks.*

frame set of shelves. *1591: one owld frame with five glasses xvjd.*

framed furniture made with a frame as opposed to boarded or solid construction. For examples see BOARD; JOINED; TABLE; TURNED; STOOL.

frampald, franpald, furpald, thrempold J.O. Halliwell, *Dict. Archaic Words,* gives 'poles to be reached *fram* or *from* the hedge'. The forms furpald and thrempold, which seem to be the same word, rather cast doubt on this derivation. Whatever they are, they are not large or expensive; as all examples cited are connected with SOLES, the wooden yoke or bow put on the neck of cattle to attach them in a stall, 'frampald' might be a part of the sole, or perhaps shackles, hobbles, or trammels. *1302: xxiiij soles & lx thrempold vijd. ob. qu. 1319: in furpaldes & soles xjd. 1320: in sol & franpald iijd. 1340: iiij soles & j frampald [to attach cows ½d.].*

frankincense aromatic gum from trees of the genus *Boswellia,* also from firs and pines, particularly the frankincense pine, *Pinus taeda. 1587: j li. & a half of Franckynsence iiijd.*

frankpledge in Anglo-Saxon England each vill was divided into tithings of ten men, members of which stood surety for the behaviour of the others. This was continued and extended after the Conquest. View of Frankpledge, held usually at the COURT LEET of the manor, made sure it held good. The head of frankpledge was the capital pledge.

franpald see FRAMPALD

fraungyd fringed

freasse see FRIEZE

83

frecherynge fresh herring. *1525: lxv frecherynge.*

freesador, frizado woollen cloth with raised nap; fine kind of FRIEZE. *1555-6: iijs. iiijd. for a Coatcloth of blewe freesador...And of xxs. for lynyng & makinge up of the same coat. . . iijs. iiijd. for a Coatcloth of prple fresadore.*

freestone any fine-grained sandstone or limestone that can easily be cut or sawn. See ASHLAR. *1541-2: dyggyng of freston & calyon in the said late abbey. 1619: masons...tooke downe Freise Stone at Coxford.*

French barley barley skinned and with the ends ground off. Pearl barley is steamed, dried, and ground between millstones set high to take off the husk, and is finer ground than French barley. *1647: for 1 li. of French Barly 1s.*

French eaves eaves with a gutter. *c.1620: french eaves and dutch dormers. 1621: [bricklayers] hewing setting and Finishing of 37 yards in lengtht of French eaves at 12d. the yard.*

French hood small close-fitting hood worn at the back of the head, curving round to the ears; sometimes a small front peak. The tail was often stiffened to lie flat on the crown, or stand up and forward. Fashionable 1530-1600, thereafter worn by widows and old women. *1537: ij Frenche hoods wt the byllmts for Kat'yne & Anne.*

French lock possibly shackle for a horse's feet. *1671: 2 french locks 2s. 6d.*

French oven possibly a version of the DUTCH OVEN. *1692: a french oven. 1734: One french oven 2s. 6d. 1738: tin French Oven 1s. 6d. 1756: brass French oven.*

French pin ornamental pin with decorative head, much more expensive than common pins. *1587: half a doz french pynns vs. ...I doz french pinns viijs...iiij papers of pynns xvjd.*

frere friar

freston see FREESTONE

fret(t) thripples or movable rails of a CART. *c.1331-3: in frett' [and nails 12d].*

fret(t)work carved decorative work of intersecting straight lines, especially on ceilings of late16th-17th century. *1665: hart larth for the frett work seeler...the frett worke seelings.*

friar's grey grey of the shade worn by the Franciscans. *1601: 10 yards dim' of fryers graye at 2s. xxjs.*

fricacy, fricassee meat sliced and fried or stewed, with sauce; small animals or birds cut in pieces; the pan in which fricassee was prepared. *1709: 13 fricacy pans.*

Friday book newsbook or paper bought, but not necessarily published, on Friday. News-sheets of the 1640s include *Mercurius Aulicus* (royalist), *Mercurius Britanicus* (parliamentarian), *Mercurius Politicus*, and *Mercurius Pragmaticus*. *1647: for the Fryday Booke 2d.*

frieze friezing, frizzing, or cottoning meant raising the nap on woollen cloth by rubbing. Friezes were used for petticoats, linings etc. High frizzing raised a nap of small curls by rubbing one side of the wet cloth with an iron rubber. Generally friezes came from the Midlands and Wales. *1531: ix yds white fryse for coats for Mr John, George Banyard & Lawrence navell vjs. 1533: for Furryng of John Walpoles Russet gowne & ditynge of the Fryse xvjd. 1601: 18 yards of course grey frise at 13d. 8 yards dim' of blacke manchester frise at 10d. 1603: v yardes and a quarter of white Freezed blanckett.*

fring frying

fringe narrow band of material from which threads of silk, cotton etc. hang, either loose, tasselled, or twisted. *1466: for grey lynen cloth and sylk frenge for the hers. 1647: 6 yards of deep fringe at 1s. 4.d p yard. 7 yards of smale fringe at 2d. p yard. 1649: 7 yards of cald Fringe at 1s. 4.d p yard. 10 yard & halfe of top Fringe at 1s. 9d. p yard. 6 yards of stoole Fringe at 6d. p yard.*

friture syringe Fr. *friture*, frying; syringe for injecting meat with oil or fat. *1745: copper friture syringe.*

frog *Prompt. Parv.*: 'Frogge, or froke, munkys abyte (frok, monkes clothinge, J.W.)'. Long habit, with long, wide sleeves (L. *froccus*), worn under the *cucullus* until the late Middle Ages, when the two garments appear to merge. *1466: For a cope called a frogge of worsted for the Prior of Bromholm xxvjs. viijd.*

frosting fitting horses with frost-nails, to prevent slipping in icy conditions. *1649: for horses frostinge 6d.*

fruit dish, fruit trencher dish or wooden trencher, often painted, for serving and eating fruit. *1582: halfe a Dussen frute dysshes. 1593: 1 dozen & 6 frute trenchers with boxes & 1 voider knife.* See TRENCHER.

frunture frontier, armed resistance. See FORSLET.

frysadoe rough 'frizzed' woollen cloth. See FRIEZE. *1595: ij stuffe gownes & one of frysadoe.*

fudder see FODDER

fugre ?figured. *1459: j jakket of sateyne fugre.*

fukke mast, fuk, fucksail ON *fok*, driving. Foremast, foresail, jib. *1465: paid for a Fukke maste, iiijs. iiijd. 1466: a fuk maste for the said Kervelle iijs. iiijd...ij seyle yerdes for the Fuk and the museyn.*

fulle ON *full*, cup, large drinking vessel; small pan. *1466: ij ketelles calde a Fulle iijs. iiijd.*

fuller's earth hydrous silicate of aluminium, used for cleaning cloth. *1747: for Fuller's Earth 6d.*

fulling cloth was beaten to clean it and thicken it, by hand and mechanically at fulling mills. *1499-1500: [making] le fullyng stokke [at Sileham 23s. 4d.].*

fulmer a grooved tool in which iron is shaped by being hammered into the groove. *1592: One hatche mandrell and a fulmer.*

fur OFr. *forre*, sheath, case; axle-box, iron lining of the nave of a wheel. See CART. *1562: puttinge in of a payer of fures into the new well. 1621: a pair of new wheles 1 li. 3s. 4 fellowes 6 spokes for ye old 7s. 5 furres in ye wheles & 5 li. pith & ½ li. tallow for ye nafes 2s. 4d. 1647: for 1 new Furr, & for makeinge it fast 2s. 4d. 1663-4: spoiling in the furrs. 1738: four stone two pounds of Run Furrs 2s. 6d.*

fur to fix strips of wood to floorboards, rafters etc. in order to make them level. *1620: taking up the ould bords and Furring up the Floore leavel and bording the same with deales planed and well layed.*

fur, furrs see FURZE

furindeal, furrendeal, -dale see CHEST; DEAL

furk see FORK

furlong see ACRE; ROOD; PERCH

furniture apart from the usual meaning, anything that furnishes or equips a plough, horse, door etc. *1587: a womans sadle wt ye furniture. 1595: the furnyture belonging to a payer of tryse. 1597: [saddlery] a furnyture of russet velvet & cloth of Sylver together. 1648: a snack & furniture 1s. 6d.* [for door].

furpald see FRAMPALD

furr-manderell see MANDREL

furrmaker man who cut and prepared FURZE. *1621: To the Fyrremakers 23 li. 17s. 6d.* [rate was 1s. per hundred bundles of furze].

furze gorse or whins, *Ulex europaeus*. Cut for fuel, particularly for brewhouse, ovens, and brick clamps and kilns. Usually reckoned in bundles. *1507-8: fellyng v lodes of fyrres xd. 1536: a hatchet for the baker to hew furrs wtall. 1592: Two loodes of furres xvs. 1598: furrez & woode xxs. 1620-1: For digginge & bindinge 4300 Furres 3 li. 13s. 9d. 1621: for 2400 Furres makinge 1 li. 4s. 1656: new setting ye Pyracanthus Dike and finding of ye Fur Lair to back it with.* See LAIR.

fustian, fuschine, fushine, fustyn different types of cloth, ranging from coarse cotton and linen to mixtures of linen and silk. Fustian of Naples was a cropped, dense VELOUR of linen and silk. *1552: ij tunicles of douned fustian...& oon vestyment of fustian in napes. 1588: [bed] tester & vallance paned with Satten of bridges & fustyan of Naples. . . ij Cotes of plate j covered with yellowe fustyan, thother with crane colored fustyan xxxiijs. iiijd. 1597: one fustian blankett, Long 3 yards di', lat 2 yards j qrter. . . [bed] one fustyn of fower brethes. 1620: one large Blankett of holmes fustian. a millian Fustian Down bedd.*

fyeing fan see FEY

fyller, filler see THILLER

fyrrett possibly a long-handled implement to recover a ferret. *1595: a Fyrrett a dygginge staffe Twoe nightstaves.*

Threshing by flail 1760s - note fan hanging on wall

Elizabethan kitchen fireplace, with hake suspended from gallow balk, spit turned by weight, and latchpans

86

G

G a gross, 12 dozen or 144. *1589: v G pins at vijd. - ijs. xjd.*

gad measure of iron or steel, roughly ¾ cwt. or 84 lbs.

gad long iron nail or spike. *1331-3: [fitting] viij gadd ferr' [to mend wheels and carts 6d.].*

galaches see GALOSHES

galingale aromatic root of *Alpinia* and *Kæmpferia* genera, used in medicine and cookery; also roots of *Cyperus longus* or English galingale. When cooked, is pinkish and smells of roses. *1562: di' li. of Ganingall ijs.*

gall marble-like growth on trees, especially oak, produced by the gall-wasp puncturing the bud and laying eggs; the irritation stimulates the formation of tissue in the shape of marble galls, which contain a concentration of tannic acid. They were used in tanning and for making INK. Marble galls originated on the Turkey oak, *Quercus cerris*, introduced in 1735, and spread to the English oak; before that the galls were imported. *1562: Payde for galls for my La: ijd. . . coprosse & galles vjd. 1592: a li. of not gales viijd.*

gallabok see GALLOW BALK

galle see GALLYPOT

gallery long room, usually on upper floor of large house, used for indoor exercise, portraits, storage etc. *1593: Stuff in the gallery 1 Carpet frame with the furniture 3 Cheese Rackes 12 black bills 6 boore speeres & 1 pece of old male xviijs. viijd. 1597: The best Gallery [contained 2 forms, 3 chairs, window cushion, carpet, close stool].*

gallow balk, galleybalk, gallibauk, gallows the usual definition is an iron bar or wooden balk fixed across the chimney over the open hearth, from which HAKES and pothooks hung. It is a very common entry in probate inventories. However, *fixed* furnishings were not normally included (see TABLE), which seems to nullify the theory that the balk was part of the structure of the chimney. Perhaps the 'pair of gallows' could be seen as an iron chimney-crane, or a pair of them, which would be attached to the structure of the chimney but would also be removable. This still leaves the problem of why gallow balks, where 'balk' suggests a large timber beam, should be included in inventories of movable furniture, to say nothing of the interpretation of the apparently hybrid phrase 'a pair of gallowbalks'. Perhaps the use is similar to 'balk' as the beam of a balance. See p. 86. *1591: payre of Gallows with hookes thereunto belonging. 1591: gallowtre. 1591:[hall] one Gallowe bauke. . . [parlour] payre of gallowebakes thre hokes & one Andiron. 1593: one payer of gallowes to hange potts on xijd. 1595: payre of iron gallowes. 1685: one gallibauk and hakes. 1736: one pair of dogirons two speets two heakes & gallabok 6s.*

gallon measure of capacity based on the volume of 8 pounds of wheat and 8 pounds of wine. The cubic capacity varied according to the substance: ale was 282 in^3, corn was 268.43 in^3, later 272 or 272¼ in^3 (Winchester measure), and wine was 231 in^3 for centuries but only legalised in 1707. The Imperial gallon of 277.274 in^3 was established in 1824, when all other gallons and bushels were abolished. A gallon contains 8 pints or 4 quarts, and there are 2 gallons to a peck and 8 gallons to a BUSHEL.

galloon, golowne narrow close-woven ribbon or braid, of silk, gold or silver thread. *1708: a parcell of Silk Gowlones 1 li. 10s. 1724: blew golume 3d.*

gallypot, gallipot pot for ointments etc. usually of glazed earthenware but sometimes of silver. *1465: a galy pott iijd. 1513: iij Galypotts. 1593: Closett by the Chimny in my La: Chamber 1 deske 1 little old Caskett 1 runlett wth some wine in yt glasses gally potts drinking glasses. 1649: 2 greate gallepotts 4s. 2 - 4 li. galle potts 1s. 2 - 2 li. galle potts 6d. 1763: [surgeon and apothecary]*

Gally-pots painted on Blinds for ye Window Shutters £1 1s. 6d.
gambale gammon, leg or haunch of pig. *1618: ij fliches gambales of baken one pece of hanged beefe vjs. viijd.*
gambeson decorative padded tunic worn over (or sometimes under) body armour. *1352: [2 pairs of quissas and gambesons].*
gammon backgammon. See TABLES. *1737: A pair of Gammon tables with the Appurtenances.*
ganingall see GALINGALE
garbage offal, entrails of animals. *1562: a cutting knife for garbage xvjd.*
garbrasse, gardebras additional piece of armour placed on upper part of gauntlet, or fastened to elbow plates. See WARE BRACE *1459: j garbrasse.*
gard, guard decorative trimmings of braid, velvet etc. probably derived from guarding the edges from fraying. *1588: an olde blacke clothe garded wth velvet. 1588: yellow carsey to guard the souldiers coats wth. 1592: An old damaske Cloake wth ij gards of velvet xs. 1597: soldiers Coats 2: redd garded with whyte.*
garderobe OFr. *garderobe*, keep-robe; chamber for clothes, stores etc. generally secure; also occasionally a privy. A term obsolescent by the 16th century. *1310: [repairing the carpentry of the kitchen] garderobe [and chambers]. 1314: vertivell [for the door of the] garderobe [of the great chamber]. 1335: [1 lock with key for the door of the] Garderobe jd. 1362: [lock for the door of the] garderob solar'. 1546: The New Garderobe...Tholde Garderobe... The Chamber entring in to the said garderobe.* See WARDROBE.
gardeviance, gardevyant OFr. *garde* and *viande*, meat; originally a food or meat safe, then a chest for holding valuables, travelling chest. *1459: j fedderbedde j bolster ij blankettes j gardevyaunt ij cosshonys of blewe saye. 1463: to brynge home my lordys gardevyence Fro London.*
gardnap see WARDNAP
garget, gargitt root the root of *Helleborus fœtidus*, bear's foot or stinking hellebore, a cathartic remedy for boils, spots, and worms; the root was also inserted into a wheezy cow's dewlap. *1647: gargitt rootes 2d.*
gargett Fr. *gargate*, throat; inflamed condition of throat and neck, in cattle, pigs, poultry. Also applied to inflammation of the udder. *1655: drinching & blouding 38 Bullockes for ye murrain & Gargett. 1664: [heifer] died of the gargett wch sett in her chest.*
garlek garlic. *1325: vjd de Garlek [sold].*
garnet a hinge of ⊦ form. See CROSSGARNET. *1483: for iiij garnettes for the said bene in the pantry xijd.*
garnish OFr. *garnir*, to provide, prepare; a set of vessels for table use, usually a dozen of each piece. See PEWTER. *1522: A Garnische of newe pewter.*
garnished adorned, furnished. *1597: a payer of Aundyrons garnyshed wth Latten. a payer of tongs lykewise garnished.*
garret, garit, garythe 1. OFr. *garite, guerite*, watchtower, turret. 2. Room on top floor of house, or in the roof-space; often used for storeroom, or servants' beds. 3. An outbuilding. *1367: [roofing] le Garit. 1382: [thatching the walls] dil garyt [up to the hall door]. 1383: [thatching and cresting] le garyt. 1685: in the Garret chamber one bed as it standeth 1 li. sheets knapkins table cloathes and other lyning 20 li. 1745: the Salone Garretts [8 rooms above the saloon, mainly servants' bedrooms].*
gartering in the 16th and 17th centuries garters were tied below the knee to secure stockings; they could be silk, taffeta, cloth of gold, or plain worsted. *1587: xlix yards of cullard garteryng ijs. jd. iij dozin & a halfe of gartering iijs. vjd.*
gasking lace see LACE
gast see GEASON

88

gate L. *gate*, Fr. *jatte*, bowl, trough. Treated as an English word by the 14th century. Wooden vessel constructed of staves. *1310: j gate & j bolle. 1318: ij gates [for carrying mortar]. 1321: [binding] j gate jd. 1352: [2 great] Getys. 1498-9: pro iij gettes viijd ob.* See GOTCH.

gaud, gawded, gawdee a gaud was a large ornamental bead on a rosary. Gauded, gawded: ornamented, adorned. *1484: my peir bedys of calcidenys, gaudied with silver and gilt. 1507: a payr bedys of Corall, gawded wth sylver, and an other payr beds gawded wt Casteltyns. 1513: j peyir beedez of blake Gette Gawdeez of sylv' & gylt. j pare of Gette Gawdeez of whyt Amber.*

geason, gast, geest OE *gæsne*, barren. *1603: Fowre milch beast and two gast hefers ix li. 1620: eighteene ewes with ther lambes & five geest sheepe.*

geioun see GUDGEON

geld to castrate; transf. meaning to cut, throw down. *1649: geldinge of fower shotts 6d. 1664: gelding of four thousand eight hundred & 85 molehills xlvijs. viijd.*

gelding castrated male horse. *1593: 1 old gray amblinge geldinge xlvjs. viijd. 1 gray Cotch geldinge iiij li. xs...1 black cart gelding wth a ringe on the offer buttocke xxxiijs. iiijd...1 white gelding called the millhorse xiijs. iiijd.* See STONED.

gelly jelly. *1655: 1 Gelly Bagg 6d.*

gelt see GELD

gemel, gemew, jemmel, jemowe OFr. *gemel, gemeaus*, twin. 1. HINGE with pin-plate and hanging-plate of identical size. *1321: iiij gemell [for 1 chest in the lord's pantry 5d.]. 1588: a short settle of waynscotte with a backe havinge locke & Jemowes. 1588: ij payer of gemowes for ye vyce dore...viijd. 1648: 2 payer of Jemmell 6d.* 2. Double ring which could be divided at wedding or betrothal; one of a pair. *1515: a gemewe spoon.* See GIMMER.

Geneva Bible English translation of the Bible, first printed in Geneva in 1560. Based on the GREAT BIBLE but influenced by Calvin and Beza, it was very popular in the reign of Elizabeth. *1595: A Geneva Byble, an olde Testamt, & other bookes with a drynkyng glasse viijs. iiijd.*

gesern, gisarme, gizzern a BILL with long shaft and long blade, in line with the shaft and sharpened on both sides. *1450: with boresperis, swerdis, and gesernys.*

gesse chamber guests' chamber.

get see GATE

gette jet, either the mineral or the JET of a barrel etc. See GAUD.

geyl, geylfat see GYLE

gial, timber see GILL

gibfork a two-pronged harvest fork. See FORK.

gice, giest see JOIST

giladge, gildfat see GYLE

gill quarter of a pint; sometimes a half-pint, when a quarter is termed a jack.

gill a female animal, such as a ferret, mare etc.

gill, timber pair of wheels connected by strong axle, for transporting tree trunks or large logs. *1752: 1 Timber gial.*

gill, jill mechanism for preparing and combing flax and long wool. *1734: One Jill and Weights 5s.*

gillyflower OFr. *girofle, gilofre*, clove; clove, clove-scented pink *Dianthus caryophillus*, and other like plants e.g. wallflower, stock.

gilt gilded: covered with a thin layer of gold, either of gold leaf or deposited by a chemical process, the base usually being silver. 'Parcel-gilt': partly gilded. *1459: a saltsaler like a bastell, alle gilt with roses, weiying lxxvij unces. ij everes gilt pounsed with floures and braunches, weiyng xxxix unces. 1588: One Bason and Ewer of sylver and psell gilte...ij potts dowble gilte with one cover.*

gimmel, gimmel fede ring see GEMEL; JOINTED

gimmer form of GEMEL: a HINGE with the two parts of equal size. Cross gimmers were in the form of a X with the pin through the centre. *1648: 2 payer of Cross gim^rs 2s. 6d....snack & furniture 1s. 6d. 1665: gimmers for the little doores by the leads xij paire.*

gimmer a ewe between the first and second shearing.

ginnet, jennet a carpenter's adze.

girandole branched or bracket candle-holder, usually on a wall, and often backed by a mirror. *1792: A pair of gilt Girandoles.*

girder a main beam. *1622: Carpenters... framinge of C ioyces to 3 Summers & ij Girders.*

girdle belt of cloth of varying widths. *1513: J Tyssue Gyrdyll wt long harnez J rede Gyrdyll sylv' & Gylt Damask corde J lytyll Gyrdyll wt sylv' & D gylt wt breydyn corde. 1587: xiij yellow wasts gyrdells ijs. viijd. ij broad wasts yellow xiiijd. xv jd. gyrdells xijd. i doz small wasts xxd. 1589: ij dozen & halfe of girdells at ijs. xd. - vijs. jd.*

girdle to cut round the bark of the trunk of a tree, either to kill it or to make it more fruitful. *1633: succidit div'es arbores...anglice cut downe and gurddled div'se tymber trees.*

girt web woven material from which girths for horses were made; strong broad tape for upholstery. *1655: for girt webb 2s. 6d.*

girt window The Builder and Architect's Companion (1727) has 'Girt and Lutheran [i.e. luthern, LUCARNE, or dormer] windows, made of oak' differenced from sash windows. In other contexts, 'girth' has the connotation of convexity, so perhaps it is a small bow window. *1781: A girt window.*

gittern gut-stringed and plucked musical instrument, predecessor of guitar and from *c.*1600 synonymous with it.

glaive, glathe, gleave OFr. *glaive, gleive*, lance; weapon with long tapering blade, sharpened on one edge, mounted on long shaft; possibly also sword, broadsword. *1450: with curesse, brigaunders, jakks, salettes, gleyfes, bows, arowes, pavyse, gonnes, pannys with fier. 1588: vj gleave staves xxs. 1593: 2 ptisans 3 holberds 1 pollax 1 glathe.*

glass up to the 18th century a glass was not neccessarily a drinking glass, but could mean a container made of glass. *1595: ij glasses with rose water...an aquavite glasse. 1602: a glasse of preserved Apricocks. 1612: a chest of glasse xxxs.*

glass, window crown glass: very thin glass made of silica, potash, and lime, formed in circular sheets by blowing and twisting. Plate glass: much thicker than crown glass. Made on a cast-iron bed, and then ground and polished. A. Clifton-Taylor, *Pattern of English Building*, says it was first made in England under French supervision in 1773, but it was certainly in common use well before that date. See PLATE GLASS; WINDOW. *1737: 8 Squ' of plate Glass. 15 Squ' of Crown glass. At Read's 10 Quare.*

glasskeep safe or cupboard for glass. *1626: a glasskeep ijs.*

glasswright, glasewryte a glazier. *1501-2: To a glasewryte for mendyng of a wyndowe js. jd..*

glathe, gleave, gleyfe see GLAIVE.

glavelyn perhaps the lance or bill form of GLAIVE; or a javelin *1584: j olde glavelyn.*

glayser glazier.

glister see CLYSTER.

glot, gloat see EEL.

goaf, gofe, goffe, golf, gove, gulfe + stead ON *golf*, floor, apartment. The bay of a building, particularly a barn; hence the quantity of unthreshed corn etc. in the bay. Goafstead etc. = the bay itself, with the corn contained in it. The actual amount varied, of course, with the building. As a verb, means to stack. *1417: William Waleys for Golvyng att Cossey xld. 1587: a golsteade of haye xls. 1591: one govested of sedge xvjs. 1593: on golfsted wt Rye, pease, feaches & barleye. one other golfe of myxlin. 1593: j gulfe of wheat & rye. 1593: 3 gofesteades* *barley [200 coomb].* *1594: barley in the sheves unthreshed and threshed. in an other golfesteade nexte that barley certeyne mixtlyn thresshed & lyeinge in the Chaffe.* *1597: j gouestead of Rye [25 coomb] j gouestead of barleye [20 c.] j gouestead of otes [20 c.] j gouestead of branck [20 c.].* *c. 1628-30:* [barley unusable for malting was] *goaf burnt rotten & not merchandizable.* *1637: wheat & mixtling one gouestead to thrash 60 combes 50 li.* *1655: ye hay Golfe.* *1719: A Barn of 4 Golfe steads and one middle stead to be built upon the heath.* *1743: Two Golfsteads of Barley...At the end of the old Barn, One large Stack of barley One pease and Vetch stack Two Golfsteads of Barley one Golfstead of Rye and a part of a Golfstead of the same.*

goat, goud Goats are not normally mentioned in inventories, and are rare in any Norfolk documents. *1599: two towe combes a pece of gouds wolle.*

godderd OFr. *godet*, drinking-cup, goblet. *1596: a godderd of pewter.*

goge jug. See GOTCH. *1592: v gret ston goges xvd.*

goggle spectacles, often constructed so as to correct a squint. In the quotation the association with other items suggests an ANTIGUGLE. *1787: One dozen tea Spoons, a pair of Tea Tongs, a Silver Goggle, a Silver Punch strainer.*

gogones, goionys see GUDGEON

gold of Venice gold thread, woven into textiles and decorating harness etc. *1465: di' unnce of goold of Venyse ijs. vjd.* *1506: a bald sorelyd hors, with a deep trapper full of long tassels of gold of Venys...a sorelyd hors, bald, the harnes of Venys gold, with a deyp frynges of half zerd of lengh.*

golf see GOAF

goloshes over-shoes worn to protect boots or shoes. In the 17th century they had wooden soles and were fastened with buckles. *1465: a payr shone and a payr galaches.* *c.1650: a paier of gren lacshooes and goloshooes 5s.*

golowne, golume see GALLOON

golving see GOAF

gome to gum, polish. *1573: wax, resell & turpentine to gome the livery beddes.*

gong see PRIVY.

gong a tool. *1590: ij fils wt a wrest & gong.* See WREST.

gong a set, gang. *1382: gongs de Felghes [sold with] gonge de spoks.* *1636: 8 gonge of Carte Fellows. 3 gonge of Carte spookes.*

gongfarmer man who cleaned out the GONG or PRIVY and sold the contents.

goodman master, head of household; man under the rank of gentleman, especially yeoman. *1647: Goodman Fishpooles man.* *1654: Goodman Oates.*

goody married woman of the yeoman and lower classes. *1654: Goody Jackman.*

goose, green young goose, older than a gosling and up to a year old. *1593: [22-29 April] for x grene geese iiijs. iiijd.*

gorge small pitcher or jug. *1671: Earthen Whight ware...3 small gorges.*

gorget, gorgit 1. A piece of armour, sometimes articulated, worn below the helmet to protect the throat. *1588: x Burganetts & x gorgetts.* *1597: 4 Curetts: 4 headpecs: 4 gorgetts. 4 black Corsletts: wherof 2 want their gorgetts. a launce Armor whyte wthout the gorgett.* 2. A collar or ornament worn round the neck. 3. A channel-shaped surgical instrument.

gotch large pitcher, big-bellied jug, usually of earthenware. See p. 241. *1639: you are a Swill-bellied knave a gotch-bellied knave.* *1649: 2 gotches & 1 Jugg.* *1705: a stone pott & gotch with other Holland ware.* *1738: [stoneware] Seven Blue and White Gotches 1s.*

goter see GUTTER

goud see GOAT

gove, govestead see GOAF

gowlone see GALOON

goyce see JOIST

gradual see GRAIL

grafting saw short saw, sometimes double-edged, used for cutting fruit trees for grafting. *1592: one cutting sawe one wynber* [WIMBLE] *on grafting saw.*

grail, gradual book containing all the music sung by the choir in the medieval mass.

grains alkermes, kermes, or scarlet grain insect, the female of *Coccus ilicis*, which used to be thought a berry, and supplied red colouring; later applied to cochineal, the dried bodies of the insect *Coccus cacti*. See GREYNED; ENGREYNED; KERMES.

grains of Paradise the seeds of cardomum, *Amomum meleguetta*, of West Africa, used in medicine and as spice. *1498-9: j libra Greynys xiijd. 1587: i box & the grayns withit xviijd. 1589: iij qzters of graynes xijd.*

grange L. *grangia*, barn. In the Middle Ages generally just a barn, but the term was beginning to be used for an isolated farmstead by the end of the 16th century. *1509: And also my Grange in the same parisshe. 1593: Implmts howshowlde Stuff and necessaries remaininge at the Grawndge...all and ev'ie chamber hawle & office of the saide Grawndge. 1594: [house] lately cauled by the name of the man'e of Nowers & nowe come'ly cauled the Graunge.*

grapes There were vineyards in Norfolk in the early Middle Ages, but manorial records show most of them petered out in the first half of the 14th century, due to the competition of French wines and to a change in the English climate that made vineyards unproductive, at least of ripe grapes. Harrison (1580s) and Parkinson (1629) noted the lack of English vineyards, the latter attributing it to the fact that the climate was not so warm as it had been. Grapes could still be grown in an orangery or greenhouse. See F.A. Roach, *Cultivated Fruits of Britain*, 1986, 249-61. *1712: 21 vines for the uper part of the walls. c.1720:* [list of best fruits to be considered for planting at Houghton] *Vines - Tulep, Perle, White Muscadin, White Muscat or frontiglian, Black Muscat, Annernat, Burgundy, Gennotin, Bricke grease, palot melier.*

grass fish, grash fish. The OED gives an 1885 quotation for grass fish as the eastern *Nemichthys*, swimming upright amid 'grass'. The only *Nemichthys* in European waters is the snipe-eel, *N. scolopaceus*, a very long and thin eel, hardly a good food source. An alternative might be a green variety of cod *(Gadus morhua)* - Cotgrave 1611: *'Morŭe, the cod, or green fish. Morŭe verte, green fish.'* - or another green-coloured fish. See MULWELL. *1583: ij grasses vjd. 1655: for 12 Sandlins 3 Grash fish 3 whitins 3 Codlins 8 Crabbs & 5 Lobsters 5s..*

grass hook sickle for cutting grass. See HOOK. *1665: grasse hooke for the gardiner.*

grate 1. Grating, often of timber, in a watercourse or moat to act as a sieve. *1433: [enlarging] le gretelay [and cleaning the watercourse]. 1619: Carriage of v^{xx} ix lod Sand, ij lod Stone, 9 lods Bricke, j Chalder lyme from Creake, j lode morter To his howse for ye Slewce ther, j lode hurdelles, 4^r lod Aldcopoles to the Buildinge & for Carriage of ye Weddinge grate liijs. viijd. 1665: [sawers] piller for the grate at the Moat & Newater 30 peeces.* 2. A cattle-grid. *1539: ye grate owt of ye chirch yard into ye feyer stede, both ston work, yerne & ty'byr xxvs.*

grate a closed CUPBOARD, with a grate or lattice front, to store bread and other food and utensils. *1584: [parlour] Twoo breadgrates. 1593: In the Closett by the Chimny in my La: Chamber...1 duble grate. . . [pastry] 1 bread grate. 1649: a small grate 2d.*

grate 1. A grid-iron. *1620: an Iron grate for Buttered meats.* 2. Fire-grate, generally coming into use with the adoption of a raised grate for coal fires. *1636: i grate for coales & i riddle belonginge to it.*

grater kitchen utensil for grating, e.g. making breadcrumbs. *1745: bread grater.*

grave OE *grafen*, dig. *1619: for 5 daies in gravinge Flagg vs.*

grease until modern times greasing with tar was favoured for the treatment of scab on

92

sheep and for smearing on cuts, bare patches etc. In the autumn sheep were greased all over with a mixture of tar and butter or tar and soap as a protection against scab and the weather. *1647: for the greaseing of 143 hoggs 13s. 4d. for 8 li. sope to mix a monge their tarr 2s. 4d.*

great, by the work done for a fixed price by bargain for the whole task. *1622: Worke by the Greate. 1733: When he workes what he has taken by the great he pays them [his workmen] the same.*

Great Bible the work of Matthew Coverdale, using Matthew's Bible (1537), which was a revision of the work of William Tyndale. In September 1538 the Great Bible was ordered to be placed in every church, but in fact it was not issued until 1539; an extensively-revised edition was issued, with a preface by Cranmer, in 1540, and was often called Cranmer's Bible. See GENEVA BIBLE.

greediron, grediron see GRIDIRON

green geese see GEESE.

greet spykyng see NAIL; SPIKING

gressing, grece, grecing, greese, greys, grise L. *gressus* or *gradus*, step. Stairs. *1484: a litel white bedde that hangeth over the gressyngs for a trussynge bed. 1519: emendyng the Greys. 1613: mending of the grisings iiijd.*

gretelay see GRATE

greyned dyed with GRAINS, that is, scarlet. See ENGRAINED. *1459: j broken gowne of sangweyne, graynyd with the sleves...j gret rollyd cappe of sangweys, greyned...iiij hoodys of sangweys, graynyd.*

gricke, black Fr. *grièche*, grouse. Cotgr. 'poule griesche, a moorhen; the henne of the Grice, or Moorgame'. F. Greenoak, *All the Birds of the Air*, 1979, 103, gives 'grigear' as a name for the hen black grouse. Sir Thomas Browne: 'The Heathpoult common in the north is unknown heere as also the Grous, though I have heard some have been seen about Lynne'. *1593: a dussen stints & a blacke Gricke. . . iij black gricke iiijd. ob.*

gridiron, grugne, grydyl iron grid, sometimes with legs and handle, for cooking in front of open hearth. *1313: j grydyl [bought] ijd. ob. 1313: [making] j grydyl jd. ob. 1592: a spete and a payer of cobyrons a brundit a grugne and a frien pan ijs. vjd. 1602: j grediron. 1743: one Gridge Iron.* See ROAST IRON.

grift fruit tree grafted on to a vigorous base stock. *1665: Bought of Katherine Locke widd. Sept 6th, nine grifts, seu'all rose bushes.*

grigge hook possibly hook for suspending EEL above the fire.

grindstone, painter's a ledger, a block of marble or some other close-grained stone on which solid pigment is ground with a muller, a large stone shaped like half an egg. *1602: a paintrs grindestone wth a muller xviijd.*

grint stone grindstone. *1709: [smith] two Grint stones as they hang 16s.*

grisings see GRESSING

grosgrain, grosgram, grogryn coarse fabrics made of large twills of worsted, mohair, and silk; practically the same as CAMBLET. *1593: 1 cushin ymbroyderd uppon blacke grogryn.*

grope see GRUP

grospykyng see NAIL; SPIKING

gross twelve dozen, 144. *1647: halfe a groose of tobacco pipes 1s. 6d.*

groundsill, grouncellyng, groundseele horizontal timber forming the footing of a timber-framed wall. See DORMAN. *1509: xvjd....for ij Groundsyllys . 1536-7: le grouncellyng of the Hall. 1593: ij groundsells ijs. 1611-2: heweing & saweinge of groundsells xvd. Thirtie foote of Tymber for groundsells xvs. 1662: groundseele & stoods & broches & sparres & dogs 15s. 6d.*

ground table foundations of masonry or brick building. *1620: The ground table already sett* *about the house conteineth in length 805 foote wch at 10d. the foot 33 li. 10s. 10d. 1620: hewinge...300 fotte of grownd table att 4d. ye foote.*

grub axe, grub iron axe or axe-like tool for grubbing up roots. *1597: ij long cutting sickles a grubb yron and iiij didalls iiijs. vjd. 1745: three old Netts, two Grub Axes.*

grugne see GRIDIRON

grup(p) ditch, trench, small water channel. *Prompt. Parv.* 'Gryppe, or a gryppel, where watur rennythe a-way in a londe, or watur forowe'. Forby: 'a trench, not amounting in breadth to a ditch. If narrower still, it is a *grip*; if extremely narrow, a *gripple*.' *1306: [digging] ij grop' [length 1 perch 2s. 7d.]. 1310: [making] de gropes in le launde. 1418: [making] Grupp' [around the hall]. 1544: A plancke to ley ov' the grope at the Hethe.*

grydyl see GRIDIRON

guard see GARD

gudgeon 1. Iron or steel pivot or spindle on which wheel etc. turns or gate swings. See HINGE. *1313: [nails] staples, guggens [and other things of iron for the house near the gate]. 1318: ij guggens & ij plat'. 1328: j Geioun [with iron nails 4d.]. 1355: guggoun [for the gate of the postern 1d.] 1387: gogones plates viroles staples & hespes. 1665: Virrells gudgirons & plates for a crudbarrowe xviijd.* 2. Iron joining adjacent stones in masonry.

gugg jug

guggen see GUDGEON

guilder the man who gelds animals. *1654: the Guilder... for guildinge him [a Bulkin] 1s.*

guild, guile see GYLE

gulf see GOAF

gull throat, mouth; shaft of brick-kiln. *1665: pulled downe bothe the gulls at the brickell being decayed, lengthened and wrought up the same againe to save fireing.*

gullet fish of undetermined species; the roe of a fish. *1654: 2 Couple of salt fish more wth souls & Gulletts & 1 Lobster & 6 Crabbs.*

gum punch out, reset the teeth of a saw. *1579: for Gummyng of a nother sawe. 1665: One sawe guming setting and sharping.*

gunfis, guncis, gunfus, gumfis, gumphis the hook, or crook, part of a HINGE for a door or gate, the eyed part being the VERTIVELL. See GUDGEON. *1256: [repairing the gates of Grettum] & in Gumphis] for them 5½d.]. 1264: [lock for the door of the granary with mending the door] & gunffis & vertivell.*

gurking see JERKIN

gusset a piece of flexible mail used to fill in joint between two pieces of plate armour. *1481: for ix gussetes, xd. a piece ixs. iiijd.*

gutter gutter, channel, drain, rainwater gutter. Materials might be wood, brick, masonry, or lead. Several quotations refer to thatching the gutter, which might be a covered channel or sewer, or even a euphemism for the privy or jakes. *1278: [making] j gutter [under the fowl-house with daubing the wall of the house 8d.]. 1292: [two cartloads of stone for] j guter [of the well]. 1296: [thatching] Gotores [of the lord prior's chamber with cresting 14d.]. 1299: [thatching] j Guter super Solar. 1306: [thatcher working on kitchen, wall against chamber, & bullock house] & goter [of the hall and chambers 21d.]. 1313: [mending the lead] del gotore [near the chapel 3d.]. 1323: [carpentering] del gotere. 1335: [panel of boards for] guttera [in the bullock-house 12d. Carpentering the said gutter for two days 6d.] Cxxx durnayl [for it 5d.]. 1380: [repairing] le gottuer dil chymne dil cam'e. 1466: to the plomer for a gotter.*

gwnys gowns. *1449: sume frese to maken of zour child is gwnys*

gwypcord whipcord

gyffne given

94

gyle, geyl, giladge, gild, guild, guile, gyld wort fermenting during the process of BREWING. Gyle vat, fatt, etc. is the VAT or tub in which the wort fermented. *1397: [hoops for] le mashefat & Geylfat. 1513: J masshepane J Gylyngfatte. 1588: Browen: one Mashe fatte, one gilde fatte, one worte Tubb, one Coler. 1595: one gyld fatt. 1606: a mashefatt a giladge fatt and a Coler xxs. 1647: for the new Guilevatt 6 li. For new shooteinge the other fatt and for 2 new hoopes 1 li. 10s. 1787: a Marsh Tub and two Guile Tubs.*

gylhouse house or room where the gyle was produced; brewhouse. *1321: [j lock with key bought for] Le gylhous iijd. ob. 1403: [house called] Gylhous.*

gynne bolt, bar. *1619: ij iron Gynnes for the dore.*

gyrkin see JERKIN

gystis see JOIST

Processing hemp 1760s

H

Haburdine, habblurdine   large kind of cod, used especially for salting. *1583: Habblurdine one^C iij^{xx} xvij.*

habergeon   coat of plate or chain-mail, without sleeves. *1454: jakks and saletts, and rusty habyrjohns.*

hatchet, hachet   OFr. *hacete, hachette,* dim. of *hache,* axe; small axe used with one hand for trimming trees, splitting small wood etc. *1278: j hachet emp' ijd. ob. 1312: j hachet vd.*

hagge   see HAKE

hagesaw   hacksaw, for cutting metal. *1591: j hagesaw & j short sawe.*

haggard   hawk caught after assuming adult plumage; wild, untamed. *1602: a haggard Jerfalcon.*

hair   sieve with bottom of finely-woven hair, for straining liquids, especially for use in the malt-kiln, where it is usually termed a kill-hair. See KILLHEYER. *1526: hayer yt he made my Mrs malt wt xs. vjd. 1587: a haire on the kell.*

hair   was used to give body to interior plaster. *1607-8: for fower bushelles of heare for the Guilhowse xxd. 1649: 2 bushells of hayre 1s.*

hair, hair-cloth   hair, e.g. goat's hair, was incorporated in various types of cloth; and see HAIR LINE. *1498-9: xviij yerdes of hayre iiijs. viijd.*

hair-button   button made of horse or other animal hair, closely woven over a wooden core. *1589: ij grosse of heare buttons at vjd. js.*

hair line   washing line made of hair for drying fine linen. *1655: For a Hare line for ye wash maids use 2s. 6d.*

hake   adjustable hooks incorporating a ratchet on which the POTHOOKS or S-hooks hung above the open hearth; usually found in pairs. See p. 86; GALLOW BALK. *1588: one longe barr of Iron wheron ye haggs hange. 1592: Two payer of hakes in the Chymney. 1637: One Crosbarr of yron in the Chimny wth 2 haks & 2 esses vijs.*

haketon   padded jacket or jerkin worn under mail; jacket of leather plated with mail.

halberd, halbard, holberd   a develpoment of the early-medieval battle-axe, the halberd had a broad, shallow axe-type blade, with a spike on the opposite side and a lance-head above it, mounted on a shaft 6-8 feet long with a spike at the bottom end. Armed: the shaft covered with leather or cloth to stop it becoming slippery. Black: blackened steel. White: polished steel. *1592: Two blacke Halbards with studs armed vjs. viijd. Two playne white Halbards armed wth white mocadowe vjs. one playne Halberd xijd.*   c. 14

hale   tent or hut, sentry-box. *1597: A Hale. A tent, wth the Chamber: & buttrye.*

hale, hall   a pot-hook. *1589: one stayned cloath & one hall in the chimbrie. 1590: ij dogges of yron one hale a fyer panne a paier of tongs & A payer of bellows. 1692: One Iron barr in ye Chimny one hale one fire pann & tongs.*

halfpace   step, floor, platform; broad step at landing between two half-flights of stairs. *1732-3: Cleaning ye steps and Gallerys & halfpaces of ye Great Staircase &c.*

half-headed   see BEDSTEAD

hall   in the medieval house the hall was usually the largest room, and was often free-standing or detached like the CHAMBER, KITCHEN etc. It was used for eating, heating, cooking, and social purposes, and in Anglo-Saxon and early medieval times for sleeping. The medieval hall was usually single-storey, with a central hearth or a hearth with a smoke-hood or flue near or against a wall, but from the 15th century it was often ceiled over and a room - SOLAR, chamber over the hall, hall chamber etc. - placed over it. Even as late as 1600, however, a considerable percentage of houses still had an open hall with no overhead chamber. The hall occurs in the vast majority of inventories of the 16th and early 17th centuries, but it becomes less common as a major room in the small or medium-sized house after 1700.

hallowmass, hallowmes 1st November, All Saints' Day. *1539: att ye rekenyng att hallowmes for ye drykyng.*

halling, hallyng tapestry or painted cloth for the hall. *1459: j hallyng of blewe worstet, conteyning in lenthe xiij yerds, and in bredthe iiij yerds. j hallyng with men drawen in derke grene worsted.*

hallywater sprincle, - sprinkell see HOLYWATER SPRINKLE

halmes alms. *1461: it is an halmes dede to do hym good.*

halter rope or leather strap by which horses or cattle were led or tied up; complete harness for the head. *1593: 5 dudfin halters 3 unwinked halters. 1736: Five Bell Halters Ten plain Halters...Five Large double Rane Hemping Halters.*

hambletree, humbletree, ampletree wooden beam fixed by a central hook to PLOUGH or HARROW, and with a hook at either end to which the HORSE-TREES, smaller beams, are fixed to be drawn by the horses. *1592: viij weedinge hookes with c'tayne hambletrees & staves. 1746: six harrows with iron Starts & Hamble Trees fit to go. 1746: old iron humble trees & clavers. 1836: wood for horse trees & ample trees.*

hames piece of wood or metal curved in a flat Ƨ-shape to fit over the collar of a draught horse and to which the traces are attached; usually in pairs.

hammer the varieties of hammer are too numerous for a work of this nature, and in any case are not usually distinguished in documents before 1800. A marking hammer was used as a punch to mark trees etc. *1683: [124 ashes and elms] All marked with the markinge hammer of the said Robert Walpole now all felled.* The hammer, called a maul, used in fighting was mallet-shaped with a spike projecting from each face. See HORSEMAN STAFF.

hammerbeam roof roof in which the principal rafters are braced by a vertical post mounted on the end of a short horizontal beam, which itself is joined at right angles to a short vertical post fixed to the wall or resting on a corbel.

hammer →   ← wall   corbel →

1620: making a new roofe...conteining in lenght 44 foote and a halfe or thereabout. And in width 126 foote from out to out being Framed with a Halfe story 5 Foote high above the Floore being a hammer beame Roofe.

hamper in the Middle Ages, large case, trunk, box; from *c.*1600 wicker basket. *1616: one Truncke 3 coffers a hamp a boxe. 1720: one pair of Hampers.*

hanckell see HANGELL

hand board, hand screen handscreen to protect the face from the heat of the fire. *1593: 1 plate for lights & 1 handscrene. 1738: A Japan Hand Board 4s.*

hand churn see CHURN

hand cup hemispherical vessel, about 9 inches across, with short handle at the side, used for scooping liquid out of a tub. *1737 [dairy] one hand-cup.*

hand saw small-toothed saw that could be used with one hand. *1592: a long sawe a belt a Rabbet a cutting saw two handsawes with other tooles.* See SAW.

hangeldes see HENGLES

hangell part of the apparatus over the open hearth; differentiated from pothooks and the iron bar or GALLOW BALK, it was possibly a variant of the chimney crane or HAKE. *1587: one spytte one gred Iherne & the pott hanghylles vs. 1592: two payre potte hooks two hanckelles one bare of iron. 1595: iij paier of Hangells with a Iron bar.*

hangen see HANGING

hanger, hanker short sword, usually with slightly-curved blade sharpened on the outer edge, used for hunting, travelling, and as a general-purpose weapon. *1595: ij swords one hanger one daggard and a longe knyffe xiijs. iiijd. 1636: Eighteen hangers. 1738: A pair of pistolls (one without a Lock) and Four Swords (one without a Hilt) A Large Hanker £6 6s.*

hangeule, hanghylles see HANGELL

hanging tapestries, painted cloths, and leather hangings were common furnishings, particularly in larger rooms, up to and beyond the 18th century. Some were of considerable size. 'Hangings' might also refer to curtains, or the furnishings of a curtained or posted bed. See ARRAS; BEDSTEAD; TAPESTRY; TIRE. *1513: The hangyngs of ye chaunbr wt whyt lenen cloth. . . J rede hangyng. 1537: iij clothes to hange in the parlor, at ixs. iiijd. a cloth, & in the hall xxviijs.. . . v clothys for the hanging of the pler iij li. vs.. . . to Willes wiff for tyer for the plor hangyngs vd. . . . for an old hangyng xs. of the Hey Hall at Westacre. 1589: A payer of steyned hangens for A bedd ijs. iijd. 1593: hangings...of dornix of blacke & yellowe & 1 painted ou' the Chiminye wth Armes xxs. 1597: iij pecs of hangings ymagery of tapestry lyned with Canvas wch bene in depth 3 yards qrter: in length one vj yards iij qrter, onother iij yards & thother v yards di. . . one Ladder to take downe the hangings. . . the hangings of dornix 3 yards in depth 14 yards in length. 1636: Mr Godsalles Chamber hanged wth guilte leather. 1647: to John Wright for 6 daies & halfes worke 3s. 6d. to Richard Froste for helpeinge him to doe up the hangings 6d. 1671: To Bowers for taking downe the hangings & mending of them & packing them up 4s. 6d. 1684: for the hanging of Malls closett 1 li. 19s. . . pd for scouring 95 ells of Tapestry hang' 2 li. 7s. 6d.*

hangingiron the HAKES or HANGELL from which to suspend the pothooks. *1513: ij peir pothooks J peir panhooks iiij hangingeirons J rostyng iron.*

hanging lock padlock, a form of LOCK used from early times; lock for securing horses. *1599: [harness] vij snaffles. ij smale hanging lockes. 1619: ij hanging locks 8d. 1649: 2 hanginge locks for the barne dores 2s. 4d.*

hankin see HANGING

hapharlot, hopharlot a coarse coverlet made of poor material. *1613: an old trendle bedstead one sheet and a hapharlot and an old matres ijs. vjd.*

harburyone see HABERGEON

hardbowe, hardbeam hornbeam, *Carpinus betulus*, a hard wood used for the teeth of gear-wheels, ox-yokes, etc. *1590: one hundred hardbowe bord iijs. iiijd... three pecs of groundsilles & iij plancks vs.*

harden, hardeyne, hurden coarse linen made of 'hards', the hard fibres of HEMP and flax. *1513: J hardeyne sheete in ye kitchen. 1537: xxix yerds of white hurden cloth at ijd. ob the yerd. 1592: viij payer of tearen & harden shetes.*

harding mortar quick and hard-setting mortar. *1664: plaistred the windowe in the wine siller wth harding morter.*

harletree OE *heorr*, *heorra*, harre, har, the pin and socket HINGE of a door or gate; hartree or harletree is the beam of the door which turns on the har. *1401: [2 sawers sawing for 10 days for the door of Fring barn] iiij harletree raybetes shortbetes. 1584: fyve hartres xij ioyce and certen pailes. 1729: a peice of oak 14 foot long for a harletree Barndoor.*

harness clothes, garments; attachments, means of joining e.g. buckles. *1513: j tyssue gyrdyll with long harnez.*

harnessed trimmed, ornamented. *1459: j bollok haftyd dager harneysed wth sylver, and j chape thertoo. 1484: a girdell of black, h'neised wt silver gilt and enamelled.*

harnser see HERON

haroyne see HARROW

harquebus, arquebus portable gun, usually matchlock, varying in size from a short handgun to a small cannon, mounted on carriage or rest when in use. The term was obsolescent by *c.*1660, when it had been replaced by the CALIVER.

harrateen stiff linen furnishing fabric imitating damask; a worsted version had been produced by 1719. *1730: Blue Harrateen furnishings &c in a bed. 1756: One Bed and Bedding with Green Harrateen Furniture and Window Curtains.*

harringe harrowing. *1665-6: a weeke harringe of oates.*

harrow, harrows L. *hercia.* Wooden frame, square, triangular, or ⌷ set with teeth of wood or iron and pulled by horses or oxen to scuffle the ground, break clods, and cover seed. 'Iron' or 'wooden' usually refers only to the tines; iron-framed harrows from the late 18th century. *1342: [mending sieves] & j haroyne ijd. 1401: [repairing] ij herciar' cu' tyndes [of iron 2s. 6d.]...[1 new wooden harrow 5d.]. 1417: ij plowes ij harowes goyng all day sewyng Ry. 1587: One paire of yro' harrowes one paire of timber harrowes. 1597: Harrowes one payer wth yron tynes: an other payer wth treen tynes. 1618: j payer of eyerne harrowes one payer of tryinge harrowes. 1636: Thre payre of harrowes one olland harrowe. 1647: 1 payer of new wooding Harrowes 4s...1 new Bauke for ye Iron Harrow 1s. 6d.* See p. 243.

harrow sled sled or sledge on which harrows were transported. *1593: 4 iron harrows wherof one is broken 2 wodden harrows & 1 harrowe sleede xs.*

harry carry, harry cart, hurry curry two-wheeled, single-horse CART, long, low, and narrow, originally made in the reign of Henry VII for use in the narrow 'rows' of Yarmouth. *1591: cart called a hurrycurrye. 1592: an harry cary for water & an ould cart book. 1593: Hurry Carry. 1595: j harrye carte.*

harth hearth. *1664: dormans for the harth peece.*

harthens, harthings L. *harolum, harta, harca* withies, willow or osier rods; hurdles made of withies. Withies were also used for the upright rods of a timber-framed wall. *1264: [collecting] harthing & squewes vjd. 1264: [rods] & harthins jd. ob.*

hartichoke see ARTICHOKE

hartre see HARLETREE

hartshorn a source of ammonia, made from shavings of the antlers of male red deer (hart). *1665: Hartshorne ij oz of Mr Smith vjd.*

harvest up to the 20th century labourers were often paid by the farmer for the whole harvest, that is an agreed lump sum rather than by the actual time taken to gather the harvest. At Houghton in 1647, for example, 'gatherers' were paid at the rate of 6d. a day on 23rd August, 6th, 9th, 16th, 17th 23rd, and 27th September, with 'rakers' paid on 24th and 27th September, while on the 27th one man was paid 'his Harvist wages' of £1 5s, five more their wages of £1, and four more theirs of 16s. At Oxnead in 1655, however, payments for harvest were spread over the period 6th August to 15th September, the workers obviously being paid week by week rather than in a lump sum. In the 19th century most harvest wages were paid at the end of harvest, and provided the only large sum of money that the agricultural labourer was likely to receive during the year. Manorial accounts show that in the 13th-15th centuries, at least, the lord of the manor provided food for the labourers (who were mainly those obliged by feudal custom to perform harvest services) for the whole of the harvest period, usually four weeks centring on the beginning of September, and the custom of providing food in the harvest field carried on in some parts until the 20th century.

harvest basket large basket or hamper in which food and drink taken out to the harvest workers. *1738: An Harvest Baskett 1s.*

harvest bottle large bottle in which to take ale or beer to the harvest workers. *1592: Two harvist botles xd. 1606: A bottell for harvest of wood. 1738: wooden harvest bottle.*

harvest gloves leather gloves or DANNOCKS provided by the master or lord for the harvesters. *1500-01: for harvest glovys iiijs. vjd. 1647: 16 payer of Harvist Gloves 11s. 6d.*

harvest pudding chest box to take food to the harvesters. *1756: three pitching Forks, two unpitching Forks, and Ten rakes, two Harvest Pudding Chests.*

hasp hinged plate, with a slot that passes over a U-shaped projection on the post to fasten a door, gate, or lid. *1319: staples haspes & specke. 1326: j haspe [for the well 1d.]. 1335: [2 hanging locks and 2 keys] iij staples & j hespe. 1648: 4 stolpes & hespes 6d. 1671: a hesp for ye Coale yard gate.*

hasp, hesp hank; quarter of a spindle of yarn. *1587: i hespe and a q' of packethred vjd. 1593: 5 hespes of linne' yearne & 2 reeles xxd.*

Hasting seed oats early-ripening variety of oats. *1654: six Bushell of Hastinge seed Oats for ye Common.*

hat palm the leaves of the palm trees *Thrinax argentes* and *Copernicia cerifera* were used for making hats. *1654: Apple trees...Pear trees...Hatt parmes 6d. Turky Beanes 6d.*

hatch 1. Small door opening within another; door divided horizontally. *1608: one dore with a hatch and locke and key.* 2. A trapdoor. 3. A sluice. See HECH.

hauldfast see HOLDFAST

hauserope 1. Hawser, cable for mooring or towing ships. *1579: for a roape to drawe up pyles viijd. for a haumserope ijs. for a nother roape for the Fery boate vjs.* 2. OE *hals, heals*, neck, that is a rope for the neck of a horse or other beast. *1621: hausrope for the carpenter. 1648: 1 new hausrope & Lop rope for the Tryces. 1649: mendinge the hooke to the hausrope 8d.* See HORSEROPE.

haver oats.

haver an alternative word for IMP or EKE, that is, a plaited roundel to increase the height of a beehive. See BEESKEP. *1654: for 4 Bee Hives and 6 Impes or Havers 5s.*

hawk flat piece of wood with a handle, either on the end or underneath, used by plasterer or bricklayer to carry a dollop of plaster or mortar. *1819: Hawk for bricklayer.*

hawk's hood hood to cover the hawk's head when out hawking. *1595: A hawkes hoode.*

hawk's mewe place where the hawks were kept. *1544: loke for the hawksmewe dore.*

hawk's perk perch, often free-standing like a bird-table. *1597: a broad foot of a hauks perke. 1608: [hall] a haukes pearke.*

hay OE *hege*, hedge. By the 17th century it might mean a dead hedge. *1313: [making] j haye ad methelwodedyck viijd. 1330: [mending] haye [at the bailiff's chamber 8d.]. 1364: [making] j haye [on the fosse of the wood containing in length 78 rods 12s. 10d.]. 1663-4: stoped gapps in the hayes in thentry.*

hay OFr. *haie*, net; NET for catching rabbits, birds etc. Described by Nall as being 30-40 yards long by one yard wide. *1519: Paid to Stephen Percy for a haye of l fadom [50 fathom, 300 feet] long, xs. 1593: a pece of an old haye 12d. 1596: his master Rumbelowe who was the warrener at Bylney did loke for him to have hayed with him that night for connyes...I am no more lyke to goe as hayinge.*

hayer see KILL HEYER

hayfer see HEIFER

hayhold, hayhole room under the hayloft. *1665: made a going up unto the hayloft out of the hayholde...made a new door for the hayhole...planchered the hayhole.*

hayre see HAIR

haysel, hayseel, hay siel hay + ME *sele*, season. Depending on the weather, the hay harvest preceded the corn harvest by a few weeks. At Oxnead in 1655 the haysel lasted from the week ending 7th July to the week ending 11th of August. *1639: in the time of haye seale. 1655: Hay siel. The Charge of mowinge and Hay making this weeke coms to 7 li. 3s. 11d. 1664: a wett hayseele.*

head house the main part of a dwelling-house, particularly the front range as opposed to the backhouse or leanto part. *1672: mending ye rufe of ye head house. 1675: 4 days of thacking ye head house on ye north side. 1829: The Headhous to have Ceiling with one Coat on Lath plaster...The Roof to be of English Timber & covered with red Pantiles rollpointed over the Headhouse & interlathed over the Leanto.*

headkerchief kerchief worn around the head. *1474: iij hedkercheffes pris xijd.*

head of plough see PLOUGH.

headmere headland. See MERE. *1586-7: le heademeere [leading towards] le grange.*

headpiece helmet, usually plain without visor. *1597: 4 Curetts: 4 headpecs: 4 gorgetts 1625: musket...Bandeleres & heade peece.* See ALMAYN RIVETT; MORION; SALLET; SKULL.

headsilver common fines, fines levied in the manorial court; capitation fee. *1648: For Signeinge money at the Leete 8d. for headsilver this year 4d.* See SIDESILVER.

headstall the part of the bridle or halter that goes round the horse's head. *1665-6: a headstall & hussingell*

hearen, hearing see HERRING

hearinge hair. See SIEVE.

hearnsew, hearnes, hernshaw see HERON

hearth floor of the fireplace; basket or grate for the fire; smith's forge. *1664: dormans for the harth peece. 1709: 1 steel hearth & dogs of the same.*

hearthstaff a smith's long metal poker. *1595: fyve payer of tongs a harthestaffe and a punch ijs.*

hearth tax created by Act 14 Chas. II c. 10 1662, abolished 1689. A half-yearly tax of one shilling for each hearth in the occupation of persons whose house was worth more than 20s. a year. Paid by the occupier, not the landlord. Persons too poor to pay either church or poor rate were exempt, as were those in a house worth less than 20s. a year or not having other property worth more than 20s. a year, nor an income of more than £10 per annum. Charitable institutions and industrial hearths, apart from smiths and bakers, were also exempt. By the revision in 1664, 16 Chas. II c. 3, landlords of exempt leaseholders were made liable to pay, also all persons with more than two hearths. The Norfolk assessments for 1664 and 1666 are printed in vols. 15 and 20 of *Norfolk Geneaology.* See CHIMNEYMAN.

heart lath see LATH

heavill see HEDDLE

hecferd, heckforth see HEIFER

hech, heck the crook, consisting of a pin on the end of a long thin wedge driven into the doorpost, forming the fixed part of a simple HINGE. The hook or fastener to secure the door. See GUDGEON; GUNFIS; VERTIVELL; VIROLE.

hech, heck from OE *hec*, the lower half, or perhaps the whole, of a door divided horizontally. See HATCH. *Prompt. Parv.*: 'hec, or hetche, or a dore'. *Ortus Vocabulorum* 1500: '*Antica*, a gate, or a dore, or hatche. *Est antica domus ingressus ab anteriori.*' Cotgr. 1611: '*Guichet*, a wicket, or hatch of a doore'. Forby: 'hack, half-hack, a hatch, a door divided across'. *1313:[mending] j vertivell ad le hech [of the hall ½d.]. 1318: j hech [for the granary door]. 1319: [making] j hech [for the malt-kiln door 3d.]. 1320: gunfis vertivell & [key for] j heche [for the hall door 12d.]. 1321: [4 oak boards for] j heche [for the stable door 4d.]. 1323: [making] j heche [for*

101

the kitchen door with] gunfis & vertivell.

hechnail 1. nail for use on a door or HECH, it is distinguished from doornail and may have been smaller. 2. nail whose point could be bent or hooked over. Cf. DEADNAIL. *1321: xij^C Lattenayl xxxlx spyks viij^C Lx splentenayl clx hechenayl iijs. xd.. . . in C splentenail & Lx hechnayl iijd. 1335: In iiij^{xx}x durnayl [for the door of the carthouse and the pigsty 3d.]. In lx hechche nayl [for the gate of the] pinfolde jd. ob. 1335: xx hechchenayl [for] vertivell [of the doors of the orchard ½d.]. in xxx durnayl [for the door of the kitchen 1d.].*

heckle, heckell, hackle comb for combing and splitting flax and HEMP. It was fixed to a board or table and the fibres were drawn through the wooden or metal teeth. *1590: a wullyn whele...a heckle...a Clock Reele.*

heddle, heavill, heavell in a loom, thin cords stretched vertically between two horizontal pieces of wood separating the warp threads to allow the shuttle to pass through the warp. *1602: the heavill & the sla att iijs. iiijd. a lombe with heavill & sla vs. . . .2 Elbrod darnocke heavell iijs. 2 owld wolsaye heavell iiijd.*

hefferd, heffker see HEIFER

heggeyng hedging, trimming, cutting, or planting hedges. *1522-3: for iij dayes heggeyng goyng to his owne borde xijd. for iiij dayes hegging wt ye borde xvjd.*

heifer young cow before it has calved. *1562: For the custome of xxiiij hefkers j bull boughte at Gyslinge fayer vd. 1589: one hecforth. 1595: one hayfer one yearling calfe xlijs. 1595: iiij yearlinge heckferds.*

hemp *Cannabis sativa* was widely grown in Norfolk until the 20th century for its fibres, processed for linen, canvas, string, rope, and other purposes. The fibre comes from the sheath of the stem. The female plant bears the flower and the male the fruit, but up to the 19th century they were described the other way round, the male being termed fimble or female. The 'male', really the female, was thought to produce the finer fibre. The stages in preparation are:-
1. Harvesting and drying.
2. Retting or rotting by immersion in water, usually in pits, to dissolve the natural glue holding the fibres together.
3. Drying.
4. Crushing to separate the fibres from the core, usually by beating with a SWINGLE or mallet.
5. Pilling or pealing the beaten hemp.
6. Beating again, in bundles, with a mallet or BEETLE on a BUNCHING block.
7. Heckling or combing with a HECKLE. The long fibres produced the best yarn, and the short fibres, discarded during heckling, were known as tow (also applied to all hemp fibres).
8. Spinning, weaving, making rope etc.
See pp. 95, 242, and Nesta Evans, *The East Anglian Linen Industry*, 1985.
1328: in Femelyngs canobi ijd. 1509: ijd for hempe to bynde wt splents. 1589: iiij^{or} combs of hempseede xxvjs. viijd. a thousand of hempe & femble iij li. xs. 1591: for 4 com' of hempesed 1 li. 19 hondarde of hempe & fembell 5 li. 1592: of hemp shofes ccc xs. 1592: hemp in the shove. 1595: hempe ryvene & unryvene. 1606: hympe unpillid vijd. 1647: [16th May] the widdowe Curtis for 3 stone of Hempe pilling 2s. 1647: [18th October] Bunchinge of 5 stone Hempe 1s. 8d. 1649: [12th March] for the bunchinge of 6 stone of hempe 2s. 1649: 3 bushells of Hempseede 16s. 6d.

hempyard, -land, -stall the land where hemp is grown. *1595: Yard or hemstalle.*

hengle, hengell simple pin hinge, especially the female part attached to the door or gate. See GEMEL; GUDGEON; GUNFIS; HECH; HINGE; VIROLE. *1392: v hengles [with nails for the* *door of the cowhouse and gate 14d.]. 1393: [1 pair] de hengels [of iron for the dairy door 5d.]. 1424: [1 board for the kitchen window 7d. Paid for] hengelys hokys [with nails for the same hanging board 4d.]. 1525: To the loksmythe for le makyng of the Engyllys for the carollys j li 2s. 1588-9: ij payer of hokes & hengyls for ye dores ijs. sneckes Ryngles and staples for ye same dores viijd. ij payer of gemowes for ye vyce dore of the same howse viijd. 1648: hookes & hingells & vardell 3s. 4d. 1662: paire of hoockes & hingells for the clay house dr 2s. 8d.*

hen puller It. *pollajio*, hen roost; poultry loft or roost. *1665: [in hoghouse] for daubing a ptition ijs. making a hen puller there ijs. vjd.*

heryedyn harrowed. *1428: The tuisday sand ye wedenysday heryedyn to rie.*

hermaphrodite often written 'morfrey' or similar. A wagon that could be converted into a TUMBREL, the front pair of wheels being small and detachable from the cart body, which had a large pair of wheels towards the rear end. Cf. CART. *1802: 2 Waggons £15 1 Hermaphrodite £2 2s. 1836: one hermaphrodite carriage.*

hern see HERON

hernished harnessed, decorated, mounted. *1474: a payr of hernishede knyffes xijd...a Knyff harnyshid with sylver xijd.* See HARNESSED.

heron, hern, harnser, hearnshaw, hearnes, herensew the grey heron, *Ardea cinerea*, was a popular object of falconry, and was eaten. *1533: v herns & a popeler of store. 1593: j herensew xijd. 1600: 4 Hearnshawes. 1619: for Clyñinge an hearnesis nest vjd.*

herring line fishing line for herrings. *1591: hearen lynes with pikes. 1647: 48 yeards of Heareing Lyne 3s. 8d.*

herring the herring, *Clupea harengus*, was eaten either as white herring, which were either fresh or salted (in barrels) but not smoked, or as red herring, which, from the 13th century, were soaked in brine, then strung up and smoked before being packed into barrels. Bloaters were steeped in brine or laid on dry salt for 24 hours, then smoked over an oak fire, leaving them moister than red herring. Kippers were herring split open, rubbed repeatedly with salt and then dried either in the air or in smoke. Other fish besides herring could be kippered. Shotten herring were those that had spawned, that is the females without the roe. See CADE; LAST. *1468-9: ij laste of shotyn heryng, price the cade iijs. viijd. xj marc. 1505-6: vj barell of full heryng iij li. vjs. et ij barell of schoten xviijs. 1560: vj ba' of whyt heryngs at xvjs. viijd. the Barell...iij Cads of Read heryngs at viijs. vjd. the Cade...one stycke of flemyshe heryngs xxs...Ciiij^{xx}xvj duche heryngs at vj p jd. to fylle up the barrell iijs iiijd.*

herritree see HARLETREE

hersel, hearse L. *hercia, herpicem*, harrow; originally a triangular frame, like some forms of HARROW, made as an elaborate framework to carry large numbers of candles over the bier or coffin, or fixed permanently to a tomb.

hesp see HASP

heyford see HEIFER

heyned heightened. *1557: sche repared the bakhous an inheyned it...she heyned the stepul...the seid Ele...be new roved, leded and glased, and the walles therof heyned conveyently and workmanly.*

hind household servant, domestic; labourer. *1665: the Hinds Hall.*

hinderland cloth, perhaps from the interior of Germany. *1465: a pece of Hynderlond, prise the elle jd. ob., conteynenge xxiij elles.*

hinge the common hinge in the Middle Ages consisted of the GUDGEON, or GUNFIS, the upright or male pin or hook of iron fixed to the post, and the VIROLE or HENGLE, the female part which fitted over the pin. The plates or VERTIVELLS were the iron bands running horizontally from the virole across the door or gate. The *sera, serula, cerule* etc. was a bolt, lock, or catch. *1320: ij platis & j guggen. 1387: gogones plates viroles staples & hespes.*

103

1391: in plat Gogines verolys & cerelys [for] le Wodeholgate xvjd. The terms were also used for similar components in other situations: *1665: virrels gudgirons & plates for a crudbarrowe xviijd.* See also HECK.

hippocras, ipocras red wine spiced with ginger, cinnamon, and GRAINS of paradise or less expensively with pepper and clarified honey. The name came from the resemblance of the bag through which it was strained to the sleeve of Hippocrates.

hirnewegge iron wedge.

hoale see HALL

hobby, hoby ME *hobyn*, whence OFr. *hobin, hobi.* A small or medium horse, perhaps originally a breed from Ireland, Wales, or Scotland; a riding-horse, pony. *1463: to hele the grey hors wyth, and the hoby... for a sorellyd hoby xxs.*

hobyte see OBIT

hocke hook. See POTHOOK. *1597: one payer of pote hockes.*

hoe there were two basic varieties of hoe. 1. The thrust hoe, a development or sideshoot of the breast plough; the modern type is the Dutch hoe, in which a blade more or less in the same plane as the shaft is pushed through the soil. 2. The draw hoe, MATTOCK etc. in which the blade, on a straight or swan neck and at about 80° to the shaft is drawn through the soil. This was the main type used in garden and field until the 20th century. *1306: j howe iiijd. 1315: j howe ijd. ob. 1665: two howes for the garden ijs. 1692: One turnib-hough. 1713: a how a muddskupett 1s. 6d.*

hog young boar in its second year; a castrated boar. *1603: A sowe two barrowe hogs and two piggs xxxs.*

hog, hoge, hoggs sett, hoggyssede see HOGSHEAD.

hogget, hog a yearling sheep. *1588: Ewes, wethers & hogges. 1595: six skynnes of hogge shepe.*

hoghe a hedge. *1313: [making] del hoghe [on the bank].*

hogshead a capacity measure of 63 wine gallons or 52½ Imperial gallons; the container itself. Sometimes abbreviated to ho'. See BREWING. *1513: J hoggyssede. 1588: xviij hoggesheads. 1619: for 2 hoggs setts wherof the Coper Cutt & made the aforesd Tubbes. 1648: 11 nayle barke hoopes set on to the Hogsheades 2s. 4d. 1663: repairing two old hoggheads making two barrels of them.*

hog stool hog-backed, that is with a humped seat. *1720: one hogge stool & two Payles. 1741: Cheese Fats, Breeds, a Hogstool, Butter Killer, & Bowl.*

hog's yoke wooden frame to put round pig's neck to stop it getting through hedges. *1620: 2 pitchforke shafts 1s. & 10 hogs yoks 18d.*

holberd see HALBERD

holdfast 1. Iron crook jammed into a hole in bench or anvil to hold wood or iron under the crook when two-handed working is necessary. See p. 108. 2. S-shaped iron hook. 3. Iron strap. 4. End of iron tie-rod. *1590: one hould fast one vice. 1649: 1 hauldfast 4d. 1663-4: [smith] four holdfasts & mending two phanes on the pspect. 1665: a holdfast for the glazier. 1819: 2 new holdfasts 6s.*

holl OE *hol*, hollow. The ditch of a ditch-and-bank; the bank was the deek or DIKE. Cleaning out the ditch was OUTHOLLING.

holland linen cloth, originally from Holland. *1465: v elles of fyne Holond for ij shertes for hym selffe, prise the elle xxijd. 1474: a stomaucher of a zerd of gode new hollond cloth xd. 1589: iij ells of brown hollond. 1593: 2 longe Tablecothes of Holland & 2 square clothes of hollonde xxvs. 1637: 80 pr of sheets whereof 3 p of holland sheets. 1688: Twoe Holland Board cloathes and three dozen Holland Knapkings.*

Holland tile the early name for PANTILES, imported from Holland from the 17th century and made in Norfolk from *c*.1700. *1636: At the stayres foote thre or foure hundred holland tyle Coope & six ladders. 1683: Holland tyle 6000 at 2 -15-0 : 16 - 10 - 0.*

holmes a FUSTIAN cloth made in Ulm, Germany, and from the 17th century made in England. *1589: one pece of holmes fusten.*

holywater sprinkle club with spikes on all sides, with a fanciful and grim resemblance to the medieval holy water sprinkler, which was a waterpot, pierced with small holes, on a short staff. See p. 108. *1597: a staff or Clubbe called a hallywater sprincle... A Crackt staffe or Clubbe called a hallywatersprinkell.*

hondarde see HUNDRED

hood, French small close-fitting hood worn on the back of the head, with a flap at the back often turned up over the head. *1537: ij Frenche hoods with the byllymts.*

hook see HECH

hook 1. WEEDING HOOK. 2. Crescent-shaped tool, for cutting grass, or light hedging. See SICKLE. 3. Draw HOE, draught hook. 4. Hook for pulling off thatch in a fire. 5. Fireside implement. See HAKE; POTHOOK. *1306: j sythe & j hok vijd. ob.[ij sickles ijd. ob. retoothing ij sickles ob. q']. 1588: a sholve a mattocke a drafte hoke a come & a heckell. 1593: one bill one hooke.*

hop common medieval measure of capacity containing two bushels (16 gallons); the vessel itself. See BUSHEL; GALLON. *1352: j bussell j hop.*

hop hoop. *1561: hopynge and spyllynge of that barell xd.*

hopenet net on a hoop; keep-net. *1482: ij hopenetts, prise viijd.*

horschon horseshoes. *1482-3: ij dozeyn le horschon xiiijd. 1504-5: xix dozen horschon xjs. jd. and for settyng of horschon and remevyng xxiijd.*

horse frame on which to dry linen etc.; stand for pressing iron; stand for barrels. *1592: [bolting house] Item ther on oweleded horse 4d. 1709:[laundry] 2 linen horses...3 horses to set irons on. 1738: [brewhouse] A Tunn Horse.*

horse chain chain for horse traction; chain to secure horse. *1593: 2 paire of horse chaines & lockes.*

horse clog large block of wood to which horse was secured to prevent wandering. *1747: two cart ropes horse clog plowline.*

horse leech a horse doctor. *1533: to a horse leche iijs.*

horse lock a shackle, FETTERLOCK, to prevent horse straying; transferred to mean padlock, HANGING LOCK. *1595: fyve hanginge lockes horsse lockes & horsse cheynes ijs. vjd. 1603: 1 £ of cheynes with a horse locke js.*

horseman staff 1. A war HAMMER, a three-foot shaft with a spike and hammer-head opposite each other and a spike at the bottom end of the shaft. 2. A flanged mace. *1589: two coats of plate & an horseman staff.*

horsemeat fodder for horses. *1582: Horsemeate 4d. 1595: pease for horsemeat. 1603: heye & fetches for horsemeate.*

horse mill grinding mill powered by a horse, attached to a beam, circling the central millstones. *1595: a horse myle with one pair of stones. 1595: fower horse myll stones. 1647: beatinge on the stones of the horse mill.*

horse pick implement for removing stones from horses' hoofs. *1819: New horse pick 6d.*

horse rope literally rope to attach horse; but see HAUSROPE. *1648: 1 new horse rope 2s. 6d. 1649 a new horse rope 3s. 6d.*

horseskep skep or large basket for horse fodder; pannier. *1328: ij horseskeppes vjd.*

horse tree 1. Whippin, or swingletree: cross bar, pivoting on centre, to which traces were attached to draw a plough, harrow etc. See HAMBLETREE. *1374: [5 pairs of] seles cu' ij* *horsetres.* 2. Beam on which timber was placed for sawing. .

horsewele wale: ridge on horse collar. *1585: horseweles, ropes, iiij syves.* *1908: I was told by one of the workmen that the rolls or ridges of a horse-collar between which the hames lie are called respectively the fore-wale and the after-wale.* See HAME.

horsing block mounting-block, from which to mount a horse. *1733: The Whitby horsing Block at Collonade.*

hose, hosen, hosenne, hosh, hosyn stockings, although up to the early 17th century hose could also mean breeches. As stockings, hose usually covered from the thigh to the sole of the foot, but sometimes reached only to the ankle. Boot-hose were stockings worn under boots to prevent chafing the fine stockings next to the skin. Stirrup-hose were long over-stockings without soles and kept in place by a stirrup under the foot. Trunk-hose, round-hose, French hose were breeches sewn to the stockings or NETHERSTOCKS.

hoswyfe housewife. See HOUSEWIFE CLOTH.

hot water 1. Spirits. *1636: [plate] one hot water bottle.* 2. Medicinal compound for horses. *1654: hott water for ye Grooms 3 pints 15d.*

hough see HOE

hough the hock, the hind-leg joint between tibia and metatarsus. *1654: for 5 Bacon Hoggs heads 10s. 8d. sparibbs 5s. 4d. feet and houghes 5s.*

hour glass instrument in which sand trickles from an upper to a lower glass chamber at a predictable rate, usually emptying the upper chamber in an hour. A cheaper alternative to the clock, but even so not very common in the inventories of the 16th and 17th centuries. An hour glass symbolised mortality. *1634: one ower glasse.*

house sometimes means a room, detached room, service room or workroom.

household bread In the Stiffkey Hall account of 1593 the 'hoshold' BREAD was baked in relatively enormous loaves costed at 4d. each as against the manchet, the finest bread, at 5 for 4d., cheat (large loaves of second quality) at 1¾d. each, and yeomans (the staple bread of the establishment) at just under 1d. each. The household bread would seem to be the coarsest, made of the residue of the siftings of the flour, and probably used for the lower servants, animals etc.

houseling cloth long, narrow plain linen cloth held by communicants in the pre-Reformation service to prevent the bread falling to the ground. See HOWSELE.

house of office the PRIVY. *1665: making clean the house of Office by the parlour being fowle.*

housewife cloth coarse linen or woollen cloth for household use. *1465: xx elles of hoswyffes clothe, prise the elle vd. 1560: xxij yards iij qu'ters of hoswyfe Cloth at xvjd the yard. 1598: xx yarde of new huswiffe cloth xs. 1771: pair of housewife cloth sheets 7s.*

hovel open shed, outhouse, poor cottage; workshop. *1664: stowed an oake beyond the hovell in the parke.*

how see HOE

howell cooper's plane with a sole-plate convex lengthwise, used on the inside of casks. *1613: 3 axes 3 percers 4 shaves three crowses fower adses 3 howells and other tools in the shoppe.*

hower hour

howke see HOOK

howsele, housel OE *húsl, húsel,* sacrifice. The consecrated elements; to give or receive the sacrament. *1478: it is butt an esy cure to kepe, For ther ar natt past xx* ᵗⁱ *persons to be yerly howselyd.*

hoy English: single-masted small ship, rigged fore-and-aft, for coastal and passenger trade. Dutch/Flemish: two-masted. Any small ship. *1495: an hoye of Dorderyght. 1573: a hoye. 1602: the hoye and divers other pinckes weare putt to sea.*

huch see HUTCH

huckaback, huckabagg thick LINEN cloth of northern English manufacture, with alternate weft threads raised to provide a rough surface. *1738: Four Huckaback Table Cloths 16s. Eight Coarse Huckaback Towells 2s. 1751: five dozen Huckabagg Towells. 1764: Thirty nine Dozn & Eleven Damask Napkins, Fifteen Dozn & half Huckaback D⁰. 1788: A Diaper Table-Cloth, a huckabick D⁰.*

hucyrne hook-iron, the crook or male component of a simple HINGE. *1343: iiij hucyrnes [for the doors of the hall 1d.].*

huke hooded cape, originally for women; a close fitting gown. *1459: j jagged huke of blake sengle, and di' of the same.*

humbletree see HAMBLETREE

hundred for the problems associated with the interpretation of C (centum) as 100 or 120, see C. Similarly, 'hundred' can also mean 100 or 120. Up to the 18th and in some cases the 19th century board etc. was almost always reckoned by the long hundred, i.e. 120. See LAST. *1557:* [liberty of pasturing five hundred sheep] *accomptyng syxe skore shepe to ev'ry hundreth shepe. 1594: sheep of all kindes...One thowsande or there abowt at vj ˣˣ to the hundreth and at xxx li. p'ce for the hundred so all CCC li. 1592: one hundreth of oking boorde. 1599: viij studds v hundeerd bords. 1665: for planing 240 score and 6 deal planke for planchering in wch by square measure 6800 feet at six score to the hundred.* 'Hundred' can also mean one hundred bundles etc. *1647: for 100 Reede 3s.* It can also mean HUNDREDWEIGHT. *1562: for C Inglishe yarne* [iron] *& half a hundreth viij li. of Spanish yearne at xiijs. viijd. thundreth xxjs. vjd. 1591: 19 hondarde of hempe & fembell. 1621: iij Barrels Tarras...weighinge 7 C 3 quart att ijs. vjd. C. 1671: 6 honderd and a halfe and 14 pound of Spanish Iorne.*

hundredweight 8 stones or 112 pounds = 1 hundredweight (cwt.); 20 hundredweight = 1 ton. But see R.D. Connor, *The Weights and Measures of England*, 1987, 134.

hurden see HARDEN

hurdis light wall, parapet, originally of hurdles. *1363: [made] dil hurdis [of the well with boards attached upon the same well].*

hurres etymology and meaning uncertain. Possibly windfallen trees or branches. *1654: for 2 old Oaken Hurres 8s... . for a parcell of Ash Hurres out of Sam's medow 2 li 10s. 1655: rootinge up some Hurres. 1656: for small hurres and 3 rootes... an old fallen hurre ash.*

hurrey, hurry small load of corn, hay etc. See HARRY CARRY. *1584: ij hurreyes of haye and ij hurreyes of fitches.*

hurrycurry see HARRY CARRY

hurt shoulder of an axle, against which the NAVE of the wheel rubs.

hurtiron, hurtyrin iron plate to protect the HURT from wear. See CART. *1310: ij hurtyrines ijd. 1312: In j hurtyrin jd....in viij cluts ij lynpinnes & ij hurtyrynes [bought] viijd.*

husbandman tiller of the soil. Up to 18th century the word denoted a smallholder, small farmer, a step lower than a YEOMAN, perhaps with the implication of rented rather than freehold land. In larger establishments, a worker on the home farm. *1593: the husbondmens chamber* [3 beds]. *1654: to James Bell and Tom Thompson 2 Husbandmen their Qrs pay ended at Xtmas day last of 3 li. 10s. p man.*

huss dogfish *Scyiorhinus canicula*, nursehound or greater spotted dogfish *S. stellaris*, whose rough skin had various uses, including polishing arrows and ivory and making shagreen. Perhaps also HOUSEWIFE cloth. *1753: one small Piece of Huss Lining 3d.*

hussey housewife.

hussingell surcingle, girth for horse to keep cloth or load on back. *1665-6: a headstall & hussingell 1s. 6d.*

107

hustlement household furniture, lumber. *1591: other hustlement xs.*

huswife housewife.

hutch chest, usually on legs. Bolting-hutch: chest specifically for bolting or sifting flour. *1455: ryfled his huches. 1588: payer of quernes wth the stale and the hutch. 1590: One great Chyst...a lytle huche ijs. vjd. 1590: in the pler chamber a huche and iiij coffers iijs. iiijd. 1592: a boultinge hutche. 1616: one hutche...3 coffers a hamp a boxe. 1617: one hutche with beddinge in yt.*

hydromell mixture of honey and water, recommended for application to wounds and as a base to carry medicine. *1680: a hydromell 1s.*

hymnal in the medieval church, a book of the words and music of all hymns sung at canonical hours.

hympe see HEMP.

hyrdel hurdle, made of osiers or willow. *1482-3: viij doseyn lez hyrdel viijs. viijd.*

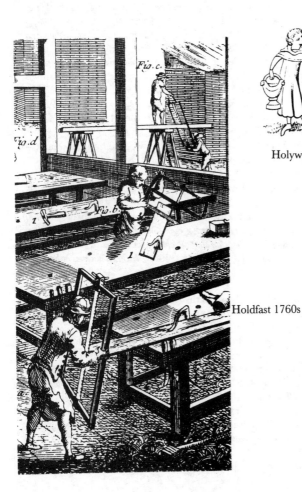

Holywater sprinkler 15th cent.

Holdfast 1760s

Holywater sprinkler

I

I the Roman i = 1 in arabic numerals. In manuscripts, it is written j when = 1 or a terminal figure, and i when combined with j for a figure more than one e.g. ij = 2, iij = 3, viij = 8, xxj = 21. See C; D; J; L; M; V; X. As a letter, up to the 18th century i was often used for j, e.g. Iohn for John, ioyner for joyner (joiner).

ieren iron. *1631: One Ieren wegh.*

image statue, not necessarily religious. *1764: An Alabaster Image on a pedestall.*

imagery textile embroidered or woven with figures. *1588: one coveringe of Imagerie. a Coverlet of ymagerie. 1590: coverlet of corse Imagery. 1597: iij piecs of hangings ymagery of tapestry. . . A Counterpoynt of Imagery Arras.*

imp a young shoot, sucker, slip, seedling.

imp a woven ring of straw, rush, or osier used to heighten beehive. See EKE; HAVER. *1654: for 4 Bee Hives and 6 Impes or Havers.*

indenture see p. 243

inderlin interline, inner lining. *1589: ij ells & di' of inderlins.*

Indian does not necessarily mean 'coming from India'. 'Indian' furniture may be (a) from India or the Middle East (b) from China or Japan or (c) JAPANNED work, that is painted work imitating far-eastern lacquer, but made in England. *1709: White Indian dimity curtains. . . 2 Indian pictures. . . Bed of Indian silk lined with a striped Indian silk. . . 11 Indian pictures in the panels. . . 2 Indian firescreens. 1745: One India chest One India Cabinett and Skreen. . . White Work't India Bed* [actually English needlework].

infield land continuously in cultivation (including fallow year), as opposed to outfield, which was cultivated for short terms e.g. 3 years and then reverted to rough pasture. See also BRECK.

Inglishe, Inglyce English. *1595: Inglish waxe xij poundes viijs.*

ingin engine. *c.1620: for making an ingin to draw up tymbr 1 li. 5s.*

ink writing-ink was made from crushed or powdered oak-GALLS (Aleppo galls seem to have been the best), logwood, iron sulphate, gum arabic (to stabilise the mixture), copper sulphate, sugar candy, and water, in the proportions 8: 4: 4: 3: 1: 1: 96. Other recipes existed. Indian ink was lampblack or fine soot mixed with gum tragacanth, and made waterproof by suspension in a weak solution of shellac dissolved in borax. The addition of salt or cloves prevented mould forming.

inkhorn container for ink, originally a small horn, often supplied with pen. *1590: iiij payer of ynkehornes wth pennes vjd.* See PENNER.

inkle linen tape used for strings, garters etc.; stronger material for harness. *1565: iiij head stallis of brode Inkle wth knopps & tassells. 1587: iiij li. of cullarde Inckell xvjs. 1589: ij li. x ounce of corse inckle at xvijd. - iijs. ixd. vj ounce of HW inckle at iijs. iiijd. - js. vd. . . v doss of colored Incle at iijd. - xvd. 1648: Canvas to make baggs on & Inkle for strings. 1655: 5 doz Inkle 16d.*

inset house this puzzling term is of infrequent occurrence. The only one of the normal meanings of 'inset' that might be relevant is 'recessed'; insit, that is a tenant, is just possible. Most of the houses in which the term occurs are small and poorly furnished, apart from the parsonage at Kirstead (see quot. 1709). Most inset houses contain a bed, and were evidently living and usually cooking rooms, with from two to five other rooms. *1593: In the insyte fyer house. 1709: ye pars house Consisting of an Insett house with their Romes vis a hall a kiching, a litell parlour & panterie over ye seler with Chameres over them all One backhouse & butery with Chamberes over them* [1716 terrier of the same house implies that the bakehouse and buttery are a separate building].

instrument a document, particularly a legal one.

inventory by Stat. 21 Hen. VIII c.5 (1529) wills submitted for probate had to be accompanied by an inventory of the goods of the deceased person, male or female. An inventory was also required if the person died intestate. The inventory had to include all movable goods and chattels, money, debts, valuables, clothes, livestock, standing crops, grain, and felled timber. Possessions not covered included wild animals such as deer and fish, furnishings attached to the building or fixed to the floor, property held in the name of the widow, heirlooms, land, buildings, and perishable food and drink. The items had to be assessed in value by three or more 'prisers', usually neighbours, including at least one person of similar rank or status to the deceased. As the rate of probate fee depended to a large extent on the value of the goods in the inventory, the valuations are not altogether reliable. It is important to remember that the valuations are of the *secondhand* value of the goods, and even the contents of shops are usually assessed at approximately ⅔ to ¾ of their retail price. Inventories are sometimes accompanied by executors' accounts, which can serve as a useful check on the actual value of individual items. In most houses except the smallest the prisers list the contents of each room under the name of the room.

iorne, ioroon, iringe see IRON

Irish stitch W. Hogarth, *Analysis of Beauty* (1753): 'Retiring shades... gradate or go off by degrees...There is a sort of needle-work, called Irish stitch, done in these shades only, which pleases still, though it has long been out of fashion'. *1597: a walnuttree chayer wth yrish stych nedlework.*

iron in Britain, iron came from various locations, the chief being the Weald, Gloucestershire, Wales, and the North. It was also imported in quantity from France, Spain, Prussia, and Scandinavia. See L.F. Salzman, *Building in England*, 286 ff. Spruce iron came from Pruce or Prussia. Small amounts of iron were obtained in Saxon and early medieval times by smelting the ironstone conglomerate found in N. Norfolk. *1562: for C di' & v li. of yearne viz C frense yearne & the rest ynglishe yearne at xiijs. the C xxjs. vijd. . . for C Inglishe yarne & half a hundreth viij li. of spanishe yarne at xiijs. viijd. thundreth xxjs. vijd. . . for vij ends of Inglish Iron wayenge Ccxiiij li. at xijs. the Cth xxvs. vjd.. . . for viij ends of spruse Iron wayeng CC iij qrters iij li. at xiijs. iiijd. the Cth xxxvijs.*

iron, box iron box iron: large hollow pressing iron, in which a red-hot triangular lump of iron, the heat, was placed. Flat iron: solid iron, heated directly on the fire or stove. *1647: a smoothing iron 2s. 8d. 1709: [laundry] an iron to set the boxes upon...5 box irons, 3 horses to set irons on, 10 heaters...6 flat irons. 1738: Two Boxes Irons and Stands and four heats 5s. A Large Ironing Board 1s. 6d. a smoothing iron 4d. 1779: Two large Box Irons with Heats & Rests. Two smaler do.*

iron maid clothes horse; washerwoman's dolly; trivet. *1771: Iron maid, ridling pan 2s.*

isinglass firm, white, transparent substance, almost pure gelatine, made from the air-bladders of certain fish, especially the sturgeon, and used in cooking for jellies, glazing, clarifying liquids etc. and for making glue. Inferior kinds were made from the horns and hoofs of animals. Not to be confused with waterglass, which is a solution of silicate of soda used for preserving eggs, painting etc. *1530: di' li. of issinglasse.*

issue plaster plaster for an issue or discharge of blood, matter etc. *1747: 2 Boxes of Issue Plaisters 2s.*

iwyn yewing, yew. *A muskett a sheefe of Arrowes iij Iwyn bowes & a Coate of plate xxs.*

110

J

J interchangeable with I or i in texts before the 18th century, and with i in Roman numerals. In manuscripts, almost invariably used as the terminal digit in Roman numerals e.g. iij (3), viij (8), xxvij (27). See I.

jack short, close-fitting, sleeveless jacket, often of quilted leather, sometimes plated; a coat of mail. *1448: jakkys & salettis. 1459: j jakke of blakke lynen clothe stuffyd with mayle. vj jakkes stuffyd with horne, j jakke of blakke clothe lyned with canvas mayled. 1464: a Walsh jakke cueryd wyth blakke Fusteyn...a Scottysh jakke cueryd wyth blakke Fusteyn. 1537: ij pound of twyn, for the jacks...iij elnes of canvas, for yr jack xiijd...to the taylour for the wurke man shippe of iij jacks ixs. iiijd... twyne, for yor jacks vjd...makyng of plats for the jacks iiijs. ijd...for ij skins to cov' yr jacke ijs. viijd. 1597: Skulls 6 Jacks 10. 3 olde Jacks: 14 foreparts of olde Jacks. a new twylted Jack.*

jack black jack, large can or jug, often of leather. *1592: iij ston cupps & j lether Jack. 1751: Two Pint and four half Pint black Leather Jacks lined & tipp'd with silver.*

jack oscillating apparatus over the open hearth for suspending pots, kettles etc., driven by an iron or lead weight, the jack-iron, geared to a flywheel (fly-jack); sometimes it drove the spit. A smoke-jack had a fan in the chimney turned by the heat rising from the fire. *1588: one Jackhorne of leade. 1589: a Jack to turn the spitt vd. 1618: Jacke for a bason of water. 1753: 1 Iron Horse, Fork, small Fly Jack, & Tongs 2s. 1764: one Jack pulleys & weights.*

jagged ornamented by being cut into jags; pinked, slashed. *1459: j jagged huke of blakke sengle.*

jamb the side of a window, doorway, fireplace etc. *1621-2: 88 foot of Jambe stone 10 inches broade and 11 inches thick.*

jane see JEAN

jane the gean or wild cherry, *Prunus avium*. *1664: beat down a jane wch stood into the siller.*

japanned, Japan genuine oriental lacquer work became popular in the late 17th century but was very expensive, so a European substitute, known as japanning and using layers of shellac polished with tripoli powder, came into use. Documents rarely distinguish between the genuine and the substitute. The quality of japanned work declined around the middle of the 18th century. See INDIAN. *1709: Japan corner cupboard. . . Japan Wainscot . . . Japan door...10 black Japan mouldings for hangings. . . Japan knife tray...Japan napkin tray. 1779: One small Japan Waiter. a Japan Dish. Japan Flat Candlestick..*

javelin light spear with steel or iron point hafted or bound to a long light shaft and thrown by hand or with a thong. *1537: di' li. of blacke cruell for the javelyns xijd. 1592: j blacke bill & one Javelin.*

jean, jane from Geane, Genoa: heavy twilled cotton cloth. *1589: v yards of Jane fusten.*

jeinger ginger. *1593: Sinamon & Jeinger.*

jelyflower see GILLYFLOWER. *1593: 5 peeces of old hangings of tapstrye worke wth Jelyflowers xxs.*

jemmell, jemowe see GEMEL

jennet Fr. *genet*, Sp. *jinete, ginet*: small Spanish horse. *1597: j Cannon bytte for the Jenete.*

jerfalcon, gerfalcon a large falcon, especially the white gerfalcon of Iceland *Falco Islandus*. *1602: a haggard Jerfalcon.*

jerkin close-fitting short coat or jacket, often leather, for men; out of fashion by 1630. The military jerkin, with high waist and deep skirt, was in use 1620-65. *1598: a gurkyn and a payer of Rounde hose for a man. 1612: j old Gurking.*

jersey washed and combed wool spun on a small wheel, and used for the finest work, often being combined with silk.

111

jet 1. A spout, nozzle, tap. 2. A large water-ladle. 3. Bowl, trough. See GATE. *1591: ij getts & j flote. 1593: [bakehouse] 3 old boulters & 1 iett. 1606: one hogshead, one tunels, one Jeth. 1656: 2^C hoopes making 15s. and for ½^C hogsheads hoopes...2 pales 2s. 3 jetts 2s. 2d. 1664: mended the tunnell, staved the jett.*

jewe, iewe ewe. *1598: xxiiij copelles of Jewes and lames 6 li. 13s. 4d.*

jewrye jury

jice see JOIST

jill see GILL

jog, jogg 1. A board made of two parts JOGGLED together. 2. A leftover piece of timber. *1663-4: one board stock 13 inch broad 18 foot long 19 boards and one jogg.*

jog a small cartload.

joggle to join two pieces of stone or wood by inserting a slip of stone, metal or wood into mortices cut in the adjacent faces, or by a blind mortice-and-tenon joint; the joint itself. See JOG.

joined, joint made by a joiner rather than a carpenter; with sophisticated joints. For applications see CHAIR; FRAMED; STOOL; TURNED. *1459: j junyd stole. 1593: 1 ioynde stoole. 1603: A Joined Cubberd and a Lecture xs. A framed Table two framed Formes and Fowre ioined stooles vjs. viijd. A ioyned Presse with a paire of virginals uppon it xs. Two turned Chaires.*

joiner, jointer 1. A long plane for dressing the ends of boards. 2. A tool for making joints in masonry and brickwork or smoothing the mortar. *1590: iij Joynturs.*

jointed ring a gimmel or gimmel fede ring, from L. *gemellus*, twin, and *fides*, faith: ring that separated into two halves, sometimes interlocked; the fully-separating version used in betrothal and marriage until the later 17th century, when it was superseded by the single band ring. See GEMEL. *1689: a Joynted ring in my little trunck.*

joist, giest, jice, gice horizontal timber forming the support of a floor or ceiling, or timber of the appropriate dimensions. Bearer-joist: the main beam running across the middle of a floor/ceiling, into which the common joists are mortised or let. *1445: how manie gystis wolle serve the parler. 1593: one dorman two halfe dormas bords & giests with partition. 1662: laiving [lathing] of Jice...7 jice at 9 foote long & 3 6 foot long at 2d. the foot 9s. . . a gice for the [chancell] stooles 6d. 1663-4: joyce stock 8 foot long. 1664: cutting one four inch planke & cutting the same into three joyce. 1665: 6 seleing gice over the stares and closit at 3 fout and a half longe at 3 half penc 2s. 3d. 2 gice at 6 fout long a pece used over the paler Chamber at 3 haf penc the fout 1s. 6d.*

joll jowl. The jaw, or cheek, or throat and neck; the head of a fish. *1655: a Joll of salmon 5s. . . a Joll of salmon 3s. 6d.*

jorrum large bowl, hence the name applied to the feature like an upturned bowl between the pedestal and shaft of an Elizabethan/Jacobean chimney shaft. *1620: The 4 stacks of chimnyes in this rainge of building From the upper floore to the Jorrum & base of the shaftes.*

joystemer agistment. See AGIST. *1466: for the joystemer of a strese of schepe.*

julup, julep Fr. *julep*, L. *julapium*, from Persian *gul-ab*, rosewater. Sweet drink, containing medicine. Bezor: counter-poison, antidote, especially the concretion in the shape of a round stone formed in the stomach of certain mammals, originally the Persian wild goat and some antelopes. The chamois provided German bezor. Hysterical julep: hysteria was formerly thought to be caused in women by a disturbance in the uterus and its functions. *1680: A Julup 2s. 2d... The Bezor Julup 2s. 10d. 1729: An Hysterical Julep 2s.*

junyd see JOINED

K

K because of the similarity of sound, many words beginning with c are written with a k, e.g. kart, kounter, kowl. The reverse is also true, e.g. cichen for kitchen.

kaii 1. *Prompt. Parv.* 'Key, or Knyttynge of ij wallys, or trees yn an unstable grownde'. 2. A quay, wharf. *1326: [made] del Kaii [under the malthouse 13d.]*

kailer see KEELER

kali see CALE

kalke chalk.

kanevas see CANVAS. *1313: [8 ells] de Kanevaz [for the table 17d.].*

kartehous carthouse, cartshed. *1309: [mending] Kartehous. 1313: [barley in] le Kartehous. 1318: [thatcher and his boy for 15 days working on] Le Malthus & kartehous [and barn and walls].*

karteskeppe skep, large basket for use on the cart. *1310: [making] j Karteskeppe.*

kaudrum see CAULDRON

kayles see SKAYLES

keachinge see KITCHEN

keel flat-bottomed cargo sailing-boat or lighter with a single square sail, especially in use on Norfolk waterways; superseded by the wherry. *1579: carryeng of freston unto the keele. 1612: for two keeles and about 3 quarters of a keel of Cambridge Clay v li. xvijs. vjd.*

keeler, killer, ciller etc. OE *cælan, célan,* to cool. Originally a wide, shallow wooden tub or bowl, used for cooling liquids like milk, and later for purposes such as washing. *1341: [made] ij keler [out of 1 tine 4d.]. 1342: [making 1 cade] & kelere [new]. 1444: iij vasa vocata kelerys. 1588: vj staves, a plowbeame, ij leavers, a wymble, a kill heare & a block. . . ij soes and an olde Killer. 1595: a masshefatt iij soes a kailer a bulting hutche. 1597: 2 Kyllers to wasshe the plate in. 1625: a salting killer for the cheese. 1637: one old keeler or fleshtub. 1648: 2 hoopes set on a Ciller & the bottome putinge in 8d. 1709: a dish killer...a butter killer. 1738: A Deep killer for Hamms.*

keelman the worker of a KEEL. *1621-2: To March the keeleman for bringing 8 fodder of lead being 67 piggs and charge of Loding &c 1 li. 2s.*

keene, kene see KINE

keep safe, small closed cupboard. *1591: j keepe wth locke & key ijs. 1603: A Glass kepe. 1762: a keepe 2s. 6d.*

keeping parlour Arthur Young (1804) has the keep-room as the main room of a cottage, but this use is not apparent in 18th-century Norfolk inventories. William Marshall (1787): 'The lower class of Norfolk farmers, however, are the same plain men [as elsewhere] living in a great measure with their servants. Another class live in the kitchen with their servants, but eat at a separate table; while the upper classes [of farmers] have their "keeping rooms" and other commodious apartments.' *1779: the keeping parlour /fireplace, set of 8 chairs, 2 tables, bureau, 4 mirrors and a 9 foot square carpet].*

keg small barrel, usually containing less than 10 gallons. *1530: a cagge of elis. 1594: ij iron kegs. 1595: a cagge with some sope.*

kell, kelled see KILN

kempt OE *cemben,* comb; combed. *1631: 3 pound of Cempt wooll & 2 stone of uncempt wooll.*

kennel, cinell often in sense of 'kennels', that is multiple housing for dogs. *1672: ye dogs cinell.*

ker car, carr; pond, pool, fen with bushes; osier bed. *1354: [fishpond] in le ker.*

kercher kerchief: square of linen, silk etc. worn flat round the neck and over the shoulders, or used as handkerchief. Yard kercher: 3 feet square. *1588: v neckerchers, v* *childrens neckerchers... ij yard kerchers, ij corner kerchers.*

kerchyng see KITCHEN

kerdil belt or GIRDLE for carrying quiver of arrows. *1481: for the casis xiij, and for kerdils.*

kermes the pregnant female of the insect *Coccus ilicis*, from which a scarlet dye was made. The 'kermes mineral' of the 18th century was antimony trisulphide. See GRAINS; SCARLET.

kersey coarse cloth woven from long wool, originally from Kersey in Suffolk and occurring in many varieties. *1459: ij payre hosyn of blakke keyrse. 1592: [kerseys: Devonshire, Hampshire, Northern, Suffolk; ash, black, blue, checker, green, grey, russett, sea green, sky colour, stammell, white, yellow]. 1620: one large greene Kersie Chayer.*

kervell, karvyle, carvelle a carvel, a type of small fast ship, originally from the Mediterranean and lateen-rigged, used in England from the 15th to the 17th century. 'Carvel-built' is with the boards of the hull laid edge to edge, not overlapping as in 'clinker-built'. *1463: the werkemen that werke on the kervell.*

ketch catch. *1663-4: one ketch for a windowe.*

kettle vessel, usually metal, for boiling water and cooking; until the 18th century it was was a pot or cauldron, sometimes covered, and without a spout. A fish kettle was oval, with a perforated plate to raise the fish off the bottom. *1326: j chetel [of bronze 2s.]. 1532: j bruyn chetyll. 1588: one olde flatte copper ketell iijs. iiijd. 1589: a lardge copper kettell j li. ij longe kopper kettells xvjs. viijd. 1592: viij ould hanging chetylse smale & grete xs. 1597: ij greate hanging keatles with biles & iiij smale hanging keatles with biles viijs. 1603: ij kytles xs. ij lesser Kytles viijs. 3 lytle Kytles iijs. iiijd. 1620: copper kettles vij. one other large copper bryne kettle. brasse kettles one...lattin kevers for kettles v. 1764: Seven fish Kettles & plates to them.*

keychine see KITCHEN

kicking see KITCHEN

kid small wooden tub for flour. See KIT. *1738: Two flower Kidds 2s.*

kidd faggot long faggot of small branches. *1595: v score faggots of wood & x kidd faggots.*

kil, kill, killen see KILN

kilderkin, kinderkin cask of half-a-barrel capacity for liquids, that is 18 gallons (ale); for butter, half-barrel containing 112 lb. butter, 132 lb. gross. See BARREL; GALLON. *1588: vj kyndyllkyns iijs. iiijd. 1592: Two ferkins a kilderkinne. 1593: 1 kinderkyn wth verges.*

killer see KEELER

killheyer cloth, of hair or fine thread, laid on floor of the MALT-KILN, on which the sprouted barley was spread and dried by hot air flowing from the furnace in BREWING. See also KEELER. *1526: hayer yt he made my Mrs malt wt xs. vjd. 1590: an old killheyer. 1603: j old kyll heyre ijs. vjd.*

kiln the word implies a structure. Up to the 16th century most BRICKS were burnt in clamps, that is rows of dried but unburnt bricks were set up and the spaces between the rows filled with combustible material; the whole was ignited and covered over for a few days, then opened and the burnt bricks removed. Brickkilns usually operated by indirect heat; the dried but unburnt bricks were stacked in the kiln, which was in the shape of a truncated cone or a rectangular box, and the hot air was conducted into the kiln from the tunnel in which the fire burnt. Limekilns were used to burn chalk to make quicklime, which was then slaked to become, with sand, a constituent of mortar. A typical limekiln was circular, with a central funnel-shaped chamber packed with alternate layers of chalk and fuel. See p. 116; SAFFRON. *1663-4: hope [helped] to drawe a kelled of bricke. 1713: 1 killen of brick.*

kilnhouse, malt kiln building in which barley was dried by heat after steeping and sprouting. See BREWING. *1377: [one lock with key for the door] dil kylnehous. 1392: [thatched] le*

114

kilhos [and stable].
kinderkin see KILDERKIN
kin OE *cine, cinu* crack, slit, chink; perhaps a tool like a bradawl or chisel. *1590: j crow ij kines iij Joynturs.*
kine, keene, kene, kye plural of cow; cattle. *1591: xiiij Milch Kyne. 1592: xv mylchkene.*
kinyng the CONEY or rabbit. *1459: redde panne of kinyng skynnys.*
kip, kippe beam, kiptree, of a PLOUGH; roller of a draw-WELL.
kipchit see PLOUGH
kipling tub Nall: 'Kiplin. The palate, gullet, sounds and other perishable parts of the codfish, cut away and cured separately from the body. Flem. and Dut. *kibbeling,* cod sounds and clippings'. *1738: A Kipling tub.*
kirtle male tunic or coat; female gown, skirt, or outer petticoat. *1513: j Kyrtyll of Chamlett for an Awt' cloth. 1 Kyrtyll of blak wurstead. 1 kyrtyll of tawny wursted. 1593: 1 holle Curtle of crimsone vellett wth a uppbody of yellowe sackinge iij li. vjs. viijd. 1602: Three gownes j kirtle three petycotes.*
kit circular staved and hooped small tub, with handles for carrying. See KID. *1709. a kit. 1779: Two Dinner kits. a Flour kit. 1787: Flour tub & kitt... salt kitt.*
kitchen in the earlier Middle Ages the kitchen was the place for preparation of food, not necessarily for its cooking - some cooking at manor-houses was done outside, not least to get round the problem of large open fires in timber-framed, thatched buildings. The control of fire developed through the widespread use of internal flues and permanent hearths, and by the 14th century most cooking was done in the kitchen. See p. 117. The kitchen implements and utensils in inventories of the 16th century show that it was the main cooking-place, although they also occur in other rooms, notably the hall. The spelling of the room is very variable e.g. cechin, cettchen, chatching, chitchin, cichen, cything. Apart from some specialist developments, the equipment changed little between the 13th and the 17th centuries. By the 17th century the largest kitchens had specialist ranges, although these were still basically open hearths - see quot. 1620 - and some large kitchens had their own water supply, sinks, and drains. See DRESSER; SINK. *1310: [1 wall] in le kychene croft. 1513: In le Kechyn. 1530: stocke of kerchyng knyves. 1620: [kitchen] A fier grate before the Range Chymney...twoe Iron hacks in the boiling Chimney...an Iron grate for Buttered meats. iij bigg square Spitts [and six other spits.]. 1647: 2 payer of stockings for ye kicking boyes.*
kitchener one employed in the kitchen; the clerk of the kitchen, that is the person in charge of provisioning a large household. *1597: The Cooks Chambr:..The Kytcheners Chamber. 1654: ye Kitchener 6 weeks at 4s. p weeke.*
kittle see KETTLE
knacker slaughterer of horses and cattle for hides, hoofs, and dogs' meat. *1621: To the knacker for sundry things bought and for worke xiijs.*
knapsack, snapsack bag of cloth or leather for personal carriage of small articles. *1654: 9 yds of Cloth at 9d. for 6 Knapsacks 6s. 9d. & ye making 12d.*
knatt equated by Thomas Browne with the KNOT. *1655: 4 redshanks 3 knat & 4 soalls . . . 12 knatt 1 Pluver 4s. 6d... some small fish 18d. and 7 knatts 2s.*
kneading trough shallow trough for kneading dough for BREAD, usually standing on four legs. See MINGING.
knee a naturally-bent timber, particularly of oak, for use in shipbuilding and in roofs. *1465: for xxxiiij great kneis, prise of every kne sawed and hewed, iiijs.*
kneeler the return of the dripstone at the spring of an arch; projection between the slope of a gable and the corner of the wall beneath; crow-step. *1620: top stones and knelers for the gable ends on the long court.*

115

knife a specialised tool taking many forms e.g. *1466: vj knyves in one shethe ijs. vjd. 1595: A table knife of wood. 1597: 5 broad knyfs wth whyte hafts...2 great broad knyfs wth black hafts...3 small knyfes one carvingfork with whyte hafts. 1636: Two minceing knives...one scraping knife. ,1637: 2 clivers a shreading knife. 1649: 12 new knives for the Butler 10s. 1671: A case knives & forks, with a Tortoiseshell Knife, and pruning Knife 1 li. 1s. 6d...a case of knives 12s...a Buxhorne knife 1s. 1709: 20 knives & Forks, 6 oister knives.* See FORK.

knop, knopped, knopte knob, knobbed. See SPOON. *1601: twelve silver spones knopped wth Lyons gylt...three playen silver knopped spones.*

knot the knot, *Calidris canutus*, a wading bird, winters along the coast of Britain, and was consumed in relatively small numbers during the autumn and winter months. Sir Thomas Browne: 'Gnats or knots a small bird taken with netts grow excessively fatt. If being mewed and fed with corne a candle lighted in the roome they feed day and night, and when they are at their hight of fattness they beginne to grow lame and are then killed.' *1593: for vij knutes xd. ob. 1655: 2 corlewes 8 knatts & 9 soales.*

knott, knotthe, knotch, knoth, knuth bundle of small branches, prunings, rods etc. *1313: xiiij knotch [of rods bought for the walls]. 1412: x knotthes [of rods and bindings]. 1663-4: some knotts left by James Browne. . . bratling of the tops of the said [fallen] trees & knotting them.*

kovyrpayn see COVERLET; COUNTERPANE

kussyne see CUSHION

ky- many words were written with a y instead of an i or e after the k.

kye key. *1584: A hanginge box to putt in Bookes wth locke & kye.*

kye see KINE

kylhayre, kylle hair see KILLHEYER

kyndyllkyn, kynnekyn see KILDERKIN

kype safe, box, KEEP. *1289: ij kypes [for salt and flour].*

kyplyne see PLOUGH

kyppe cap or cape. *1533: for a kyppe of lambe iiijs. viijd.*

kyllern see KEELER

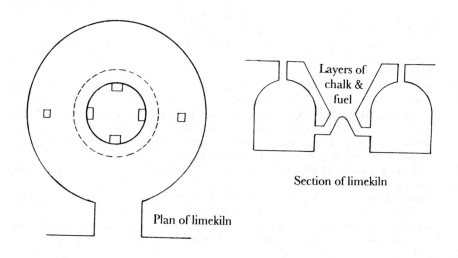

Layers of chalk & fuel

Section of limekiln

Plan of limekiln

116

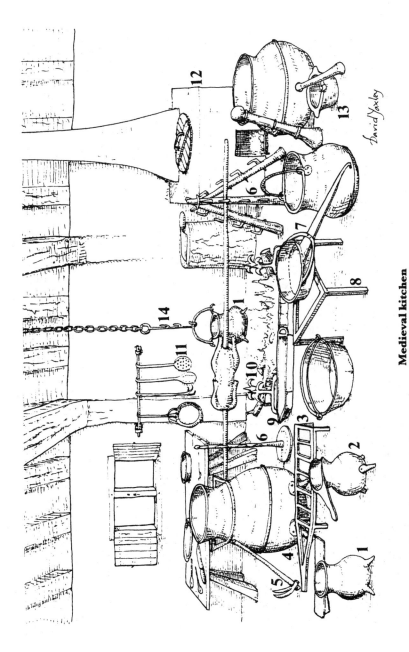

Medieval kitchen

1. Pot 2. Potenett 3. Gridiron 4. Cauldron 5. Fleshhook 6. Andiron 7. Frying pan 8. Tripod
9. Latchpan 10. Dogiron 11. Scummer 12. Lead 13. Mortar and pestle 14. Hake and pothook

L

L, 1 Roman numeral for 50, e.g liij = 53, lxx = 70, xl = 40. See C; D; I; J; M; V; X.
£ see LI.

lace lace could be woven from any combination of linen, jersey, worsted, silk or hair. Bone, bobbin or pillow lace was made by hand using a conical 'pillow' and bone bobbins, and was generally introduced by immigrants from Mechlin and Lille after 1563, before which date needlelace or needlepoint lace, made by looping and knotting threads, was the main English method. Copper lace was copper-coloured, dublittin lace was for doublets. Loom lace was introduced by Flemish immigrants in the reign of Elizabeth and one of the early centres of production was Norwich. Statute lace was made according to an Act of Parliament. *1589: ij dozen di' of narrow say lace at xd. [a doz.]. vij yards & di' of loome lace at vjd. [doz.]. v yards of lome lace at iiijd. [doz]. iij ounces of lace at xviijd. j dozen & di' of lace at ijs. [doz.]. v ounces & j qzter of silke lace at xviijd. [doz.]. ij dozen & x yards of hart lace at vjd.[a doz. yards]. j doss of bone lase iijs. vjd. vj yards of bone lase at ijd.[a yard]. xiij doss of narrow dublittin lase at vijd. [doz.]. iiij doss of statute lase at xd. [doz.]. j doss & di of small lace iiijd. 1592: in startwe laesse & therede xxs. 1593: 1 black vellet Curtle wth an uppbody of vellet layde wth blacke bugle lace xiijs. iiijd. . . 1 old windowe Cushin of black vellett with silver bone lace iijs. iiijd. . .1 canapie of black vellett wth Copper lace. 1595: bobbyngs to weave boane lace. . .iij lasyng needelles of sylv' & a ball of crystall* [to concentrate the candlelight]. *1597: one chayer cou'ed wth Crymsyn velvet layed wth bone lase of golde.*

lach, lachthe see LATCH; LATCH-PAN
ladd see LADE
ladder, leather, lether, lathegres OE *hlæder.* Most ladders consisted of staves or rungs between two uprights, but occasionally a single pole had the staves threaded through it ╫╫╫╫ . DEAL was particularly useful for long ladders, but other timbers were used. *1359: j Lathegres xd. 1591: j lether. 1593: 3 longe Leaders & 2 shorte leaders viijs. 1604-5: an oke to make a ladder for the towne vs. vjd. 1605-6: boringe the ladder pec & for the sawinge xvjd. Fower foote of Tymber for ladder stafes xxd. 1649: 2 peeces to make leathers on 5s. 1655: one Ladder peece 20 ft 4d. 1663-4: [smith] one winding bond 7½ foot long for the long deale ladder & nayling on the same.*
ladder, cart open-staved framework for the sides, front, and back of a flat cart. *1663-4: made a new cart ladder & a new bitt for the cart.* See BIT; CART.
lade, ladd channel to the mill-race; a ladd net was stretched across the lade. *1597: a didall and iij Ladd nettes.*
ladele ladle. Usually of wood in the Middle Ages. *1312: ij ladeles ob.*
lading place where ships loaded and unloaded; shed of light construction. *1600-2: The entry from the hall into the kitchen. The rof being a lading all rotten & standing upon undersetters decayed for want of tileing.*
lagher see LAIR
lair, layer live hedging material, e.g. WHITETHORN, FURZE (firr, furr), and blackthorn *Prunus spinosa*, usually rooted slips, seedlings, or saplings. *1386: [bringing] lagher [for the bank]. 1654: Laying a treble Lair. . . whitethorn lair. 1655: 600 Lair 2s. and 2C Birches 5d. . . 2 Alesham Lair gatherers. . . gathering and setting it with furr Lair. 1656: outholling scouring and findinge furr lare for 271 Rod. . . new setting ye Pyracanthus Dike and finding of ye Fur Lair to back it with. 1676: weeding the Laire. 1677-8: for grafting & pruninge ye Laire 2s. 1681: for 6000 laire wanting ½ a hundred 1 li. 4s.*

laiving see LATH

lame lamb. *1598: xxiiij copelles of Iewes and lames.*

lamp Up to the 18th century lamps of the following types were in use:-
1. Floating-wick: a wick of cotton or fibre floating in an open dish or vessel of glass or pottery filled with animal oil, particularly fish oil, or liquid tallow.
2. Cresset: shallow vessel of stone, pottery, or metal filled with oil, the wick having one end in the oil and the other lying in a channel at the edge of the vessel. Some cresset lamps had more than one vessel and channel.
3. Open pan: often metal, hanging from chains or supported on a pedestal, with the wick enclosed in a tube or channel and burning fish-oil, whale oil, or liquid tallow.
4. Spout: an enclosed reservoir for oil and the wick in a tube or spout.
See F.W. Robins, *The Story of the Lamp*, 1939 repr.1970.

lampade an oil-lamp. *1321: [1 potell of oil for the] lampade...j cord ad lampade.*

lampas swelling of the lining of the roof of a horse's mouth behind the front teeth. *1664-5 [smith] burning the grey mare of the lampas ijd.*

lamp black almost pure carbon collected from the soot formed by a LINK or torch and mixed with gum to form a pigment. See INK. *1665: 2 barrels of lamblack 6d...1 box of lamblack 3d. [with pumice, putty, emery, resin, beeswax, and brimstone] to be used by the stone cutters for the working pollishing and sementing of freestone to marble chimney peeces.*

lance early on lance was synonymous with spear, but from the 14th century usually meant a horseman's spear. Usually of ash, a lance was about 14 feet long with a small pointed head; from *c.* 1320 a funnel-shaped steel plate, called a vamplate, protected the hand, and from *c.*1400 the shaft was thickened before and behind the hand to form a grip. Demi-lance: light lance; light armoured horseman.

lance armour armour of a mounted lancer; black: painted with black rust-resistant paint; white: polished steel. *1597: 2 Launce Armors black complet. 2 Launce Armors whyte complet. Rem. at Wrights of Norwch Armorer.*

lance gay OFr. *lancegaye*, using Arabic *zagaye, arzegaye.* (assagai). Light throwing lance with a point at either end, in use from the 14th to the 17th centuries. *1459: j launce gay.*

land stone stone found on the surface of the land; flint. *1829: The walls to be built wth Land Stones wth Red Bks at the angles.*

landry see LAUNDRY

landskip Du. *landschap*, painting of the countryside. *1709: 2 Landskips over the doors. 1764: A Landskip over the Chimney piece.*

langedebief Fr. *lange de bœuf*, ox-tongue. HALBERD, medium-shaft weapon with a head shaped like an ox-tongue. *1454: jakkes, saletts, langedebiefs, and boore speres.*

langell, langeld, langoll horse hobble. *1332: [31 pasterns] & langeldes iijd. 1417: ij payr langell jd. 1587: a broken paire of langelds. 1590: paire of Langolls with a lock. 1590: j payer of Langeles iiij old horse collers.*

langell rug, blanket. *Prompt. Parv.:* 'Blankett, lawngelle. *Langellus.*'

langell necklace, pendant. *1513: j peir bedde langells of sylu' Gylt Gawdeez.*

lanncetyll long SETTLE, backed bench. *1513: j lanncetyll* [one in parlour, one in chamber].

lantern lanterns used either candles or fish-oil, whale-oil, or vegetable oil. The spelling 'lanthorn' came from association, as the windows or lights were often of thin plates of horn rather than glass. *1326: [mending] j lanterne ijd. 1595: cheste with lanterne hornes in it. 1655: for a Bladder of Oyle to ye Lanthornes use 1s. 8d. . . 2 Lanthornes 2s. 10d. 1701: one tynn lanthorn.*

lantern small ornamental structure in the form of a dome or cupola on top of a tower or chamber; the pierced or open sides were sometimes glazed. *1620: In the Joyners chamber by the Lanthorne. 1621: In the roofe towards the front where the lanthorne stands. 1665: hewed timber for the lanthorne to be sett up upon the pspect and began to frame for the same.* See PROSPECT.

larder OFr. *lardier,* lard. Originally the room in which meat, bacon, lard etc. was stored. By the 16th century the larder was a general food store. Wet larder: where moist foods such as 'wet' fish pickled in brine or meat that needed cool, damp conditions were stored; the floor was strewn with rushes and sprinkled with water. Dry larder: store for food that did not need especially cool or moist conditions, e.g. cheese, bread, and kitchen utensils. See PANTRY. *1330: [mending the walls of the kitchen] & Lardar vd. 1352: [in the larder: 2 troughs for salting meat 1 block for cutting meat]. 1593: In the Larder 1 beefe tubbe 2 dresser bordes 3 tressells 1 Chopping blocke ijs. 1608: In the drie larder a boultinge tube a knedinge trough. 1620: [carpenter] making ptissions in the pastry and larder with a floore to separate the wett from the dry. 1764: Dry Larder - Three Dressers, one Table, Three Shelves [and 8 sieves, 28 copper stew pans, frying pans, 9 pudding dishes, 9 copper pots, 7 fish kettles, 13 saucepans, 2 coppers, 4 tart pans, 8 pudding moulds, 16 earthenware pans, 6 stone jars, etc.].*

larder basting-ladle for spit-roasting. *1593: a latten larder & an yron to sett before the latch pans.*

larding pins metal pins to slide into large joints of meat to carry lard and fat into the middle. *1764: case of larding pins, eighteen in number.*

largess Fr. *largesse,* liberality. Gift, usually money, particularly in harvest time. Thomas Tusser (1580): 'Give gloves to thy reapers, a larges to crie'. Forby: 'A gift to reapers in harvest. When they have received it, they shout thrice the words "halloo *larges*", an obvious corruption of the words "à la largesse", a very ancient form of soliciting bounty from the great; not of thanking them for it.' The reapers joined hands in a ring, with the cheer-leader outside. *1655: Largesses: A Largess given H. Empson men by my Mr 2s. 6d.*

last a measure of quantity. *Fleta* 1290: 'a last of herrings consists of 10 thousands and each thousand of 10 hundreds each of six score' (= 12,000). Nall: 'Last of Herrings. Nominally ten thousand fish; but being counted in long hundreds of 132...amount actually to 13,200'. *Tomlins' Law Dict.* 1835: 'A last of white herrings is 12 barrels; of red, 20 cades or thousands; and of pilchards, 10,000; of corn, 10 quarters, and in some parts of England, 21 quarters; of wool, 12 sacks; of leather, 20 dickers, or ten score; of hides or skins, 12 dozen; of pitch, tar, or ashes, 14 barrels; of gunpowder, 24 firkins, weighing a hundred pounds each'. Other lasts and variants: 10,000 bricks; 20 coomb of corn (see 1721 quot.); 12 quarters (24 coombs, 96 bushels) of corn; 200 hides of leather; 100 gloves. *1341: j Last & viij^c [turves cut]. 1468-9: ij laste of shotyn heryng, price the cade iijs. viijd. xj marc. 1536: a last of barrells to tun bere in, that is to say a dozen barrells. 1713: six Last of wheat £78 five Last of Barley £30. 1721: Delivered to Cornel Worpole 1 last of oats £5 10s. @ 5s. 6d. p comb. 1738: Three Last & Seventeen Combs of Barley Threshed which want to be screned.* See CADE; COOMB; HERRING.

latasyng see LATTICE

latayne see LATTEN

latch perhaps OFr. *lache,* lace; the cord or lever on a door which, when pulled, lifted or pressed, raises the SNECK, the horizontal bar that falls into a socket; the sneck itself. *Prompt. Parv.*: 'Latche, or snekke'. Palsgrave 1530: 'Lache, or snecke of a dore, *locquet.* Latche of a dore, *cliquette, locquet.* Sneke latche, *lacquet, cliquette.*' *1274: [mending] j lachis [for the hall door]. 1319: ij Lattches [for the window of the chamber 1d.]. 1345: [1 pair] vertivell snecke lachthe [of iron 11d.]. 1354: j latche [of iron for the great gate 1½d.]. 1608: a locke & key latch &*

snatch. . . iij seu'all dores latches & snatches.
latch see LATCH-PAN; LYE
latch-pan OE *læccean*, to catch; pan placed underneath the spit to catch the drips; dripping-pan. *1588: a brode Iron to sett before a latche panne. 1593: a latten larder & an yron to sett before the latch pans. 1649: a tyninge latchpann 1s. 8d.* See pp. 86, 117.
latch spoon probably a basting-ladle used with the latch-pan. *1604: 20 pewter spoones and pewter latchspoone.* See SPOON.
lath the spring (first wood, then steel) of a CROSSBOW. *1595: iiij new Crosebow lathes rough and untempered viijs.*
lath thin narrow strip of wood made by rending, riving, or splitting balks of oak, ash, chestnut etc. along the grain. Heart lath came from the heart of the tree and provided the best wood. Many uses, but principally as a base for plaster in ceilings and walls, and as horizontal supports for tiles, slates etc. on the roof. *1313: in M lattes iijs. iiijd. 1323: [nails for] flewes & Lathes [for the hall, chamber and chapel 5s. 5¾d.] iiij^C Lattes [for the said houses]. 1400: [wage of 1 man cutting ashes and oaks for] le Latthclever viijd. 1407: [daubing and repairing the furnace] & latthanch [lathing] [upon the malt-kiln]. 1509-10: xiiij^C hertlath vijs., et v^C saplath xxd. 1621-2: For 21000 Lath rendinge to the Lathrender 2 li. 12s. 6d. 1648: 6 bunches of hart larth 15s. 1662: plainchering...& laiving of Jice. 1664-5: fetched cliff for pale & larth to the Larthriver. . . stubbed up a decayed oake in the pke for larth & pale. 1665: hart larth for the frett work seeler.*
lath brick long narrow brick used for malt and grain-kiln floors. *1721: Lath Brick 1 li.*
lathe a machine for turning wood and metal. A pole-lathe is operated by using the spring in the stem of a young tree, which was held bent over by a rope or cord that drove the spindle or centre for the turning operation. A treadle lathe is powered by the foot on a small platform which, by means of a crank and wheel, turns the spindle.
lathe ON *hlaða*, barn. *1320: [repairing] del middellathe xiijs. xd. [thatching] del middellath [in total 7s.].*
lathegres see LADDER
lather see LADDER
lath nail small iron NAIL for nailing laths to batten or rafter. *1298: xviij^C lattenayl xjd. ob. 1313: In mmv^C de lattenayl xxd. 1343: viij^M de Lattenayl vjs.*
lattas see LATTICE
latte see LATH
latten, lattin, latting OFr. *laton*, brass. A yellow alloy resembling BRASS, of copper, tin, and a little lead, imported in sheets from the Continent, and used for utensils, decorative work etc. *1459: fountayne of latayne to set in pottys of wine. 1552: ij grett candelstyckes of laten, & iij lyttell payer, veyn [weighing] C di'. 1552: one lectern of laten weyng by estimacon C di' at ijd. the li. 1593: a letten Chaffingdish a latten morter & ij latten Candlestickes. 1597: 2 latten plates for lights. . . a payer of Aundyrons garnyshed with Latten a payer of tongs lykewise garnished. 1688: latting dripping pann.*
latthanch see LATH
lattice wood or metal laths criss-crossed with the diamond-shaped spaces in between usually left open, used for windows that need to admit a certain amount of air, e.g. dairy, corn chamber. *1319: in tyngelnayl as Latys jd. 1335: Latyznayl [for the window of the malt-kiln]. 1537: lattas for the corne chamber wyndowes. 1539: bordyng & latasyng of ij of ye stepyl wyndows. 1584: A wyndowe lettis. 1648: 8 new letteses to the corne Chambr windowes 6s. 1699: Wyer Lattice for the Cheese Chamber window.*
laund OFr. *launde*, wooded ground; wood, open space in wood, glade. *1295: [carpentering 1 gate of the wood near] launde vd. 1310: [making] gropes in le Launde xxd. . . [making barres and*

hedges] in Le Launde. . . [herbage and meadow] in Le Launde. 1325: [digging] j waure in Le Launde. 1397: [cutting thorns for a hedge made] in le launde.

lavender a washer, washerwoman. *1415-16: [wages of] Christine Lauender [for washing clothes of 15 monks as well linens as woollens for the whole year 15s.]. 1466: to the lavender at London for washynge xvd.*

laver wash-bowl, wash place. *1459: j laver weiyng xxiiij unces* [plate]. *1513: laver of laten. 1535: [repair of] le lavers. 1591: one Lavior xijd. 1595: A laver of pewter fixed to the well.* See p. 241.

lavure see STAFF

lay to re-steel, particularly a cutting edge. *1648: [smith] a hachet layeinge 6d. 1648: a Mattocke layinge 1s. 1649: a Coulter layinge... a belt layinge.*

layer see LAIR

leach vessel with tiny perforations, used for making LYE and for separating cream. *1663-4: mended the leach in the washouse. 1709: 3 milk leach upon frames.*

lead a material with a wide variety of uses in building and household: roofing, gutters, pipes, utensils etc. 'Shooting' lead is casting the molten lead over a bed of sand to obtain a sheet. See FODDER; POUND. *1619: [for clock] for shotinge ix stone di' Leade at vijd. ye stone. 1621-2: To March the keeleman for bringing 8 fodder of lead being 67 piggs and charge of Loding &c. 1 li. 2s. 1665: made a pitt to run lead in in the scullery for the plumers. . . pulled downe a lucome covered with lead next the best garden.*

lead The medieval lead *(plumbum)* was either 1. A tank or cistern. 2. A milklead or cooler. See LEAD, MILK. 3. A vat for steeping barley before malting. 4. A large cooking-pot or cauldron. 5. A form of washhouse 'copper' (see p. 117). 6. A lid, see also LEED. David Yaxley, *The Prior's Manor-Houses*, 1988, pp. 53-4 has a full discussion of these meanings, which were still in vogue till at least the 18th century, as the following examples show. *1500-01: to the plomer for makyng of the grete leede...xijs. ijd.. to cleyman hangyng the grete leede iijs. iijd. 1513-4: to cleymen werkyng in the bakhous iiijs. xd. to them for hangyng of ledes vjs. vijd. 1584: twoo Leads xxvjs. viijd. 1597: brewing lead with a cover. 1637: [yard] one washing leade. 1647: in the Yard. One good and Sufficient Pumpe with a Lead att the foote thereof. 1662: a day about hanging of the Cooler & a Coper leed 1s. 6d. 1709: a pot lead. . . one copper & leads. . . a leaded pan, 2 milk pans. 1743: [brewhouse] One Copper with Doors and barrs and two Copper Leeds one other Copper with Leeds.*

lead, milk large flat vessel, usually of wood and sometimes lined with lead, for cooling milk. *1685: Two milk Leads. 1688: One Milke Ledde and one salting traie. 1743: One milk Lead.*

leading staff staff borne by a military commander; truncheon. *1592: [with weapons] a leadinge Stafe. 1637: a captaynes leading staff.*

leaning height the height from the floor to the flat horizontal surface formed by the thickness of the wall on the inner and lower side of a window. *1621: In the leaning height of the cant windows and dead lights is conteined 320 feet 2 briks.*

leantree lean-to, a low building standing against the side of a larger structure. *1665: boarded the sides of the leantrees going into the best stable.*

leap OE *léap*, basket. See CHAFF-LEAP; SEED-LEAP; SKEP. *1483: for makenge of lepes and othir gere for the kechyn to kepe ynne eles. 1498-9: [for] ij grete lepys xviijd. [and for] ij skeppys vjd. 1505-6: the leep maker iiijs. 1619-20: one Leape or greate Basket & a Fann 4s. 4d.*

lease, lease and release see p. 243

leather see LADDER

leather, white light-coloured leather, soft and pliant, dressed with alum and salt to retain its natural colour. See TANNING. *1595: a whitt leather hyde.*

lecter coffer box with a sloping lid to contain a book e.g. the Bible.

122

lectern, lecture, leytrun stand on which to lay a book. Standard furnishing of churches, even before the Reformation, but also found in private houses. *1315: [making one] leytrun [for the chancel 17d.]. 1588: one lectorne to laye a booke uppon. . . standinge lecterne of timber. 1603: A Joined Cubberd and a Lecture.*

lectuary see ELECTUARY

ledder leather. *1587: a chest covered with Ledder iiijs.*

ledge see TABLE

ledge 1. Horizontal member of a door, gate etc. 2. A length of timber, shorter than a BOARD. *1579: x longe ledges xxd...ix ledges of ashe xviijd...lxx ledges of Espe & pople vs. vjd...ij longe ledges of Espe viijd.*

leed a lid. *1649: a leede & dash for a hand Churn 1s. 8d. 1685: two iron potts with pott leeds two iron kettles 1 li. 6s.* See CHURN; LEAD; OVEN.

leednayl see nail

leenge see LING

leet Possibly from OE *læte* connected with *læten*, let. See COURT LEET. *1648: leet fee & side silver due to the mannor of Snetsham.*

legend, legendary a book containing readings from the Bible, homilies, sermons, and lives of the saints in the unreformed church.

lenggys see LING

levant taffeta see TAFFETA

leveray see LIVERY

ley see LYE

leytrun see LECTERN

li. abbreviation for *librum, libra* pound (money or weight). So xxiij *li.* = £23 or 23 lb. In money, the form li. (occasionally lb), placed after the number, was used until the early 18th century, when the fancy capital L, written as £, came into use. This sign was at first also placed *after* the number, e.g. 23£, and was not generally placed *before* the number until the later 18th century. The abbreviation lb. or lbs. for pounds weight came into use at the same time as £.

libel 1. A little book. 2. A written paper. 3. A formal document. 4. Statement of allegations in civil and ecclesiastical courts of plaintiff instituting a suit. 5. A published document containing a defamatory, treasonable, or immoral statement.

liberate, writ of warrant either for payment of annual pensions etc. granted under the Great Seal, or for delivery of lands, goods etc. in sheriff's custody.

lift ledge according to Forby, a lift was a rough gate of sawn wood not hung but driven into the ground like a hurdle; a ledge was the horizontal member of the gate. *1802: Hurdles and Lifts £1. 1819: 8 lift ledges sawed @ 2d.½.*

liggen form of the verb to lie.

light an oil-lamp or candle perpetually burning before an altar in the pre-Reformation church, and the subject of many bequests in wills. *1487: I bequeth to the sustentacon of the lyght, brenyng be form the patyble upon the perke...xijd. 1490: to the Plowlyght of Sygate xijd. 1506: to the sepulchre lyght of Hunworth vjd. 1517-8: the light... upon the perk. 1518-9: For the lygth upon the herse ijd.*

limbeck Fr. *alembic*, from Arab. *al-ambīq*, still; the head or cap of a STILL, with a beak or pipe that took the vapour to the condensing vessel. *1589: one Lymbeck prised iiijs. 1606: a limbeck xiijs. iiijd. 1745: beck over the Copper. beck under the marsh tub.* See p. 209.

lime kiln see KILN and p. 116.

lime pit 1. A pit in which hides were dressed with lime to remove hair etc. in the process of TANNING. *1591: hydes in the lyme pit xx.* 2. A chalk pit, especially one producing chalk for lime-burning.

limn, limm to paint, illuminate, especially in gold; to paint in watercolour. *1597: An auncyent costly Chayer folding Carved & tharmes of Fraunce lymmed.*

lincewoollse see LINSEY-WOLSEY

linen cloth woven from flax, or HEMP, which has greater tensile strength. See HARDEN. *1459: j brode pyllow of lynen clothe...viij pelowes of lynen clothe of a lasser assyse. v of the lest assyse. . . j pece of lynen clothe, countyng lenthe and brede iiij^{xx} ellys* [100 yards] *and the tone ende kit and nought enselyd and the other ende hole. 1562: To Peter woode of Yaxley for weauinge of xxx yardes of lynen clothe wth iiijd. for wyndinge iiijs. 1593: Fine Lynnen remayning in my La: chamber in a chest under the north windowe . . . Corse linnen remayning in a danske chest. 1595: a stole to smothe lynnyng on.*

linen wheel spinning wheels could be used for both linen and wool, but a linen wheel generally had a smaller wheel than that for wool.

lines cords stretched between the frame of the BEDSTEAD to support the bed. *1587: vij bedd lynes vs. iijd.*

ling the plant ling, *Calluna vulgaris*, was widespread in Norfolk. The word was used for heathland, sometimes under the term BRUERY, derived from the Fr. *bruyère*, heather. Brooms were made of heather and ling, which were also strewn as a floor-covering. *1498-9: for hewyng of lyng iijs. iiijd. 1654: 3 markum brooms 1s. 6d. 1 dozen of Ling 18d. 2 mopps 16d.*

ling *Molva molva*, a long-bodied deepwater fish growing to over 6 feet; also the more slender blue ling, *Molva dypterygia*. See WEASEL LING. Ling were usually dried and salted. *1415-16: [16 salt fish called] leenges [bought 15s.]. 1484: xviij lenggys & di'. 1499-1500: [for] Clxxxxxx lyng price of the hundred liis. iiijd. 1593: in Linge fish 3 warpe xijs.*

linghouse building to house heather or ling; house on heath. *1300: [clearing out] Lynghus.*

link sausage. *Prompt. Parv.* 'Lynke, or sawcistre'. *1625: a Cake and Cheese a fewe pudinges and linkes. 1654: 1 li. Linckes and 2 Porketts heads. 1655: 4 dozen Linckes 4s. . . 5 Couple Linckes 7d.*

link torch made of tow and pitch, or sometimes tallow or wax. *1587: xiiij lynckes iijs. xd.*

link pan a pan, sometimes with divisions, in which LINKS or sausages were cooked. *1734: two Link panns. 1753: 1 small Pr of Dog Irons, Gridiron, Maid & 1 Small Link Pan 2s. 6d.*

linnail, lynnail see NAIL

linsee tray tea-tray, or butler's tray on stand, perhaps from name of maker. *1751: Two Copper bottle Cisterns, eighte Linsee Trays, Six Voiders.*

linseed linseed oil was obtained from the seed of flax, and was used in medicine, as the medium for oil paint, as waterproofing, oil fuel etc. *1649: 1 pint of lynsett oyle 8d.*

linsey-wolsey, linsey cloth with a linen warp and woollen weft; the fabric of tartan, which word was derived from Fr. *tiretaine, tiertein/tartein* in Flanders. *1648: 1 yard & halfe of Lincewoollse. 1763: a linsey coat.*

lintel horizontal beam forming the head of a door or window. *1374: [making one] Lintil [for the barn door and hanging] le durestall [of the said barn]. 1410: [carpenter placing] linnt' [in the great gate].*

liquorice the rhizome (liquorice-root) of *Glycyrrhisa glabra*. Spanish or Italian liquorice came from *G. echinata*. *1560: one pound of Lyckoras bought at London by William Bullmer iiijd. ob. 1647: 1 li. of green Liqouris 2s.*

list border, edging, strip; narrow cloth. *1584: [cushions] iij of dornycks & one of lysts. 1753: 1 Towell & 1 Matting of List 1s.*

livery the giving of clothes, food, allowances etc. to servants. The giving of clothes led to the sense of a standard set of clothes for servants. *1513: alle my s'vants leverye paid. 1588: xvj* *payre of Liu'ie sheets at viijd a paire.* See also BEDSTEAD; BOARD; CUPBOARD; SADDLE; TABLE etc.

livery bow the plain coarse long-bow. *1591: Twoe lyvery bowes & one shefe of arrowes & one showtinge glove iiijs.*

livery pot large pot for serving drink. *1597: 2 liv'y potts gylt.*

livery saddle saddle decorated in distinctive colours. *1597: iiij*ʳ *new white lyvery sadles. j grene lyvery sadle fringed.*

load a load of FAGGOTS was 60.

load cart OE *lád,* way, journey, road. *Prompt. Parv.:* 'Loode, or caryage. *Vectura.' Ortus Vocabulorum, 1500: 'Plaustrum, vehiculum duarum rotarum,* a lode, or a wagon.' A baggage wagon. See CART. *1591: a load cart, a dung cart.*

lobster stoat (allusion to the club-like tail). *c.1490: for fere hangyd up among other mysdoers and forfaytours, as wesellis, lobsters, polkattys, bosarts* [buzzards] *and mayne currys* [many curs].

lock the stock lock was contained in a stock or wooden block, screwed, nailed, or bolted to the inside of the door. A more sophisticated version with a metal stock had evolved by the 18th century; modern name rim-lock. The mortise lock is a development of the stock lock, fitted inside the upright of the door. The padlock or HANGING LOCK, sometimes called the heart lock from its shape, is equally ancient, dating from the early Middle Ages, and is closely related to the barrel-lock, a tubular lock. A plate lock is a stock lock, or a lock in which the works are pivoted on a metal plate. See FETTERLOCK; OVERWHART. *1616: v stoke lokes with kyes. 1619: ij hanging locks 8d. 1663-4: six heart lockes iijs. one large stocke locke ijs. three stocke lockes iijs. . . one plate locke for a woodhole. 1709: 3 brasse locks. . . 2 iron locks. 1745: Two Iron Rim'd Locks to Doors. . . Two Brass Locks to doors.*

lockram a variety of linen, allied to buckram, originally from Locronon, Brittany. *1589: vij ells & j qter of lokeru'*

lodge, logge ME *loge, logge,* hut, arbour, small house, shed, outhouse; gate-lodge, hunting-lodge. Some medieval hunting-lodges were quite large. *1327: [thatching and cresting] del Logge [in the park]. 1376: [thatcher for 24 days thatching on] lougg [house in the wood].*

lodging chamber bedroom, CHAMBER.

lofeday see LOVEDAY

loft, loffe attic, room in the roof-space; see ATTIC; FALSE ROOF; VANCE ROOF. Lofts often contained beds for servants, and stores like bacon and utensils. Some were simply staging at the end of a larger room e.g. the hall, but lofts over chambers must have been in the roof space, and lofts over e.g. the parlour in a 1½ storey house were in the roof. *1584: Greate Parlor...Loffe over that Parlour. 1589: Loft over the Parlour. . . loft over the kitchen. 1590: loft of the house. 1590: ye chamber & loft at ye halls end. 1595: In the Chamber ou' the plor...In the loft there.*

loftmill raised, high mill. *1288: [making an iron head for] Le Loftmill.*

lokman possibly 'lockman', person charged with the care of the gaol. *1293: [expenses of] le Lokmen xxd.*

lom lamb. *1474: a gown furret with blake lom xs.*

lombardie lumber, rubbish. *1620: other lombardie ther.*

lond land

loose mouth a type of horse's bit. *1597: iij olde bytts Item one trenche xj loose mouthes v snaffles.*

lop rope probably from sense of lop = hanging loose. *1648: 1 new hausrope & Lop rope for the tryces.*

lor: ? a species of shellfish. See PERIWINKLE. *1648: [31st Jan.] 1500 Lor: from Thornham at 6d. p 100 . . . [21 Feb.] 760 Lor: from Thornham 3s. 9d.*

lorimer a maker of horse-bits, mounts for bridles, spurs etc. *1469: to a lorymer of London* *for vj brydille bittes, price the pece xiiijd.*

lothirdle, lothyrdle perhaps from L. *lotio*, washing, sheep-dip; hurdles for the sheep-dip. *1256: [122; cleyes & xiij lothirdles [& 69 pales 11s. 5¼d.]. 1318: [80 cleys 5s. 1½d.] vj Lothyrdles ixd.*

loveday day appointed to settle dispute by arbitration. *1459: Lord Skalys hathe made a lofeday with the prior and Heydon.*

lown to lower. *1664: drayned by the ditch... to laye the ground drye & lowned the water there.*

lucarne, luccum, lucome, lukum OFr. *lucane*, opening in roof, skylight, dormer. *1582: the ruffe and five lucombes, viz three on the east and two on the west. 1662: making of doors & window stoth [studs] & mou' of the lukums in the drieng Chamber. 1665: studded up the sides of all the lucomes on that side of the ruff ou' the best gallery towards the best garden. . . They pulled downe a lucome covered with lead next the best garden by the pspect, larthed and plastered the sides of the lucome towards the thundring gallery...pulled downe brick on the sides of the lucome in the armory chamber. . . repaired two cornishes & sett three neckes & balles unto one lucome...cutt & hewed brickes and balls almost enough for the three other lucumes.*

lufflod livelihood. *1461: gyffe a way menys goods and lufflods.*

lumberry lumber. *1626: in lumberry iiijs.*

lump CLAY LUMP, dried, unfired bricks of clay and chopped straw, usually about 15 by 6 by 6 inches, built into a wall with mortar/clay joints and covered with plaster, mortar, or bitumen.   A surprisingly hard, thermally-efficient wall, cool in summer and warm in winter, clay lump must be protected from damp.   The last clay-lump houses in Norfolk were built just after the First World War. *1721: Lath brick 1 li. 4000 Lumps 6 li.*

lump lumpsucker fish, *Cyclopterus lumpus*. The roe is a substitute for caviar. Sir Thomas Browne: 'A Lump or Lumpus Anglorum...by some esteemed a festival dish though it affordeth butt a glutinous jellie and the skin is beset with stony knobs.'

lustring, lutestring broad silk fabric double or treble in weft and given a gloss by rolling and finishing. Most silk fabrics - taffeta, satin, velvet - could be 'lustrated'. *1730: 12 yds white Lustring Broc. Col. £9...18 yds Rich White & Silver Lustring £63...15 yds Richest broad Bla. French Lustring £7 10s. 1751: A Bedstead with Lath bottom Decker Work Furniture the Curtains lined with Yellow Lustring compleat with Shalloon Case curtain & Rod. 1792: Four green silk Lutestring hang down Curtains.*

lye OE *léag, léah*, bath; alkalised solution made by leaching water through wood ash and used for fabric washing. The straining-cloth and the ash were contained in the lye-latch or leach, a perforated wooden box resting on the top of the lye-tub or trough. See BUCK. *1591: one wycker basket for lye. 1595 a lye trowgh. 1737: One Lye-Latch.. 1741: a Ly Tub, Leech, 2 Wash-killers.*

lym lime. *1386: [5 quarters] de Lym.*

lymbrennere lime-burner. See KILN. *1415-16: Willelmo Spynk lymbrennere de Crowmere.*

lymond a lemon. *1481: lymondes ix li. - ixs.*[i.e. 9 lb lemons cost 9s.].

lyncloth, lincloys linen, sheets. *1474: ij payre of lyncloys viijd...ij schertis and a quarter of lynclothe ijs. vjd...a stomaker of lenclothe.*

lyne line, rope. *1299: j lyne [of 30 fathoms 5d.].*

lyng see LING

lynpin linchpin, the pin passing through the end of the axle to keep the wheel on. *1312: ij lynpinnes cu' ij hurthyrynes.*

lynsett see LINSEED

lythe, lygth see LIGHT

M

M, m abbreviation for L. *mille*, one thousand, plural *milia, millia*; the Roman numeral for one thousand, either 10 x 100 for the decimal HUNDRED, or 10 x 120 (long hundred). The Assize of Weights and Measures *c.* 1302/3: 'But a Last of Herrings containeth ten Thousand, and every Thousand containeth Ten hundred, and every Hundred six score' = 120. The value of M needs to be worked out for each item at different periods, but it would seem generally that when C = 120, M = 1200. See C; D; I; J; L; V; X.

mace the dried outer covering of the nutmeg. Large mace was unpowdered. *1530: a pownd of clowes & masez vs. vd. 1587: j li. vj oz of large mase xjs. 1647: 4 oz of L: mace 4s. 8d.*

mace ale ale flavoured with mace. *1605: a draught of mace ale.*

madder the roots of madder, *Rubia tinctorum*, introduced from Asia by Anglo-Saxon times, were used to provide a bright red dye. *Rubia peregrina*, a native of S.W. England, produces a rose-pink dye. *1303: [planting] madur xd. [cutting the same 4d.].*

made fish see MAID

madox see MATTOCK

maid fish young of skate and THORNBACK. *1593: [25 June] ij Thornebacks & ij maides viijd. 1655: 1 tornbacke 10 made Fish.*

maid iron fireside implement, toasting-iron, trivet, slice. *1708: frying pann & maide. 1717: one sawce-pan, a frying pan and a maid iron. 1753: 1 small Pr of Dog Irons, Gridiron, Maid & 1 Small Link Pan 2s. 6d.*

mail, male OFr. *male*, bag, wallet, travelling trunk. Palsgrave 1530: 'Male, or wallet to putte geare or stuffe in, *malle.*' *1465: Item, I shall telle you a tale, Pampyng and I have picked your male and taken out pesis v. 1522: to Edward Owseley for a male that he bought for my master vs. iiijd.*

mail, male in terms of armour, mail generally means chain-mail, that is, armour formed of interlocking steel rings, or scale-armour, formed by small overlapping scales, but is sometimes a general term for any body-armour including plate armour.

malepillion packsaddle which could be fitted behind the ordinary saddle. Forby: 'stuffed leathern cushion to carry luggage upon, behind a servant attending his master.' *1595: one sadle with A malepyllyon & ye furnyture to ye same. 1647: for malepillinge & male gurths 2s. 2d. 1738: A Male pillion 6d.*

mall rake possibly 'mall' in the sense of an alley or garden walk; a mole-rake, for spreading mole-hills; a malt-rake, for turning malt. See BREWING. *1738: Three pitch Forks Three Small Forks Six Old Rakes A Mall Rake.*

malmsey, malvoisie OFr. *malmesie* from L. *malmasia*, a corruption of Gr. place-name Μονεμβασια (Monemvasia) where the strong, sweet wine originated - later from Spain, Madeira, and the Canaries. *1545: for a bottell of Malmesey xijd. 1584: halfe a Rundlet of Malmsey.*

malt see BREWING

maltbins, -bings wooden bins in which malt was stored. *1310: [mending the daub of the furnace with lead] & del Maltbynngs vjd.*

maltfloor the floor of the malt-kiln. *1309: [made] le maltflor.*

malthouse the building where the malted grain was stored prior to use in brewing. Distinct from the MALTKILN. See BREWING. *1300: [mending the great chamber] Le Malthus [and walls near the postern]. 1310: [1 lock bought for the door] dil Malthaus ijd. 1313: [kiln] & le malthous. 1557: a good malt-house with a soler. 1647: in the Malthowse, Shutt wyndowes to every Light with Sufficient Locks and Keyes: One to the dores And to the Chambers belonginge to the said*

Malthowse every of them shutt wyndowes with like locks and keyes.
maltkiln the building in which barley for BREWING was sprouted and dried in heat.
maltskep large basket for carrying malt. *1312: j maltskeppe & j corbell vijd.*
maltstool stand or trestle on which the malting and brewing tubs rested. *1352: j maltstol.*
mancheat, manchet, manc' see BREAD
Manchesters woollen cloths originally from Manchester. FRIEZES had on one side a tufted, curly nap raised by iron rubbers to give a hard, rough feel. Rug is another name for frieze. INKLE was a narrow linen loom-made lace. *1589: iij doss of Manchisters at xxd.*[a dozen]. *1601: 8 yards dim' of blacke menchster frise at 10d...11 yarde dim' of Manchester Rugg at xd. a yarde. 1654: One peece of Manchester Inckle 20d.*
mande see MAUND
mandilion loose thigh-length overcoat with a standing collar and hanging sleeves, put over the head and buttoned only on the chest. After 1620 it was called a mandeville and used only as a livery. *1590: a Cloake A mandilion an ould fryse gowne. 1590: One Mandilion of velvet wth golde Lace xxvjs. viijd.*
mandrel the arbor or axis on a lathe to which the work to be turned is fastened; an iron cone, two to four feet high with a slot for the pincers running from tip to base, around which rings can be shaped by a blacksmith. A furr-mandrel was for shaping the iron for the FURR or axle-box. *1592: three mandrells one hatch mandrell & a fulmer. 1665: two bolsters & one round mandrell for his use in the shopp. 1674: 1 mandrel 3s. 1709: a Furr-mandirell wei' half an hundred at 2d. ℔ lib. 9s. 4d.*

mandrel

mandyltre mantletree, the lintel over a fireplace. *1588-9: for ij mandyltres for ye howse iiijs. iiijd.*
manfere, marmefare MLWL has 'man-fares (pl.) (?) small boats 1326'. This sense has not been found. Perhaps a collection, boatload, set of nets. *1591: xvj marmefare of netts xvj li. 1595: One manfere of netts.*
manger, mangour, mangur feeding-trough for horses and cattle. *1313: [mending] mangurs [for the horses]. 1407: [repairing] Les mangours.*
maniple narrow double strip of coloured cloth that pre-Reformation priests wore on the left arm, reaching to the knees.
manna opt sweet pale yellow or white juice from the bark of the manna ash, *Fraxinus ornus*, chiefly from Sicily and Calabria and used as a laxative. *1680: Manna opt. oz. i 1s.*
mantle blanket or plaid worn by the Irish till the 17th century. *1573: a Irish mantell xvjs.*
mantle friese broad worsted cloth, friezed. See FRIEZE. *1530: iiij yds q' mantyll fryse for jerkyns & a payer of sloppys iiijs. xjd. ob.*
mantlet woollen horse-blanket. *1352: ij monteletts.*
manual portable book containing the order of administration of the sacrament and sacramentals in the pre-Reformation church.
maple the field maple *Acer campestris* had little value as a timber-tree except for the burrs, which were turned to make MAZERS, large bowls. It was heavily coppiced for rods. *1319: de mapeles [cut in the wood and sold 19d.]. 1332: In sraggyngs [of oak & ash, alder] & mapel xxd.*
maple bisk from the 16th century at least biscuit was baked at home, but maple biscuit, flavoured with maple sugar or syrup from the sap of an American or European variety of *acer*, was imported. *1647: half a pound of Maple Bisk 1s. 2d. . . . Sittuorne, Eringes, & Maple Biskett.*

128

mapolte see MAPPLE

mapple a mop. *1466: for thrommes for pyche mapoltes ijd.*

March beer a particularly strong ale or beer brewed in the month of March. Used also as a cattle medicine. *1654: 4 brewings makinge of march beer & 2 of small. 1655: Bullocks drink. 24 qts of March beer to drinch ye Bullockes.* See DRINCH.

marchpane marzipan, a paste of powdered almonds mixed with sugar and moulded into a cake; sometimes came in a small cask. *1526-7: to ye ald'man for messpane ixd. 1593: j march paine xiijs. iiijd.*

maribone marrowbone

mark tally cut on a wooden stick; mark made on wall etc. of workshop or shop to indicate debt or credit. *1583:[smith] some of the markes in the shopp, due x li. xvs. jd. 1584: Detts by the shoppmarkes xxxv li.*

mark, m. the sum of 13s. 4d., used in accounting, was set in Norman times at 160 pence at the ratio of 20 sterling pennies to the ounce and 8 ounces to the mark, at a time when the pound was 12 ounces; so a mark = 13s. 4d., or ⅔ of a pound. Fractions (half a mark 6s. 8d., a quarter mark 3s. 4d.) or multiples (2 marks 26s. 8d., 4 marks 53s. 4d.) were in common use up to the early 18th century. Many of the valuations in INVENTORIES were made in terms of the mark rather than the pound. There was no English coin called the mark, but at various times in the late Middle Ages and 16th century a coin with the value of 6s. 8d., called the NOBLE or ANGEL, was struck, together with a half- and quarter-noble.

marketsteed marketstead, marketplace. *1587: [aforesaid forum formerly called] le m'ketsteed.*

marking pan pan for dye or paint for stencilling marks on cattle, etc.

markum perhaps from malkin, maukin, a familiar and derogatory diminutive of Matilda, and used from the 16th for a slattern, servant, scarecrow: a bundle of rags etc. fixed on the end of a staff to clean out a baker's oven. *1654: markum broom & 4 whisks.*

marl clay with a variable percentage of carbonate of lime, varying in colour from blue-grey through brown to a dull red. Used from Roman times to condition and fertilise the soil. Many Norfolk parishes contain marl-pits. Marl was also used in brick-making. *1266: [throwing] marle [on 1 acre of land 2s. 3d.]. 1313: [herbage in] le Marlepyt. 1671: for one days worke of 5 men uncovering ye marle pitt one day pumping water 6s. 1736: A marle Pump 8s.*

marmefare see MANFERE

marrow spoon long narrow spoon for extracting marrow from bones. *1734: One silver Marrow spoon [sold for 10s.]*

Marseilles quilt stiff cotton fabric, quilted, sometimes used also in garments. *1751: The Marseilles Quilted Bed Chamber. A Lath bottom Bedstead with Marseille Quilted Furniture bordered Needle Work lined with Callicoe. . . A Four Post Bedstead, with fine Wrought Work Furniture on Marseilles Quilting lined with Green Lustring. . . an India Marseilles Quilt..*

marsh see MASH

martell a hammer. After the 15th century a war-hammer. *1319: j martell ij Wynbles & ij pcents iijd. ob. 1326: j martell ijd. ob.*

martens the fur of the pine-marten, *Martes martes.* The fur of the beech-marten, *M. foina*, was called FOINS. *1459: j gowne of bleue felwett upon felwet longe furrid withe martyrs and perfold of the same. 1590: One Cloake of blacke velwett faced wth sables and lyned wth Martyns vij li. . . one large grogreyne Cloake lyned wth Squirrell and faced wth Martyns iij li. 1592: Furre to face a gowne & iij Payer of Martyns xxs.*

martyrology book containing short lives of the saints and martyrs used in the unreformed church. *1459: j mortellege covered withe white ledes.*

129

mash in brewing, malt plus hot water, forming the wort. See BREWING. *1779: a Jet Mash stirrer an Ironbound Mash tub & Stand.*

mash tub, vat large wooden tub containing the mash, often with pierced false bottom. See BREWING. *1397: [hoops bought for] le Mashefat & Geylfat. 1415-16: in vj hopes [bought for] le Mayshfatte ijs. iijd. 1588: ij mosse Fattes. 1593: 1 marshfatt. 1595: a Mashinge fatt. 1745: one Large Marsh Tub...beck under the marsh tub. Two Large and two Lesser Oar's to Marsh Tub...1 Marsh Tub, and a Wood Pump to D°.*

mashing stick see MASHSTERELL

mashing stool stand on which mashvat was raised. *1603 i mashinge stoole & i kyller. 1617: one swilling tub twoe mashing stooles one tunell.*

mase see MACE

mashsterell mash-rudder, oar to stir the mash. *Prompt. Parv.*: 'Maschel, or rothyr, or maschscherel. *Remulus, palmula, mixtorium.*' Withal's *Dictionary* 1554: 'a rudder, or instrument to stir the meash-fatte with, *motaculum.*' *1444: j par des trustelles, j trow, ij bolles, j morter, j thede, j temse, j mashsterell, j tankard. 1751: four Mashing Sticks.* See BREWING.

maslin see MIXTLIN

mat in the garden, a kneeling-mat; a mat to cover frames, cloches etc. as protection against frost; mat to cover ground to prevent weed-growth. *1745: An Hundred Matts, most old, half worn out.*

mat(t), nat 1. A woven mat of rushes or sedge used between the bedcords and the featherbed. *Prompt. Parv.*: 'Matte, or natte'. At Thornage Hall, 1593, half the 28 beds had a matt. *1593: 1 feild bedstede corded 1 matt.* 2. A mat for kneeling on or covering the floor. Woven rush mats were used as a floor-covering by the 15th century. *1649: 2 bed natts & Matts for 2 stooles in the Church 5s, 6d...matts for three stooles in the Church 1s. 6d.*

match 1. Candle or lamp-wick. 2. For igniting gunpowder of firearms: slow match was hemp cord impregnated with saltpetre and lime, quick-match was cotton wick impregnated with saltpetre or a coating of prepared gunpowder. *1592: Three bunches & certeine roules of match iijs. iiijd.*

matting woven or plaited rush, straw etc. matting for overall floor covering in large houses was popular and widespread from the Middle Ages to the 18th century. *1649: 40 yards of Mattin at 4d. ob. p yard. . . 1 peece of mattin 20 yards square 15s. . . mattinge the green chamber 1s. 6d... yellow nayles 200 tacks 200 & Taynters 100 1s. 4d.*

mattock, mathook tool made in several forms, but basically a wooden shaft or handle with a socketed iron or steel head, having on one side an adze-like blade with the edge at 90° to the shaft, and on the other a pick-like point. Used for digging, breaking up soil and stones, etc. *1592: ij madoxe of iron.*

mattress OFr. *materas*, derived from Arabic *al-matrah*, place where something is thrown. From the Middle Ages a canvas case stuffed with straw, hair, flock etc., above the MAT and beneath the sheet. *Prompt. Parv.*: 'Matteras, undyr clothe of a bed' may confuse it with the mat, but it is possible that some early mattresses were not stuffed. At Thornage Hall in 1593 only one bed out of 28 had a mattress; this was a livery bed, at £21 the most valuable bed in the house. See BEDSTEAD. *1459: j rynnyng bedde with a materas.*[and 4 other mattresses mentioned]. *1463: for iij materes xs.*

maund, mand, maunt OE *mand*, OFr. *mande*, large wicker basket, with handles. *Prompt. Parv.* 'Mawnd, skype. *Sportula.*' Caxton, in the Boke for Travellers (c.1484), equates the maund with the CORBELL: 'Ghyselin the mande maker (*corbillier*) hath sold his vannes, his mandes (*corbilles*) or corffes.' Cotgrave 1611: '*Manne, mande*, a maunde, flasket, open basket, or pannier having handles.' *1459: ij maundys. 1583: one Mande & a batleder. 1592: maunde for*

130

clothes. *1592: washing maund.* *1597: fishe maund.* *1602: a mande of great Quinches.*

mazer, maser OHG. *masar,* excrescence on tree. OFr. *masere, masre,* veined, variegated. Hard wood, originally MAPLE burr, made into a bowl; from late Middle Ages could be metal. *1479: a grete maser with a prend* [repaired crack] *in the botom, and the armes of Seint Jorge, weying xv unc' j quarte & di...a lytil maser with a foote, weing vooj unc'* *1501: a maser wt a brode bonde, and a Prynt of Jhus in the botom.* *1518: a standynge maser.* *1584: an old maser.*

mazerene, mazerine name perhaps derived from Cardinal Mazarin (d.1662). Deep plate, usually of metal. *1709: 10 Mazerenes.*

meal cheese a meal is the amount of milk given by a cow at one milking. Two meal cheese was made of the morning new milk and the evening cream milk. See CHEESE. *1655: Old 2 meal cheese.*

meal, meat fickle or **fiddle** see FICKLE

mealpillion see MALEPILLION

meals ON *mel-r,* Islandic *möl,* sandbank; sandhills by the shore. *1588: passage in a cock boote from the steathe to the meeles.*

medley, medly cloth woven in different shades. *1504: tawney medly gowne Furred wth whight.* *1601: 6 yards dim' of a light medly Carsey at 18d.*[per yard].

melewoghe, methewolle middle wall. See WOWE. *1393: j methewolle [in the dairy house made new with splints and splintnail in total 3s. 9d.].* *1397: [2 daubers daubing the lead furnace and kiln and making] j melewoghe [in the same house for 5 days].*

meleyn see MILAN

mellilot dried flower of the yellow melilot, *Melilotus altissima,* used in plasters and poultices. *1680: Mellilot Haulfe lb 9d. the unguent 4d.*

melting ladle a ladle used to handle melted LEAD. *1621: melting ladle for the lead.*

mercer dealer in textiles or mercery, especially silk and velvets; sometimes small ware in fabrics. *1592: certen m'cery boxes wth the remnaunt of small wares iijs. iiijd.*

mere, mire OE *gemære, mære,* boundary, bank, balk, mark. The mere or mere-balk was a narrow strip of land separating adjacent holdings in the common or open field. *1706: take care to plough up ye mires and to lay it level.* See HEADMERE.

meslin, mestelyon see MIXTLIN

messpane marzipan. See MARCHPANE.

messuage originally a plot of land with building on it; house-plot.

mesynfate see MASH

metefetle, metesetell see FICKLE

methewolle see MELEWOGHE

mew past tense of mow; mowed. *1665: mew the nettles in the spongs. . . mew the low orchard and part of the brecary.*

mexling see MIXTLIN

middellathe see LATHE

middlestead the middle portion or MIDSTY of a barn, where the threshing was usually done. *1584: In the middestead 1 stand of Rye ixs. iiijd.*

middel-, middilspiking see SPIKING

midsty, midelsty the middle portion of a barn. See MIDDLESTEAD; PYCK. *1298: [1 stack near] midsty [towards the east].* *1300: j midsty [in the barley barn].* *1312: [produce of the town tithe by threshing of] j midsty [produce of the tithe] del pycks.* *1350: [from the stacks against] le midelsty [on the west part...from the stacks before] le Piks [on the west part].*

Milan steel made in Milan, for armour. *1464: a salat wyth a vesere of meleyn.*

milch neat, milch kine cows. See KINE.

milk house dairy. Before the 18th century cows were generally milked either outside or in the cowshed.

milkloth linen cloth to act as milk sieve. *1302: j milkloth jd. ob.*

milk sieve milk was passed through a sieve of coarse cloth into the COOLER or milk-pan. Cream was also passed through a strainer into the churn. *1313: j mylcsive ijd. 1319: j milcksive ijd. ob.* See p. 72.

milktongs an extending trellis or Jacob's ladder XXXX on which milk sieves etc. were rested over the milk-pan. Cf. CHEESE-TONGS. *1592: one payer of mylk tonges.*

milk tray large shallow vessel for cooling milk. *1588: xxx mylke bowles, and treyes xs. 1745: marble milk trays. lead milk trays.*

mill a hand-turned mill or large QUERN for household grinding was common up to the 18th century. See p. 72. *1592: a myll in the backhouse.*

mill, horse mill powered by a horse attached to the top stone walking round in a circle. *1593: one horse myll wth ij payer of stone.*

millcote structure housing the mill. See COTE. *1386: [reparations] dil Millecote [this year in daubing plastering thatching].*

Millian of Milan, the centre for making cloth of gold, with gold and silver wires woven into the fabric. *1589: j peece of millian fusten. 1620: a millian Fustian Down bedd.*

million a very large number, not necessarily counted. *1589: iij small boxes & j^C million nedell nedells viijd.*

million melon, *Cucumis melo*, grown in England from Elizabethan times at the latest. *1592: ij myllions & some onyons.*

mill iron, mill pick mill-rind, that is an iron tool for dressing the millstones and giving them a rough surface. *1590: iiij mylle picks. 1616: three millyrons.*

millsty see STY

minging, minking mingling, mixing, usually dough, in a minging trough. *1588: mynggyn trowe. 1592: an old minging boll. 1593: 1 minging trowgh. 1631: minging killer. 1738: Minking trow.*

miniver Perhaps from L. *minutus* little + vair. 1. A plain white fur from the Siberian squirrel *Pteronys volans*. 2. A white fur artificially spotted, with smaller spots than VAIR. 3. Stoat or ermine, *Mustela erminea*, whose white winter coat with black tail supplied the fur ermine. Cotgrave 1611: 'miniuer, the furre of Ermines mixed, or spotted with the furre of the Weesell called gris.' *1465: a longe goune of cremyson velvet...furred with menever and purselled wyth ermyn. 1465-6: xx tymbre of menever, prise the tymbre xvjd. 1513: J Gowne furyd wt calabyr and myn Ss of vyolet.* See TIMBER.

mink minikin baize, a friezed white woollen cloth, was invented in the 1570s. The fur of the European mink, *Puterius lutreola*, was in use by the 15th century, and perhaps minnke say was a woollen cloth patterned or textured to resemble mink. *1552: one Bere cloth of minnke say xxd.*

Minster, Munster. mynster linen cloth originally from Munster. *1589: iij ells & di' of mynster at ixd.*

mire see MERE

missal book containing everything for the pre-Reformation priest when saying mass.

Mississippi table Mississippi was a game like bagatelle, in which balls were hit against the side cushions of a table to go through numbered arches at the end. *1792: a Mississippi table.*

mistlin see MIXTLIN

mitter the head of an alembic, LIMBECK, or STILL. *1781: a Latch pan, Tunnell, Copper Mitter,* *two Guile Tubs.*

mixtlin mixed grains, particularly wheat and rye, either sown together or mingled after threshing and ground into flour for bread. *1417: iij combe of mestelyen. 1537: thresshyng & dyting of xxij comb & ij bz of mixtylion...iiijs. xjd. ob. 1592: x^m acres of Rye & myxtelyne. 1595: in meslyn fower cōbes ls.*[50s.]

moat moats were widespread in medieval Norfolk in areas where there was a sufficient water supply and the geological conditions to maintain it at the surface. Information about the creation and maintenance of moats is scanty, and dating them is problematical. Circumstantial evidence e.g. mention of bridges in medieval manorial accounts is often the only clue to the existence of a moat. It is unsafe to assume that every moat surrounded a dwelling house, as some may have been used as animal enclosures. House-moats were useful not only for defence but also as fishponds, water supply, and sewers. *1406: [carriage of fresh fish for] le moat de hyndrygha'. 1665: a grate to stand before the sluce at the moate & sett them downe boared a plugg to let the wast water out of the moate. . . pulling downe the old bridge over the moate betweene the best garden and tarris walle. . . working up the mouth of the sinke going from the plour into the moate. . . for rearing up the new wall in the moate agt the woodyard & little orchard being five score yards long and 7 foot high...viij li. xvs. for turning an arch in the moate from the sluce 15 yards long which round within taking bottome & all is 2 yards soe in all 30 yards.*

mockadoe It. *maccaiaro*, probably referring to an Arabic word for goats' hair. Mockadoe was a LINEN, JERSEY, or silk fabric, originally imported from the Low Countries but by the 1570s woven in Norwich and elsewhere by immigrant Flemish weavers. Plain mockadoes had an even pile, tufted ones a pile raised in distinct tufts. *1588: one foulte chayer of blacke & redd Mockadow...ij little stooles covered, the one with tuffed Mockadow. . . one filde bedsteade wth the tester of saye, and Curtens of Mockadowe. 1591: curtain of changeable mockaddowe with the curten irons. 1592: Two playne white Halberds armed wth white mocadowe vjs. seaven scarfes of mocadow vs. xv scarfes of yellow and blewe mocadowe. 1597: a cushion of tuft Moackadoe.*

mohair from Arabic *muχayyar*, selected, chosen; cloth of the hair of Angora goats. By the 1630s watered grograins or mohairs in woollen worsted cloth were being made in Norwich and elsewhere. The English mohair was transferred to French as *mouaire*, now *moire*. *1709: a yellow mowhair bed. c.1730: 61½ yds of fine broad yellow Mohair* [for] *three pair of window Curtains. 1792: Crimson Silk Mohair Bed Chamber. . . 2 crimson silk mohair hangdown Window curtains. Eight Chamber Chairs with crimson silk mohair seats & cases.*

moiety a half, half-share. *1599: his part and moyetie of one Caliv' Furnyshed.*

molehills molehills were, and are, an annoyance, hindrance, and hazard in fields, pasture, park, and garden, and were 'gelded' by being spread, thus removing the obstacle and spreading good soil over the surface. *1664: to George Page for gelding of two thousand two hundred & 48 molehills in the pke at seu'all times from the 9th of Jan: until the 4th of Febr: xxijs. v.d* [and to other men for gelding another 6595 in the same period]. . . *to a moletaker of Newton Feb: 1 for taking of six dozen moles in the brecary old orchard parkes entreys woodyard & pke ixs. To Willm Weyard of Earlesoame for taking of Eight dozen & a halfe there at 16d. p dozen xjs. iiijd. . . began to harrowe molehills in the pke Feb: 13th and 20th. . . spredding the molehills & cow dung.*

mole spade, molle spade narrow-bladed spade for digging out moles and laying traps. *1584: one molle spade one belte.*

molestaff, molepick, molespear forked and barbed staff to spear moles as they work near the surface. *1590: one mowlepyck. 1592: one molstaffe.*

molten molten grease is a disease of horses, in which the fat of the body, melted down by violent exercise, is mixed as an oily discharge with the dung. *1664: [gelding] died molten & rotten.*

133

monstrance open vessel of silver to expose the host or communion bread in the pre-Reformation church.

montelett see MANTLET

moon lamp or candle with globe or moon-shaped reflector. *1751: a Moon, a Lantern.*

mop mops, made of strips of cloth or braided cotton, were relatively expensive in the 17th and 18th centuries. *1649: 1 mope 9d. 1654: for 2 dozen Broomes 2s. 6d. 4 Moppes 3s.*

moraley morello cherries, dark acid fruit producing coloured juice and used for preserving and for cherry brandy. *1709: 16 moraley Chires.*

moreen woollen or wool-cotton mixture cloth, the pattern impressed by metal shapes, used for curtains, bed furniture etc. *1779: Four Post Bedstead with Green moreen Furniture.*

morfry see HERMAPHRODITE

morion helmet without beaver or visor. Various forms, as with a narrow rim, or (Elizabethan) with a wide curved brim rising fore and aft and a heavy ridge running front to back. Also called cabasset. *1588: Murryons, ij stele cappes. 1597: Murryans for musketts 10. Murryans one graven & gylt: & ione graven & sylvered.* See p. 136.

morris dance from Moorish. *1459: j clothe of arras, of the Morysch daunce. 1513: j clothe of murrez dannse.*

Morocco stirrups see STIRRUPS

mortar bowl-shaped vessel of stone, pot, metal, or wood, used with a pestle for grinding and mixing. *1326: ij mortar xijd. 1593: 1 morter of bell mettell wth a pestell of yron vs. 1592: on morter waieng xlv li. & pestell iiij li. xiiijs. 1595: a pestell & a morter of brasse. 1618: one woodinge Morter with an eyerne pestell viijd. 1620: one morter of pottmettle with an Iron pestle. ij stone morters with a wooden pestle. 1636: one silver Morter and pestle.* See p. 117.

mortellege see MARTYROLOGY

mortgage see p. 243

morysch daunce see MORRIS DANCE

mosquet, musketta, mukate small oriental prayer-mats. *1751: two Fire side Mukate.*

mosse fatt see MASH

moster develers see MUSTER

mould screen screen or sieve for soil, often in the form of a rectangle 4 to 5 feet long supported at an angle; the soil was thrown against it. *1738: a Mould Skreene 7s. 6d.*

mould board see PLOUGH

moulding in addition to the architectural meanings, curtains, tapestries etc. hung from mouldings of gilt or lacquered (japanned) wood. *1709: 10 black Japan mouldings for hangings.*

mouldingboard board or table on which bread and pastry was made. *1352: [1 trough for pastry] j moldingbord. . . j moldingbord [with trestles]. 1591: j mouldinge bord. 1591: a Coule, A mouldinge table, A knedinge troughe.*

mourey see MURREY

mourning ring ring given and worn as a memorial to a dead person. *1738: A Mourning Ring 10s. 6d.*

mousetrap a typical mousetrap of the 16th-18th centuries was a small cage with a shutter-type door, let down when the mouse, inside, tipped a balanced platform. Another form had bait suspended from a catch that operated the door. In both forms the mouse had to be removed and killed. In another type (see p. 136) a snare was released by the incoming mouse. Another type had a heavy block of wood that crushed the mouse when the platform or catch was touched. *1709 [laundry] 6 tables, 3 stools, a mouse trap.*

moynel see MULLION

muck-crome, muchock, muchook, muckhook a crome or hook for pulling about and gathering muck, in the shape of a fork with 3 to 5 prongs bent at right angles to the long shaft. From at least the 13th century the prongs and socket were of iron. *1300: [making] j muchok jd. 1306: [making] j mukhok [of iron 1d.]. 1363: [making 1] muchook [anew 1d.]. 1593: 1 mucke crome. 1712: 2 mucke forkes 1 mucke crome.*

mudfish lamprey or young lamprey, either *Petromyzon marinus* (lamprey or sea lamprey), *Lampetra fluviatilis* (lampern or river lamprey), or *Lampetra planeri* (brook lamprey). Sir Thomas Browne: 'Lampetra Lampries great and small found plentifully in Norwich river and even in the Citty about May whereof some are very large and well cooked are counted a dayntie bitt collard up butt especially in pyes.' *1655: one Couple of mudd fish 1s. 4d. . . 6 Butkins 6 mudd. 1656: 1 Barrell larg of mudd fish 22s.*

mudscuppet, -skuppet shovel with a concave blade for digging out waterlogged ditches. *1591: one sholve one wat'skepe one mudd skuppett. 1713: a how a muddskupett 1s. 6d.*

muell rabbits rabbits from Methwold, a well-known provider of superior rabbits, known as mule or muel rabbits after the old pronunciation of Methwold. See CONEY. *1655: 6 Couple of muell Rabbets 12s... 10 Couple of Rabbetts from Felbrig 16s. 8d.*

mukate see MOSQUET

muller see GRINDSTONE

mullion OFr. *moinel, moynel, monial,* mullion; vertical bar or pillar dividing a window. *1465: for iiij moynels to the same bay window, prise of every pece ijd. 1619: in the middle of every 4 light window one principall munniall containing in measure 194 Foote wch at 6d. the Foote cometh to 4 li. 17s. 1621: principall munial in the cant square & carroll windows. 1621-2: windows...frames of tymber, and no munnells of stone..*

mulwell fish L. *mulvellus,* OFr. *muluelle,* cod. Cotgrave 1611: '*Morue,* the cod, or green fish, a lesse and dull-eyed kind whereof is called by some the morhwell'. *1459: ij saltyng tubbes viij lynges iiij mulwellfyche.* See GRASS FISH.

muniall, munnell see MULLION

munition military equipment. *1594: a corslet fullie furnished...wth the rest of his munition.*

murrain an epizootic cattle disease, contagious and characterised by fever. *1655: drinching & blouding 38 Bullocks for ye murrain and gargett.* See GARGETT.

murrey L. *morum,* mulberry, OFr. *moré,* mulberry-coloured: purple-red. Transferred to mean cloth of the colour. *1466: iij yerdes of murrey engreyned, the yerde ixs. 1513: vj zards iij qrters murrey. 1597: one teaster of murrey velvet paned wth clothe of golde riche & wth the lres HR in golde.*

murrez dannse see MORRIS DANCE

murryan, murryon see MORION

muscadine, muscadyn L. *muscatus,* Provençal *muscat,* flavoured like musk. Muscadine wine. *1584: A quarter of a pype of Muscadyn.*

musels *Prompt. Parv.*: 'Musselle, *Morcellus, bolus, bucello.*' Morsel, small piece, BOLUS or pill. *1324: in musels [for the cows 1½d.].*

mushel see MUSSEL

musket It. *moschetto,* Fr. *mousquet,* small hawk, sparrowhawk. The basic musket of the late 16th and 17th centuries was a matchlock, that is the powder was ignited by the application of a slow-match or combustible cord. The barrel was about 4½ feet long, and when fired the weapon was rested in a Y-shaped rest with the end stuck in the ground. It fired lead balls weighing between 1⅓ and 1⅝ ounces. The use of the rest declined during the Civil War as muskets became lighter and more manageable, and some were fitted with wheel locks, the powder being ignited by sparks produced by a metal wheel grinding against pyrites, or SNAPHANCES or flint-locks, when a piece of flint was brought sharply against a steel. A bastard musket was probably a lighter type. *1593: A musket rest wth a rapyer blade in yt ijs. 1597: Murryons for musketts 10: & mowlds 10: Flasks 10: touchboxes 10: muskets 10: Rests 10. 1600: For xxiiij muskettes wherof xij bastard muskettes at xxxs. a pece. 1625: A muskett wth a rest Bandeleres & heade peece.*

musketoon short-barrelled, large-bore musket in use from the Civil War period. *1745: 12 Muskettoon's, 7 of them Riffled Barrells.*

muskle see MUSSEL

musrell, musrol nose-band of a bridle. *1597: a Musrell.*

mussel OE *muscle*. The edible sea mussel, *Mytilus edulis*, was taken and eaten along the coast in some numbers. In the Stiffkey Hall accounts of 1593 mussels occur only from 22 Jan. to 2 Apr. The freshwater mussel (family *Unionacea*) is much larger. *1545: for mushels ijd. 1593: for muskles iiijd.*

mustard cultivated white mustard *Sinapis alba* was introduced as a crop in early Roman times. It is not clear how much mustard was grown locally and mentions of it as a crop are rare before the later 18th century, so presumably some at least of the seed for grinding was imported. Black mustard *Brassica nigra* was grown in the Fens from the 18th century. Mustard QUERNS are quite common in inventories up to the 18th century. *1595: a payer of musterd quernes.*

muster develys, moster develers OED derives this term from Montivilliers, Normandy, but other sources derive it from Fr. *moitié de velours*, half velvet. A mixed grey woollen cloth. *1465: a fyn gowne of muster dewyllers furryd with fyn bevers. c.1474: a cotte of moster develers. 1484: my must' develys gown, furred with Black.*

myn see MINIVER

mynggen see MINGING

mynyng mining, quarrying. *1335: in mynyng [stone for 17 days one man 2s. 1½d.].*

myssayle see MISSAL

mystelon see MIXTLIN

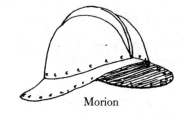

Morion

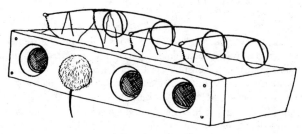

Mousetrap 1676

N

Nag small, light horse. *1505: my blacke curten nagge. 1588: amblinge nagge. 1593: one sorreld nagg called shitt xvs.*

nail as a measure of weight: 8 lbs. Measure of length: 2¼ inches, or one-sixteenth of a yard. *1522: iij quartrs & a nayle of blacke clothe. 1598: Worsted fustyans shall contayne in length x yardes & in breadthe an ell wantynge the nayle.*

nail there were many types of iron nail made for different applications, and those given below are only a sample. Nails were usually purchased by the HUNDRED for the larger nails or the thousand for the smaller, or by weight. The 'hundred' was generally the long hundred of 120, and the 'thousand' was ten hundreds that is 1200. They were made either by the local smith or bought at the local fairs and markets, having been made at well-known nail-making locations e.g. Birmingham. Hand-made nails were made from slender rods of iron forged to a long square taper; the end of the rod was put through a nailheader or NAIL TOOL and broken off at the correct length, the head was formed by hammering, and the nail and tool quenched. Occasionally 'nail' means a wooden nail - see SPIKING. A full discussion of the nomenclature and use of nails in the Middle Ages is in L.F. Salzman, *Building in England*, 286-317.

batten large, expensive nail for nailing battens. *1648: 200 batten nayles 5s.*

boat the purpose-made nails used in more modern times for boat building were either not available or not thought necessary in some medieval construction. *1319: [making boat] iiij^C de sennayl [for the boat 3s. 1d.]. C spiks vd. iij qr de durenayl iijd. hethnayl id. ob. vj gross [nails (clavis) for] le botme jd. C Wrongnayl [for the boat 3d.].*

brasen brassed, possibly brass-headed. A bully nail was round-headed, bulbous. *1648: 60 brasen bully nayles 8d. 1649: 400 brasen nayles 1s.*

burnish nail with a burnishable head, for upholstery work. *1648: 60 smale burnish nayles 3d.*

cask small nail for attaching the hoops to the staves of barrels. *1647: 100 of cask nayles 2d.*

ceiling small nail for the 'ceiling' or panels of a room. *1662: seeling nayles 1000 2s.*

cob from cob in the sense of 'rounded', therefore a nail with a large round head. *1647: pallett nayles boults cobs & shews.*

great large nail. *1648: great nayles used by the Carpenders 6d. 1664: 20 lb. of great nails at 4d. vjs. viijd.*

lath small-headed short nail for nailing LATHS to rafters, joists, posts etc. *1544: for v thousand lathe nayle at xd. the M iiijs. ijd. . . for ij Thousand lathe nayle bought at Derhm at xijd. the thousand ijs. 1647: 2000 Larth nayles 3s. 9d. 1663: 30000 learth nayles at 13d. xxxijs. vjd.*

lead nail with a broad flat head for fastening lead. *1498-9: for leednayl js. vijd.*

linnail linchpin of axle. *1306: ij wereyren & ij linneil iijd.*

price nails were often described by the price per HUNDRED e.g. tenpenny nails cost 10d. a hundred (120); the designation might remain when the actual price went up. *1545: to the Smith of Swanton for ijC of iiij peny nail viijd. a hunderd of iij peny nail bought of him iijd. 1579: for C iiij penny nayles at viijd. the C viijd. 1663: 6m: 5^C 10d. nayles at 6s.[the hundred] xxxixs. 11m: 6d. at 3s. 2d. xxxiiijs. xd. 13m: learge 4d. at 2s. 4d. xxxiiijs. xd. 2m: double 10d. at 12s. xxiiijs.*

rose square-shanked nail with a large head in the shape of a flattened four-sided pyramid. *1367: Rosenayl & Dornayl xiiijd. 1587: double buckles, rose-nayles and other sorts of nayle. 1709: Bick-iron & Rose Naile toole.*

saddler's small round-headed nail for nailing leather to the woodwork of a saddle. *1538-9: di' M^t of sadellers nayle vijd.*

schotnail, shotnail short-shanked nail. *1293: C schotnayl ijd. ob. 1342: xl shotnayl jd. 1344: CClx shotnayl vijd. ob. q'.*

sennail see **boat** above

tack small flat-headed, short-shanked nail for nailing down matting, upholstery etc. *1647: half a hundred tacke nayles 2d. 1649: yellow nayles 200 tackes 200 & taynters 100 1s. 4d.* [for matting].

tenter tenterhooks were bent nails used in stretching cloth, see TENTER. Tenter-nails (see **tack** above) may have been used to stretch the matting.

tile for nailing wooden shingles or TILES to their supporting laths, or for driving through the holes in peg or pin tiles to hang them on the laths. Some tile nails were metal, but the cheaper were wooden. *1545: xiij Thousand Tyle nayle at iiijd. the thousand iiijs. iiijd.* See TILEPIN.

tingelnail OE *tengan*, ON *tengja*, to make fast, to fasten; small iron nail. *1298: vj^c splentenayl & c tinggelnayl xd. 1300: [for boat] CC de tyngelbayl xjd. 1319: in tyngelnayl ad Latys jd.*

yellow with brass or brazen head, for upholstery work. *1647: 100 yellow nayles 3d.*

nail tool short bar of iron or steel used in making nails; pierced at one or both ends with a square-sided hole the size of the intended nail and a boss formed around the hole, so that the taper of the nail ensures that enough protrudes to be broadened by hammering to form the head. *1592: thre nayle tooles and a cart nayle toole.*

napern, napronne see APRON

napette napkin. *1474: v napettes vd. iij hedkercheffes, pris xijd.*

napkin essential tableware for middle and upper class households from the Middle Ages onwards. *1584: halfe a dosyn table Napkyns stryped wth blewe ijs. ix old playne table Nakyns xiiijd... xiiij dyop table Napkyns iijs. iiijd. ix old corse table Napkyns xijd. 1764: Thirty nine Dozn & Eleven Damask Napkins, Fifteen Dozn & half Huckaback D°.*

napkin press enclosed CUPBOARD for napkins and linen.

nat, natt, nate straw mat for bed or for use in the garden. See MAT. *1313: j natte [bought in the hall 1d.]. 1323: j Natte [in the chamber 2d.]. 1626: j liv'ry bedsted wth nat & cord. 1649: for the natting of yor worps: stoole & Mr Eds 2s. 8d...for new natts to the stoole wher Mr Wilcocks did sit at Church 1s. 4d. . . 2 bed natts & matts for 2 stooles in the Church 5s. 6d. 1655: 2 Bee skepps 18d. Nates 2s. 6d. 6 Hay Rakes 3s. 1666: one postead bedstead wth Nate & Cord.*

nave, nawys centre block of a wheel; hub. Nearly always made of elm. See CART. *1417: for bryssyng of a payre carte nawys vjd.* [cutting holes to receive the spokes]. . . *hopyng of a payr carte nawes. 1636: 2 payer of small naves ijs. 1664: spoiling in of spoakes putting of a new Nave. 1737: a pair of Neaves & spokes for a Pair of Plow wheels.*

neald annealled; to neal is to burn, bake, or fire earthenware. *1649: 1 grose of Tobacco pipes dubble neald 4s.*

neat OE *néat*, ox. Horned cattle. See SOUSE. *1589: mylche neate. 1593: neates rackes.*

neat's tree yoke or frame for holding cattle to be slaughtered.

necessaries household requisites (oatmeal, candles etc) out of the stock of the house as against food bought from outside (ACHATES).

necessary chair see NIGHT CHAIR

necessary house PRIVY. *1723: 6 12´ single deals for ye Necessary howse flower. 1720s: The servants Necessary is so offensive that it should be altered, and a Cestern made for water to keep it Sweet.*

neck lower part of the capital or head above the astragal or final part of a column; support of the top of an ornamental feature. *1665: Great neckes collers & balls...small neckes collers & bearing neckes & balls.*

neckerchief, neckercher kerchief worn round the neck. *1587: neckerchers & kerchers.*

nelle see ELL

nerve oil oil, made from a mixture of herbs, wax, tallow, and frankincense, rubbed on horse (or human) to alleviate strain, bruising etc. *1592: iij li. nervoyll xviijd. 1665: nirve oyle for the sorrold horse iijd. 1672: a pounde of Nerve oyle 8d.*

nest of drawers, boxes early form of CHEST-OF-DRAWERS. *1633: A spanish nest of boxes. 1723: A nest of drawers a Looking Glass and two tables 1 li. 5s.*

net nets were important for catching fish and birds. Nets for fishing include 1. Casting net, for taking fish from pond or moat; probably similar to pit net. 2. Dragnet, dragged through the water or along the bottom. Probably the same as the ground-net. 3. Flue, drag or trammel-net, which could be set in a narrow channel, or used as a herring-net. 4. Ladd net, either weighted with lead, or for use in a channel or LADE. 5. Pit net, for use in pond or pit. 6. Setnet, fastened across stream or channel and into which the fish were driven. 7. Trammel, a long narrow fine-mesh net sandwiched vertically between two larger-mesh nets, with floats and sinkers and held in place by poles. The fish go through one large-mesh net and are trapped in a bag of fine-mesh which goes through the large-mesh net on the other side. 8. nets for sea-fishing, usually dedicated to a particular type of fish e.g. herring. ¶ The birding net or HAY was a long narrow net drawn across heath, field, or dune. *1584: fyftene mackerell netts two spyrling netts, also tenne hearring flewes & nyne nynestores hearing nettes, with warropes 9 li. xs...One setnett, two ancres with all that long to it iij li. 1589: one lytell ould botte one Dydall one ould pyt neate and one tramell. 1590: a nett to take Roockes at xvjd. 1597: a didall and iij ladd nettes xvjd. 1602: j Grounet ledes and hockes and rodes xxxxs. j lente of a grownete three pound xs. j lettell setnet and rodes iiijs. ij peces of tramell lent viijs. brest poles tramele polles more in poles ijs. 1654: Mendinge ye Dragg-nett 6d. Paid for Siel Band line for ye Nett 14d. . . 1 capnet 10d. 1771: a partridge net 3s. 6d. silk quail net 3s. a casting net 7s... hawking net 1s. 6d.*

netherstock, -stocking a stocking for the lower part of the thigh downwards. *1588: blacke silke netherstoks...sameel silke natherstockes. 1589: x payer of ladds netherstockes vjs. viijd. 1603: two paire of nether stockings.*

night box see CLOSE-STOOL. *1745: [little parlour] One Night Box.*

night chair, night stool, necessary chair a CLOSE-STOOL in the form of a chair. *1751: a Mahogany Necessary Chair & Earthen Pan* [and Walnut ditto]. *1779: a night chair. 1792: walnutt tree night Chair. . . a wainscot night stool.*

night mug mug in the bedchamber for use at night. *1787: two night Basons, night Table, two night Mugs, hand Bason, night Stool with pewter Pan.*

night staff watchman's staff, long pole. *1595: a Fyrrett a dygginge stafe twoe night staves.*

night stool see NIGHT CHAIR

night table dressing table, wash stand, bedside table. *1764: One night table. 1792: a walnut tree night Table.*

night tray tray for use in the bedchamber. *1787: Mahogany Night Tray.*

niles see NOILS

ninepins the game of skittles, in which nine skittles, usually of wood, are bowled at. A popular game at inns. *1649: for nine pinns 2s.*

noble, nobill a gold coin, introduced by Edward III in 1344-6, with a face value of 6s. 8d.; there were also half and quarter nobles. In 1464 the value of the noble was raised to 8s. 4d., and in 1465 the RYAL or rose-noble, with a value of 10s., was issued. The ANGEL, value 6s. 8d., was issued in 1466. By the mid-16th-century the noble had settled at a value of 6s. 8d., which continued throughout the 16th and 17th centuries. See MARK. *1464: in goolde lxiiij nobles, and in sylvere vij noblis, summa totalis xxix li. . . The wyche xl marces my mastyr is content in noblis, saff that he toke my mastyr the nobylle for viijs. iiijd. 1517: to my lady Fenkill, a bowed*

139

nobill, for a token for to prey for my sowle.

nogg strong beer. OED quotes Prideaux 1693: 'A bottle of old strong beer, wch in this countrey [Norfolk] they call "nog" ', and *Lond. & Country Brew.* (1743): 'In Suffolk and Norfolk they run very much upon a light brown, or deep Amber colour'd Butt-Beer, which in the latter place is called Nogg.' *1738: In the Nogg cellar: Five Hogsheads of Mild Nogg £3. In the first Bing Seven dozen and a Half of Mild Nogg £1.*

noils short ends and knots combed out of long wool. *1603: one parsell of nyels ijs. viijd.*

nonsuch seed nonsuch was a species of lucerne, *Medicago sativa,* introduced into Norfolk in the late 17th century and extensively grown for fodder; it could be cut several times a year. *1712: not taking more than three crops of Corne & laying them down with Clover or Nonsuch at least three years before the end of their terms. 1741: A parcell of Nonesuch Seed Valued at 2 : 10 : 0. 1741: a Stack of Hay part of it Nonesuch thrash'd.*

nonnys nuns.

norden northern, particularly cloth. *1592: xiij yards greene Norden at xxd. a yard... ij yards norden green Carseye iiijs. viijd.*

Normandy glass Normandy was one of the best sources for coloured and clear window-glass. The case, chest, or cradle of glass was one seam of 120 lb. or 48 square feet. *1619-20: for 12 Cases of normandy glasse 19 li. 11s. 6d.*

northern steer long-horned black cattle, driven down for fattening in Norfolk. *1594: ij Fatte northen steeres.*

nosing exposed, rounded, projecting edge of the tread of a step. *1732-3: mason pulling down nosings & slips & coves &c.*

Nottingham Nottingham stoneware, made throughout the 18th century, had a russety-brown surface with a sheen. *1709: 2 earthern Notingham Tea pot.*

nouche see OUCH

novel disseisin literally new dispossession. A tenant thinking himself unjustly deprived of his holding could obtain a writ ordering the sheriff to summon an Assize of Novel Disseisin, at which 12 jurymen would give their verdict on the case. It was gradually used for longer periods and as a mechanism to establish title. *1451: Sir Thomas Tudenham...ful synnefully causid a writte of novell dissessyn to be brought ageyn John Aleyn.*

number thread a superior sewing-thread. *1648: 2 knotts of fine number thrid 10d. for oz. 1 of thrid 4d.*

numerals, Roman see C; D; I; J; L; M; V; X.

nuncupative will an oral, not a written, will

nursery room set aside for the rearing of children; ground set aside for rearing young plants, trees etc. *1597: The Nurcerye* [2 beds with bedclothes, 1 hanging, table, 4 stools, form, cupboard, fireirons, STARCHING PAN]. *1654: Given at Sprowson to Sr Thomas Corbetts man 2s. and another at his nursery. 1725: To two Nursarys containing 20 Acres with the wast ground occasioned by them, which I paid for 3 years as Marl'd land £27.*

nut cup cup formed of the shell of a coconut mounted in silver or gold. *1593: j nutt cupp with a bole.*

nutt see KNOT

nutts the pancreas or caul; the penis; bull's or ram's testicles. *1654: Nutts and sweetbreads.*

nyels see NOILS

140

O

Oak the dominant oak in Norfolk is the English or pedunculate oak *Quercus robur*, which in good conditions produced not only a fair amount of straight timber but also the elbowed forms useful in shipbuilding. Most of the timber for building was English oak. The durmast or sessile oak *Quercus petraea*, native to north and west Britain, grows naturally straighter. In 1445 Agnes Paston wrote to Edmund Paston in London to procure joists of a 9 by 7 inch scantling for the chapel and parlour at Paston 'for here can non seche be hadde in this conttre'. See BOARD; INK.

oar long flat wooden poles used in BREWING for working up the malt in the mash-tub. *1745: Two Large, and two Lesser Oar's to Marsh Tub.*

ob. L. *obolus*, a halfpenny, used in Roman numeration. Normally placed after the d. *(denarius)* in writing pence e.g. viijd. ob. = 8½d. See D.

obit ecclesiastical office, usually a mass, of the pre-Reformation church, performed at the anniversary of a person's death for the good of his or her soul. Sometimes an obit would be established for a number of benefactors of a church. *1505: I wyll have an hobyte kepte for me and my Frendys yerly in Hunstanton Chyrche att suche daye as it shall happyn me to depte. 1547: ye obyte daye of all ye benefactours.*

obligation legal written contract to pay money or perform an act, with conditions and penalties. Often found in an INVENTORY as part of the deceased's estate. See BOND; DEBT. *1598: one obligacon of v li.*

ocar see OCHRE

occupy do, perform, use. *1518-19: For colers beyng ocupyed in the howse viijd. c.1594: Fitt & Speller doth not occupie baking but ther wives only. . . John Lee of Fakenham is a cordiner & did occupie the trade of a cordiner.*

occupy to have sexual intercourse, fuck. *1623: Yr Nephew Brooke hath almost occup: his fine wife to death. 1639: [man] did occupie mother Botteret agaynst a Barrells head until he made all the Beere turne to Beeregood...the sayd Thomas did fuck Jeremy Botterets wife agaynst a Barrells head until he made the Beregood fly out at the Bunge hoale. 1639: did occupie her under a bushe.*

ochre pigment ranging in colour from light yellow to brown and red, derived from earth or clay containing iron oxide. Usually purchased by weight. *1511-12: for red oker and other colors js. iiijd. 1619-20: 15 li. oker 2s. 6d. 42 li. oker 2s. 8d. 1655: for 12 li. spanish white & 12 li. of Oker 2s. 8d.*

office, house of see PRIVY

oil oil for LAMPS was usually fish-oil or whale-oil, but vegetable oils e.g. linseed were also used. *1467: for oyle de olyve for harneys iiijd. 1482: for iij qrtes oyle for to scower harnesse xd. 1505-6: for lampe oyle xxxjs. for mete oyle xs. 1533: iiij galons of oyle iiijs iijd.*

oilfloorcloth canvas oilcloths, coated with a mixture of paint and oxidised linseed oil and decorated in simple patterns, were in use from the 1720s until they were superseded by linoleum in the mid-19th century. Oilcloths could be repainted as the pattern was only on the surface. *1764: [Little Dining Parlour] an oilfloorcloth.*

oker, okyr see OCHRE

oking oaken. *1591: three hundred of Oking bord.*

olland Forby: 'arable land which has been laid down in grass more than two years'. Nall: 'Lay ground, old land that has lain untilled, and is newly ploughed.' *1636: one olland harrowe. 1671: for Breaking up of 8 Acres of Orland in Bircham Breck.*

olliett Fr. *oiellet* eyelet. Twill cloth, often of linen and JERSEY wool mixture, woven to leave a perforation or 'eyelet' at the crossing of warp and weft. *1589: ij yards of crymson olliett at xijd...xj yards of narrow colored olliett at xijd.*

olsom cloth, probably linen, from Aylsham. *1465: xxiij elles of olsom, prise the elle iijd.*

onynn onion. *1300: onynns [sold 6d.].*

orange Seville or bitter oranges were imported from Spain and Portugal in the Middle Ages, but from the 16th century sweet or China oranges brought from Ceylon by Portuguese traders were imported. Fruiting orange trees were grown in England in orangeries or heated greenhouses by the 16th century. *1655: For 6 Lemons 8d. 12 Oringes 18d.*

orange water, orange flower water imported from France and Portugal and made locally from the second half of the 17th century, orange-flower water was used as an alternative to rosewater as a flavourant in cakes, biscuits, sweets, and wine. *1697: To Alice Spalding for 2 gall: of Cannary for the Making Orrange Water 16s.*

orange wine wine made from, or flavoured with, oranges. *1738: A Ten Gallon Cask of Orange Wine 8s.*

orchyerd OE *ort-geard, oregeard, orceard*, lit. vegetable-yard; L. *hortus*, garden. Orchard. *1299: [prunings] in le orch yerd [sold 6d.]. 1302: [lock for the gate] del Orchyerd.*

ordinal in the pre-Reformation church, a book containing the order of service for any day of the year.

ordinary eating-house, tavern, or room used for eating as well as drinking.

ories, orince see ORRIS

orland see OLLAND

orne horn. *1590: a drincking ornes.*

orphorian a stringed instrument, a type of CITTERN, played with a plectrum. *1603: one base violerne one treble violerne One Orphoorian ls. [50s.]*

orphrey ornamental strip of rich cloth to cover the seam of the chasuble in the pre-Reformation church.·

orrery clockwork instrument to demonstrate the motions of the planets round the sun, named after the Earl of Orrery, for whom the instrument was made after the original was invented by George Graham *c.*1700. *1792: An Orrery & with compass &c by Rowley in a wainscot case lined with baise.*

orris Silk lace with interwoven gold and silver threads. *1595: [on bed] on Cou'inge orince worcke. 1637: One large carpet of silke orres & a side board cloath of the same six silke orres quishons 2 large windowe quishons of the same lined wth green taffetye.* See also ARRAS.

orris the iris, especially *Iris germanica* and *I. florentina*. The rhizome smells like violets, and when powdered was used as a medicine and perfume.

orts fragments of food, leftovers of cattle food; fodder; an allowance of money to buy fodder. *Prompt. Parv.* 'Ortus, releef of beestys mete.' *1498-9: to the plowman for ortes xvjd.*

osier a species of willow, *Salix viminalis*, from the pliant branches of which baskets, hurdles etc. were made. *1313: Osyeres [sold 7d.]. 1328: faggot & osieres [sold 9s.]. 1654: Of Wm Mitchell of Aylsham for ye Osyers, besides 6 dayes worke of himself and his men, plantinge ye Osyer ground at ye Parke and 9500 setts valued at 6s. 8d. p 1000 and 6 Basketts for weedrs.*

Osinbrigg, Ossenbridge Osnabrück, Germany, gave its name to a coarse linen or fustian. *1589: xiiij ells of osinbrigg at xd. 1592: in buntgynes & ossing bryges pyckelyng xxs. 1738: Twelve Yards of whited Ossenbridge Cloth at 8d. a Yard.*

osmond, osmund superior quality of iron, or possibly steel, imported from the Baltic and particularly Sweden in small bars and used for fish-hooks and arrow-heads, etc. *1504-5: for a barell of Osmund vijs. viijd.*

ouch, nouche OFr. *nouche*, OHG *nuscka, nuscha*, buckle, clasp, brooch. *1467: a nowche of* *goolde set with a fyne safyre, a grete balyse and v perles. . . iiij owches of goolde garnyshed with iij rubyis, a saphyre, an amytes, an emerawde and xv perles .*

outholling cleaning or fyeing out a ditch or HOLL. The 'DIKE' or deek was the bank formed of the soil dug from the holl. *1655: outholling at ye Park dike. 1656: a quantity of outholling worke at 2½d. ye rod, they gathering and settling it wth furr Lair. . . scouring, outholling, Backing and settlinge of a dike. 1719: ditching & outholling.*

outlet way out of building, portal, postern. *1620: For piling plancking making the centers Roofes & floores lintles and dores of the two outletts adjoyning to the front East and West.*

outlode a lode is a watercourse or channel, and the outlode is the discharge channel of a watermill. *1403: [cutting] planks [of oak for] les Outloddeles [of Eaton mill].*

outrid, outshot, -shut back room, lean-to, shed. *1498-9: for nayll for the outschote viijd. 1606: In the Outrid* [cheese press, saddle, box, baskets etc.].

oven bread ovens of the 18th century and earlier can be found alongside the open hearth in many Norfolk houses. The bread oven consisted of a raised floor and a brick dome, with a small door and no flue. The oven was filled with a faggot which was lit and allowed to burn itself out; the ashes were then raked out, the inside lightly cleaned, and the bread or other food inserted to bake or cook in the heat stored in the brickwork. From the 17th century ovens with iron doors, fire-grates underneath, and flues were built alongside the open hearth, kitchen range, or grate. *1709: [pastry] 3 ovens with iron doors and frames.*

oven leed, lid 1. A large pan or pot for use within an oven. See LEAD. 2. An iron 'lead' or large pot inverted over the food to be baked and placed in or alongside the fire. *1636: one oven leede and a ladle. 1637: Twoe yron ovenleeds.*

overbody upper or outer bodice for a woman in the Tudor and early Stuart period. *1599: hir Overboddies smockes and Aprons 4s.*

overman foreman. *1349: [harvest] j ou'man vj cartar [2 stackers].*

overw(h)art, overthwart across, transverse, oblique; for timber, overwhart cuts were sawn across the grain, not along it. Overthwart ploughing: to plough at right angles to the existing furrows. *1664: for hewing and cutting ov'whart cutts of a popple blowne downe. 1665: they cutt over whart cutts & hewed ij stockes of timber at the pitt.*

overwhart lock pivoting window catch to secure casement against the frame. *1663: making of thirty and eight casements...all of them having overwhart lockes...more to him for six ringles and one locke on seu'all other casemts.*

owelede old

ower glass hour glass

oxen bullocks, castrated BULLS, were used for draught purposes at all periods, but in Norfolk horses were the main motive power from the early Middle Ages for PLOUGHS, HARROWS, CARTS, carriages etc. There was a plough-team of oxen at Paston as late as *c.*1900. *1597: Draught Oxen vj. 1655: at plough wth Bulls and Harrowes at Barly Siel.*

oyer and terminer commission appointed to hear and determine cases or indictments of serious crimes such as murder and treason at the assizes.

oyle aisle. *1664: heading up the chimney in the Oyle of Brome Church.*

oynnyng onion

oyster oysters were common along the Norfolk coast up to the early 20th century. Small oysters were eaten raw, larger ones were pickled, stewed, roasted or baked. 'Cut' oysters were already opened. In the Houghton accounts of 1647-9, only May and June were without the purchase of oysters; in 35 out of the 42 weeks in the period 5th July 1647 to 24 April 1648, 9770 oysters and 1 barrel of oysters were bought, an average of over 230 a week. *1545: [2 Aug.] iiij^C smale Oysters viijd. . . [21 Sep.] for iij^C Colchester oysts vjd. 1647: 1* *barrell of greenfield Oysters 2s. 6d. 1648: 200 of greate Oysters 2s. 200 smale Oysters 2s. 1655: 200½ uncutt oysters 6s. 3d. & 2 ^{C} Cutt 4s. & 2 Barrells of Colchester 5s.*

oyster knife knife with a short strong blade made for opening oysters. *1709: 6 oister knives.*

Types of Plough (see pp. 158-9)

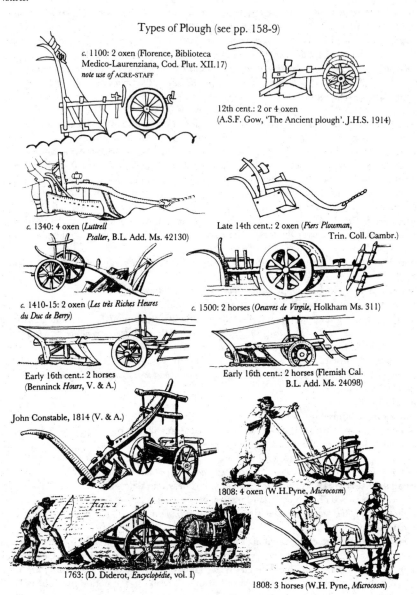

c. 1100: 2 oxen (Florence, Biblioteca Medico-Laurenziana, Cod. Plut. XII.17)
note use of ACRE-STAFF

12th cent.: 2 or 4 oxen
(A.S.F. Gow, 'The Ancient plough'. J.H.S. 1914)

c. 1340: 4 oxen (*Luttrell Psalter*, B.L. Add. Ms. 42130)

Late 14th cent.: 2 oxen (*Piers Plowman*, Trin. Coll. Cambr.)

c. 1410-15: 2 oxen (*Les très Riches Heures du Duc de Berry*)

c. 1500: 2 horses (*Oeuvres de Virgile*, Holkham Ms. 311)

Early 16th cent.: 2 horses (Benninck *Hours*, V. & A.)

Early 16th cent.: 2 horses (Flemish Cal. B.L. Add. Ms. 24098)

John Constable, 1814 (V. & A.)

1808: 4 oxen (W.H.Pyne, *Microcosm*)

1763: (D. Diderot, *Encyclopédie*, vol. I)

1808: 3 horses (W.H. Pyne, *Microcosm*)

144

P

P with a stroke through the stem, p̱ is a contraction, meaning that -er or -ar has been missed out, e.g. p̱fect, p̱close, p̱son (person, parclose, parson).

p' contraction meaning that -ra, -re, -ri, -ro has been missed out, e.g. p'sent, p'dict, p'sed, p'ved (present, predict, prised, proved).

packsaddle saddle for use on a packhorse to carry bundles or packs. *1352: j packesadel.*

pad see PARSER

pageant cart, structure in which a medieval or Tudor play took place. *1565: A Pageant, yt is to saye, a House of Waynskott paynted & buyled on a carte wt fowre whelys. A square topp to sett over ye sayde House.*

pail up to the 19th century pails were generally of wood but sometimes of bronze, with either ears or a BILE for the handle. Cleating is fitting with a metal plate or hoop, 'bayleing' is fitting with a bile. *1593: one bunche of lathes and one payell. 1603: six brasse pots, a brase payle. 1648: payles bayleing & cleatinge.*

painted cloth canvas, cloth, or linen painted with patterns, designs, coats of arms, or figures was found in the houses of all but the lowest class of the 16th and 17th century. A cheap substitute for tapestry, painted cloths were hung on the wall, above the fireplace, about the bed, and behind the table, and were usually the same as STAINED CLOTH. See also HANGING; TAPESTRY. *1584: a paynted cloathe to hange before the chymney. 1587: iij pictures of painted clothe the cullers decayed. 1589: a paynted clothe prised at iiijs. 1593: the hangings there of dornix of blacke & yellowe & 1 painted ov' the Chiminye with Armes xxs. . . 4 peces of painted hangings & 1 pece of Tapstry hanging xls. 1595: One posted bed, with Tester & a paynted cloth xs. . . a paynted cloth called a descloth* [see DOSSER] *iijs. iiijd. 1597: a pece of paynted clothe at the bedds hd.*

painted paper pictures, pages of illuminated manuscripts; if found in an inventory, painted paper would not be wall paper, as anything stuck to the wall would not be included. *1613: divers painted papers...in painted papers in Storyes ijs. vjd.*

paiser person who peises or weighs; the scales or weighing apparatus.

paisers a jemmy; pair of pincers. *1625: j percer j paier of paisers.*

pale thin, short piece of timber for making pale fences, palings, or gates, either riven (cleft, CLIFF, split see RIVE) or sawn, and joined together by rails. Pales could be pointed at the top end. See BERDINGS. *1391: palys [for] le Foderyng byng [of the cows]. 1405: [making] le pale [from the hall gate]. 1419: [making door] & palys [between the 2 pigsties]. 1591: ryven pale. 1593: vij^{xx} and xv pales vijs. vjd... viij rayles xd. 1595: in borde planke & sawen pale xs.... xxx sawen pales. 1595: A palinge wimble. 1662: pailing the lords Close...the greene yard pailes. 1664: hope* [helped] *to cutt cliff for pale. 1664: hewed 2 board stockes and 3 pale stockes, repaired pales on the spong. 1738: Four Rails of spire-headed pale 1 li. Seven Bunches of Oak Larth 14s. A Pale Gate 1s. 6d.*

pall 1. Fine rich cloth. 2. A robe or cloak. 3. A cloth spread over altar, coffin, or hearse.

pall an apron. *1619: viij leather Palles or fronts 3s.*

pallace, plaster of plaster of Paris.

pallad, pallet a flat board with a handle, for carrying newly-moulded bricks. *1664: they carryed straw sand Bricketables formes pallad boards to the Brickell. 1665: made pallad boards and a bartlement mould.*

pallate, palate sheep's head. *1655: Pallates and sheepes Tongues 2s. 6d. . . 3 doz ½ Pigeons & 3 pallates.*

paller, pallor, palor see PARLOUR

pallet moulded headpiece of boiled leather.

pallet see BEDSTEAD; PALLAD

pallisado pale, pale fence. See PALE. *1720: Garden Gate & Pallisadoes.*

paloster see PILASTER

pamment, pament from pavement: paving tile or brick. Of varying dimensions. The medieval flooring tile was about 5 inches square and ³/₄ inch thick, plain or glazed, or with impressed and glazed designs on the upper surface. From the 16th to the 19th century pamments were up to 12 inches square and 1¹/₂-2¹/₄ inches thick; the 'quarry tile' of the 18th century and after is of the same thickness but only 9 inches square. Pamments are usually of a dull red body, but vary with the type of brickearth, some being almost white. See PATHING TILE. *1618: iiij hundred of brecke & xx pamments vjs. 1671: for 9 ᶜ Pamments & 3 ᶜ Brick 3 li. 11s. 6d.*

pampilion 1. Fur of an unidentified animal used for trimming. 2. A rough, coarse cloth. *1601: a yarde of pampilion iijd.*

pan from the late 17th century many cooking-pans had specialist functions, or at least were referred to by their function e.g. DRIPPING, FRICACY, PUDDING, SAUCE, stew pans.

pane panel of cloth. *1597: one wyndowe Curteyn of saye: 4 panes redde & greene.*

pane, panne see COUNTERPOINT

pannage payment exacted by the lord of the manor from tenants for the right to pasture swine in the lord's wood.

pannell 1. A large wicker basket, sometimes with a lid, for transporting goods, one slung on either side of a horse. See PED. 2. A rough saddle; pad to go under the saddle. *1592: a pannell. 1625: j owlde carte j parnell iij ladders. 1714: a payer of pedds a pannell 5s. 1752: 2 Pannells 1 waggon cover.* See p. 242.

pannier a large basket for transporting goods by horse; see PANNELL. *1310: iiij panyers [sent for carrying eels 3d.]. 1320: in j panyer [bought 1¹/₄d.].*

pantile roof-TILE curved in a ~ section across the width, to overlap its neighbour on one side and be overlapped on the other, and hung on a horizontal LATH by a small protrusion or nib at the top end of the tile. See p. 166. Some are pierced just below the nib for a nail or oak peg. Pantiles, Flanders, or Holland tiles were imported from the Netherlands in the second half of the 17th century, and were being made in Norfolk by about 1700. By the 18th century roofs were measured and estimated by the square, that is 100 square feet, with 170 pantiles to the square. The size and curve of the tile varies with the individual kiln, but a typical 18th-19th century pantile is 14 inches long by 10 inches broad and about half-an-inch thick. Black, dark blue, dark green, and brown glazes were sometimes applied to the upper surface. Partly because the method of hanging relies on the weight of the tile keeping it in place, a pantiled roof has a much shallower slope (30-35° from the horizontal) than a thatched roof (65-70°), giving far less space in the attic. Pantiles will hang on a roof formerly thatched, but the slope renders them liable to be shed. The ridge of a pantiled roof is covered with ridge-tiles of a ∩ section. *1683: The Holland Tyle 6000 at 2 - 15 - 0 pr m' 16 - 10 - 0. 1722: [new barn] 13,142 No. of Pan Tiles Laid on att 20s. p m. [thousand] 13 li. 2s. 10d. 1728: 87 pantyles 26 roof tyle 260 flatt tyle.*

pantler L. panis, *bread*; originally the baker, later the person in charge of the bread etc. in a large household.

pantry L. *paneteria*, OFr. *paneterie*, from L. *panis*, bread. Originally the room in which the bread was kept, but by the late Middle Ages many other items of food, kitchen utensils etc. were stored in the pantry. *1319: [1 key to the door of the] panterie jd. 1647: in the pantree Fowere dressers Three shelves whereof one a hanginge one.*

146

paper up to the 19th century all paper was handmade. Linen, and later cotton, rags were rotted in water for 2-3 weeks, then chopped up and pulped, either by hand or by a hammer or roller powered by water-wheel or windmill. The pulp was spread in a mould in a thin, even layer over a fine wire mesh, often containing a wire outline which made the watermark by thinning the layer, and confined by an open frame, the deckle. When the pulp was evenly spread the deckle was removed, the mould was inverted, and the mushy pulp laid on a sheet of felt; another felt was spread over the pulp and another layer of pulp laid on it, and so on. When the pile was about 18 inches high it was pressed to remove the water, and the sheets of paper separated and hung up to dry. This produced 'laid' paper with an uneven surface; from 1750 a woven wire mesh for the moulds produced 'wove' paper with a smoother surface. Paper was sized with gelatine to prevent the spread of ink. The first papermaking machine was patented in 1807, and softwood pulp was used increasingly from *c.* 1850. The several varieties and qualities of paper are sometimes mentioned in documents, although the use is not often stated. It was sold in QUIRES (25 sheets) and REAMS (500). See CAPPAPER; PRIVY. *1538-9: xvjd. for di' reme of whight paper. iiijd. for di' a bundell of grey paper. 1578: graye paper* [for gunpowder]. *1647: 1 quir of Cap pap 4d. for 2 quir of white pap 9d. 1649: halfe a Reame of Duch pap 6s. 1 whole Reame of other pap 7s.*

par see PAR-YARD

paradise L. *paradisus*, from Old Persian *pairadaesa*, enclosure. Park, pleasure ground, monastic garden. *1557: the litel soler on the sowthe ende of here chaumber stondyng in to the paradise.*

paradise stock slow-growing apple stock on to which other fruit-trees were - and are - grafted for dwarfing. Originally from America, it was first recorded 1526. Trees could be planted 9 feet apart on the square or 6 foot apart in a single row, compared with 18-24 feet for those grafted on seedlings. *1712: As for 30 of thes duarfs appls it is proper to plant Crabs in ther plises and then to graft on them the nixt year and the other 10 may be parades stoks for presant berang the name of thos on Paradise stoks*

> The Gross Rembour of it 2   The Red Calvollo of it 2   The Ladys appl of it 2
> The Grey Reynett 2   The drapdor of it 2

parament, parmt ornament, decoration, richly decorated hanging or garment. *1591: ij paynted parmts one over a table & one over a Cupbord wth two wyndowe Curteyns & a Curteyne rodde.*

parcel a quantity, not necessarily parcelled up. *1711: a parcell of cheese 5 li. . . Three pcells of hay 7 li. . . A pcell of old corn 2 li.*

parcel gilt silver partly gilded, usually on the inner surface of a cup, bowl etc. See GILT. *1588: One bason and Ewer of sylver & psel gilte. 1593: A bright Armor pcell guylt complete.*

parcelled striped, with applied strips. *1513: A gown of Tawny lynyd wt satin of dyapez & prsolyd with blak velvet.*

parclose partition, open screen shutting off space in area; in a church, for a family seat or a side-altar; a screen. *1451: And all that tyme Waryn Herman lenyd ovyr the parklos and lystynd what we seyd. 1506: I bequeth to the repacõn of the pclose ovr the rode lofte unto the roof of the seyd church xls.*

parer 1. A mattock or similar tool for breaking the ground. 2. A sharp knife, used for paring wood, leather etc.; a pruning knife. *1593: [gardener's chamber] 2 parers 1 paire of sheeres.*

parget, spargett OFr. *pargeter, parjeter*, to throw or cast over; to cover a wall with plaster or parget. Now usually applied to ornamental plastering rather than plain work. *1517-18: spargetynge of the howse xs. jd.*

paring, paryngh trimmings, prunings, small branches. *1314: de paryngh in Estwood [sold 32s. 2d.]. 1319: in paryng [of trees 2d.]. 1374: [underwood] De schraggs & Paryngs [of oaks and oak saplings].*

147

Paris see TOUCH

parish ecclesiastical in origin, the parish was the area, with set boundaries, served by a single parish church, to the upkeep and running of which every piece of land within the boundaries contributed through TITHES. The concept of the parish was reinforced in the 16th and 17th centuries, when it was used by successive acts of Parliament as the unit to administer the poor law under the supervision of justices of the peace. The parish was finally secularised in the local government reforms of the 19th century, culminating in the setting-up of parish councils after the Local Government Act of 1894. See TOWN.

parlour OFr. *parleor, parleur*, room for speaking, as in the monastic parlour, the room in which members of the stricter orders were allowed to converse. In houses, the parlour was a private room set apart from the hall, great chamber etc. for the use of the family and in late-medieval and early 16th-century times was called 'Le Drawt' or a similar term indicating withdrawing or privacy. This sense has remained in larger houses until the present day, but from the 16th century, in houses of a size less than the greatest, 'parlour' was a common name for the ground-floor bedchamber, usually without a fireplace, and this use remained throughout the 17th century. A COUNTER is often found in the parlour in this period. The 18th century saw the parlour gradually lose its bedchamber connotation to become a room for sitting or eating: the dining-rooms on the Grand Storey or state floor at Houghton were the Common Parlour and the Marble Parlour. See DRAWING ROOM; DRAWT; WITHDRAWING CHAMBER. *1445: Wetith of yowre brothere John how manie gystis wolle serve the parler and the chapelle at Paston. 1513: In le plor J bedsted [and bedclothes, curtains, hanging, 2 counters, settle, 2 chests, 2 coffers, 3 forms]. 1593: the great plour...the Seled plor...the grene plour. 1665: for planch for the pallor cubord 6d. 27 deales for the paller flore at 16 penc a deal. 2 dayes and a half abought the palor...the plancher over the Paller...stuf for the fram of the paler Tabel 5s. 3d.*

parlour chamber normally the chamber over the parlour.

parman 'par' was an enclosure for animals, pen, fold, yard; the parman was the man looking after it. *1647: [at sheep-shearing] to 3 parmen.*

parpen, parpent, parpoint ML. *parpenus*, OFr. *parpain*, perhaps perpendicular. Squared stone passing through thickness of a wall so that both ends or sides appear. *Chambers's Technical Dict.* 1958: 'Stone wall construction in which the squared stones are laid as stretchers, with occasional courses of headers.' *1621: The Great gate in the inner court is brought up to the height of the arch with ppoint Ashlar... the peeces are brought up wth ppoint Ashlar after the manner of palosters with there pedistalls and capitalls and turned over with a semicircle of stone ppoint to the james of 8 foote over the spantrills of the arch... [porch door] enlarged with stone workmanship and carving with ppoint Janme and a vause.*

parrak, parrok fence, hurdles; the space enclosed, paddock. *1288: [1 hedge between] pinfold & parrak. 1298: [carpentering the gate of the] parrok & [the gate near the bridge 6d.].*

parrel, parelle, pareylle band or collar of rope, chain, or iron fastening the yards to the mast in a sailing-ship. *1466: a trusse parelle, and ij smale parelles xxd... for ij systers for the mayn pareylle ijd.*

parser see PIERCER

partable owned by more than one person. *1603: one ptable sowe in the hands of Gregorie Moore. One other ptable sowe in the hands of Thomas Belward. 1721: for partable wheat in the straw... at 10s. p̱ Comb.*

partisan foot-soldier's weapon developed in the 15th century: a long shaft with spear-shaped tip, often two feet in length and double-edged, and one or two short blades projecting at right angles to the spear for parrying. In the counterfeit or false partisan the blades were absent but there were lugs at the base of the spear to check penetration; it was also used as a BOAR-SPEAR. *1588: one ptyson staffe iijs. iiijd. 1593: 2 ptizans 3 holberds. 1597: one Counterfett Partysant or boar Speare. . . 9 Counterfet ptysayns.*

partle partable, divided. *1590: the ptle chamber.*

partlet, patelet in the 16th century a collar, neckerchief; later a small lacy band or collar to fill the space between a woman's ruff and bodice. *1513: j patelet of blakke velvet.*

partre peartree, pearwood. *1729: for a Black partre frame the inside Guilt with gold and Glass to a painting on paper 4s. 6d..for 5 Black partre frames one the inside guilt with gold & Glasses to the Sd Drawings 9s. 6d.*

parvis, pavis square, slightly convex shield of board or iron, big enough to cover the whole body as a defence against arrows; used particularly by crossbowmen and in sea-fights. Still in use against firearms in the 16th century. *1450: bowes, arows, parvyse, gonnes. 1459: vj wifles, Item j rede pavys. 1466: ij li. generall [paint] to paynt wyth pavyses iijs...a li. of whygthe led iijd..for a li. of rede lede, to the said pavyses ijd.*

parvise originally a court in front of a building, later applied to a porch, particularly a church porch. *1476: I prey yow as ye se hym at the parvyse and ellys where.*

par-yard, par enclosure, yard for animals. See PARMAN. *1621: a padd locke For ye parr gate xd. 1746: In the Parr Yards. Eight Home bred Cattle come three years Old 24£. Ten Budds come two Years Old very small 12£ and Eleven Budds come 1 Year Old 7£.*

Paryce, Paris see TOUCH

pashell pestle used with MORTAR; large pestle-like tool for breaking HEMP or clods. *1592: on pashell & on tow comb. 1592: the pasheling house. 1597: an yron pashill. 1598: one dabbing firke one paysshell.*

passer see PIERCER

pastern, pastrun shackle, hobble of rope for horses, fixed just above the hoofs. *1332: xxxj patruns & langeldes iijd.* See LANGELD.

pastly parsley

pastry originally the room where the paste of flour and water or milk was made for bread, cakes, biscuits etc. to be baked in the BAKEHOUSE. By the 16th century the pastry was also a general store for food and utensils. *1590: pastery [with bakehouse, larder]. 1745: Pastry: 1 Boulting Mill, two Kneeding Troughs,1 Flour Bing, and one Bran Bing, 2 Dresser's, and three shelves, 1 Ladder, 2 Cupboards.*

patching tile see PAMMENT; PATHING TILE

paten, patent shallow plate on which the consecrated bread was laid at the communion. The chalice is often paired with the paten. *1552: One payer of chalys with a patent of Sylver parcell gylt weing xj ounces and iij quarters of an ounce at iijs. viijd.* [per ounce].

path to pave. *1557: pathed the chirche and the quere.*

pathing tile paving tile, PAMMENT. *1589: Of the more sorte of the Largest patching tyle by estimacon one thousand and a halfe xvs...of the Lesser sorte ixs. 1589: ij^c pathyn tyle xs.*

patible, patyble L. *patibulum*, forked yoke placed on the neck of a criminal; gibbet, cross, the horizontal bar of a cross. *1487: to the sustencon of the lyght brenyng biforn the patyble upon the perke* [cross on the rood-loft].

pattens *Prompt. Parv.*: 'Pateyne, fote up berynge'. 1. Slippers. 2. Wooden clogs. 3. High shoes or overshoes, to raise the feet out of the wet and mud, consisting of a wooden sole raised on an iron ring. Pattens were used by the 14th century by medieval priests to cure cold feet in church. In 1464 the patten-makers of London petitioned the king to repeal the Stat. 4 H.V. which forbade them to use aspen wood, which was the best 'and lightest tymbre to make of patyns or clogges'. *1464: a payre patenys iijd. 1474: a gyrdyll, a payre of patanys iiijd. 1593: certin Alders for to make pattens. 1711: Mopps, Candles, Shott & Pattens 1 li.*

patty, patty-pan 1. Pastry in a small pan. 2. The pan itself. 3. A mushroom shape of metal or pot to support the centre of the piecrust when baking. *1745: 2 Dozen Copper Patty pan's 3 Dozen Tin Tart D°. 1787: Three China Patty's for Pickles.*

paunce piece of armour covering the abdomen. *1352: [one pair of] paunces & brassarts.*

paunce pot pot with paunch-like or bulbous shape. See POUNCED. *1588: j paunce pot.*

pavement paving tile, brick, or stone. See PAMMENT. *1591: certein pavement iijs. iiijd.*

pavier pavior or layer of paving. *1620-1: To Richard Nicholson the Pavier 5 li.*

paving tile brick or tile for flooring. See PAMMENT; PATHING TILE. *1620: Pavinge Tyle v^C at iijs. iiijd. C [per hundred] - xvjs. viijd.*

pawler see PARLOUR

paysell, payshell see PASHELL

pax, pax-bread in the unreformed church, small plate or board commonly bearing a picture of the crucifixion or relics of saints, kissed by the priest and congregation. *1459: j paxbrede. 1547: A payer of paxes of Sylver p̱cell gylte.*

payell see PAIL

payer pair. A good illustration of the theory that in the 16th and 17th centuries dipthongs were pronounced sounding all the vowels. 'Pair' is usually spelt paier, payer. Cf. chayer, fayer, dayerie etc.

paytrell see PEITRELL

pear plum several different varieties of pear-shaped plums were grown in the 17th and 18th centuries. See PLUM. *1647: for peare plums 6d.*

pearmain OFr. *permain*, from L. *parmanus*, of Parma; variety of pear known in England since at least the 13th century, and of apples e.g. Worcester pearmain from at least the 16th century. The 'Catholicon Anglicum' MS of 1483 has 'A Parmayn, *volentum*, Anglice a warden,' but F.A. Roach, *Cultivated Fruits of Britain*, p. 122, says the WARDEN was raised by the monks of Wardon, Bedfs., in the 14th century. *1602: a bushell of pomeroies & pearmaines.*

pearser, perser see PIERCER

pease pick pea-hook, a crooked iron head on a long handle for pulling up pea-plants. *1592: a syeth & a sickle & a Pease Pik & 2 weding hooks.*

peast pastry. *1764: one peast brush.*

pech see PITCH

peck a measure of capacity: two GALLONS or a quarter of a BUSHEL. Also the measuring vessel. *1352: j peck [of straw]. . . j pecke [bound with iron].*

ped basket, pannier, or PANNELL, usually in a pair, with lids, slung on either side of a horse. *1592: iiij payer of pedds iiij pr of wantons. 1593: one payre of bakers pedds. 1601: a pedfull of Crafisshes. 1603: xv payer of peades xxijs. vjd. [new]. 1714: a payer of pedds a pannell 5s.*

pedestal base of a column, statue, vase etc. *1733: The uper bed of Whitby Caps to pedestalls in East & West front.*

peel flat, wide blade of iron or wood on long handle used for putting bread, cakes etc. into an OVEN. *1593: [kitchen] 1 iron peele. [pastry] 1 wodden peele. 1673: a pie peele 1s. 1745: 9 wooden Peels, two Iron D°.*

pegtile see PINTILE

pegyn pigeon. *1525: for xxj pegyns vd.*

peistr' L. *peisa, peisia*, weight; counterbalance or weight of a shallow WELL using the beam system of drawing water. *1350: [repairing] le peistr' [of the well]. 1407: [repairs] dil fonts [with] j peystr' [made new].*

peitrel, peytral, paytrell, peystrelle OFr. *peitral*, breast-plate; armour to protect horse's breast; leather strap round the breast. *1464: a croper, a peystrelle, and brode reynys.*

150

1474: a sadyll, a paytrell and a brydall and ij gerthis xs.
pel stake, pale. *1264: j pel [of iron for the fold 4d.].*
pelew, pelowe see PILLOWBEER
pelle see PEEL
pelleax see POLEAXE
penetes see PENNET
pencel Ofr. *pencel*, reduced from *penoncel*, a diminutive of *pennon*. Small pennon, usually on the end of a lance or pole. *1459: ij pencellis of his armys.*
penceling painting with a brush or 'pencil'. Brushes, especially artist's brushes, were called pencils until the 18th century. *1621: rayling, penceling & contoring of wall & stearecases.*
pendon pennon, flag, banner. *1556: Payd for a yd & di. of yellow Buckram to make a Cote for ye Pendon Bearer xvjd. 1565: A Cote of yellow buckram wt ye Grocers arms for ye Pendon bearer.*
penn the barrel of a gun, transferred sense from 'pen' (L. *penna*, feather) - quill-like pipe. *1595: a Corslett a fowling peece caliv' a petronell penn & div'se other pcells of Armoure & weapons.*
penner, penninghorn metal, horn, or leather case for pens. *1463: for a pener and a ynkorne iijd. 1531: a pennere and an Inkhorne ijd. 1587: v hornyng pennynghornes xvjd.*
pennet, penetes It. *pennito*, OFr. *penites*, barley-sugar. *1592: vj oz. of penetes vjd.*
penthouse, pentice, pentis OFr. *apentis*, L. *appendicium*, appendage. *Prompt. Parv.*: 'Pentyce, of an howse ende.' Addition to a house, with a roof of one slope only; roof over beehives, ovens etc. See p. 28. *1319: [daubing the said walls] & del apentis xxiijd. 1665: two pentices for the two ovens. 1681: 9 skeeps of bees with Stooles and penthouses 6 li.*
pepper long pepper: the immature fruit-spikes of *Piper (chavica) officinarum* and *P. longum*, dried and ground into powder. White pepper: fully ripe, dried berries ground into powder. Black pepper: berries dried when not quite ripe and ground. Peppercorn: whole, dried berries of *P. nigra* and allied species. The berries, if received whole, would be ground in pepper-querns. *1444: unum par dez pepyquens. 1500-1: for long peper ijd. 1562: a qter of longe pepp xijd. 1587: iij oz of longe pep xviijd.*
perafrase paraphrase. Erasmus' *Paraphrases of the New Testament*, translated and published by Nicholas Udall, was ordered by Edward VI's Injunction of 1547 to be set up in all parish churches, where the parishioners could read it. *1591: one byble vjs. one perafras iiijs. 1603: one bible & one Pherofreses viijs.*
perch a lineal measure, dating from Anglo-Saxon times, of 5½ yards (16½ feet) or 7 yards (21 feet), used up to modern times, and often known as a rod or pole. There were 40 perches to the furlong and to the ROOD, and an ACRE was 40 x 4 perches.
perch 1. A perch for a hawk or a bird. 2. A wooden bar to hold lights or to form the cross-piece of a screen. 3. A clothes-horse, rail for garments. Caxton, *Boke for Travellers*: (*c*.1484): 'on the perch hongen your clothes, mantelles, frockes, clokes, cotes, doblettes, furres, wyntere clothes and of somer'. See PERK; pp. 166, 241. *1310: [making] j perche [in the hall with nails 6½d.]. 1597: broad foot of a hauks perke.*
perfume cloves cloves were used in pomanders and a PERFUMING-PAN for sweetening the air. *1649: perfume cloves 6d.*
perfuming pan OED quotes Bulleyn *Dialogue against Pestilence* 1564-78: 'Forgette not sweete perfumes of Rose water, cloves, maces, vinegar in a perfuming pan'. *1637: 1 pfuming pann.*
periwinkle the shellfish, winkle, *Littorina littorea*. At Stiffkey in 1595 winkles were bought only in April and May. See LOR.
perk as PERCH 1-3; loft, rood-beam; frame against which sawn timber was stood to dry. *1487: to the sustentacon of the lyght brenyng biforn the patyble upon the perke. 1496: To ye newe*

edificacon and repacon of ye perk there v mrks. 1527: the light...upon the perk. 1587: the shelves of the shopp ijs. the swift & the perke iiijd. the lanterne & the sockyt iiijd.

perryll ? pearl. *1474: a box with sylke and perryll ijs.*

persian cloth woven in England of Persian silk for lining bonnets, cloaks etc. *1730: 16 yards white persian £1 4s.*

pertrich partridge. Until the third quarter of the 17th century the only partridge was the English or common partridge, *Perdix perdix*, now called the grey partridge, although the adjective 'grey' dates only from the 19th century. In the Stiffkey accounts of 1593, 12 partridges were bought on 14 July, 16 'spent of our store' between 1 Jan. and 26 March and another 148 of store between 24 Sept. and 31 Dec. This suggests that partridges may have been kept as domestic fowl. No partridges appear in the Houghton accounts of 1647-9. Sir Thomas Browne, writing in the middle of the 17th century: 'there bee heere very great store of partridges yet the french Red legged partridge is not to be met with'. The red-legged or French partridge, *Alectoris rufa*, was introduced in the 17th century and apparently did not colonise successfully until 1790, but it is now much more numerous than the native species. *1466-7: to a man that brout pertriches ijs. iiijd. 1593: to duckes man for bringing a dussen ptridges ijs. vjd. . . [store] ij dussen partiches viijs.*

pertrykur English form of L. *pertricarius*, partridge catcher. *1321: [expenses] j pertrykur [for 6 days].*

pestle, pestell a leg of meat. *1464: a quarter beffe and ij pestelle porke ijs.*

pestle see MORTAR; PASHEL

pesyn peas

petticoat 1. For men: up to the 16th century a short coat worn under the doublet. 2. For women: usually a skirt, worn either as a visible garment or underneath an outer gown. *1593: 1 peticoate of Crimsine buffin lyned wth Crimsine bayes xiijs. iiijd. 1598: one redd blanquett peticoate.*

petronell L. *pectus*, breast. From *c.* 1450 a handgun; by the end of the century the term was superseded by HARQUEBUS. In the 16th and 17th centuries a petronell was a short carbine or long pistol, used by cavalry and fired with the butt resting on the chest; the soldier using a petronel. *1588: For skarfes and capps for petronelles. 1591: the halfe of a petronell vs. 1595: a caliv' a petronnell penn.*

pettipointstitch also called bent stitch. Embroidery where each stitch is made diagonally across the threads, working either horizontally or diagonally. *1636: one Cushion case of pettipointstitch.*

pettystall pedestal. *1665: 2 scrowls, one pettystall, one stone to wash hands at.*

pewter silvery-grey alloy of tin and lead in the proportion of 4:1 by weight; other metals are sometimes added or substituted for lead. Being relatively cheap, this was the main metal for domestic tableware up to the 18th century. It was often inventoried by weight rather than number of utensils, and sometimes the set of pewter was referred to as a 'garnish'. As it could be recast the worn-out pewter was exchanged for new vessels. 'Counterfeit' means made to a pattern. *1464: bowt of the pewtier...di' a garnyshe of counterfet vessellys, conteynynge xxix li. prise the li. iiijd; and di' a garnyshe of playne vessellys, conteynenge xliiij li., prise the li. iijd.; and ther of my mastryr payd hym in old vessellys, c li. prise the pound ijd.; and the same tyme my mastyr toke hym in mony, iijs. vjd. 1465: a garnyshe of counterfet vessellys, that is to say, xij platers, xij dyshes, and xij sawsers xiiijs. 1513: J pewdymorter wt a pestell. 1588: In Pewter thre chardgers, xxxj platters, Lvij dishes, xxxiiij smale dishes, xij smale plates, L Sawsers, xviij porryngers, xiiij pewter Candlestickes, ij basons, ij Ewers of pewter, ij pewter pecys, two Washinge basons of pewter, ij standinge potts of pewter, v owlde plates, and vij chamber pottes, prysed vj li. 1592: A box wth two*

152

stamps for pewter...a danske pewter pott...A Garnish of pewter wth his Crest on it xxxiijs. iiijd. 1593: Pewter wayed to the Cooke 6 stone 9 pownde. Pewter weide besides to the howse 10 stone 9 pownde v li. ijs. 1595: [yeoman] In pewter One Charger xxxij platters xxxiiij Dysshes v platters xx porryngers one peece iij wasshinge basons one Cullinder iij Frute Dysshes xix sawsers ij pewter potts iiij li. 1637: a sisterne of pewter...voider of pewter. 1648: changinge of Fortie pound of Pewter vjs. viijd. 1647: One pewter case wth Fower drawers locks and keys. 1662: for 2 posts for the puter Case & Silinge 1s. 6d. 1668: For one pewter case with drawers Full Furnish with pewter 5 li. 10s. 1764: A Chest of French pewter, with Townshends Armes, engraved in a Mantle, Viz Twenty two dishes, One Fish plate, Six dozen plates, one dozen and a half, Soup dº, Four dozen pewter dishes, Nine Dozen plates, one dozen pewter rings, Twenty eight Cheese plates.

peygys pigs

peyk see PIKE. *1525: for iiij peyks ijs. xjd.*

peystrelle see PEITREL

phan see FAN

phane vane. *1664: mending two phanes on the prospect.*

pherofreses see PERAFRESE

pheasant there were pheasants in Roman and Saxon England, but probably only in captivity. This was *Phasianus colchicus colchicus*. The pheasant with the white-ringed neck, *P. colchicus torquatus*, was introduced in the 11th century in captivity, but was feral by the end of the Middle Ages. Accounts of the 16-17th centuries suggest that the pheasant was not common in Norfolk: only 10 were bought for Stiffkey Hall in 1593, and none appear in the Houghton accounts for 1647-9. The pheasant is not mentioned in Sir Thomas Browne's account of Norfolk birds. Pheasants have a very low success rate in breeding in the wild, and it was not until the later 18th century, when breeding them for shooting became an established practice, that they became common. *1467: xij fesauntes, pryse xijs. 1533: to Fulm'ston s'vante for bryngunge iij fesands. 1588: cloth feson color. 1593: To Mr Funting his man for bringing a brase of phesants vjd.*

phillye filly

piccher man who pitches the corn on to wagon or stack. *1329: [harvest] j piccher.*

picforke see FORK

pick the bar-tailed godwit, *Limosa lapponica*, also called the SCAMBLE. *1593: iij picks ixd. 1655: 6 Pluver 4 Pickes 1 Corlew.*

pick, pick-axe implement related to the MATTOCK for digging, breaking clods, loosening stony or clay ground, etc., usually with a point on one side of the head and a narrow blade on the other. See p. 242; PICOYSE. *1352: j pickax.*

picker toothpick or earpick. *1671: a picker, a box combe, an ivory knife 2s.*

pickerell, pikerell see PIKE

pickle stand stand to hold various types of pickle. *1781: 2 pickle stands.*

pickling cloth, picklin, pyghtelyng Forby: 'a sort of very coarse linen, of which seedsmen make their bags, dairy maids their aprons, &c.'. Cloth used in the pickling of meat in brine. *1415-16: [8 ells of cloth] de Pyghttelyng vijd. 1665: picklyn cloathe ell wide 23½ yards at 9d. p̄ yard.*

pickters pictures

picther see PITCHER

picoyse, pikoys a PICK-axe. *Prompt. Parv.* : 'Pykeys, mattocke.' *1273: [mending] piccosier' iiijd. 1300: [making] j pycose jd. 1313: j picoise[bought 8d.]. 1335: [smith] ij pikoye [repairing 4d.]. 1344: [laying] j pikoys [with steel bought for the same 1d.].*

pie plate large plate on which to set a pie for the table. *1589: a Pye plate.*

153

pier, peer square pillar on either side of door, window, gate, arch etc. *1665: sawing of two drawing pl: of a post stock for a peere for the gate betweene the Cort yards 11 foot long 18 inches square.*

piercer, parser 1. A gimlet. 2. A carpenter's brace, into the jaws (pod, pad) of which metal bits could be fitted for boring. *1319: j martell ij wymbles & ij pceurs. 1546: for parserpods jd. 1584: a wymble a parser a hammer a shave. 1590: v passers and vij old bits. 1590: viij parser podes & xxv other smaule toules. 1593: one thixell ij pearsers ij wimbills. 1654: a Passer-Bitt 2d.*

pier glass tall mirror, originally for the space between two windows. *1709: 1 glasse Peer between the windows. carving round the Peer between the windows. 1764: a Large pier Looking Glass, over the Chimney piece. Two Small d⁰.*

pig oblong ingot of iron, silver, lead etc., of no specific size or weight. *1621-2: 8 fodder of lead being 67 piggs.* See FODDER.

piggin, pigen small wooden PAIL with one longer stave projecting above the rest to form the handle. See p. 72. *1709: 2 piggins. 1764: one handle Pigen.*

pightle, picle, pitle, pixhtell small angular enclosed piece of ground. *1587: Lease of a Pixhtell.*

pig iron 1. Iron in a pig - see above. 2. An iron plate hung between the spit and the fire when the heat from the open hearth was too great. *1709: a pig iron. 1723: two spitts a Pigg Iron Barr and Hake. 1745: one Poker, two Pigg Iron's. 1764: Two Gridirons Three Pigirons.*

pike the pike or luce, *Esox lucius*, found in ponds, moats, and rivers, was one of the staple fishes of the Middle Ages and after. Sir Thomas Browne: 'The Rivers lakes and broads abound in the Lucius or pikes of very large size'. William Harrison in 1587: 'The pike as he ageth, receiveth diverse names, as from a fry to a gilthed, from a gilthed to a pod, from a pod to a iacke, from a iacke to a pickerell, from a pickerell to a pike, and last of all to a luce.' As the most usual form in accounts is 'pickerell', this may have been the common term for all ages of pike. *1293: vᶜ pykerell [bought for stocking the ditch [moat] of the manor 16s. 3d.]. 1312: xxj pykerell [bought 3s.]. 1319: xx pikerell & mˡmˡ de Roches [bought for the fishpond 5s. 6d.]. 1319: ij pykes [bought for the stews 12d.]. 1502-3: pro pykerell [and eels and] pyk [for different weeks 4 li. 14s. 4d.]. 1582: pickerells iij bo' pric ijs.*

pike a 10-inch steel pointed head mounted on an ash shaft up to 18 feet long, Developed in Switzerland in the 15th century, and used by English foot-soldiers against cavalry in the 16th and 17th centuries. Controversially issued to the Home Guard in the Second World War. *1595: one pycke and ij halfe pyckes wth other staves vs. 1597: A Corslett furnyshed: lent to Mr Wootton: p Tho Philpott: but no pyke.*

pike pan long, narrow oval pan for cooking pike. *1459: iij pike pannys of brasse.*

pikerel(l) see PIKE

pikforc' see FORK

pilaster pillar of rectangular section abutting or engaged to a wall.

pile large wooden stake, pointed at the lower end, driven into river, pond, moat etc. to act as support for bridge, building, pier etc. *1388: [3 days making] pyles [for the same bridge 8d.]. 1579: one hundred alder pyles. 1620: For plancking and piling the scullery and chimneyes in the moat...For the piling and plancking of the foundation of the fourth turret or butterace. 1621: a Crane to drive downe pyles.*

pile powder medicine for piles (hæmorrhoids). *1537-8: xxjd. for iij li. of pyle powder.*

pillar, piller upright bar of a window, MULLION. *1664: new finished the pillers & cheekes that were decayed about the said windowes. . . finished seu'all decayed places on the borders & pillers of the said windowes, repaired the piller of a windowe in the Armory chamber and mortred the glasse there.*

pill, pilling, pilled the bark or rind of HEMP was pilled or peeled from the stem, usually

154

after it had been broken or beaten. *1594: pilled hempe in a chest in weight ij stone xij li. viijs.*
pillion 1. A light saddle. 2. A cushioned pad behind the saddle for a second rider. See
MALEPILLION. *1597: j womans pillyon. j male pillyon with male girths. 1636: one saddle, 1 pillyn.*
pillory an instrument of punishment for offenders in relatively minor matters. A wooden
frame of two movable boards with slots enclosing the wrists and neck, mounted on a post
so that the offender had to stand. *1328: [repairing] le pillori.*

pilloster see PILASTER

pillow from the Middle Ages pillows were stuffed with down (the best), feathers, flock,
wool, herbs, or straw. A pillow could also be a cushion or a padded movable seat. *1597:
2 Longe Cusshyns Case of clothe of golde...one olde Cusshyng Case of clothe of tyssewe Itm a pillowe longe
for one of them Itm one longe pillowe of redd leather.*

pillowbeer pillowcase, pillow-slip. *1513: iiij corse pelewbers v fyn pelewbers. 1595: fether
pillowes wth beeres.*

pin metal pins, usually of steel, were very common, from the very small gold-plated pins
used for pinning ruffs together to the large ones e.g. French pins used for ornament, but
being of small value were not usually included in inventories. *1587: i dozin pynnes vijs. iij
papers of pynns xijd. half a doz. french pynns vs. certeyn loose pynns ixd. i doz. french pinns viijs.*

pin peg for hanging hats and clothes. *1751: a boot Jack & row of Pins.*

pincers tool for grasping, holding, nipping, comprising two legs joined together by a pin.
1587: ij payer of pynsins j payer xijd. 1590: Axe, hatchet & pynsers.

pindar man, chosen by manor court, in charge of impounding stray animals. *1712: We
chose for Pindar Francis Jackson and allow him Two pence a head for ev'y Beast hee shall lawfully pound.*

pinfold sheep-fold; pound for stray animals. *1312: [mending the walls round] le pynfolde
[garden and other places]. 1318: CC de middelspiks [for the kiln and for] le pinfolde. 1342: [wall on
the south part] dil pontfolde.*

pink small square-rigged ship with narrow overhanging stern; any narrow-sterned small
ship. See HOY.

pinpillow pincushion. *1513: J pynpelowe of prple velvet wt xd. J pynpelowe of Grenevelvet wt iiijs.
ijd.*

pinson high thin-soled shoe of fine leather, worn with PATTENS. Obsolete by 1600. *1465:
a peyr botys and pynsons iijs. iiijd. 1537: a payre of pynson shoyse vjd.*

pinson see PINCERS

pint unit of liquid volume measurement, 34.66 in³ imperial. Two pints = 1 quart, 8
pints = 1 GALLON. Fresh butter was always measured in pints, salt butter in pounds.

pintile see FLAT TILE

pintle OE *pintel*, the penis. Penis; transferred to a bolt or pin. *1637-9: shewinge his pintle.*

pin trace see TRACE

pipe butt, measure or container of wine, 126 gallons. In general, a large barrel. *1352: j
pipe [for bread]. 1463: a pype of Gaskyn wyne, the pryse is v li. 1584: A quarter of a pype of Muscadyn.
1636: forty foure hoggesheades thre pipes. 1637: a cooler 2 dales 2 pipes & other brewing vessels.
1738: Two Wine pipes One Water pipe 14s. See TERCE.*

pipe cylindrical conductor of liquid; of lead, wood (especially elm), or pottery. See PLUG.
*1396: [plumber making] j pype [for] le cist'ne [with] sood [bought]...[carpenter for 2 days making a
paling fence before] le pipe [of the said cistern 8d.].*

pipkin small or medium-sized three-legged pot, usually of earthenware but sometimes of
bronze or iron. *1562: iiij pypkins & iij ladles vijd. 1583: Pypkings iij bo. pᵉ viijd. 1593: a dussen
pipkins ijs. 1671: [white earthenware] 3 galand pipkinge.*

pistolet the Italian town of Pistoia was famed for iron and steel; the adjective from the town was *pistolese*, which was applied to a dagger or short sword, and its diminutive *pistoletto* was transferred to a small hand HARQUEBUS, or pistol. *1588: iij cass' of pistoletts & one more xlvjs. viijd.*

pitch black or dark brown substance, viscous when heated and hard when cold, made by boiling or distilling tar or turpentine and used as a waterproofing agent, for branding animals, and for LINKS. See BRAND. *Prompt. Parv.*: 'Pyk, or pyche'. *1300: in xij li. picis & tar [for the boat 15½d.]. 1466-7: al my spesche and tere. 1500-1: iij ston' of pycch ijs. 1595: tarre. A pytch pan, brands. 1665: One barrell with pitch...in wch 30 li. wch was burnt at the fire for the triumph at Brome for his Maties birth day & restoracon' iijs. 1665-6: 3 li. of pech 5d.*

pitcher large jug or ewer, usually of pottery, normally with a lip or spout. *1264: iiij pichers jd. q'. 1264: in pichers [and cups against the coming of the new lord 4s. 4d.]. 1326: ij Picher jd.*

pitcher man that pitched the sheaves of corn on to the cart or stack. *1327: [3 carters] ij picther [1 stacker].*

pitchfork see FORK

pit net see NET

pitole pithole, pit, pond. *1665: hanging the gat at the pitoles.*

pit sand see SAND

pix see PYX

pixhtell see PIGHTLE

piye possibly PITCH. See Z. *1417: in Rosyn & piye [bought for the cistern 1d.].*

placard, placket 1. A thin plate of armour worn over or under CUIRASS. 2. An apron or petticoat. 3. An attached pocket. 4. An opening at the top of the skirt. *1522: for makyng of a payer of forstockes & placard iiijd. 1588: one preme cote [armour] covered wt wrought velvet wt placards therto belonging.*

place brick 1. Moulded BRICK laid out to dry on a 'place' before firing. 2. In the 19th century, an underfired brick from a kiln. *1621: Carriage of ij mil^s plase Brick att 5 lod.*

plad plaid, twilled woollen cloth with checked or tartan pattern. *1745: Plad Room. One Bed Bedstead and Plad hangings . . . one Pair of Plad Window Curtains.*

plaintain water the plantain, *Plantago major*, was said to cure all manner of diseases. Nicholas Culpeper 1653: 'The juice, clarified and drank for days together...helps excoriations or pains in the bowels, the distillations of rheum from the head, and it stays all manner of fluxes, even women's courses, when too abundant'. The leaf stopped bleeding, and the seed was used against dropsy, falling sickness, yellow jaundice etc. *1654: 1 pinte of Plantaine Water wth a jugg 9d.*

planch PLANK, BOARD. *1665: dowe for planch for the pallor cubord 6d.*

plancher floor, platform, upper floor, staging, roof. *1313: [clates for] Le plauncher [of the house above the gate]. 1323: [carpenter for 3 days making the door of the cart-house] & Le plauncher [of the solar, dairy and mending the fowl-house 12d.]. 1521-2: of ye costs For the plawncering of ye kechyn...For CCC Fett of borde ye p'ce iiijs. vjd....For C peces of tymbyr ye p'ce iijs. iiijd...For ye Dormant ijs. iiijd. 1585: on the plancher. 1591: a bording bed fastened to the plancher wth nailes. 1600-2: The plancher rotten by rayne falling through the roofe being uncovered & the leades not repayred. 1607-8: for j & fortie foote of board to make the plancher xijs. 1663-4: planchered pt of the vance ruff. 1665: to make an end of the plancher over the Paller...shored up the plancher. . . take up the plancher from under the flatt leads ov' the painting chamber.*

planchering flooring, putting in a wooden floor. *1446: the plawncering of ye Kechyn...For CCC Fett of borde ye p'ce iiijs. vjd...For C peces of tymber ye p'ce iijs. iiijd...For ye Dormont iijs. iiijd... For caryng of ye borde from town iiijd. 1662: plainchering of the washhouse. . . plainchering the Chancll stooles 2s. 3d. 1665: for planing 240 score and 5 deal planke for planchering in wch by square Measure*

6800 feet at six score to the hundred.

planchering speken floorboard nail. See PLANCHER NAIL. *1665: planchering spekens 5 pound 2s. 6d.*

plancher nail ⌐-shaped floorboard nail, square in section with tapering stem. *1343: m¹ C de planchernayl iijs iiijd.*

plank at some periods, a plank was thicker than a BOARD, which seems to have had a maximum thickness of 1-1½ inches - see quot. 1664. *1344: Lx durnayl [for] plankes [on bridge]. 1397: [cutting] plankes [for the gates of] Le Launde. 1402: planks [of oak for] les Outloddeles. 1664: sawing of one two inch planke stocke 12¼ foot long 11¾ inch broad...one inch board stocke 13 inch broad 12¼ foot long...cutting one four inch planke & cutting the same into three joyce... Two drawing planke of the Eavesboards...One stocke of deale 2 inch thicke 10 foot long 12 inch broad 10 planke.*

planyng a carpenter's wooden plane. *1595: ij vices ix planyngs.*

plash to interlace bent-down branches and stems to form a hedge. *1679: 2 workmen to plash the hedges behind the garden.*

plass plaice. *1647:12 plasses 5s.*

plaster of Paris originally prepared from gypsum of Montmartre, which when dehydrated by burning is $2CaSO_4.H_2O$. Used as mortar and for moulds, casts etc. *1485: [5 stone of] playster paryce. 1621-2: To Stanion in full of 203 yards of plaistr of paris 21 li. 15s.*

plat, plot map, plan; to draw. *1582: where there is a plat drawen for the erreccion and settinge upp of a newe stable. 1620: iij Daies Drawinge platt for the Bridge 22d. p die . . . 5 daies in plattinge at 22d. p die. 1621: buteth endways one the garden acording to the plote.*

plate armour consisting of plates of steel or iron; MAIL was composed of rings or scales. *1352: [one pair of gauntlets of] plates. 1588: ij cotes of plate j covered wth yellowe fustyan, thother wth crane culored fustyan xxxiijs. iiijd. one cote of Plate xs.*

plate timber beam laid horizontally, as in sole-plate (at base of wall), wall-plate (beam under the eaves). *1728: 2 pieces for plate 14' long. 1730: 12 Plates 11 ft Long 5 in. by 10 in. 6 Plates 12 ft 6 Long 5 in. by 10 in. 2 Plates 32 ft Long 5 in. by 10 in.*

plate for lights flat support for CANDLES, using a spike or socket. *1588: Two copper plates for Candelles. 1589: j plate to set candeles on iiijd. 1592: Two hanginge platts xijd. 1593: [hall] 4 plates for lights. 2 great plates for lights belonging to the great plour ijs. viijd. 1602: Two Laten Kandelstickes & A latten plate to sett a lyght in.*

plate glass a French invention, used in England from the beginning of the 18th century but only manufactured in England from 1773. Though flat compared with CROWN glass, it was thick, heavy, and expensive until 1838, when a method of polishing the thinner and cheaper sheet GLASS was discovered. *1737: 8 Squ of plate Glass put in & 15 Squ of Crown glass.*

plate lock lock in which the works pivot on an iron plate. *1620: [smith] a plate lock with a double key and a single key 1 li...a plate lock with two key-holes 1 li. 1664: one plate locke for a woodhole door by the plour vjd. See LOCK; STOCKLOCK.*

plate of venison the thin part of the breast of a deer. *1593: give' to my Ladie butts man for bringing a plate of venison xijd. 1665: One bucke killed this day Of wch sent to Culford j plate j haunch j shoulder & the umbles One plate given to Mr Brampton*

platter large flat dish or plate usually of TREEN (wood) or PEWTER; sometimes silver. *1459: [silver] xij platers, weiying xjˣ xij unces. 1468: iijᶜ platers, price the c, iiijs. 1584: iij Trene platters wth other Trene vessell. 1584: halfe A dosyn pewter platters iiijs. 1589: 17 platters 16 pewter dishes eleven trencher playtz 3 platter playtz. 1595: [pewter] xxxij platters xxxiiij Dysshes v platters. 1649: a woodinge platter for to make Capons meate in 3d.*

plauncher, plawncher see PLANCHER, PLANCHERING

playing tables board or table for playing games, particularly backgammon. *1588: payer of playeinge table.*

playse, playz plaice, a right-eyed flatfish, *Pleuronectes platessa. 1306: in playz ijd.*

playstr wall-plaster. *1386: playstr [bought 8d.].*

pleasure-ground the formal garden next to the house in the 17th and 18th centuries. *1745: A Moveing Scaffold in the Pleasure Ground.*

plete to plead in legal sense. *Early 16th cent.: non of ye brothers and systers zall plete wt othyr for no manr of cawse.*

plodd see PLAD

plonkett see PLUNKET

plot see PLAT

plough by the 13th century the plough in general use in Norfolk was a two-wheeled plough drawn by 2 horses, and this remained the norm until the 20th century. See pp. 144, 242. Arthur Young (1804) wrote that the wheelless or swing plough was used in the S.W. of the county. Oxen were occasionally used. In inventories and accounts of the 16th and 17th centuries ploughs were of low value, often only a few shillings. They were usually described as 'a plough with the furniture or gear', and a 'plough' may often have been the basic beam without wheels or fittings. The ploughmaker or ploughwright made only the basic plough; the wheels were supplied by a wheelwright or ploughwheelmaker. The main parts of the traditional wooden plough were:-

beam the main longitudinal beam of the plough, to which everything else was attached.

breast the front of the mouldboard; the mouldboard itself.

cock or foot Fitzherbert 1523, of the wheelless plough: 'The plough fote is a lyttell pece of wodde, with a croked ende set before in a morteys in the ploughe beame, sette fast with wedges, to dryve uppe and downe, and it is a staye to order, of what depenes the ploughe shall go.'

coulter the vertical knife that cut through the soil.

head 1. The share beam - the beam or frame to which the share was fixed. 2. The front of the plough, that is the assembly of the wheels to which the draught harness was attached.

kipchit, kipchip, kipchep the share-beam or head.

lines the cords or leather straps forming the reins or controls between the draught beasts and the ploughman.

mall the hammer or the mallet carried on the plough to break clods.

mouldboard the wooden or (later) metal plate, slightly concave, that turned the soil after it had been cut by the coulter and share.

sele iron or wooden part of the horse-collar, to which the draught harness was attached.

share horizontal pointed iron blade that cut the soil and transferred it to the mouldboard. Also called the vomer.

sheath, skeath, skerche, skife Markham 1613: 'The skeath is a piece of wood of two foote and a half in length, and two inches in thickness; it is driven extreamely hard into the plough-beam, slopewise'. It held the beam and the share-beam together.

shottell, shuttle bolt or bar to secure the share and mouldboard to the beam.

staff staff with a small iron spade-like head, used to clear the share, coulter and mouldboard of soil. See ACRE-STAFF; SPANISH STAFF.

tail handle or handles of the plough, held by the ploughman.

tem L. *temo*, main beam of the plough.

trace ropes, leather straps, chains by which the plough was attached to the collar or yoke

of the draught beasts.
vomer see share

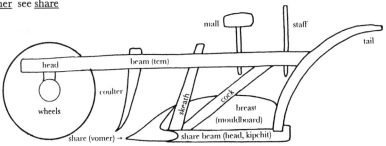

Diagram of a two-wheeled plough, showing the main parts

1306: j kipchit vd. ob. 1343: [making] iiij kippes iiij [heads] vj skerches [and making 10 pair of] seles. 1482-3: [for 5 pairs] lez plowelynys xjd. . . [for 6 pairs] lez trayses & plowelynes xvjd. 1584: j plough & ploughgeere wth two collers. 1589: one plought wth ij payer of plought trace. 1593: 1 other plowe wanting sheare Coulter & beamenayle. 1597: one bullocks plough: 2 horse plowes. 1636: 2 plows at 3s. pese... 6 plow beames at 6d. pesse...14 plow tayles at 3d. pese...30 plow heads and skifes at 2d...9 brestes For plowes at 2d....3 plow Cockes at 6d. pese...In the home yardes...12 plow beames at 6d...56 plow Tayles at 3d...514 plow heads brestes and Skifes. 1647: 2 new plowes heads & shottell 8s. 1654: a new Plough 4s. 6d. and 2 heades 1s. 4d. 1655: 1 plough beame 1s. 11d. 2 heads 1 breast and 1 Skife 2s. 8d. & 2 pair of plough wheeles 3s. . . Barraway and Ant. Garrett 6 [days] a peece at plough wth Bulls and Harrowes in Barly Siel. 1662: plow starf 9d. 1738: plow sales. 1802: 2 Pair of Plough Collars and Seals 10s.

plough possibly a domestic version of the barley-plough, a narrow shovel for turning the barley when malting; a dustpan. *1709: 4 plows, 5 brooms, 2 brushes.*

plough scot, plouscot customary payment to the lord for the use of a plough and team. *1313: in Candelscot jd. in plouscot jd.*

plough steer ox, bullock for pulling the plough. *1631: a paire of plough steeres.*

plover the green plover, lapwing, or peewit, *Vanellus vanellus*, occurs in household accounts, as, does the golden plover *Pluvialis apricaria*, and the grey plover *P. squatarola*. The baste plover has not been identified. *1593: grey plover. . . green plover. . . ij teales a wigin a baste plou'.* See PUET.

pluck heart, liver, and lungs of an animal. *1593: a qt of Veale & a plucke ijs. xd.*

plug tree-trunk bored through to form a waterpipe to act as a conduit or drain. *1665: one other plugg peece for the moate 10 foot long 8 peeces 43s. 6d. . . almost fitted the two trunkes for the pluggs to let the water out of the moate...laid downe the trunkes & fitted up the heads of the sluce to let the water out of the moate & finished the pluggs...boared a plugg to let the wast water out of the moate.*

plum throughout the Middle Ages plums were generally split and sun-dried. The damson in its several forms was the most popular. With the revival of fruit-growing in England in the early 16th century new varieties were introduced; in 1597 Gerard claimed to have 60 varieties in his garden. Many introductions and varieties followed. *1715: Fruit Trees in the Beach Garding. Plums. 2 Morocco   3 whit pedrigon   2 Musal   3 blew perdrigon   2 Fortheringham   6 Green Geage   3 queen Mother   2 Emperial.*

plumbe see CLOCK

plunket, plonkett OFr. *plunkié, plonquié,* a woollen cloth of a lead-grey or light blue colour; the colour itself. *1466: j brode clothe of plonkett xlvs. vd. 1481: xij yardes Plounkett chamlet at iiijs. iiijd.*

159

plush see PLASH

pod, pode, pad see PIERCER

points ties, tagged lace to keep breeches, hose etc. up, or to attach pieces of armour. Cf. Shakespeare *1 Hen. IV.* ii.4: '*Fal.* These nine in buckram that I told thee of, - *Prince.* So, two more already. *Fal.* Their points being broken, - *Poins.* Down fell their hose.' *1463: j doseyn armynge poyntys iijd. ij doseyn red poyntys iiijd. 1589: i grosse of lether points xd.*

poke, poake, pook small sack, bag. *1488-9: for the poke iiijd. 1591: iiij boult pooks. 1592: one bushell poocke. 1599: a maunde a pooke sack. 1595: viij saking pookes. 1738: a Linen Poke 6d.*

pol *Prompt. Parv.*: 'Pol, or head. *Caput.*' *1386: j pol [for] le Chymene iiijd.*

polayn, polerne piece of armour to cover the knee. *1588: one blake Armore of Proofe, one Burganet, one Gorgett, & ye poleernes xxxiiijs. iiijd.*

poldavi, poldavy derived from Poldavide, on the coast of Brittany. A coarse stout canvas, used *inter alia* for sailcloth. Manufactured in England from the middle of the 16th century. *1481: French cloth, that is a piece poldavy of xx yerdes iij quarters.*

pole-axe, pollax, pollex, pollux weapon of varying forms: 1. A short-staffed cavalry weapon with a broad axe blade and a sharp point opposite it. 2. A staff 5½-7 feet long with a spike at either end and a broad axe blade and a hammer-head or spike opposite it. *1449: ij or iij schort pelleaxis to kepe with doris. 1465: Sum of hem havyng rusty polexis and byllys. 1584: A Pollex iiijs. vjd. 1593: 2 ptizans 3 holberds 1 pollax 1 glathe xvjs.*

polleson piece of armour for the head or shoulder. *1459: j garbrasse Item j polleson Item, vj payre grevys.*

pollett small POULDRON, armour to protect the shoulder.

pollett small pole. *1266: viij pollett [for the wall of the barn 12½d.].*

pomatum scented ointment, especially for dressing the hair. *1747: paid for a pot of pomatum 6d.*

pome-citron, pomcidron, pumsitturne large CITRON. Barnaby Googe, *Heresbach's Husb.* 1586: 'If they [citrons] be very great and rounde like Pompeons, they call them Pomcidrons'. *1649: Orenge & Lymons 4s. 6d. for 1 li. pumsitturne 5s.*

pomegranate the fruit of *Punica granatum*, native to E. Asia and N. Africa, and valued as a dessert, a treatment for oral ailments, and, because of its abundant seeds, as an aphrodisiac and aid to fertility. *1466: for xvj pongarnettes ijs. vjd.*

pomell stonemason's square punch.

pomell ornamental knob or ball at the summit of a building, top of a tent-pole, flag-pole; finial. *1343: iij li. rosine [and wax for varnishing the] pomel [of the hall].*

pomeroy 'apple of the king.' Variety of apple, grown from the 16th century at the latest to the 19th century. *1602: a bushell of pomerois & pearmaines.*

pomp see PUMP

pongarnet see POMEGRANATE

pontfolde see PINFOLD

popeler *Prompt. Parv.* gives 'Popelere, byrd (or schovelerd...). *Populus* . . . Schovelerd, or popler, byrd (schoveler, or popelere, K. scholarde or poplerd, S. schones bec, or popler byrd, P.) *Populus.*' The shoveller, *Anas clypeata*, is a migratory duck which, among other names, is also known as the spoonbill. The true common white spoonbill, *Platalea leucorodia*, breeds in Holland and may have bred in England before the draining of the fens; it could have been known in 15th-century England, although the hangings on which it features may have been imported. See SHOVELER. *1459: ij clothis portrayed full of popelers. . . j hangyng clothe of Popelers. 1533: iij popelers of store...v herns & a popeler of store.*

poplar, popple, popling the native black poplar, *Populus nigra*, now uncommon in

Norfolk, may have provided much of the poplar board in the Middle Ages and later. The white poplar or ABELE, *P. alba*, is an early introduction. Poplar wood is soft and light and not easily split by nails, and was used in building, coachbuilding, and for tiles. *1410: iiij popylbordys viijd. 1579: lxx ledges of Espe & pople vs. vjd...for xxvj hundred lxxxxix fote of pople boarde at vs. iiijd. the hundred...ij popul bords of xv foot viijd. 1620: 19ˣˣ fotte & 10 sawinge of Popple Bord to be used for makeinge Tyle xjs. iiijd. 1655: a parcel of Alders in ye wood besides 60 Pople setlins. 1664: popling board & planke. 1664: for hewing and cutting ou'whart cutts of a popple bloune downe at Samuel Newsons fearne in wch was vij loads & nine foot at 2s. p̄ load xvs and for cutting of the ground end iijs.*

porch provided shelter to the entry of a barn, granary, house, church etc. In 16th and 17th-century houses the porch, usually of flint or brick, often has a useful small room over it. *1354: [C nails for repairing] porche [of the granary 3d.]. 1365: [carpenter pulling down] j Porch [of the barn]. 1367: [cutting] Bordes [of oak and making] dil porch [for the door of the hall].*

porenerse see PORRINGER

porkett young pig; more specifically, a fat pig. *1654: a Porkett 12s. 6d. and halfe a Porke wth the head 7s. 1655: 2 piggs to fatt for porketts. . . a whole porkett 1 li. 2s. and for a side wghd 25 li. 4s. 2d. . . 2 porketts 1 li. 12s. and for 8 rosting Piggs 13s. 2d.*

porpoise the porpoise, *Phocæna communis*, now *P. phocœna*, was - and is - a visitor to the Norfolk coast, and was eaten. *1465: fore a pece of porpays ijs. 1530: to John Millers s'vnt, in reward for bryngyg of a pece of purpose iiijd. 1593: to Brownes sonne of Beeson for bringing a purpose they founde ijs.*

porrage peas peas for porridge or thick soup. *1582: Porrage pease ij bz bo. iijs. iiijd.*

porringer from the earlier *potager, poddinger*, bowl for pottage. Small bowl or cup, usually with two handles, and often of silver. *1592: Syxe rounde Porringers with TB* [Thomas Butts] *ijs...Fower porringers wth eares & TB xijd. 1592: in porenerse fyve xxd. 1593: six Pewter Porrengers ijs. 1595: [pewter] xx porryngers. 1636: two double silver porringers one of them wth a cover one single silver porringer. 1648: 6 white earthern porrengers 2s. 9d.*

pors see PURSE

portal panelled partition within a doorway containing an inner door; a partitioned-off corner. *1608: one portall wth latch & snatch.*

portflask belt for carrying a powder-flask. *1592: Eleven porteflasks of seales skynne & ij of Buffe iiijs.*

porther', porcher' see BERCHER

portifory a breviary; all the books of the medieval church services in one volume.

port mentell, portmantoo a portmanteau, case or bag for carrying clothes, especially on horseback. Cf. MALE. *1593: one port mentell ijs. 1593: One Portmantoo and payer of Bootes vs.*

portpain small cloth for carrying bread to the table without touching it with the hand. *1467: xij elles of lynnen clothe for portepaynes, pryse the elle vd.*

poryshe porridge. See PORRINGER. *1598: Fyve old pewter poryshe dysches xxd.*

posnet, poscenet, posenete small to medium-sized long-handled cooking pot with three feet. *1310: j pede j poscenet jd. 1352: ij potenetts [of which one holds 1 gallon and the other half a gallon]. 1591: a little posenete. 1592: iij Letyll posenetese ijs.*

posset hot milk curdled with wine or ale, often heavily spiced. Sometimes used as a medicine. *1605: Take two ounces of syrrup of Damask roses, two ounces of syrrup of Ruberbe, and one ounce of syrrup agrick mixt together, and a third part taken in possit ale will serve for a good purge. 1625: I hope thow dost not eate of those possetty curdy drinkes which howsoever pleasinge to the pallett it maybe for a time, yett I am perswaded are most unwhollsom and very Clogginge to the Stomake and apt to brede surffits by reson thay doe not redyly disgest but many times doe corrupt in the stomake. 1637: [silver] one* *posett peece wth a handle & Cover.*

postell small post. *1321: raftres & ij postell [bought for the kitchen 6s. 8¾d.].*

postern door to the side of the main door or gate; back door, side door. *1318: [fixing] C bord [upon] postern' viijd. xv bords [for roofing] post'nre xjd. 1355: guggonn [for the gate] dil postern jd. 1368: [fitting one] thresshwale [to] le post'ne [of the great gate].*

pothold pothook; BRANDLET. See COOK'S HOLD. *1590: iiij potholds.*

pothook cooking-pots were hung above the open hearth from pothooks, which were suspended from a bar or HAKES in the chimney. Pothooks are usually described as a 'pair'. See p. 117; ESS. *1597: one payer of pote hockes. 1619: ij pair of pothakes j paire of potthookes.*

poticarie an apothecary

potkin, potekyne a small pot. *1301: ij potekynes [and 4 bowls for the dairy 4d.].*

pot lead, potleed see LEAD

pot metal an alloy of copper and lead, 4:1 by weight. *1620: one morter of pottmettle.*

pottage soup, usually thickened with meat and vegetables.

potted fowl potted meat became popular in the mid-17th century. The selected meat was cooked in the pot, then sealed in with lard, suet, or butter. *1664: James Browne rod with a letter for fowle &c to Sr Henry Bacons of Lovingland & returned to Norwich for potted fowle he had spake for at Mris Felthams but was disappointed.*

pottinger small bowl or cup for soup etc. See PORRINGER. *1709: 2 little pewter pottingers.*

pottle, potell, poteller a measure holding 2 quarts (half a GALLON); a large drinking pot or container, of silver, pewter, pot, or leather. *1321: j potell [of oil]. 1459: ij potellers of oon sorte, weiying iiij^XX xiij unces. One potell potte, of anothir sorte, weiyng xxxv unces. ij potellers, with my maisters armes on the liddes, weiyng lxxij unces. j potell potte, with braunches on the lidde enamelled, weiyng xlix unces. 1464: a potelle of ypocrasse xxd. 1465: fore vj potelle pottes of leder vjs. 1481: xviij potel tankards iiijs. a dousen.*

pottle pan small deep cooking pan. *1591: one litle pottle panne of brase 4d.*

pouldron, pauldron piece of flexible armour for the shoulder.

poult, pout the young of domestic fowls. *1665: Turkie pouts of Tho: Watson six bought by Robt Myles wife at 10d. a peece.*

pounced metal embossed by striking from the other side; répoussé. The tool for embossing was a pounce or punch. *1459: xij platte peces, pounsed in the bottom. . . j stondyng cuppe, pounsed with floures. 1520: iiijd for a pownse to make wt the pewter. 1588: thre other bowles pownced. ij cuppes of silver pownced.*

pound unit of weight of 12-16 ounces, varying according to article, period, and region. The avoirdupois pound of 16 ounces was established by the 15th century. The 14th-cent. waxpound seems to have been a standard pound probably of 12 ounces; the leadpound was a STONE of 6 pounds, and a leve ponde a stone of 7 pounds. *14th cent.: Sex waxpunde makiet j ledpound. xij ledpunde j fotmel. xxiiij fotmel j fothir of Bristouwe...Sex waxpunde makiet j leedpound. xviij leedpund j leed bole. xviij leed boles j fothir of the Northleondes, ys haat xc and xiiij leed punde, that beeth xix hundryd and foure and fourti wexpunde...Sevene waxpund makiet onleve ponde one waye, twelf weyen on fothir, this aveit two thousand and ix score and four wexpund, that beeth thre hundryd and twelfve leedpound.* See R.D. Connor, *The Weights and Measures of England,* 123-132 and *passim.* The monetary pound was 20 shillings (240 pence). See £, LI.

powalyes poles, posts. *1401: [cutting timber namely] powalyes bordes & bases. 1423: [carpenter repairing the door of the lord's barn and putting in the same door] bases & powalyes.*

powdering trough, tub, vessel vessel for salting or pickling meat in brine. *1584: A powderinge tubb. 1595: a Powdering Troffe. 1636: one pouderin trowe one pouderin vesell. 1692: a pcell of porke in the powderinge tub.*

powtenere possibly a kind of bag. *1474: a powtenere with a payre of bedys of jette.*

praise, prayse, prise to value, apprise. The neighbours who compiled the probate INVENTORY of a deceased person were termed the praysers, prisers etc.

prekette see PRICKET

premere see PRIMER

press a large CUPBOARD with doors; often shelved. The 1648 quotation seems to indicate a 'trouser-press' function. *1546: two close cobords and a presse...The presse gallerie. 1584: One cloth presse with two chests & thre coffers xxxs. 1588: a cubbert presse wth iij locks xs. 1588: presse to laye in clothes vjs. viijd. 1589: a presse for letters iiijd. 1591: one presse cubbard xs. 1591: a presse wth a glasse case vjs. viijd. 1592: An open Presse iijs...a Presse wherin his apparrell laye vjs. viijd...The Presse wherin the armor lyeth xs. 1597: a great presse for sadles. 1603: A ioyned Presse with a paire of Virginalls uppon it xls. 1648: a presse wth scrues & drawers 1 li. 10s. 1709: Napkin presse with 4 drawers...3 presses for linen. 1751: a Deal Press full of drawers.*

press board, pressing board board for pressing CHEESE. *1352: v chesfat ij pressingbord.*

press board, press table for pressing or ironing cloth. *1592: One ould presse bourde.*

pressing iron smoothing IRON used by tailors, clothworkers, housewives etc. *1615: Pressingyron and sheeres. 1625: ij pressinge Irons 1 paire of shires.* See BOX-IRON.

prevy see PRIVY

prick see PRICKWOOD

prick to ride, ride fast, from 'pricking' the horse with spurs. *1459: j prikkyng hat covered withe blake felwet.*

prick a shooting-mark, bull's-eye; a target; target-shooting. *1464: my masterys lossys att the prykkys viijd.*

pricket a buck in its second year; its straight unbranched antler.

pricket a spike on which a CANDLE was fixed; the candle itself. The distinction between a pricket and a candlestick is not clear, although they were clearly seen to differ in 1459; the 'candilstik' cannot been of the socket type, as 2 'sokettys' are also mentioned. *1459: ij prikettys of silver, weiyng xxvij unces et di'. . . a candilstik, a priket and ij sokettys of silver. 1552: v prikettes of laten.*

pricket a pointed finial on a building. *1612: for 3 pricketts of Iron for the gable ends iijs.*

pricket roastiron a SPIT on which the meat was impaled on prickets or spikes. *1593: a rostorne...one prickete Rostorne.*

prickwood, prick wood from the spindle-tree, *Euonymus europæa*, the dogwood, *Cornus sanguinea*, or the hazel, *Corylus avellana*, used for the thatcher's BROACH or brotch, a thin sharpened rod with a notch or fork at the blunt end to secure the longitudinal SWAYS or bindings, the rods or cords that bound the thatch to the roof. Superseded by iron hooks in the 19th century. *1328: in prickes [for thatching 23½d.]. 1371: [rods] & p'kkes [for thatching the house]. 1392: prikkes & swyes. 1647: 2 bunches of prickwood & j of byndeings 1s. 6d.*

prikele iron spike for the top of a gate. *1344: xvj prikeles [of iron for the gate of the purpresture].*

primer devotional book for the laity in the unreformed church. *1474: j premere ijs.*

print mould for impressing a pattern on butter. *1587: ij butter prynts. 1601: three smale printes of plaistr of paris.*

pritchel sharp-pointed tool for punching holes, especially in horseshoes. *1592: One stamp one prychell two hatchstaves.*

privy the bog, gong, jakes, house of easement, HOUSE OF OFFICE, NECESSARY HOUSE etc. The privy would often stand over a shaft leading to a cistern or tank, or the moat. The shaft would be swilled out at intervals and the cistern emptied. Before the advent of cheap paper the wiping material was a bundle of rags, wool, cotton etc. on the end of a short stick, with a pail of water for rinsing it. Inventories of houses seldom mention privies as they usually contained few or no movable furnishings. See CLOSE-STOOL; GARDEROBE; WARDROBE; WATER CLOSET. *1561: to the Duchemane for makyng cleane of le chapell Chamber prevy ijd. 1663: a deale & a halfe to bottom the privy 1s. 10d. 1665: making clean the house of Office by the parlour being fowle.*

probate inventory see INVENTORY

processional book containing the music for the reponsaries and anthems sung in procession before mass in the unreformed church.

proctor an executive official of the ecclesiastical courts.

procuration, proxage, proxy annual payment from a benefice in commutation of payment for the entertainment of the bishop. *1537: Ingaldesthorpe Benefice. Itm pd the xiijth day of June, for senage & proxage for this yere ixs.*

procurator an attorney; someone having power of attorney.

proof armour that has been tested or proved for strength. *1588: One Blake Armore of Proofe, one Burganet, one Gorgett, & ye polernes xxxiiijs. iiijd.*

prospect viewing-place or gallery on top of a house. *1665: studded up the sides of the lucome on theast side of the pspect. . . hewed timber for the lanthorne to be sett up upon the pspect & began to frame for the same.*

proxage, proxy see PROCURATION

proxy letter of attorney, authorising one person to act for another.

proyne a prune. *1483: iiij li. proynes.*

pruning, prunings loppings, toppings, branches. *c.1730: The Pruning of ye Scotch fir to be savd for fencing round Houghton.*

prygge see SPRIG

psalter the book of psalms for singing or reading in church. The Book of Common Prayer used the translation by Miles Coverdale. *1598: one Saulter booke xxd.*

puck see PUKE

pudding cart offal, refuse, or muck cart. *1756: a pudding Cart and three old wheels £2.* See also HARVEST PUDDING.

pudding pan deep pan for boiling puddings. *1709: 3 pudding pans.*

puet, puitt normally the peewit, green PLOVER, or lapwing, *Vanellus vanellus*. Browne: 'Larus alba or puets in such plentie about Horsey that they sometimes bring them in carts to Norwich and sell them at small rates, and the country people make use of their egges in puddings and otherwise. Great plentie thereof have bred about Scoulton meere, and from thense sent to London.' This seems to be the black-headed gull, *Larus ridibundus*, called 'puet' because its feeding habits are the same as the lapwing's, though its call is very different. *1593: to mr pries man for bringing j dussen di' puitts xijd. 1602: xij puets.*

puff a puff-ring was hollow, not solid; counterfeit. *1603: a seleinge Ringe with a puff.*

puke MDu. *puuc, puyck*, best woollen cloth; as adjective probably means 'best'. Soft, smooth cloth made from carded wool. *1464: my mastyr gaff to Jamys Hobard a longe blakke gown off Puke, the wych cost my mastyr xlijs. 1466: j yerde of pewke for ij payr hosen ixs. 1476: that same gowne off puke furryd with whyght lambe. 1597: iij yardes and a quarter of blacke puke blankett.*

puke dark brown or black colour produced by the action of COPPERAS on GALLS.

pulebere see PILLOWBEER

Pulham work, pullam originating from Pulham St Mary and Pulham Market, this was an expensive woollen cloth used for coverlets, bedhangings, and curtains, charac-

164

teristically decorated with a BIRD'S EYE pattern. *1593: coveringe of pullhm worke with birds eyes. 1602: two quysshens of Pulham worke.*
pulle pillow. *1593: iij pulles one pulebere.*
pullerie, pullery poultry
pulling a pulley. *1588: ij stoppes on Great roppe & A pulling.*
pulyve, polyffe a pulley. *1465: for iij grete polyves ijs...for a bowlyne polyve vjd...for vij smale polyves xiiijd. 1468: iiij pullyes xvijs. viijd.*
pump hand pumps were in use from the late 15th century, with leather washers and valves in wooden or iron barrels, raising water 15 to 20 feet from wells by suction. The waterwheel and the horsewheel pumps, developed in the 17th century, could raise water from a much greater depth - the Houghton well of the late 1720s, with a horsewheel pump, was 116 feet deep - and the steam-driven pump was available from the middle of the 18th century. *1589: the Pomp house. 1626: iij spitts j pumple Iroron ij latch pans. 1647: halfe a bende of Leather to mend the pumpe 2s. 10d. 4 days worke of 2 men aboute it and a new spoute 3s. 1647: In the Yard. One good and Sufficient Pumpe with a Lead att the foote thereof. 1648: Kempe of Walsingham for his Jorney & scoreing the water pipes 5s. . . Mendinge the Pumpe they findeinge leather & makeinge a new sucker 5s. 4d. 1676: one days worke of 5 men uncovering ye marle pitt one day pumping water 6s. . . to May ye Pump man 1 li. . . pd Stibbard for mending ye Pump &c 3 li. 15s. 1685: R Calfe for leather for the Pumpe.*
pumsitturne see POME-CITRON
punch short upright timber to support a beam. *1664-5: Two punches for the dovehouse aulter xijd.* See ALTAR.
punde see POUND
pur, purr a poker, used almost exclusively with COAL and not wood fires. A pur was often included with a CHALDRON of COAL sent down from the Newcastle area in the 16th and 17th centuries. In the early 17th century it is not common to find evidence of the use of coal in a household, and even some of the larger houses used only wood or charcoal. *1626: 1 cradle for cole wth fire pann & pur...1 fier forke. 1647: One Large Iron peele a rake and twoo Iron purrs. 1649: the kiching fyre purr mendinge 1s. 2d. 1676: for my parlor Pur & riddle 6s. 6d.*
purfle, purfill OFr. *porfil*, border, edge; embroidered or decorated edge; to border, trim. *1487: A purfill of ermyns of ij skynne depeth, and iij yardys and an half long.*
purle twisted thread of silver and gold wire used for bordering and embroidery. Purle silk was silk embroidered or woven with purle. *1459: donge of purle sylke.*
purlin longitudinal roof timber, resting on or joined to the principal rafters half-way or a third and two-thirds up the slope of the roof, and acting as bearers for the common rafters. *1730: 4 Purlings 11 ft Long 10 by 8 [inches]. 12 Purlings 25 ft Long 10 by 8.*
purloyned, purlinned with purlins. *1620: being a hammer beame Roofe and purloyned, with gable ends.*
purpoint see PARPEN
purpoint, purpoynt, pourpoint OFr. *porpoint* means perforated; hence it was applied to materials that were quilted, that is thinly padded and sewn through and used particularly for bed-coverings and quilted clothing, e.g. doublets. *Prompt. Parv.*: 'Pur-poynt, bed hyllynge' [covering]. However, judging by the quotation, some purpoints were used as hangings. See COUNTERPOINT. *1459: j purpoynt white hangyd. . . j purpoynt white, with a scuchon after an horse wyse, visure and braunchis of grene.*
purpose see PORPOISE.
purpresture, purprys, purpoys strictly an illegal enclosure of another's land, but used for any recent enclosure. *1312: [making ditches] del purpoys. 1321: [pruning trees of the*

165

ditch] del purprys xjd. 1323: [mending the ditch and bank around] Le Purpis xijd. ob.

purs purse. 1474: j purs in the bedstead with xxs... a purs of welvet viijd.

purvey provide. 1484: I will that myn executōs pveye a stoon of Marble to be leyde alofte upon my grave.

putlog, putlock short horizontal timber in an erection of scaffolding, inserted in a hole in the wall (putlog-hole) to tie in the scaffold poles, and withdrawn when the building work is finished. The putlog-hole in a flint wall was usually in the form of a trilith, two upright stones or bricks capped with another. 1619: x Cople short Sparres for putlock. 1819: ½ day chopping putlock & getᵗ scaffordˢ to Hall 2s. 6d.

putter, puter see PEWTER

puttingup stick possibly a wooden, iron, or bone stick for crimping or pinning linen, as in ruffs. 1589: vj - jd. inckhorns js. iiijd. j li. puttingupp sticks js. viijd. iiij paps of dice xd.

pyck, pyk peak, gable, gable-end, particularly of a barn. 1310: [produce] del pycks [towards the east...1 stack before] le Pycks [towards the west]. 1313: [produce] del Westpycks.

pycrilles see PIKE

pyghtelyng see PICKLING

pykkyng pitching (corn). 1417: ij men pykkyng di' day vd.

pyle, pylle see PILE

pynclicez ? 1513: [just after PINPILLOWS] ij small pynclicez of rede and vyolet velvet.

pynson shoes see PINSON

pypys rolls. 1440: I prey yow do byen for me ij pypys of gold.

pyx a box or vessel in which the consecrated bread was reserved in the unreformed church. 1459: j pyx, demi gylt weiyng xxx unces.

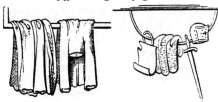

Perches 14th-15th centuries

Putlog-hole   Pantile and section

Q

q' abbreviation for Latin words meaning a fourth part, such as *quarta*, (QUART), *quarterium*, (QUARTER the volume measure), *quarta, quadrans, quadranta*, (FARTHING).

q used in some late-medieval texts in place of w. *1449: he went thedder for to aspye qhat they dedyn, and qhat felachep they hadde with them; and qhan he com thedder, the dors were fast sperid.*

quaggmore quagmire, wet or muddy place. *1664: cast straw into the quaggmore by the stable muckhill to make mucke of the same.*

quail net see NET

quare see QUARREL

quarrel, quarry small diamond-shaped piece of glass, cut from a sheet of CROWN GLASS and held in place in a window by bands or cames of lead fixed by wire to horizontal iron saddle-bars. See SOUDLETT. *1608: some 30 quarels of glasses broken. 1647: to Wortly the glasier 25 quarrells souldering & bandinge 2s. 6d. 1648: 38 quarrells put into the windows. 1664: for 37½ quarries of new glasse putt in sev'all windowes about the hall iijs. jd. 1737: at Read's 10 Quare & 6 Sqrs.*

quarrel short arrow or bolt used with the CROSSBOW. *1459: j coffyre, full of quarrellys of a smale sorte. Item xij quarrellis of grete sorte, feddered with brasse.*

quart a quarter of a GALLON, 2 PINTS. Imperial quart: 69.36 in³, wine 57.75 in³, ale 70.5 in³.

quartelette small quart; pot holding a quart. *1459: ij quartelettes of dyvers sortes, weiyng xlviij unces* [silver].

quarter a formal garden of the 16th-18th centuries was often divided into four quarters by a cross of paths or walks. See p. 168. *1709: plants for the quarters of the Willdernes...Hedges round the Quarters.*

quarter a measure of capacity, 8 bushels or 64 gallons; a quarter of a WAY. In the Middle Ages also called a SEAM.

quercus see OAK

quere, queer choir.

quern pair of circular stones, top and bottom, for grinding malt, corn, mustard, pepper etc. between their flat faces by turning the top stone with a rotary or to-and-fro motion. *1584: a payer of pepper quernes. 1597: j payer of musterd quarnes. 1597: one paire of mault quearnes & one pare of Musterd quearnes. 1599: a paier of quernes wth stalls* [stand]. *1606: one payer of old Cuernes. 1615: in the Quearne house...one paire of musterd Quearns ijs.*

quest men assistants to the churchwardens, particularly at VISITATIONS and to ensure attendance and good conduct in church. *1556: for the churchreves & the queste menes Costs when they wer before the Vysiters at Walssynghme.*

quethode, quetheworde, -woode bequest, legacy. *1517: to the new chapell on the north syde of ye chirche, of the quethword of William Damyetts. 1544: þcell of ye quethode gyffne by the testament...*

quickset cuttings, slips, or seedlings of shrubs or trees, particularly of blackthorn and hawthorn for hedging. *1619: for 2^C longe quicksetts ijs. for iij^C Di' short quicksetts xxjd. for iiij^C Elme quicksetts ijs...v^C filbert quicksetts vs...for ij^C plume setts ijs. for ij^C longe Whitethorne setts ijs.*

quilt, twilt bed-covering stuffed with down, wool etc. often stitched through to retain an even thickness. See COUNTERPOINT; PURPOINT. *1584: A Twylte ijs. vjd.*

quince the quince, *Cydonia oblonga*, was grown in Britain from at least the 12th century. Too sharp and bitter to eat raw, it was very popular from the 16th century as jelly,

167

jelly, marmalade, or candied quince. The quince tree was used as a rootstock for grafting pears. *1601: a Basket of Quinches. 1602: a mande of greate Quinches. 1648: 4 duszen Quinches 4s.*

quinnis, quynnes, qwennys see WHINS

quire OFr. *quoer, quaier,* later *cahier,* copy-book, writing book. Originally four sheets of parchment or PAPER doubled to form 8 leaves; later 24 or sometimes 25 sheets, the size of sheet being variable. *1647: for 1 quir of Cap pap 4d...for 2 quir of white pap 9d.*

quissa see CUISSE

quit rent payment by tenants of a manor to absolve them from customary manorial charges; rent paid for a particular purpose. Abolished 1922.

quoin corner-stone, or the angle of the corner of a building. *1620: hewinge...120 square Coynes att 3d. a peice.*

quoshion, quychen, quysshen see CUSHION

qwern see QUERN

qwete wheat. *1417: j lod of qwete.*

qweyer see QUIRE

qwypcord whipcord. *1423: in qwypcord iijd*

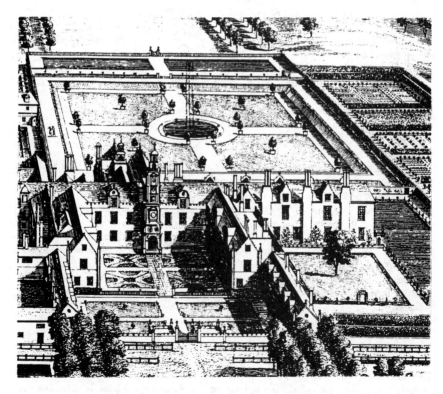

Quartered and terraced garden, Brome Hall, *c.* 1705

R

Rabet, rabat, rabbet carpenter's plane, usually for rebating (rabbeting) or grooving boards to receive a tongue, or for overlapping boards. *1592: a long sawe a belt a Rabbet a cutting saw.*

rabet, rabetting Cotgrave 1611: '*Rabat*, the staffe wherwith plaisterers beat their mortar'. Rabetting is plastering, either with plaster or clay. *1526: x lodes of clay for rabettyng of ye berne wall.*

rabbeting stool, stock stool, horse, trestle, or low bench for rabbeting boards, possibly with a clamp to hold the boards. See RABET. *1587: i Rabetinge stole vjd. 1590: a long sawe a Rabbett stock 2 Joynters. 1592: a Rabbyting stoole.*

rabestele stone for sharpening tools, a RUB. *1318: iiij rabesteles [bought ¾d.].*

rabbit *Lepus cuniculus*. See CONEY. *Prompt. Parv.* : 'Rabet, yonge conye'.

rack open frame for straw and hay above the manger in a stable etc. *1328: [carpenter making] Rackes cribbes crates [and other necessaries in the court]. 1620: [stable] with french racks and mangers.*

rack support for the SPIT, usually made of iron; see COBIRON. Wooden racks must have been well away from the fire. See ROAST IRON. *1467: in makenge of rakkes of tre to roste one xijd.*

rack irons footed upright pair of iron bars with crooks at intervals to stand on either side of the open hearth to bear the ends of the spit. *1591: one paier of Rake Irons. 1593: 2 paire of Rackes 5 hakes 1 paire of Cole Irons 1 paire of Cobirons. 1593: pair of rackins. 1637: one pr of yron racks Cont a boute 10 ornhooks a peece.* See COBIRON; REEKING IRON; ROAST IRON.

rack of mutton neck or forepart of the spine. *1620: For a shoulder & racke of mutton 1s. 6d. 1648: 1 Racke of Mutton 1s. 4d.*

radlace red lace. *17th cent.: a paier of radlace shooes 3s.*

raff 1. imported timber, mainly deal. 2. rubbish. 3. goods. *Prompt. Parv.* 'Raaf, ware. . . Ware, or chaffare. *Mercimonium*. . . Chaffare. *Mercimonium, mercatum, commercium.*' This implies that a 'raffman' was a seller of general merchandise. Raffmen were coupled with the grocers in the Norwich pageant of 1527. OED says a rafman is a dealer in timber. *1411-13: [paid to Walter Colman] rafman [for 5 trowys and 1 bolle 16d.]. ?16th cent.: This daye it is ordeyned that non occupacon, but only Raffemen, shall wtin this Citie bye any rowe talowe, and thei to make it in candell and sell it forth.*

raftre rafter.

ragstone in general, rag is hard, coarse, rough stone, unworked or almost incapable of being worked, like the ironstone conglomerate used before and after the Conquest by church-builders. *1621: which ould barne the wall of it that fronts the Courte and the end of it to the basse Courte is made of Ragestone which must be taken downe and made up new of Bricke...the walle and Roofe being Roten.*

rail the water-rail, *Rallus aquaticus*, or corncrake, *Crex crex*. Sir Thomas Browne: 'a kind of Ralla aquatica or water Rayle. . . The Ralla or Rayle wee haue counted a dayntie dish'. *1654: 1 Rail 1 Quail 5 Partridg 12d.*

rail horizontal member of a bannister, fence, wall etc.; the top of a stone wall. *1621: walle of open worke of stone 3 foote and a halfe high answerable to the bridge, with soyle and rayle of stone with pedastalls in rustick.*

raisins, reyseres, reysons solis raisins, partly-dried grapes. Great raisins are dried common grapes, small raisins are CURRANTS or raisins of Corinth, made from dwarf seedless varieties. See ALLEGANTS. *1415-16: [4 lbs. of] reysyngges de curauncis [bought 12d. . . .*

169

[10 lbs.] de Reysyngges [bought 17d.]. 1505-6: for grete reyseres ijs. ixd. ob. for reyseres of Corres, iiijs iijd. ob. 1647: 6 li. Currants 4s. for 6 li. Reysons solis 2s. 6d.

rake until the 16th century the rake was probably an all-wood implement, used mainly for gathering corn, hay etc. together. The head was 2-3 feet wide, braced against the shaft, and with long wooden teeth, sometimes projecting on both sides of the head. The distinction between DRAG-RAKE and following-rake is not clear; following-rakes were slightly cheaper, and may have been used to rake through the stubble after the drag-rakes had gathered most of the corn or hay. By the 16th century some of these agricultural rakes had iron teeth. Mechanised rakes drawn by horses had come in by the 19th century. *1310: ij rakes ijd. 1585: iiij drag rakes v folowing rakes. 1591: vij dragg rakes vij following rakes ij barne rakes iij haye rakes. 1593: 5 dragg Rakes xxd. 4 following Rakes 3 hayrakes viijd. 1595: in swath rakes handrakes. 1618: iiij dragge Rakes iij of eyerne & one tryinge rake. 1647: 3 pichforke shaftes & 12 hand Rakes. 1746: Seven Drag-Rakes 1£ 1s...ten Hand Rakes, one titter rake and One Turnip Crome.* See SWATHE RAKE; TITTERS.

rake irons see RACK IRONS

raker one who rakes corn or hay. *1342: [10 carters 2 stackers] j Rakere.*

ramping from ramp, to ascend, descend; wall going up and down, therefore = crenellated. *1665: lowning the wall...setting ramping bartlements upo' the same.*

ranell horizontal bar of wood or iron fixed across a fireplace to hang pothooks on. *1459: [bakehouse] j bulter j ranell ij payre wafer irons.* See GALLOW BALK.

range up to the 18th century a 'range' in the kitchen was a set of COBIRONS and iron bars to hold spits or pots, with perhaps a GRATE formed of iron bars, and a series of pot-stands or TRIVETS. The modern type of enclosed kitchen range was available in the 18th century, but only came into general use in the 19th century. The screw range had a screw or worm adjustment for the grate. *1709: [kitchen] 4 spits, a Jack, a fire rang. [laundry] an iron rang, 2 cheeks. 1791: screw range with turning trivets. c.1830: Kitchen. The capital Range - Complete. The oven as set with grate, stove &c &c complete.*

rat fall rat-trap, in which the rat set off a trip-switch causing a heavy weight to fall and crush it. See MOUSETRAP. *1592: on ratt falle.*

ratchet see ROCHET

ratiner, ratoner, ratuner, rattentaker rat-catcher, probably using poison and dogs. In the accounts of the Prior of Norwich's manors the rat-taking costs grew considerably in the thirty years leading up to the Black Death of 1349. *1306: [expenses] Ratoner [for 4 weeks 6d.]. 1318: [expenses of John] le ratuner iiijd. 1335:[expenses] dil Ratoner [and his servant for 1 day and night 3d.]. 1530: pd the xiijth daye of August to Peter Rattentaker for hys Fee for leyeng for Ratts of ye halff yere endyd at Michelmas next comyng xxd. 1649: for the takeinge of 18 Ratts 3s.*

rat's bane, ratten bane rat-poison, usually containing arsenic. *1533: for leyinge of ratton bane iiijd. 1587: j box of Ratten bane vjd. 1647: to Rawlyn for the takeinge of 14 Ratts 2s. 4d. to him for Rattensbane laide at two severall tymes 1s.*

ratteen thick twilled wool cloth, friezed or with a curly nap. *1753: One Ratteen Coat Unlined 7s. 6d.*

rattentaker, ratton bane see RATINER; RAT'S BANE.

rawblack thick cloth designed for warmth. *1522: a yerd of raweblacke to make a payer of hose.*

raybate see RABET

ray a worsted cloth, woven with coloured stripes; made in Norfolk in the Middle Ages, but discontinued after c.1500, when rays were imported. *1466: iij yerdes and di of ray...vjs. vd.*

ray, raying chopped straw, chaff. *1737: 1 Skreen for Corn 1 Raying Sieve 15s.*

raynes see REYNES

170

rayseburies raspberries.

ream originally 20 QUIRES, that is 480 sheets of PAPER; by the 17th century a ream was 500 sheets, perhaps to allow for wastage. A printer's ream is 21½ quires, 516 sheets. *1533: halfe a reme of papyr xijd.*

rearrages arrearages.

reconcile a rule of medieval Canon Law was that a church once consecrated could not be reconsecrated unless it had been polluted by bloodshed, fire, or the like. 'Reconciling' was the equivalent of reconsecration. *1513: I bequeth to the Reconsilynge of Upton Chirche x mrc.*

rector, rectory the office of parish priest was tied to the benefice or living, which was the income derived from glebe (the land annexed to the benefice) and TITHES, which were a tax of a tenth of all produce of the parish. In the Middle Ages, by the process called appropriation, some benefices were acquired by monasteries and other religious entities, which received the great tithes as rector and appointed a vicar (L. *vicarius*, substitute) to do the actual work in the parish, rewarding him with the small tithes. At the Dissolution of the monasteries their estates were disposed of by Henry VIII, and many rectories came into the hands of laymen, who were known as lay rectors and received the great tithes. The title and income of the rector remained with the incumbents of those benefices that had not been appropriated to the medieval monasteries, while the title and income of the vicar continued with the incumbents of those that had been so appropriated. The rector, whether clerical or lay, was responsible for the upkeep, repair, and rebuilding of the chancel of the parish church.

redgewith see RIDGEWITH

reek to pile, stack turf, peat etc. See RIG.

reeking iron iron hook on which to hang meat or fish for smoking. See RACK IRONS. *1595: viij Speets, A payer of Iron cobyrons, iij latche pannes, fower reeckinge Irons iij payer of potthookes, one speete yt ye reekynge Irons hange on.*

reel, gardener's reel wound with string or cord to enable the gardener to lay out a straight line; a garden line. *1593: [gardener's chamber] 1 rele & 1 settinge yron.*

refuse leather, refuse sheep the usual meaning of 'refuse' in this context is 'not up to standard': *Prompt. Parv.* : 'Refuce, or owt caste, what so ever hyt be'. The leather and sheepskins of the 1602 quotation bear out this interpretation, but the value of the refuse sheep in the 1713 quotation does not. Perhaps 'refuse' sheep were those that were unable to breed - see 1756 quotation. *1602: vj dozen of refuse leather vjs. vj dozen of shepes leath' vjs. ix sheepes skinnes vjs. xix refuse sheepe skines js. vjd. 1713: 240 old Weathers 150 li. 150 Sherlings 70 li. 16s. 8d. 50 Sheep hoggs 17 li. 10s. 50 Crone Sheep 15 li. 16s. 8d. 20 Reffuse Sheep 8 li. 1756: Twenty one Score Ewes wth their Lambs at 12s. p couple. Sixty Refuse Sheep at 6s. p head.*

remove horseshoe removed, or changed to another hoof. *1647: 10 shoes & 2 removes.*

reap-reeve in the open-field system, the manorial official in charge of the reaping of the demesne corn. *1353: [harvest food: 3 tithers] j repreue [1 stacker].*

resin, reson, rosen, rosell secretion from many types of tree, used for various purposes e.g. polish, glue, soap. *1343: rosine [and wax for the pomell of the hall.]. 1417: [making cistern with solder] in Rosyn & piye [bought for the same 1d.]. 1538-9: j li. of rosen for syment. 1573: wax, rosell & turpentine to gome the livery beddes. 1592: in rouseng & pycke ijs. . . xbij li. roson iijs. xd. 1665: 1 lb rosen 2d.*

rete L. *rete*, net. *1274: j rete [with cord for eels 2s. 4d.]. 1339: j Rete [of 5 ells for the weir 3s. 4d.].*

revyting hammer riveting hammer. *1592: j revyting hammer and a vyce.*

rey see RYE

reynes fine linen cloth, possibly from Rheims or Rennes. *1459: j cover of raynis, wrought* *with golde of damaske.*

reyseres, reysons, reysyngges see RAISINS

Rhenish from the Rhineland, or with the characteristics of that area. *1526: Rynnyshe wyn. 1584: A gallyon of Runnyshe wine.*

rial see RYAL

rib short for ribbon. *c.1680: 6 yd 6d. pinke pownd rib 2s. . . 1 yd ¾ 10d. blue chquer rib 10½d.*

rice imported from the Middle East from medieval times, rice was expensive. *1504-5: for ryce and anneys xxijd. 1647: for 1 li. of Rise 5d.*

ridbil perhaps derived from ON *rydja*, to clear; bill-hook or slasher. *1352: [2 forks for muck] j ridbil.* See BILL; HOOK.

riddel side-curtains of the altar in the medieval church.

riddle, ridde sieve, the size depending on the use, for sifting grain, chaff, lime, ash, embers. The larger riddles had to be supported on a riddling horse or stool. *1306: [mending] j Ridele [and 2 shovels 2d.]. 1352: j Wynewecloth and ij Rydeles. 1595: a frenche rydle. 1636: [with fireirons] one riddle. 1655: 1 Riddle for lime 1s. 4d. 1734: One Ridling Pann & stand 1s. 6½d. 1738: Two Riddles one Fan Four shovells two Rakes A Ridling Stool 9s. 10d. 1747: Eleven forks nine rakes Corn Scuppit ridleing horse & hammer 17s.* See p. 242.

riddling pan perforated pan for sifting the ash from the cinders. *1648: mendinge the Riddlein pann.*

ridgewith, redgewith ridgeband, the part of the harness of a draught-horse running across the back. *1499-1500: [for] regge wytthys xd. 1664: a new wombe rope and a redgewith waite 5½ li. - ijs. iijd.*

rigall, rygholt board see BOARD; ESTRICH

rigery from *ridgel*, an undescended testicle supposed to lodge near the back or ridge; hence a sheep imperfectly castrated, or one that had only one or no descended testicles. *1654: of Mr Smith for a score of weathers besides 6d. given back 13 li. 2s. and for 2 Rigerys 20s.*

rig to pile, stack. *1655: 18d. a 1000 for cutting & Rigging of 40000 Turfe. . . Turfe cutting and Reeking at 18d. p̱ 1000.*

rippling comb implement for cleaning seeds and dirt from HEMP and flax. *1592: one Riplinge combe for flaxe.*

riser OE *ris*, branch. To fit the upright poles into a wattle-and-daub wall; the pole itself. *1665: They made clay splented risered and daubed betweene the studds to lengthen the berne, the pticon by the hayholes, and the pticon betweene the groomes chamber & Saddle house.*

rive ON *hrifa*, rake. See RAKE. *1591: iij drage Ryves xvjd.*

rive to split wood along the grain, to create SPLENTS and PALES. *1738: A Riving Bettle.* See BEETLE.

roach, roche the freshwater fish *Rutilus rutilus* can grow up to 13 inches in length and weigh 2¼ lb., and was a popular fish in the Middle Ages. *1315: vj^c roch [for the pond 2s. 2½d.]. 1319: xx pikerell & m ^Cm^C de Roches [bought for stock 5s. 6d.]*

roast iron *Prompt. Parv.* : 'Rost yryn, or gradyryn'. See GRIDIRON; REEKING IRON. An iron plate or a set of iron bars with hooks or spikes on which small joints of meat were roasted in front of the open hearth. *1459: j roste iron with vij staves. 1592: a rostelyngierne. 1593: A rosterne...one prickete rostorne.*

rochet a sleeveless surplice for clergy. *1539: vj yards of Normandy canvas for ij rochetts.*

rod linear measure: a rod, pole or PERCH was in most cases 5½ yards (16½ feet), but a rod of 7 yards (21 feet), 18½ feet, or even 8 yards (24 feet) is occasionally met. There is evidence that some builders, particularly in towns and major buildings, used the rod as a base unit of measurement.

roftre see ROOFTREE

roll 1. A large cylinder of iron or rounded balk of wood for crushing and smoothing the surface of the soil or for rolling young cereal crops to encourage the stems to branch; a roller. *1592: 2 ould roules And 3 ould ladders iijs vjd. 1592: one rowle to rowle barley.* 2. An iron beam round which the warp or web was wound on a loom. 3. The round beams on which logs were placed in a sawpit. *1664: made two Pitt rowles.* 4. The cylinder of a winch.

rolling chamber chamber in which the rolling or pressing of clothes took place. *1592: a table And a Cou'lett in the Roulinge chamber.* See ROLLING PIN.

rolling flasket large basket on wheels or castors. See FLASKET. *1593: One Rollinge flasket a maunde.*

rolling pin a small round roller. 1. To roll out pastry. 2. In laundry, to squeeze the water out of wet cloth and smooth it. See BATTLEDOR. *1595: a flasket for Clothes a rowling pynne & a battleder. 1595: batteldors iij rollyng pynnes.*

roman, roming, roning see SAW

Rome-scot, romscot Peter's Pence or Pentecostals, tax of one penny per household paid to the Pope from the reign of William I to 1534.

rood one quarter of an ACRE, 40 square RODS/PERCHES, 1210 square yards.

roof-tile apart from the general meaning of TILE for a roof, it sometimes meant the curved ridge-tile on roofs of PANTILES or flat tiles. *1499-1500: xxiiij roofetyle ijs. 1728: 87 pantyles 26 roof tyle 260 flatt tyle..*

roof-tree the ridgepole of a roof. *1298: in xxiij cuppl' j roftre. 1661: a pece for the rouftre and 4 sparz.*

rose nail see NAIL. A rose nail tool was a tool for making rose NAILS.

rose noble see RYAL

rose water water either distilled from roses, or mixed with essence of roses, was used as a perfume or an air freshener from at least the 14th century. *1595: ij glasses wth rose water. 1631: 6 qrts of Rosewater and glasses vs.*

rosell, rosen, rosyn, roszen see RESIN

roset see RUSSET

rospyse raspberries. *1465: a botelle of rospyse iiijd.*

rost eyern, rostelyngierne, rostiron, rostorne see ROAST IRON

rother an ox

rother OE *ródor*, oar, paddle, rudder. *Prompt. Parv.* : 'Maschel, or rothyr, or mascherel' refers to the OAR used in BREWING, a flat, rudder-shaped piece of board, that is without square corners. *1595: vij^C popler bourd xxxs. iij Rothers iiijs. iiij^r or v other peces ijs.*

rough roof

rouling see ROLLING

round hose see HOSE; TRUNK HOSE

roundlet see RUNLET

rouseng see RESIN

roved roofed. *1484: I wulle that the seid Ele, in which my body shal be beried, be newe roved, leded and glased.*

rowel OFr. *roel, rouel*, dim. of *roe, roue*, wheel. 1. A small sharp-pointed wheel on the end of a spur to prick the horse into action. 2. A small roundel of leather with a central hole, inserted between the skin and the flesh of a horse to facilitate the discharge of matter. 3. The rung of a ladder. 4. The rim of a wheel.

rowel short flat board. *1506-7: [for] rowell boorde iijs. vjd. 1655: a hundred wantinge 15 foot of Rowell Bourd 3s.*

royal see RYAL

rub, rubstone, rubber gardener's rub, a length of carborundum or similar abrasive stone, usually rounded, for sharpening tools. *1502-3: for a rubbe and mendyng of a lokke ijd. c.1620: for a grinstone & a rubstone. 1654: For a Rubb for ye Gardiners use 2d. 1655: for 2 new sithes for mangs wth Rubbs virolls & hanging 7s. 1745: Six new Sythes, six old D⁰, and six Rubstones.*

rubber 1. A brush. 2. A cloth for dusting and polishing. 3. A towel. 4. A curry-comb for horses. 5. A flesh-brush for massaging and cleansing the skin. 1 and 2 are the most likely meanings to be met. *1587: iiij brushes & ij Rubbers iijs. 1591: one dussen knives & v Rubbers. 1664: Course cloath for rubbers at Norwich Apr' 2d four yards xviijd. 1709: 15 Rubbers 13 Collaring cloaths 7 Deer cloaths. 1764: Three Dozn pantry Rubbers Three Dozn House rubbers. 1792: 2 Lead rubbers some brushes & brooms.*

rufe, ruffe roof

ruff and reeve the bird *Philomachus pugnax*. The ruff is the male and the reeve the female. A delicacy; the birds were caught by netting and fattened for about ten days on bread and milk, then beheaded and roasted or boiled. *1709: ruff & reeve pans.*

ruffle-shirt shirt with ruffles or frills displayed at the ends of the arms. *1680: 1 Ruffel-shirt 4s. 1734: one sett Ruffles 2s.*

rug a thick tough woollen cloth, coarse frieze, used for cloaks, coats, coverlets etc. Manchester rugs were made from hairy Irish wool. A rug as a floor-covering did not come in until the 18th century. *1593: [on Lady Butts' bed] 1 rugg of Color redd grene yelowe & purple. 1597: 3 ruggs: one whyte: one tawny, & one Chequered: & a yellow rug...a rugg blanket. 1601: 8 yards of Narrowe white Rugg at 6d. iiijs...11 yarde dim' of manchester Rugg at xd. a yarde. 1615: one grene Rugg Cou'lett xxs. 1620: one white poland Rugg of a bredth and a quarter...a white Irish rug. a new Kelkenny rugg. Cf. Shakespeare, Rich. II. ii. 1.157: Now for our Irish wars. / We must supplant those rough rug-headed kerns...*

rumthes rooms. *1591: in other rumthes.*

run a full set. *1636: One Rune of Coch whelles 1 li. 6s. 8d.*

run fur see FUR

runlet, rundell, rundlet a measure of capacity; the vessel itself: wine 18½ GALLONS, or since 1700, 18 gallons; Imperial, 15 gallons. See TUN. Generally, a small barrel. *1306: j Rundell [bought 1d.]. 1466: For a roundlet of red wine of xv gallonys. 1584: halfe a Rundlet of Malmsey the rundlet conteyinge thre gallyons. 1647: 1 Runlett of venigr of 10 Gallons and halfe.*

runnall silk probably from runnel, stream, hence watered silk with wavy damask-like pattern. *1738: Fifteen new Runnall Silk handkerchiefs cut out but not made 1 li. 10s.*

runnell pot runnel can mean a funnel, but it is difficult to see how this could apply to a pot. See RUNLET. *1595: [in dairy] A saltynge troffe for bacon, A runnell pott.*

runnyshe see RHENISH

Rushia see RUSSIA

russell Du. *Rijsel*, Netherlandish name for Lille, where the cloth originated. Smooth satin of wool, originally imported but made in Norfolk from *c.*1554. *1552: one vestment of blak Russelle.*

russet coarse woollen cloth of grey or reddish-brown colour; the colour itself. *1459: j gowne of Frenche russet, lynyd with blak clothe. 1462: iiij zerdys and di off roset...pryse le zerde vs... makynge off a short gown off roset xxd. 1513: j Couyrlyght Ruset and whyt. 1601: 3 yardes of broad silke Russett at 4s. 4d. [per yard]. 5 yardes of sadd Russett carsie at 2s. 3 yard 3 qrters of woded Russett 2s. 2d. 11 yardes qrter of sheeps Russett at 2s. 15 yardes 3 qrters of course northen Russett at xijd*

Russia cloth linen (flax or HEMP) cloth originally imported from Russia or made from

174

Russian hemp. *1738: Six small Russia Cloth Table Cloths 7s. 6d. Twenty five Russia Cloth Towells 5s. Five coarse Russia Cloth long Towells 1s. 6d. Thirty Yards of Curdeled Russia Cloth Cut out for Towells 10s. One Hundred and forty Yards of Coarse Russia Cloth £1 5s.*

Russia leather durable leather treated with birch-bark oil. *1688: Eighteen Backe Chaires covered with Russia Leather at five shillings p peice 4 li. 10s. 0d..*

russing rush. *1595: ij russing stoles.*

rustick, rusticated 1. Masonry in which the joints between the stones are emphasised by deepening to give a massive appearance. 2. The ground-floor of a 17th-18th-century great house, in which the stone is often rusticated to provide a visual transition from the ground to the smoother masonry above. *1620: The pillosters on either side the window over the gate being in Rustick with their orders according to the Ionick.*

ryal, rial, royal rose-noble, a gold coin of the value of 10s., first issued in 1464 and current throughout the 15th and 16th centuries. The issue of 1553-4 had a value of 15s., and the rose-ryal of 1604 a value of 30s. Also half-ryal, 5s., and quarter-ryal, 2s. 6d. *1513: J ryall.* See ANGEL; NOBLE.

ryall paper a size of paper, 24 by 19 inches for writing, 25 by 20 inches for printing; a quality of paper. *1588: ij books bounde with Ryall paper.*

rydele see RIDDLE

rynnynge bed see BEDSTEAD

rynnyshe see RHENISH

ryve see RAKE; RIVE

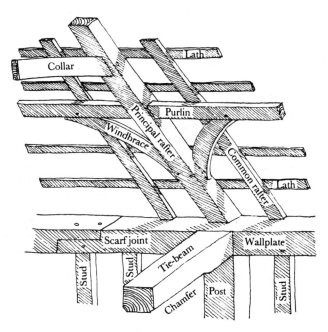

Roof structure

S

s. L. *solidus*, shilling of 12 pence; twenty shillings to the pound (see D., LI., £).

sacer see SAUCER

sack a class of white wines imported from Spain and the Canary Islands. *1545: for a bottell of sekke xijd.*

sacking, saken 1. Coarse HEMP or flax cloth used for making sacks. 2. Finer material, of mixed LINEN and silk, used for clothes. *1498-9: for a bolte of sekkene iijs. ixd. 1593: 1 fetherbedd of sacken. . . 1 holle Curtle of Crimsine vellett wth a uppbodye of yellowe sackinge iij li. vjs. viijd.*

sacring bell, sance bell in the pre-Reformation church, a bell rung at the time of the consecration of the elements in the eucharist. After the Reformation the term continued in use for a short time as the name for the bell used to summon the congregation to a service. *1459: j sakeeryng bell, weiyng xj unces. 1552: sance belle. 1568-71: mendinge the sawnce bell.*

saddle some of the varieties named in documents are:-

<u>great</u> saddle: the largest type of saddle, often armoured, for the great or war horse.

<u>livery</u> saddle: painted or stained with the colours or device of the owner, and usually for servants. *1597: iiij new whyte lyvery sadles wth girths. j grene lyvery sadle.*

<u>road</u> saddle: the ordinary saddle for a single rider with little luggage. *1603: a Rode saddle.*

<u>Scotch</u> saddle: a flattish saddle. *1597: a playne clothe scotch sadle.*

<u>side</u>-saddle for women. *1587: a womans sadle wt ye furniture xs. 1597: one syde sadle.*

<u>steel</u> saddle: armoured saddle fitted with steel plates to protect the rider's legs. *1588: iij steile sadles ij li.*

<u>trunk</u> saddle: for carrying large items of baggage. See MALEPILLION; TRUNK. *1597: j truncke sadle.*

See also PILLION; SUMPTER.

saddleleap 1. LEAP or basket to hang from a saddle. 2. A SEED-LEAP. *1499-1500: ij sadyllepys.*

saddlepole a loop to hold the CRUPPER. *1417: a sadlepole iijd.*

sadlip, sadlop, sadlup, sadlyp see SEED-LEAP

saese see SEARSE

saffron in the Middle Ages most saffron was imported from Spain, but the saffron crocus *Crocus sativus* was grown in Britain from the 15th century at the latest, although other forms, e.g. *C. nudiflorus*, have also been used for saffron. Walsingham was a notable centre for the production of saffron in the early 16th century. The stigmas of the plant were gathered and dried in a small kiln and, according to Culpeper (1653), made into 'square cakes', although the usual form is a powdery dust. It was used for flavouring (a mild honey smell), colouring - orange, yellow, and gold - and as a medicine for various conditions, notably jaundice. It was very expensive. *1517: the closes of saforne. 1585: a safferne kylle. 1587: iiij oz of saffron at xvjd* [an ounce]. *1606: a payer of mustard quernes and a Safforn kill, a whirne sive 2 saffron parers xviijd. fouer pound of safforne v li.*

sakeryng see SACRING

salad oil olive oil, used for various purposes apart from dressing salad. *1588: a pynte & a half of sallett oylle for the armor xiijd. 1619: Di' pynte of Sallett Oile for the Stone horses. 1654: for 6 swords cleansing and their scabbards making 10s. ½ pinte sallett oyle 6d.*

salamander 1. A red-hot poker used for igniting guns. 2. A flat metal plate on a handle, heated until red-hot and used to brown the top of cakes, puddings etc. *1745: One Salamander, one Poker.*

176

saler see SALT

sales see PLOUGH

sallet open helmet covering the top of the head, often with a tail to protect the neck; sometimes fitted with a visor or beaver to protect the face and throat. *1448: therfor my mastres dede us don on owr jakkys and owr salettis. 1597: Salletts olde 29.*

sallett see SALAD OIL

sallist salad. *1590: iij saucers iij Sallist dishes ij pewter saultsallers.*

saloon, salon Fr. *salon*, from *salle*, hall. The principal reception room in a great house. The name was used from the early 18th century for a room formerly called the great PARLOUR and was usually paired with a HALL. In the 18th century the saloon usually contained only chairs and a few tables, all standing against the wall, and choice items from the picture collection of the family.

salserse see SAUCER

salt as well as a seasoning, salt was essential in the days before refrigerators and freezers for preserving meat and fish. It was mined in Worcestershire and Cheshire, and also obtained by the evaporation of sea-water in shallow ponds or 'pans', or from the settling and filtering the mud of the pans for brine, which was then boiled. The inferior grey or bay salt was imported from Brittany, especially the Bay of Bourgneuf. Fish and meat were either dry-salted by burying them in salt or by steeping them in brine. *1562: for vj combz of baye salte at xxvs. the waye xvs. for one combe of white salte iiijs. iiijd.* See WAY.

salt a salt-cellar; often ornamental, and sometimes, as in trencher salt, in the form of an open dish. See p. 241. *1459: a saltsaler like a bastell, alle gilt with roses, weiyng lxxvij unces...j saltsaler, with j kever, well gilt, with many wyndowes, weiyng iiij^{xx}vj unces. 1511-2: a newe salte sylver and parcell gylte iij li. vijs. vjd. 1537: iiij salt sellers for the halle xijd. 1588: one silver Trencher Salte. 1637: [silver] j trenchr salt. j drume salt seller. j bell salt. j old fashen guilt salte.*

salt box wooden box in the kitchen to hold salt for cooking.

salt cat a mixture of gravel, old mortar, cummin, stale urine, and salt placed in the dovehouse to attract pigeons. See SALTSTONE. *1706: there is a salt Catt come from Tidd of Wells which I hope old Cole...may place accordingly in ye Dove house.*

salt fish generally means COD, LING, or some smaller fish buried in salt for preservation. *1498-9: [for] v warp of saltfyssh iijs. iiijd. 1582: Sawlte Fyshe ij^c xlvij... Sawltesamon iij qztes* [in stock] *one bo*[bought] *pr' iijs iiijd. Sawlte eles vj bo pric ijs xd. 1595: syxe saulte Fysshes.* See DRYING CHAMBER; STOCKFISH; WARP.

salting troe, trowgh, tub a TROUGH or tub for salting fish or meat.

saltstone lump of rock-salt, or a SALT-CAT. *1387: j saltston [bought for the doves 3d.].*

salve, black mixture of tar and grease for application to sheep with scab or other diseases. *1655: severall Ingredients for blacke salve 6s. 6d.*

samel, sammon brick half-burnt or underburnt BRICK. *1717: one fifth part only of the said Bricke to be soft Burnt or Samon Bricks.*

samite rich silken fabric woven with gold threads.

sampher true samphire, *Crithmum maritimum*, a seaside plant, the salty leaves of which are eaten as salad or pickled in brine or vinegar and used as a condiment, is not found in Norfolk. Samphire is the East Anglian name for glasswort, *Salicornia stricta*, which is used in the same way, and also in glassmaking. See CALE. *1649: Sampher 1s.*

sanap see SAVENAP

sance, saunce see SACRING BELL

sand was used as an abrasive for scouring utensils as well as for building. *1647: scoring sand 6d. 1710: 8 loads of Wash sand is charged 8s. & the Carriage 16s. 1 li. 4s...the 9 loades of Pitt* *sand charged wth the carriage together at 18s.*

sanders, saunders powdered wood of the sandalwood tree, used as white, yellow, and red colouring. *1498-9: [for 2 lbs. of] saunderes ijs. viijd. 1587: j box and saunders withit xijd. 1589: j qzter of sanders iiijd.*

sandling, sandlin a common entry in household accounts; either one of the sand-eels, or the dab *Limanda limanda.* See SMOULE. Just possibly the sanderling *Calidris alba*, a wading bird. At Stiffkey in 1593 sandlins were bought from Oct.-March.

sangueyn, sangweyne sanguine, blood-red. *1440: The goune nedyth for to be had; and of colour it wolde be a godely blew, or erlys a bryghte sangueyn.*

sarcenet, sarsnet very fine soft silk cloth, used for clothes and linings and as a furnishing fabric in the 15th-17th centuries. *1465: vij yerdes of wygth sarsenet for ij shertes. 1513: ij elnyes of blak sarcenes. 1588: one posted bedsteade, j tester of sarsnet. 1590: auncient of taffata sarcenet...Cloak of blacke Carle lyned with sarcenet. 1593: 5 Curtains of blacke & yellowe sarcenet & 3 Curtins of Crimsine duble sarcenett. 1597: One Large Sparver of stytched sylk: wth the trayne of redd sarcenet. . .3 curteyns of sarcenet in 10 panes black & yellow. . . [with armour] Skarfs of black & whyte sarcenet 2. 1637: j Skarlet Cloak lyned Changable sarsnett. . . an auncient of redd & white taffety sarsenet.*

sarche, sars see SEARSE

sartane certain. This and SARVES are typical examples of the Norfolk pronunciation. *1598: sartane Dishes.*

sarves service. *1590: too sarves bokes.*

saser, sasser see SAUCER

satin, sateyne cloth produced by a weaving method in which the warp almost completely covers the weft, mainly imported before the 16th century; cloths of other materials, or a mixture of silk and e.g. wool or linen threads, but with the same weaving pattern. See RUSSELL. *1593: tester & vallence of black figured vellett & russett Satten.*

satin a bridges, satin bruges a satin mixture of silk and linen, originally from Bruges, and used mainly as a furnishing fabric. *1552: iij vestmentes on of blewe Satten bruges another of greane Satten bruges. 1588: Tester & vallence of Satten of Bridges & fustyan of Naples. 1593: 1 longe yellowe Cushin of Satten a bridges ymbroydered wth black vs. 1597: One Longe Windowe Curtayn of satten abridgs in length 4 yards j qrter...ij wyndow Clothes of satten abbridges. . . one pece of satten abridges grene & orenge tawney lyned wth Canvas beinge 3 yards longe & bettr...one Curteyn of satten abridges at the stayer foot.*

sauce pan OFr. *sausse*, L. *salsa* salted. Originally a small pan with a handle in which sauce was prepared, but by the 17th century any small pot with a handle. *1648: 2 sawce panns 1s. 2d. 1709: 6 sauce pans.*

saucer OFr. *saussier.* Frequently occurring in accounts of the 13th-15th centuries, the saucer was a small shallow bowl, originally for salt or sauce, but by the 13th century a bowl for soup, pottage, or similar semi-liquid food. This continued until the 18th century, when the saucer was taken over by the tea-cup. *1459: xij sausers of silver, weiyng iiij^{xx}xv unces. 1584: vij large sawcers & vij smale sawcers of pewt' ijs. 1588: xij smale plates L Sawsers, xviij porryngers. 1592: salserse iij - vjd. 1595: halfe a dosing sacers. 1597: sixe pewter disshes fower Sassers. 1597 [with plate] 9 sawcers white 12 plates white. 1649: 1 dusen of white sawcers 3s. 1709: 16 Tea Cups & saucers. 1764: One Mahogany Tea Table with Twelve Tea Cups and Saucers.*

saulter see PSALTER

saunce bell see SACRING BELL

saunders see SANDERS

sausage traditionally made of chopped pork stuffed into small bags made from the

178

pig's intestines, sausages were being divided into individual LINKS by the early 17th century. They were often smoked in the chimney to help preserve them. The skinless sausage appeared in the 17th century; the meat was prepared and potted, and used by rolling out, moulding into shape, and frying.

sausage knife for chopping up meat for sausages. *1779: Sauceage Knife.*

sausage pan pan with shallow divisions to hold individual sausages. *1787: sauceage pan.*

sausage trough small trough in which meat was rolled before stuffing into sausage skins or using as skinless sausages. *1779: Sausage Trow. 1836: sausage trough & chopper.*

save safe, meat safe, closed cupboard with perforations, for keeping food. *1612: j save of splytter wth lock & kei.*

savenap sanap or strip of cloth placed over the main tablecloth to prevent plates and dishes marking it. See p. 241. *1352: [1 hanging table 1 canvas cloth] j savenap.*

saw saws with differentiating names are found in documents, but not all of them are identifiable. The OVERWHART saw was a cross-cut saw with a broad blade and coarse teeth and a handle at each end, for two sawyers, or a framed and tensioned pit-saw; sawyers are paid for 'overwhart cuts'. The roming, romen, roning, or roving saw has not been identified; it is differentiated from the 'long saw' - overwhart or pit-saw - and the 'cutting saw', and might be a bow-saw or the convex saw shown in late-medieval and 16th-century illustrations of carpenters at work. Shuting or shooting the saw was resetting and sharpening the teeth. See p. 242. *1592: on cotyng cotyng [sic] sawe viijd. 1593 1 rominge sawe. 1596: cuttyng sawe...on hande sawe. 1599: ij longe sawes j Romen sawe j Cuttinge sawe. 1621: a Roninge saw. 1647: a new overwharte saw 6s. 1649: an Over Whart saw mendinge 4d. 1733: Pd the Smith for battering Axes shuting Saws &c £1 4s. 6d.*

sawnce see SACRING

sawter PSALTER. *1474: j sawtere vjs. vijd.*

say cloth of fine texture, originally of linen but by the 16th century of wool or wool mixture. Used for clothes and furnishing. *1513: J Coveryng of Grenesay...J hangyng of Grenesay wt a rayle.. . iij Coteyne of Grene saye. 1588: v curtens of blew and yellowe saye...Curtens of Saye grene and yellowe. 1597: 3 Curteyns of saye good in xj panes grene & Crimson. 1604: j saye Loome wt all things ready to worck wythall. hearing line and say Reed. 1 say beame and 9 weaving shaftes...j ould say peticote j ould say wastcote.*

scaffle see SCAPPLE

scaffold a framework with a platform, on wheels, used to trim the high hedges of the formal garden. *1745: A Moveing Scaffold in the Pleasure Ground.*

scaffolder a scaffold-erector. See STAGE. *1619-20: for a staffolder [sic] 2 dayes for the plumer 2s. 4d.. . for 5½ dayes for a scaffolder for ye plumer 6s. 6d.*

scales, scoles, scoales, scooles, skalles, skoales, skoles, skolles, skolys etc. to judge from the spelling, scales must have been almost invariably pronounced 'scoles' or 'scooles' until midway through the 17th century, when the spelling 'scales' takes over. Up to the 18th century an ordinary pair of scales, of whatever size, was of the beam type, that is an iron or wooden beam balanced about its middle on an upright post, with a pan or platform at one end for the weights and one at the other end for the goods being weighed. The weights were of stone or metal, the latter being usually more accurate. The term 'pair of scales' often referred to the pans, the beam being listed separately. See STEELYARD. *1587: one payer of sope scoles. 1590: ij paire of skoles and one beam. 1591: j box wth weights & scooles for golde xijd. 1592: ij payer of skolys on of brase and ye other of wode xxd. 1592: a gret bem & skeles to it ijs. vjd. a medell bem & skeles xijd. in ieren waytes seven ston vs. in ledin waytes xxij li. in brasen waytes a li. & di. 1593: ij pare of scoles xl li. waight of lead. 1595: one Iron beame wth Scoalls*

179

& *weyghts. 1597: one yron beame & 2 great latten ballanz scoles. 1668: In the slaughter house two beames, scooles, waits and other things ther. 1677: one paire of skales. 1709: a pair of scales, an iron beam, 3 two stone weights, a 2 pound weight, an half pound weight, a two pound brasse weight.* See also SKAYLES.

scalon, scallion, shallot chibol, Welsh onion. *1279: scalon [sold 13d.].*

scamble, scambler, scambrel, skomble the bar-tailed godwit, *Limosa lapponica*. Sir Thomas Browne: 'Godwyts taken chiefly in marshland, though other parts not without them accounted the dayntiest dish in England and I think for the bignesse, of the biggest price.' Cf. Shakespeare's 'I'll get thee Young scamels from the rock' *The Tempest* II. ii. 184. H. Stevenson, *Birds of Norfolk* 1866: 'At Blakeney Mr Dowell states that bar-tailed godwits are known to the local gunners by the singular appellation of "Picks" and "Scamells". He believes by 'Scamells' are meant the females and those found singly in autumn.' *1593: [17th Dec.] a skomble & a graie plover vd. 1655: 3 scambrels 18d. . . 5 Pluver and 6 scamblers.*

scantling 1. A measuring-rod, ruler. 2. Dimensions, particularly cross-section of timber.

scapelery, scapular short cloak covering the shoulders. *c.1474: Item, a scapelery with an hodde.*

scapple, scaffle to reduce a block of stone to roughly the right size and shape. *1622: ground table...rough scaffled vizt 9 inches broad att one end & 13 inches at the other end.*

Scarborough water water from the celebrated mineral springs at Scarborough. *1738: Five Bottles of Scarborow Water 3s.*

scarf broad cloth band worn diagonally across the chest or around the waist or the headpiece by soldiers. *1588: ij oulde Scarfes one Carnation & the other blacke. 1590: One Calyver with a Cote and a skarffe. 1597: Skulls 2 covered with black clothe & yellowe skarfs bands.*

scarf cloth hung on back of chair to prevent soiling of upholstery. *1751: Six Walnutt back Stools cover'd with Tapestry, silk scarves & serge Cases.*

scarf a diagonal joint, sometimes with hidden keys, joining two beams end to end.

scarlet smooth soft woollen cloth, usually dyed scarlet with KERMES - the pregnant female of the insect *Coccus ilicis*; in the 18th century 'kermes mineral' was antimony trisulphide. *1588: Two fayer Imbroydered chayers the one of satten the other of skarlet.*

scarvy grass see SEA SCURVY GRASS

scate the fish skate, members of the *Rajidae* family, notably *Raja batis*. *1582: Scatefyshe One bo[bought] pric ijs.*

scavell a small narrow SHOVEL with the sides slightly upturned, used to clear drains and ditches. See SCOPETT. *1591: j scavell shovle*

sceled see CEIL

scepe, scepp see SKEP

schafynge disshe see CHAFING DISH

schalder see CHALDER

schamber, schawember see CHAMBER

schene a chain. *1463: my mastyr sold to my lord of Norfolke a schene of gold weyyng xix owncys and half an ownsce, the prise of every owns xxxs.*

schephous, schephus sheephouse, the building in which sheep sheltered. *1325: [making two pieces of wall behind] del schephus.*

schereman, scheres sherman, sheepshearer; shears. *1592: iij payer of owlde scheremanse scherese vjs.*

schereve see SHERIFF

schertys shirts *1450: old gownys for lynynges and old schetys and old schertys that may non lengur*

seven zu send hem hom in hast.
schofel see SHOVEL
schone, shoen shoes
schoolhouse room in a mansion in which the children of the household were taught. *1637: in the schoolhouse. . . In the schoolhouse chamb'.*
schot door-bolt. *1318: j schot [for the door of the hall].*
schotnayl, schetnayl unidentified type of NAIL. *1293: C schotnayl ijd. ob.*
schoveler see SHOVELER
schoyell a sill. See CART. *1507-8: a schoyell of a carte xiiijs. iiijd.*
schraggants, schraggator, schragg, schraggyng see SHRAG
schymney see CHIMNEY
scituat situated
scoales, scoalls, scoles etc. see SCALES
scochen escutcheon, heraldic shield; badge, keyhole-plate, gunlock plate. *1474: ij schochenes viijd. 1484: the first scochen shal be of my Husbondes armes and myn, depted.*
sconce, sconse 1. A screened candlestick or lantern; from the late 17th century, an ornamental small bracket fitted with candlesticks and mounted on the wall, often with a mirror backing. 2. A screen; partition. *1603: a bushell poke a Seeve a skonse and a fanne. 1709: 1 Pair of glass sconces...a brasse sconce. 1745: Four Brass Sconces Two Glass D^0.*
scoolray see SCULLERY
scope scoop, bowl-shaped utensil for bailing a boat; large basket, SKEP. *1326: j scope [for the boat]. 1328: j scope [for corn 1¼d.]. 1720: six Scoppes for the Lime kell 3s. 6d.*
scopett, scoppett, scuppet a narrow shovel with edges turned up for turning malt, shovelling corn, mud etc. See MUDSKUPPETT; SCAVELL. *1590: a corne scopett. 1595: ij scuppet shovels. 1718: One spade and one scuppet 3s. 6d.*
score normally = 20, but may be 21 for weight e.g. in the weight of pigs a 'score' is 20/21 lbs, and in the mid-17th century a score was 21 COOMB of grain. *1655: [receipts] wheat 10^C 2^B 0^P. Recd for half a score of wheat sold ye miller of wickingham full 6 li. 2s. 6d. . . for a score of wheat full paid viz 4^C att 11s. and 6^C 2^B at 12s. 4d. July 18 and 10^C: 2^B after 13s. and 2s. 6d. over Aug: 14. 12 li. 10s. 6d.* See C.
scot a local as opposed to a national tax in the Middle Ages; a manorial due.
Scotch carpet carpet of double-weave with no pile and reversible, popular in England in the second half of the 18th century. *1764: [Best Lodging Room] 3 Scotch Bedside Carpets. 1779: [Keeping Parlour] Scotch carpet 9 foot by 9.*
Scotch cap 1. A helmet. See SKULL. *1591: one armyn sworde a skotishe cape of stele twoe ould daggers.* 2. The Glengarry of Balmoral, a man's cloth cap.
Scotch cattle by the 16th century Galloway cattle were being driven down from Scotland to Norfolk to be fattened and bred, eventually to supply the London meat trade. *1685: five Heifers 10 li. tenn Scotch heifers 15 li. 5s. tenn Scotch steares 17 li. 10s.*
Scottish cloth 17th-century Scotch cloth was said to be made from the fibres of nettles, and 'a sort of white Sleasie Soft Cloth' used instead of the dearer callico for bed-linen and window curtains. *1589: iij ells & j qtr of skottish cloth. 1593: 3 towells of sctoch cloth viijs.*
Scottish needlework embroidery of a pattern thought to have been Scotch. *1597: 6 newe Joyned stooles cou'ed wth scottish nedleworke. . . a old fashoned Chayer ~~of walnuttree cou'ed wth scottish nedlework~~ wth snapdragons.*
Scottish stirrups see STIRRUPS
scouring see SAND
screen see SIEVE

screen 1. A fixed screen across the end of the HALL or major room to eliminate draughts, usually with a central door or opening. 2. A movable screen to shield from draughts. 3. A movable screen to shield from excessive heat of the fire. *1580: a screyne of wickers xijd. 1608: 3 skreenes. 1620: a Cubbord fastened to the Skreine. . . In the farras ou' the hall skreine a lether Stondard much other lumber. 1637: [parlour] j wicker skreene js. vjd.* See FARRAS; FORCER.

screws 1. Apparatus for raising large objects, operated by a screw-jack; a jack. 2. A bench vice. *1592: seven pair of scrues broken & whole xxs. 1647: use of his Scruesses aboute ye Barne. 1664: two paire of screwes to raise the house 2s.* See RANGE.

scrowle scroll. *1588: the hanginge of the Chambre of olde Tappestrie wth scrowles xiijs. iiijd.*

scrutore escritoire, writing-desk. *1734: One scrutore 2 li. 2s. 1756: One mahogany scrutore.*

sctoch see SCOTCH CLOTH

scuchon, scutcheon see ESCUTCHEON; SCOCHEN

scull see SKOLE

scullery, sculling OFr. *escuelerie*, from L. *scutella*, dish. Room concerned with dishes, plates, utensils for the table. Although the word dates from the 14th century it is scarcely to be met in Norfolk documents before the 17th century, the function of the room being performed by the BUTTERY, BACKHOUSE, or KITCHEN. A low-class worker in this type of room was a scullion. The scullery of 1751 quot. is a bowl or tub for washing-up or waste food. *1622: That there be a little vawlt made on the side of the Skullery under the Cole house to receive 3 or 4 Chalder of Coles, and a passage to it, out of the Scullery, to take them out. 1637: In the skullery. 1647: Paid to the Scullinge boye. 1648: paid Tho: the Sculinge his qtr wages 10s. 1706: In the scoolrey. 1751: a Copper Scullery.*

scummer, skimmer, skoomer, skummer flat ladle, often perforated, for skimming liquids. See p. 117. *1591: ij skoomers & one basteinge spoone xd.*

scuppet see SCOPETT

scure skewer. *1737: two Iron Scures.*

scurvy grass see SEA SCURVY GRASS

scutcheon eel not identified. Logically it would refer to a shield-shaped mark on the fish, but none of the true eels seems to have such a feature. 'Scutcheon' as a scale on a fish seems to date only from the mid-19th century. See EEL. *1655: 16 Lemmons 1s. 3 Cabbages 6d. Scutcheon Ealls 2s.*

scythe the traditional scythe has a curved, tapering blade, two to three feet long, sharpened on the inner edge and fixed at 90° to the shaft and canted so that it lies more-or-less flat to the ground when the scyther is using it. Up to the 17th century the shaft was usually straight, but in that century the curved shaft seems to have come into use, although the straight shaft persisted. Two handles are fixed, one near the end of the shaft furthest from the blade, and one at a convenient point down the shaft. It was sharpened by a RUB. Like similar tools, the scythe was often the property of the worker rather than of the employer. Scythes were used for mowing grass, hay, reeds, weeds, and corn, although much corn was reaped by SICKLE. As scythers in a hayfield, or mowing stubble, moved in echelon, left-handers were not welcome. See p. 242. *1306: j sythe & j hok vijd. ob. 1588: dyv'se mowinge sythes and reede sythes. 1595: ij sythes redy hange. 1597: A corne sythe, & a grasse sythe..*

sea coal is mineral COAL (as distinct from CHARCOAL), derived from the exposure of beds of coal by the action of the sea, although by the 17th century it may have been taken to mean coal brought by sea from Northumberland. It was usually bought at the port of entry, e.g. Wells, by the CHALDER. By the middle of the 17th century it was being called simply 'cole' or 'coles'. Fireplaces for sea coal generally had some sort of grate and a PUR or poker, an implement hardly ever found on a wood-burning hearth. *1484: ij Chaldr & di' of see coole. 1562: for v cobz of sea coale at xviijd the combe vijs. jd. 1592: A payer of yrons to make a seacole fyre wth ij barres ijs. . . A racke for sea Cooles wth ij barres of yron vjs. viijd. 1593: 5 Chaulder of Sea coles liijs. iiijd. 1648: for 9 chalder & halfe of Coles at 15s. ₽ Chalder 7 li. 2s. 6d. for the loadeinge of them 3s. for my Charges & spent uppon the Carters 4s.*

sea cole sea kale, *Crambe maritima*, a wild plant grown as a garden plant from at least the 18th century for its edible young shoots, blanched and eaten as a vegetable. *c.1720: Sea Coal Seed. How to Manage it.*

seal, seel, sele see PLOUGH

seal, sealing to panel; wooden panelling; See CEIL. *1544: sealynge abought in other places. 1572: keys sealings doores.*

seam OE *séam*, ML. *summa*, load, pack-horse load; standardised from the 13th century as a QUARTER, that is 8 BUSHELS. *1264: [produce of barley] viij ^{xx} & xix suma & ij B'. 1482: for treching [threshing] v seme barle xxd. 1585: one seame of barley & iij bushels nette.*

seamue commonly identified with the common gull, *Larus canus*, its presence in a household account with the description 'wild' is not easily explicable. Sir Thomas Browne: 'Here is also the pica marina or seapye, many sorts of Lari, seamewes and cobs'. *1593: a cuple of wild seamues ijd.*

sea-pie the oyster-catcher, *Hæmatopus ostralegus*. See SEAMUE. *1593: a sea pie a graie plover.*

searce, searse, sars OFr. *saas*, sive, strainer. Small fine sieve for sifting flour, straining liquids, etc. of wood or metal. *1459: j sars of brasse...j sarche of tre. 1588: one saese of latyn. 1589: a searse to drayne fysse ijs. 1592: a baskett a sercer an ale stole. 1636: i smale brasen searce. 1647: 1 searse for the Cooke 1s. 6d.*

sea scurvy grass *Cochlearia officinalis*, used as a remedy for scurvy. The least common in Norfolk of *Cochlearia ssp*. In 1653 Culpeper's sea scurvy-grass seems to be *C. Anglica*, and under 'scurvy-grass' he has *C. rotundifolia* (Dutch round-leafed scurvy-grass, which he thought had the best effect), *C. danica* (stalked scurvy-grass), *C. Grœnlandica* (Greenland scurvy-grass), and *C. Armoracia* (horse radish scurvy-grass). *1654: for sea Scurvy grass 7s. 6d.: & at Norwch 9d. 1655: a quantity of Sea Scurvy Grass 6d.*

seaxes sacks. *1593: iiij seaxes.*

second see BREAD

sedge various coarse rushes and flag-like grasses, used for horse-collars, chair-bottoms, ridging a thatched roof etc. *1320: [carrying] de segges [from the pond to the gate]. 1328: seggs [bought for burning 9s. ½d.] 1587: seigge chayer. 1621: for 4 paire plough traise & 4 segen Collers 3s. 4d. 1656: a segging Coller 3d. 1664: for putting a segging bottome into a chayer iiijd.*

sedlep, sedlupe, sedlupe, setlap see SEED-LEAP

sedyle see SETTLE

seed-leap basket or box, hung in front of the sower by a strap or cord round the neck, to carry the seed to be hand-sown or broadcast on the field. See p. 242; LEAP. *1357: j sedlep vd. 1599: one setlapp. 1603: ii old seeves & i old sadlippe. 1714: a sadlup a saw a letch a wash Baskett 3s. 6d. 1738: Two wooden Sedlopes 2s.*

seeled, seeler, seeling see CEIL

seething trough trough for seething or steeping, soaking, pickling e.g. meat in brine. *1591: a seething trowe.*

seffe see SIEVE

segamore the sycamore, *Acer pseudoplatanus*, was probably introduced by the Romans. Its wood was used for dairy vessels and, having a compact grain and taking polish well, for inlay in walnut furniture, when it was known as harewood; also as a substitute for satinwood, which it resembles. *1474: a payre of beddes* [beads] *of segamore iiijd.*

sege a seat; PRIVY. *1505: Willelmo Stapylton for skoryng seges viijd*

segen, segging, segges, seigge see SEDGE

seisin see p. 243.

sekatoure an executor

sekken see SACKING

sel, sele, seal, siel ON *sæll*, happy; season, best time. *1639: in the time of haye seale. 1655: at plough with Bulls and Harrowes in Barly Siel at 8d. a man.*

seland cloth ? cloth from Zealand in the Netherlands; or sealed, that is stamped or sealed to authenticate the quantity and quality. *1459: j pece of Seland clothe, with dyvers sealys at the endys.*

sele sill. See GROUNDSILL; PLOUGH

seled, seleing see CEIL

seler, seller cellar. *1459: Celar. In the seler, certayn vessell.*

selfer silver. *1612: j selfer spon.*

selleridge cellar. *c.1620: The Floore of the selleridge on the west side of the house. 1621: the height of the Selleredge to be 7 foote and a halfe betwen the ground and the seelling or ther abouts.*

sellore ceilor, bed canopy. See BEDSTEAD. *1474: a sellore xijd.*

sement cement; lime mortar, often including pounded brick or stone, or mixed with RESIN for waterproofing. *1663: put in sement to keep out the wett.*

sempiternum woollen serge cloth, made in the West Country from the 1630s. *1633: halfe an ell of sempeternum.*

senage see SYNODALS

sendal a fine rich silk material.

sennayl, senmail, semnail see NAIL

sensor, sensour a censer.

sequence hymns or musical pieces sung in the pre-Reformation mass.

sercer, serse see SEARCE

serge woollen fabric, little different from SAY, used for hangings, furnishing, and clothing. *1688: fower smale Backe chaires covered wth searge...twoe lowe Stooles covered wth searge.*

serpentin(e) small cannon, bore 1½ inches, often used in ships or for sieges. The chambers were movable breechblocks. *1459: iij gonnes, called serpentins. 1481: for x serpentines, and to eche of them iij chambers, weing every piece withe all that longeth to it, Cxiij li.*

serpentine powder 1. powder containing herbs e.g. dragons, dragonwort *Dracunculus vulgaris*, and FENUGREEK, used as an antidote to snake-bite and for curing skin and eye complaints. 2. gunpowder, powdered rather than granulated, used in the SERPENTINE. *1538-9: paid ijs. vjd. for vj li. of serpentyn powder.* See PILE POWDER.

serrop see SYRUP

sessor an assessor.

sesterne see CISTERN

set, sett, setling set, slip, sucker, seedling, sapling. See OSIER; SPRING. *1392: in setlyngs [cut and placed around] le Pond iiijd. 1619-20: plume setts. Elme setts. Whitethorne setts. 1654: [osiers] 9500 setts valued at 6s. 8d. p̱ 1000. . . 60 Pople setlings. 1664: made up the shreedings of settlings cutt in Mr Morses fearme ground & had them into the woodyard.*

set cloth coarse woollen cloth dyed or 'set' in woad; light blue.

setlap see SEED-LEAP

setnet fishing-net spanning a stream or channel, into which the fish were driven. Blomefield 1745: '19 appropriated Fishing-Places, which they called Setts, which were yearly allotted by the Mayor, to certain Fresh-Water Fishermen.' See NET. *1482: a sett net of ij fadom, prise ijs. 1593: j boote called the Jelivat with 3 old setnets.*

sett tool, possibly rake, in BREWING. *1692: one beer cooler 2 mash tubbs a storrer & sett 16s. 6d.*

setting chisel heavy chisel used by stonemasons. *1622: a Settinge Chysel xviijd.*

setting iron, setting stick implement with a drop-shaped end for setting small plants and seeds. See DIBBLE. *1587: bucketts & setting sticks. 1593: 1 rele & 1 settinge yron.*

setting loom, lomb loom for weaving SET CLOTH. *1319: j settingelomb [for the use of the bishop 18d.]*

setting on the eaves of a roof; junction of wall and roof. *1621: the second storye of this building shalbe 9 foote or ther abouts to the seting one of the Roufe. but over the stable shalbe but 7 foote to the seting one of the Roufe and ther shalbe no second flower...Second story 2 bricks in thicknes from the water table to the setingone of the Roufe.*

settle wooden bench with arms and a high back, often with a box or chest seat. Occurs infrequently in inventories of the 16th and 17th centuries, but revived by the Victorians. *1513: J lanncetyll* [long settle]. *1515: j longbakked sedyle. 1588: a shorte settle of Waynescotte with a backe havinge locke & Jemowes ijs. vjd. 1606: Settell with a rome for a bedd. 1637: one broken old setle a boute a yard & a quarter longe 1s. 1665: mended the settle* [in strangers' stable].

setwork a kind of embroidery imitating tapestry and used in upholstery fabrics; an English version of TURKEY-WORK. In the example cited, the top of the CHEST must have been upholstered as a seat. *1590: danske chest of setworke viijs.*

several 1. Separately, individually. 2. Privately owned land, properties etc. as opposed to common. *1595: iiij acres of pease fetches & oates as they are sev'ally sowne.*

several the vernacular understatement for 'many', e.g. referring to the crowds at the Royal Norfolk Show, 'there were several people there.'

sewell an article of cloth, perhaps connected with the sewer, the person in charge of the table and food at banquets; a tablecloth. A sewell or shewell was a scarecrow, or something hung up to frighten deer into going in the right direction at a hunt. The length argues against a possible misreading of towelles, towellys. *1459: iiij sewelles playn warke eche cont' in lenthe ij yerds dim'...ij wasschyng sewellys of warke, eche of x yerds.*

sewerte surety. *1466: became sewerte to my mastyr for the bayle of on William Valenden.*

sewet see SUET

sewger sugar. *1526: for A pownde of Sewger.*

sewker sucker, a blood-letter, leech. *1499-1500: to the sewker vijd.*

sexse sacks. *1592: iij corne sexse ijs.*

shack in general, the right of pasturage (a) by the lord's sheep on the tenants' fields and (b) by the tenants' animals on the common fields. *Phillips' World of Words*, 1706: 'Shack, (in Norfolk and Suffolk) the liberty of winter pasturage; the Lords of Manours having the privilege to feed their flocks of sheep at pleasure, upon their tenants' land during the six winter months. Also a custom in Norfolk to have common for hogs, from the end of harvest till seed time in all men's grounds; whence *to go at shack* in that country, signifies as much as, to go at large'. Shack is also grain fallen to ground at harvest; stubble. A shack-CART was presumably a stubble or straw cart. *1593: ij shacke cartes & j tumbrell xxs. 1636: one shackecart with shod wheels.*

shack trace see TRACE

shade window-blind. See BARREL. *1745: one wire window shade. 1751: twenty four old Spring Shades*

shadow or comet, in the period 1580-1610 was an oblong cap of stiff material, usually velvet, worn flat on the head and bent to fall behind and shade the neck; and at the same period and up to the 1640s a linen cap edged with lace with a rounded front, falling flat on the neck behind. *1587: ij corner kerchers, vij coyfes, ij shadowes, iiij payre of handruffes.*

shag worsted, sometimes silk, cloth with velvet nap on one side. *1590: one blacke velvett Cloake lyned with shagge xxxiijs. iiijd. 1633: ij yards and halfe an ell of shadg at 2s. 6d. the yard. 1709: A shag yellow & green bed. 1751: a Parcell of Yellow Dutch Shagg.*

shalloon woollen cloth woven from fine yarn, first made in England *c.*1640 in Hampshire, later in Suffolk and Norfolk. *1718: For a new Postilian Coat & Cap, with a Cape to the Coat, & Lined with a Sholone £3 10s. c.1730: Caffoy curtains lined with Shalloon. 1745: case curtains of red shaloon.*

shalme, shawm an early version of the oboe, with a double reed enclosed in a globular mouthpiece, shawms came in 6 sizes from treble to great bass shawm, which was over 9 feet long. *1597: one olde Chest, wth 2 vyollens & 2 shalmes.*

sham false lockplates put on doors or dummy doors for appearance. *1745: Two brass Mortice Locks to Stair Cases and Shams to D⁰. . . Four Brass Mortice Locks to Doors. Two Sham D⁰.*

shamfron see CHAMPFRAIN

shank piece leather from the lower part of the animal's leg. *1593: iiij heades of leather x shanke peces.*

shave spokeshave, carpenter's and wheelwright's drawknife consisting of a straight blade sharpened on one edge, with a handle at either end at right angles to the blade, and used by drawing towards the person. *1584: a wymble a parser a hammer a shave.*

sheaf a bundle of 30 pieces or 'gads' of iron or steel. *1341: [2 sheaves (garb') & a half of steel 22d. price per sheaf 9d. less in total ½d.].*

shear to cut corn or shear sheep. *1537: for a dayes worke of viij sherers at iijd the day in shering the whete closse. 1647: for the Clipinge of 1368 sheepe at Siderstone 2 li. 0s. 6d...to a boye for mending snips 4d.*

shear, shirr ? the female part of a bolt, or the iron rest into which the latch or SNECK on a gate or door falls. However, if related to 'shear' meaning cut, scissors, shears, or ultimately derived from the OE *scyttel*, bar, bolt, lock, possibly the latch or sneck itself. *Prompt. Parv.:* 'Schyttyl, or sperynge. *Pessulum, vel pessellum.*' See SHERINGE. *1647: Boultes & sheares wayinge 6 li. & halfe 2s. 2d. 1649: a new shirr to the latch of the gate 1d.*

shearing board tailor's board for cutting or shearing cloth. *1595: a sherynge borde. 1601: fowre sheire boordes xs.*

shearing knife a sharp knife, carving knife. *1587: a sheeringe knife a choppinge knife. 1593: 1 Cliver 1 shering knife 3 small knyves.*

shears shears consisting of a pair of wedge-shaped blades connected at the wide end by a semicircular spring were used by tailors, cloth-workers and sheep-shearers. Garden shears were of the scissor type, with handles. *1591: v payr of shermanshears. 1592: iij payer of owlde scheremanse scherese vjs.*

sheet sometimes defined by type, e.g. linen, coarse, servants' etc., and sometimes by breadth. See HARDEN; WEB. Inventories often list all the sheets of the household together and not on individual beds. *1588: xx payre of Shetes of ell brode, and of yarde brode viij paire xvij li. xxiiij paire of course shetes for servaunts v li. 1593: 2 paire of fine sheets xxs...26 paire of sheets & one odd sheete wherof 15 are abrod upon bedds v li. iiijs.*

sherding see SHREEDING

sheriff the Crown's chief representative in the county from the late 11th century, in charge of the military functions of the county, accounting for the revenues of the Crown, and being the main executive of the King's courts. The twice-yearly sheriff's tourn, around Easter and Michaelmas, in the court of each hundred reviewed FRANKPLEDGE and dealt with minor criminal cases, and the sheriff also held the monthly county court. The powers of the sheriff were reduced in 1461 when criminal cases were transferred to the Justices of the Peace, and the introduction of the office of Lieutenant (Lord Lieutenant) of the county in 1551 to be in charge of the county's defence further limited the powers of the sheriff, but with his considerable staff he was still responsible for *i.a.* the execution of writs, the empanelling of juries, and the collection of fines. Sheriffs were chosen for one year only, and in spite of the diminution of power the office remained important and prestigious.

sherivescot tax paid to support the office of SHERIFF. *1498-9: [for] scherereschot [there 4d.].*

sherman sheep-shearer.

shew ? a type of nail for studding cart-wheels; CART tyre. *1647: [smith] 4 stone 9 li of Iron aboute the carte to make staves pallett nayles boults cobs & shews at 4d. p̱ li. 1 li. 6s. 8d. for Shooeinge the wheeles & puttinge in the furrs 4s.*

shewyngehorne shoehorn.

ship vessel shaped like a ship to hold incense. *1459: [chapel] j ship, with gilt verges, weiyng ix unces. 1552: one shippe of sylver parcell gylt wayeing xj unces.*

shippin, shippon cattle-shed, cowhouse; term not often found in Norfolk. *1591: in the yard & shippin.*

shires see SHEARS

shirr see SHEAR

shist see CHEST

shittle cock, shuttlecock small rounded piece of cork fitted with a circle of feathers, used in the game of BATTLEDORE and shuttlecock, which in England dates from the Middle Ages and evolved into badminton. *1687: for shittle Cocks & Battledores 2s. 6d.*

shiver a small iron wedge; a pulley; a splinter of wood. *1621: For haspes staples shivers For the brickmakers moulds.*

shoaf, shofe a sheaf, of corn, hemp etc. *1592: of hempe shofes CCC - xs.*

shock the Norfolk word for sheaves of corn leaning together in the field, elsewhere called a stook. *Prompt. Parv.: 'Schokke, of corne. Congelima, tassis.'*

shod see CART; SHOVEL.

shoe, coal a small coal-skuttle.

shoemakers' hairs fine thread used in shoemaking. *1587: iij boxes of shoemakers heres.*

sholone see SHALLOON

sholve see SHOVEL

shooting spreading and watering clay before using it as CLAY LUMP or for wattle-and-daub. *1522-3: for iiij loode of claye cartyng & ye caryage viijs. xd. To olde Hamond for shotyng of ye same cleye by ye spase of j daye goyng to his owne borde iiijd. for tredyng of ye same cleye by ye space of a nothyr daye wt his borde iiijd.*

shooting glove glove worn by bowmen to protect the drawing hand. *1465: a shotenge glove iiijd. 1592: an olde shotinge glove a shefte of Arrowes xijd.*

shooting lead, shooting saw see LEAD; SAW

shopboard shop counter or display and serving table. *1593: one shopboorde wth 3 tressells.*

shopmark mark or tally kept in a shop to record unpaid bills or credit. *1584: Debts by the shoppmarkes.*

shore timber balk for shoring up walls etc. *1592: One ould ladder & thre Shores iijs.*

shotnail see NAIL

shott young weaned pig, under the age of twelve months. *1593: 21 shotts leane of the smaller sort iij li. 11 leane Shotts of the greater sorte lvs. 1595: vij Swyne & vij shotts ls. 1649: geldinge of fower shotts 6d. 1734: 24 shotts £6.*

187

shottel see PLOUGH

shotten see HERRING

shouldger soldier. *1665-6: paid the shouldger.*

shoulfe see SHOVEL

shove sheaf. *1592: hemp in the shove.*

shovel before the later 18th century shovels generally had a wooden blade, sometimes with an iron or steel edge. Several different types can be distinguished:-

bare without the iron edge to the blade.

casting for 'casting' clay for CLAY LUMP or wattle-and-daub walls.

corn broad flat blade for dealing with grain.

fire for removing ash from the fireplace, or a perforated type to sift the unconsumed coal from the ash.

paring for paring turf.

shod with iron or steel edge to the blade.

skomel possibly connected with scum, skim, that is for skimming turf, liquid, or muck.

skuppet, scuppet, scopit a narrow blade with flanges for cleaning out ditches, HOLLS etc. See MUDSCUPPETT; SCAVEL; SCOPETT.

1352: j cornschowele. 1465: a shodde sholve iiijd. 1482: for ij schofelis ijd. 1584: a shode sholve. 1592: a spade & muckforke skomel shovel & a muck crome xviijd. 1593 6 shoulfes wherof 1 shod. 1595: ij scuppet shovells one shod shovell...ij bare shovels. 1593: one cole fire shoulfe. 1620: fier Shovells twoe whereof the one to sift the Ashes or cinders from the coales. 1647: 1 new castinge shovell 1s.

shoveler a migrating duck, *Anas clypeata.* Prompt. Parv.: 'Schovelerd, or popler, byrd (schoveler, or popelere, K., scholarde or poplerd, S., schones bec, or popler byrd, P.) *Populus'.* See POPELER. It was also known locally as the spoonbill, but should not be confused with the true spoonbill, *Platalea leucorodia,* which is the bird referred to in Sir Thomas Browne: 'The platea or shouelard, which build upon the topps of high trees. They haue formerly built in the Hernerie at Claxton and Reedham now at Trimley in Suffolk. They come in March and are shot by fowlers not for their meat butt the handsomenesse of the same, remarkable in their white colour copped crowne and spoone or spatule like bill.' *1459: j clothe hangyng of Schovelers.*

showes, shoyes shoes

shrag, schrag, schraggs, schraggings, schraggants to lop, prune; the twigs or branches lopped off. Schraggator: the man that schrags. *Prompt. Parv.*: 'schragge trees, *infra* in schredyn...schredynge, of trees and other lyke, *sarmentacio, sarculacio.'* *1332: sraggyngs [of oak and ash alder and] mapel. 1362: [underwood] de xls. de schraggyngs. 1374:[underwood] de schraggs & paryngs [of oak]. 1387: in mill CCC fagotts [in the wood 30s. 3d. In bindings bought for the same from the] schraggator iijs. iiijd. [1 man 36 days throwing down] splentes schraggants [and setting thorns].*

shreading made of shreds or scraps; patchwork. *1637: a shreading cov'let.*

shred, shreading small length of wood attached to the end of the rafters of a roof to extend the eaves beyond the line of the wall. See FUR. *c.1620: [carpenter] a hammer beame Roofe: and purloynes, with gable ends shreds and dormers to the new roffe.*

shreed shred, strip of leather or cloth, used *i.a.* for tying and nailing up shrubs and fruit trees. *1621: 2 li. rosen 9 oz wax & shreeds and pap. 1665: 86 pecks of shreeds 2s. 6d. 1724: China dish 6s. starch 5s. 6d. Shreeds 5s. 10d.*

shreed 1. To lop, prune. *1664: made up the shreedings of settlings cutt in Mr Morses fearne ground & had them into the woodyard.* 2. To shred, peel. *1590 [kitchen] one shreedinge knyfe one clyver. 1615:[kitchen] one shreddinge knife.*

188

shruff rubbish. *1664: stubbed up chatts in the little orchard & raked up shruff.*
shucking, shogging unsteadily, in an agitated way. *Prompt. Parv.*: 'Schoggyn, or roggyn. *Agito.* Schoggyn, shakyn, or waveryn. *Vacillo.*' *1637-9: ran shucking up and down from place to place.*
shud a shed. *1705: the Shud.*
shulve to shovel; a SHOVEL. *1597: a shulve on Axe. 1664: shulved up the mucke at the berne and stable doores.*
shuting saw see SAW.
shyckforke two-tined FORK for sheaves; pitchfork.
sickle OE *sicol, sicel,* possibly related to L. *seco,* to cut; reap-hook, often with a saw-toothed cutting edge (medieval manorial accounts record the 'dentilation' of sickles); some illustrations show it in use with a crooked hand-rake or gatherer held in the other hand. Most corn from the Middle Ages to at least the 17th century seems to have been reaped with a sickle, with only short straw left attached to the ears, while the stubble, up to three feet high, was either grazed off later or mown with a scythe for fodder, bedding, or thatch. *1562: for v sickles at xd. p pece. 1591: x olde siccles & iij glasses. 1594: sex olde sykells. 1597: a mattock and a corne Sithe...ij long cutting sickles a grubb yron & iiij didalls.*
side board 1. A table standing at the side of the HALL or the main table. 2. A TABLE at the side of room, used for display, serving food, storing tableware, etc. This usage seems to begin in the 17th century. *1620: Side Boards twoe. 1637: 4 cubboard cloaths 8 towells six side boarde cloaths. . . One smale sydborde 3s. 4d. . . One syde boarde 5s.*
side silver a manorial due. See SIGNING MONEY. *1648: leet fee & side silver due to the mannor of Snetsham 9s. 6d.*
siel see SEL
siel OE *sál,* ON *seil,* rope, cord. OED quotes 1668 'for a sayle and band to ty up the Bull', but that may be SALE, a yoke, collar. *1654: mendinge ye Dragg-net 6d. siel band line for ye Nett 14d.*
sield see CEIL
sieve implement for sifting various materials, up to modern times consisting of a thin slice of wood a few inches wide bent to form a round frame, with a bottom of split rods, sedge, fibres, metal, or coarse hair-cloth, according to the fineness needed. See P. 242; SEARCE. *1318: botmyngg j syve. 1618: two payles and a hearinge* [hair] *seve. 1621: bottominge a mortar sive. 1647: new bottominge of 2 siffes 1s. 1764: Seven Hair sieves One Lawn d⁰.*
sifter, sifting iron fire SHOVEL for sifting coals and cinders from ash. *1637: a siften iron. 1709: an iron sifter.*
sifting stool framework to support a large corn or flour-sieve. *1636: 1 sadlope, 2 shovels, a sifting stoole & 9 sackes.*
signing money a customary payment at the manorial court leet. *1648: for Signeinge money at the Leete 8d.*
siling see CEIL
siller cellar. *1664: They finished the ranges of bricke worke in the wine siller...pavemented the bricke ranges to sett the wine bottles upon...pavemented the great siller...pulled downe the brickeworke & doorestall at the going into the strong beere siller.*
sindon soft silk or linen material similar to SENDAL.
singing bread the bread or wafer used in the pre-Reformation eucharist. *1459: box for syngyng brede weiyng iiij unces. 1483: for syngenge bred jd.*
sink stone paving-stone with a hollow and hole in the centre to act as a drain. *1733-4: Setting up a sinck stone making good ye paving & Working a sinck ston in ye paving under ye table &*

letting in a Washer & plugg to D°. 1734: Portland sinck Stone for ye poultry house.

sinomon see CINNAMON

siphe see SIEVE

sipris see CYPRESS

sistern see CISTERN

sith see SCYTHE

sittuorne citron, the fruit of *Citrus medica*. Before the 16th century it could include lemon and lime. See POME-CITRON. *1647: Sittuorne, Eringes & Maple Biskett.*

sizars scissors

sk- for words beginning sk- see also sc-.

skalles see SCALES

skame skein. *1602: thre skore skames of Corsse yarne.*

skatches skates. *1588: payer of Feñe skatches ijs. vjd.*

skayles, scales, kayles a form of skittles or ninepins. An act of Edward IV prohibited playing 'cloish, kayles, half-bowl, hand-in-hand and hand-out, quekeboard.' *1596: the sayd Noman was playinge at scales in the barne .*

skeme possibly related to scheme, an arch of less than a semicircle. Brick or stone coping for a wall or gable. *1665: cutt footlanes & skemes for part of the heading of the wall of the bridge. . . water table brick & skemes.*

skep, skeep large deep basket; beehive. See pp. 28, 242. *1274: j scepp [for the horses 1½d.]. 1306: j skeppe [for the stotts 2d.]. 1498-9: [for] ij skeppys vjd, et pro xiij smale skeppys xvjd. 1499-1500: xiij smale skeppys et v too eryd skeppys et ij sadllepys ijs. vijd. 1592: a skeppe to put in clothes. 1595: six skepps of Bees God Save them. 1636: bese skepes and one sithe 5s.*

skerches see PLOUGH

skewer thin wooden or iron spike for holding meat together when cooking. *1595: lytle skures.*

skeyne, skene a short dagger or long knife, used as a weapon by the Irish kerns and the Scots. *1591: A skeyne or Woodknyff ijs.*

skife see PLOUGH

skillet small pan with short legs and a handle; a pot fitting inside a separate stand that had its own handle and legs. *1588: vj skilletts iiijs. vjd. 1592: on posnet ij skilletts. 1637: j skillet wthout a Cou' & j skillet wth a Couer. 1648: 1 new skillet & Frame 7s. 6d. . . [smith] 1 new frame to a skillett 2s. 2d. 1665: [smith] one foot for a skillet.*

skink OE *scencan*, ON *skenja*, to give drink. Large pot for dispensing drink. *1589: two skinke potts iijs. iiijd.*

skoales, skoles see SCALES

skochonys escutcheons, heraldic shields. *1459: with my scochonys of armys of hym and hese auncestryes.*

skogen escutcheon. *1459: one ball of coper gilt, embrauded rechely with j skogen hongyng therbi.*

skole, scull, skull the scaldfish, *Arnoglossus laterna*, a left-eyed flatfish growing up to 7 inches long. Sir Thomas Browne: 'The passer squamosus Bret Bretcock and skulls comparable in taste and delicacy unto the soale.' *1593: skoles xxiiij xviijd. 1654: 1 skull 1 Brett.*

skolles, skoles, skolys see SCALES; SKOLE; SKULL

skomel see SHOVEL

skomer, skoomer see SCUMMER

skopit, skupit, skuppett see SHOVEL

skowpis see SKEP

skuffle garden tool, consisting of a head of three or more prongs bent at right-angles to the long shaft, and used for stirring the soil. *1745: 1 Hoe, and two Skuffle's.*

skull see SCOLE

skull a skull-cap, a close-fitting iron or steel cap worn by foot-soldiers. See SCOTCH CAP. *1591: one byll & a skolle xvjd. Twoo heade peaces & a skull Cap vjs. viijd. 1597: Skulls 2 couered wth black clothe & yellowe skarfs bands...Skulls scottish brought in newe by Jo: Graye 10. 1599: one Black Bill & one skull xxd.*

scure see SKEWER

slab the rough outside part of a tree-trunk cut to expose the centre for squaring. *1733: 4 slabs 12 foot 4 slabs 25 foot.*

slab, slabbe small block of iron or steel. In the same account as the quotation, the cost of the slabbe is 13% of the cost of the SHEAF of steel. *1341: iij slabbes iijd. ob.*

slade, slad see SLED

slake *1596: toke up the morter slake which is a crooked pece of wood used for breakinge the morter.*

slat to slate, roof. *1557: she made the cloystir on the North syde and slattyd it.*

slate grey roofing slate from the West of England and Wales was not used much before the 1840s, when the railways reached Norfolk. Before that, stone slates from Lincolnshire, Northamptonshire and other relatively accessible places were occasionally used. Out of over 80 buildings in the Houghton survey of 1800, some half-dozen appear to be roofed with stone slates.

slay OE *slege*, OScan. *slegi*, stroke, striking; a reed for a loom, a tool originally made of thin strips of wood, or reed with ends of wood, used to separate the threads of the warp and in 'beating up' the weft. *1588: lome & xij slayes. 1590: vj slayes for linen. ij slayes for wool. 1601: one paire of Slaybordes viijd.*

sled, slead, slad, sleed sledge for transporting agricultural implements such as HARROWS, small loads etc. Sladd wheels, perhaps derived from the low wheels fitted to some sledges, were probably small, solid (as opposed to spoked) wheels. See SLUG WHEEL. *1306: [made] j slede iijd. ob. 1595: ij payer of yron harrowes a plow cheyne ij sleds. 1619: ij payer of Cart wheeles, vizt Sladd wheeles for ye smalle Tumbrelles xxxs. 1626: the plow barowes with a slead. 1665-6: mending a harow sled. 1718: one Slade & a Boy to ye Cart 2s.*

sleeve armoured or mailed sleeve. *1597: Briggandynes wthout sleves...Plated sleves canvas: 23 payer.*

slickstone, sleekstone smooth stone for smoothing paper, parchment, linen, and for polishing. *1587: iij slickstones iijd.*

slide, slider coaster on which to pass bottles, decanters etc. round the table. *1738: Four Mahogany Sliders 4s. 1764: Knife Box, eight Slides, Two Dinner Trays. 1787: Two Bottle slyders.*

sling wide stout cloth support for the bed. See BEDSTEAD. *1591: j pe of bedd slings xvjd.*

slip long narrow piece of stone under the NOSING of a step, etc. *1732-3: pulling down nosings & slips & coves &c.*

slip a varying quantity of yarn etc. *1513: ix slyppes of covylyght zarne.*

sload slote, sloat: bar, stretcher, joining-piece of timber. *1579: xvj sloades to under sett the Synter.*

slops wide baggy breeches, loose trousers, working wear for sailors etc. *1530: a payer of sloppys.*

slot, slote bolt of a door. *Prompt. Parv.* : 'Slot, or schytyl of a dore'. *1410: [paid for] ij slots [to the same door weighing 3 lbs price of each lb. 2d.].*

slug wheel solid wooden wheel, not spoked. See SLED. *1598: a grinston a Cranke & old sluggs xvjd. 1621: a drug with slug wheles.*

slyver short loose coat. *1597: Coats of plate: 10. Fustyan slyvers yellow 2.*
smelt or spirling, a trout-like marine coastal and freshwater fish, *Osmerus eperlanus*, up to 11 inches long and smelling of cucumber. Sir Thomas Browne: 'Spinachus or smelt in greatest plentie about Lynne butt where they have also a small fish calld a primme answering in tast and shape a smelt and perhaps are butt the yonger sort thereof'. *1498-9: iij cades of spyrlyng iijs. 1544: for Sperlinge ijd. . . for whyte spurlynge ijd. 1590: ix herring nets v spirling nets. 1590: a old sperlin net. 1647: a dish of smelts & a dish of Shrimps 1s.*
smoke jack apparatus fixed in the chimney, having vanes that turn with the rising heat and geared to revolve a JACK or SPIT for cooking or roasting.
smoothing box smoothing-iron, BOX-IRON. *1713: three Smoothing Boxes & heets.*
smoule the sand-eel, *Ammodytes tobianus*, sometimes called the lance, a small slender coastal fish, now mostly caught in quantity to make fish-meal. See SANDLING. *1593: for smoules to Tompson on Thursdaye ijd. 1649: smoules from Lynn 6d.*
snack see SNECK
snaffle a simple bridle-bit, without a curb. *1597: xj loose mouthes v snaffles.*
snaphance, snapphaunce mechanism on musket or pistol by which a piece of flint held in the jaws of a 'cock' was brought down on a piece of steel to strike a spark and ignite the charge; also called doglock, English lock, or flintlock. Transferred to the firearm using it. *1588: ij cases wth snapphaunces liijs. iiijd. one odde snapphance xs.*
snatch see LATCH; SNECK
snathe, snaith shaft of a SCYTHE; metal or wooden loop that curves from blade to shaft of a scythe to help the mown grass or corn slide away from the blade. *1584: j sythe snathe.*
sneaker small bowl for punch. *1751: Three Bowls...and two Sneakers.*
sneap the swipe or handle of a well-pump. *1664: repaired some brickeworke by the sneape at the well. 1665: made a cover to goe against the sneape of the well pumpe.*
sneck the usual way to keep doors closed from the Middle Ages to the 20th century was by the sneck, a bar of wood or metal up to 18 inches long, that pivoted on the end attached to the door and fell into a slot fixed to the post; but sometimes it seems to have meant the lever or cord mechanism that raised the bar, which would then be called the LATCH. See SHEAR. *1310: vj staples & ij sneckes [for the doors and windows of the hall 4d.]. 1310: sneck [of iron for the door of the hall 1d.]. 1314: j snecke [for the door of the] garderobe [of the chamber 3d.]. 1328: j snecks [for the lord's chamber 2d.]. 1345: [1 pair of] vertivell snecke & lachthe[of iron for the new door of the passage to the kitchen]. 1360: j snekke [of iron with] stapul [for the door of the barn 2d.]. 1367: j snekke [bought for the great gate 1½d.]. 1544: makyng barres and Snekks. 1648: a new Snack & other things to it 1s. 4d.*
snite the snipe, *Gallinago gallinago. 1593: for a snite & a teale ijd. ob.*
soap a compound of an alkali, such as caustic soda, with fat, tallow, animal oils, or vegetable oils e.g. olive oil. Soap was being made commercially by the 14th century, and until the 18th century was used mainly in the laundry. It was usually sold in barrels as soft soap - best, white, and grey, in descending order of quality. It was used for purposes other than washing e.g. treating sheep, greasing wheel-hubs. See BLACK SOAP. *1464-5: for a li. of whygthe soppe ijd. ob. 1530: di. a barrell of Sope. 1535: a firkin of soopp. 1587: one payer of sope scoles vjd. 1647: for the greasinge of 143 hoggs 13s. 4d. for 8 li. sope to mix a monge their tarr 2s. 4d. 1649: 1 barrell of Sope 6 li. 1664: Sope for the carts by George Page xijd.*
socket holder for a CANDLE. See CANDLESTICK. *1459: a candilstik, a priket and ij sokettys of silver, weiyng xvij unces. 1649: a new sockett for to sett a candell in 4d.*
sodder see SOLDER
soe, soo ON *sá-r*, OE *saa*, cask. Large wooden tub. According to Nall, it was a large tub

carried by two men by means of a pole through its ears. See COWL; STONDELL. Other soes may have been smaller, but are distinguished from the KEELER and other tubs. *1306: j soo vijd. 1352: j sue [for milk]. 1444: ij soos leeke. 1513: j soo for water. 1592: two Charnes And a mylkinge soe. 1593: 1 soe 2 kelers 1 stander. 1599: ij^{po} tubbes iij^{or} soes & iij^{or} killers iiijs. 1603: ij sooes one temse. 1819: Guile Tub hooping 10s. & Soe hooping 3s.* See p. 72.

soket see SUCCADE

solar, sollar, soller perhaps derived from L. *sol*, the sun = room open to the sun, but a more convincing derivation is from OFr. *sol*, floor, and *solive*, beam, that is a room on a beam, the upper floor. It was in use from the Middle Ages to the late 16th century as a term for a chamber on an upper floor, more private than the HALL, and was used as a family eating-room, living-room, and bedchamber. By the late 16th century the word occurs mainly in inventories of small houses as an upstairs room, sometimes over the bedchamber and often used for storage of corn, seed, hemp, hay, nets, implements etc. *1283: [key for the door under the] solar'. 1298: [chamber under the] solar. 1299: [roofed] j Guter [upon the] solar. 1310: xvj bord[bought for] j spere in solar xvjd. 1310: v bord [bought for] j flewe solar vd. 1362: [2 locks bought for the door of the hall and the door of the] solar xd. 1382: [repaired the great] solar. 1557: a good malt-house with a soler...the litel soler on the sowthe ende of here chaumber stondyng in to the paradise. 1590: on the soller over the bed chamber...on the soller over the Kitchen. 1590: on the soller over the Hall. 1591: uppon the soller hempe unpilled. a catch of hay. 1592: soller over Chamber next to Parlour. 1592: lumberment in the soler xijd. 1634: soller chamber* [trunk, linen, grain, butter, cheese].

solder, sodder, sood, sowde L. *solidare*, OFr. *souder, soulder*, to make solid or firm. An alloy used to join metals, of varying composition: soft solder is lead and tin, brazing solder is copper and zinc. *1396: [plumber making] j pype p le cist'ne [with] sood [bought 16d.]. 1417: [making] cistern cu' sowd. 1499-1500: vj lib' sowde ijs. 1539: for remouyng, leyyng, & sowdyng of sent James Chappell vs. ij li. of sowd viijd. 1541-2: vj li. of sowde. 1753: Sixty Eight Ounces of Soddered Plate 17 li. 10s.*

sole thick leather suitable for the soles of footware. See TANNING. *1591: xxj whole soales & vij heades & ij cheeles. 1594: lx soole leather hydes prised att xxix li. vs.*

sole 1. Sill, beam, as in window-sill, GROUNDSILL, sole-plate; a horizontal timber in a building. 2. A short horizontal timber in furniture, or at the foot of a rafter resting on the WALL-PLATE. *1389: in soles [with repairs] dil Cuckestool. 1393: [putting] soles [in the carthouse]. 1553: for boords for ye Mynystryng Table ijs.; & For Sooles for the sayd Tables, xxjd.*

soling iron iron shaped to hold a shoe or boot for soling. *1597: iiij wimbles a squier & a souling yron.*

soller see SOLAR

somerley summerley, land lying fallow in summer. *1711: Tillage of Thirteen acres of Somerley fitted for Turnips.*

sond sand

sood see SOLDER

soop soup. Foreigners to Norfolk often complain, unjustifiably, that the local pro-nunciation of 'soap' and 'soup' is confusing. See SOAP; SOUPE BOX. *1709: 4 Pye plates, 7 soop dishes, 2 pewter Collinders.*

SOOPP, SOPE see SOAP

sorrel bright reddish-brown, chestnut; used as a description of horses. *1603: one bayd sorell mare xls.*

sort a quantity, large number; more particularly, 10-10½ coomb, half a SCORE. *1654: for a sort of Barly full paid 6 li. 13s. 4d.*

sosse see SOUSE

soudlett small horizontal bar fitting over the vertical bars in glazing; saddle-bar. *1410: paid for ij transen bars & ij soudletts occupied* [used] *by the glasswright in the porch weighing iij li. price of each li. ijd.* See QUARREL.

sounds OE, ON *sund*, water, swimming. The swimming-bladder of a fish, eaten and used for making glue. The bladder of the sturgeon provided ISINGLASS. *1410: for sounds to making of glew iijs viijd. 1655: 2 Fins 4s. 100 Sounds: 1s. 6d...2 Barrells of sounds...2 firkins of Sounds and gulletts.*

soupe box soap box. *1592: j soupe box & j salt boxe.*

souse the ears, feet etc. of cattle or other beasts, pickled in brine in small barrells or tubs. *1513: j sousyng tubbe. 1592: a panne for dogges sosse. 1593: xvj stonne iij li. of beiffe at ijs. le stone xxxijs. vd. ij neatts tounges xijd. for a neatts souse xd. 1593: 2 old sowce tubbs. 1647: a souse 2s. 6d.*

sousters thread see SOWTER; THREAD

sow large oblong lump of metal, particularly LEAD. *1482: for ij sowes lede, the ton* [the one] *weyinge viij^C di vij li., and the tothyr viij^C qrtr vij li. Suma xvj^C iij qrters and xiiij li. at iij li. xiij s. and iiijd. the fether Summa iiij li. xjd.*

sowd, sowdyng see SOLDER

sowgere see SUGAR

sowter, souter OE *sútere*, shoemaker. *1454: they took a man of Stratford, a sowter. 1592: a ounce of sosteres thred xijd.*

soydyer, sowdyour soldier. *1545: A Swerd & A daggarde for one of ye Soydyers yt shold have gone furthe ijs. viijd.*

soyle 1. Sill, threshold. 2. Lintel of door or window. 3. Horizontal foot of balustrade etc; sill. See SOLE. *1619: walle of open worke of stone 3 foote and a halfe high answerable to the bridge, with soyle and rayle of stone with pedistalls in rustick. 1621-2: Soyles for the said windows 10 inches broad & 9 inches thicke.*

spade a spade is normally a digging implement; a SHOVEL is for moving loose material. Until the late 18th century most spades had a wooden blade with a lower or cutting edge sheathed in iron. See p. 242. *1507-8: a spade with the schoo vijd. 1593: 6 shoulfes wherof 1 shod 2 Cutting Spads.*

spall splinter, chip, offcut. *1314: de spalles [sold in the manor 14d.].*

Spanish ash in a work of 1716 the Spanish ash was described as *Caroba barbad*. This has not been identified, but seems unlikely to be the carob tree, *Ceratonia siliqua*, a native of the Levant but known in England for the edible and medicinal carob fruit. Perhaps 'Spanish ash' was wood from the narrow-leaved ash, *Fraxinus angustifolium*, or ash timber from Spain. *1597: one brode square dycing table of spanishe Asshe.*

Spanish ashes the maritime plant barilla, *Salsola soda*, when burnt yields alkali, which was imported and used in making SOAP, soda, and GLASS.

Spanish bedstead see BEDSTEAD

Spanish blanket the Norwich Flemings introduced the soft and fleecy cloths called Spanish rugs or blankets in the mid-16th century. They were made at first of Spanish wool, but soon incorporated English wool, and were produced especially in Witney (Oxon.) and its neighbourhood. *1597: one spanysh blankett redd* [and green, white]. *1627: a payer of Spanish blanketts.*

Spanish iron generally held to be superior in quality to English iron, Spanish iron was being imported by the 13th century. *1622: for iij Tunn CC j quarter & xiiij li. of Iron dd* [delivered] *att Wells; at 13 li. 10s. the Tunn for ij Tunn xij^{CC} j qr xiiij li. therof & the other di' Tun at 14 li. 10s. beinge Spanish Iron xlij li. xiijs. iijd. 1671: 6 hondered and a halfe and 14 pound of*

194

Spanish Iorne to make Spitts and Iorne worke belonging to the Kiching.
Spanish staff seems to be a tool or implement, although use as a weapon should not be ruled out - see BILL. On the analogy of Spanish pike (needle) it might be a small or miniature staff, or a PLOUGH-staff for cleaning the coulter. See ACRE-STAFF. *1592: two billes one spanish staffe & one stoole vs. 1592: two saddles two belts a spanyshe staffe. 1592: one spanes tafe ijs. 1613: Ten ladders and a Spanish Staffe xxvs.*
Spanish white fine powdered chalk used as a pigment or for cleaning. 1686: 'Spanish white made of Chalk and Alum burnt together'. *1649: 2 stone of Spanish White 2s. 4d. 1655: for 12 li. spanish white & 12 li. Oker 2s. 8d. 1665: for one hundred[weight] of spanish white bought by him at Ipswich iijs. To Wm Legatt for bringing the same xviijd.*
spantrell, spantrill spandrel. The roughly triangular space between a round-headed or a gothic arch and its enclosing rectangular frame.
spar length of timber of medium SCANTLING, used for e.g. rafters (often listed as a couple), ladder poles, STUDS for timber-framed houses. *1306: iiij sparrs viijd. 1310: ccxvij sparres de fir [for making] j bercar lxjs. ijd. 1313: j sparre [for 1 ladder]. 1361: vij sparres [bought for] le wat'bordes [of the vicarage house 7d.]. 1590: halffe a hundred furren sparres xs...xl bume sparres xxs. 1649: 3 cupple Sparrs 20 foote longe 5s. 9 cupple 15 foote longe 10s. 6d. 1662: 7 couple of sparres for Sumer barne at one shilling 8d. the Couple 11s.*
spar, spear, sper OE *gesparrian, besparrian,* MDu. *sperren,* MLG *speren,* to bolt, shut up. *1449: and qhan he cam thedder, the dors were fast sperid. 1462: the yates of Lynne, by the Bysshop comaunement weren fast sperred and keped with men of armes...the Bysshop...made to sper the yates after hym.*
sparable see SPARRIBILL
sparflew see SPARTLE
spargetting see PARGETTING
spark a small diamond or precious stone. *1603: iij gold Rings thone a hoop tother wth a sparke of a Rubye.*
sparribill shoemaker's small wedge-shaped headless nail. *1648: hobnayles & sparribills.*
spartle, sparflow, spergle to scatter, disperse, cast at random; to coat with plaster, sparget, PARGET. *1327: in speregilling [the chamber towards the church 1½d.]. 1610-11: a loade of ould Claye to sparflowe the guildhowse xijd...ij dayes worke of Sparflewinge of ye guildhowse & Riginge of the same iiijs. 1647: 3 daies of a Mason & his sonne to spartle the Dayry Chambr. 9s. for 3 daies of their Server 3s.*
sparver see BEDSTEAD, sparver
speakins see SPIKING
specialty debts on specialty wÈre DEBTS owing by contract, sealed agreement, written bond etc. as opposed to unpaid bills, unwritten debts. *1591: due to the testator upon spetialtie iij li. xvjs. viijd. 1602: owing by John Fuller wthout specyalt xxs.*
speck, spetch patch of leather, to patch shoes. *1648: Shooes speckinge & weltinge.*
spectacles spectacles, in the form of a pair of lenses connected by a bridge, were in use by the 14th century. *1593: A payer of Spectacles silver & gilte vjs. viijd.*
speer see SPERE
speete a SPIT. This was a common spelling of the word, and probably reflects the pronunciation in the 16th and 17th centuries.
spekin see SPIKING
spending line ? line for traces or harness. See STAGE. *1648: 1 new hausrope & lop rope for the Tryces 6s. 1 bunch of spendinge lyne 1s. 2d.*
sper see SPAR

195

sperate debts are hopeful of recovery, the opposite of desperate DEBTS, not hopeful. *1708: Debts speratt 254 li. 2s. 1d. Debts Desperate 39 li. 17s.*

spere, speer fixed wooden SCREEN, fitted across the entrance end of a room e.g. a hall to screen the main part from the draught of the outside door. Probably began as short side-screens projecting from the walls, and gradually expanded until the whole width of the room was covered, with one or two door-openings. See Margaret Wood, *The English Medieval House*, pp. 139 ff. *1310: xj bord ad speres [in the hall 3s. 5d.]. xvj bord ad j spere in solar xvjd. 1328: [carpenter making] ij speres in [the lord's chamber and 1 bench in the hall]. 1389: [4 tables bought for the repair] dil speer [in the hall 15d.]. 1392: j speer [in the dairy-house].*

speringe ? a shutter; see SPERE. But see also SHEAR. *1582: fynishe, erecte and set upp all suche dorestalles, dores, windoes and speringes for windoes.*

spesche see PITCH

spet see SPIT

spett spats, oyster-spawn.

spice drawers miniature chest-of-drawers to contain spices. *1723: a pair of spice drawers.*

spice plate plate to hold spices for perfuming a room. *1459: j spice plate, well gilte like a double rose, my maister helmet in the myddes, with rede roses of my maisters armes, weiyng v^{XX} v unces.*

spigot, spigitt small pin used to stop the vent-hole of a barrel; a tap used to draw off the liquid from a barrel. *1649: 6 Reede Spigitts 9d.*

spicke spike. *1620: [smith] ankers doggs cramps spickes and bolts.*

spiking an iron NAIL. A source of 1647 says a spiking was headless. In 13th-15th-century accounts spikings were differentiated from nails and from 'great' and 'middle' spikings, but there was little difference between them in price, spikings averaging for the long HUNDRED (120) just under 3d., 'middle' spikings about 3d., and 'great' spikings varying from under 3d. to 8d., although for each category instances have been found where the price was well above the average. Possibly it was the form, shape, and purpose rather than the size or weight that differentiated them. By the 17th century the term was obsolescent, and 'great' spikings seem to have become much larger and more costly. Forby: 'a large nail with a round flat head.' For general terms for medieval nails see L.F. Salzman, *Building in England down to 1540*, pp. 304 ff.

spikings *1273: lx spikings ijd. 1273: CC spiking vjd... in M [nails for a house and] Lxx spiking ixd. ob. 1274: C spiking ijd. ob. 1295: C spiking [bought for the bridge 2¾d.]. 1300: m¹ vj^{CC} clavis* [nails] *de magno spykyngs [bought for the chancel 4s. 4d.]. 1306: C clav'* [nails] *de Spyking ad evesbord iijd. 1647: 4 speekings 4d. 1661: 300 nailes & 5 speakins & 60 gital nailes used about the house 4s. 9d. 1665: planchering spekens 5 li. 2s. 6d.* [among large collection of different nails].

middlespikings *1296: iij^c middilspikĩg [for the granary 7d.]. 1300: xxx middelspykyngs [for the malt-kiln 1½d.]. 1312: C middelspykyngs [for the barn door 4d.]. 1310: in C myddelspikyngs C grospykyngs & C tyngelnayl ixd. 1313: lx middelspikyngs [for the great door 1½d.]. 1339: xl middelspikys [for attaching] Wat'bordes [of the same barn 1d.].*

great spikings *1310: di' cent grossi spikyngs C middelspykyngs Ciiij^{XX}x splentenayl & cc de lattenayl. 1319: v^c de gross spiks xiiijd. 1344: Clx de Greetspykyng [for] Walplates [and elsewhere bought 12d.]. 1416: in longa spekyng [bought for the said barn 6d.]. 1649: [smith] 20 great spikeings 4s. 2d. 1665: 3 great spekins for the carpender. 4 cart clouts & spekins.*

spile, spoil, spyll, spyllyng to stop a hole with a spile, SPIGOT, or plug. *1562: for hopynge and spyllynge of that barell.*

spile, spoil 1. a pile, for foundations; to drive piles. 2. a large wedge. *1665: They planked & spoiled for the foundacõn for the wall to be lengthened. . . drive spoiles and laid some plank at the sluce at the Newater. 1802: Posts and Spoils £2.*

196

spindle the simplest method of spinning wool was by the spindle, a short slim rod tapering at both ends and weighted with a stone or lead whorl to maintain momentum. A thread was hand-twisted from a bundle of wool on a distaff and fixed on to the spindle, which was then revolved to twist a continuous thread, from which it was suspended. The spindle-tree *Euonymus Europæus* yielded a yellowish, hard, fine-grained wood which was used for spindles. *1595: Spyndelles & whorles.*

spinet cloth derived from Spinney in Cambs.

spirket, spirkit, spurkett hook, peg, usually of wood; possibly candle-spike (see 1601 quotation). *1601: a latten plate with two socketts and two brazen spuketts iiijs. 1608: 10 spurketts of woodworke to hange armor one. 1647: [smith] for spurketts 3d. 1819: 35 new Spirkits to larder 8s. 9d.*

spirling, sperling, spurling see SMELT

spit iron rod or bar, pointed at one end to impale the meat and stretched across the front of the open hearth to roast food. Usually supported on COBIRONS or standing DOGIRONS. The size and form of the spit depended on the type of meat, e.g. whole pig, joint of beef, chicken. On some spits a double-pronged fork with a prong on either side slid along the main shaft to hold the meat in position - see PRICKET ROASTIRON. Spits for birds or fish were shorter and lashed to a longer spit. The spit revolved slowly, turned either by hand by a boy (turnspit, TORNEBROCHE, see BROACH) or by mechanical means - SMOKE JACK in the chimney, JACK driven by weights, etc. See p. 86. The dripping fat was caught in the LATCHPAN or dripping-pan. The presence of spits in an inventory almost certainly means that there is a cooking-hearth in the room, although occasionally unused spits were stored in the BUTTERY or elsewhere. *1416: [making] dil spets [of the chamber 6d.]. 1459: ij square spittys cocnos. 1513: J Byrddespete. 1589: a Jack to turn the spitt vs. 1620: iij bigg square Spitts ij lesse square spitts ij flat spitts ij roundspitts. 1738: skrew spitt. 1745: lark spit.*

splent splint, LATH, possibly WATTLE; longish, slender rod, used in walls and tied in with yarn or string. Palsgrave 1530: 'Splente for an house, *laite.' 1310: xᶜ broch & C splents xviijd. q'. 1319: in splentyncks [for the middle wall 13d.]. 1387: [one man 36 days cutting down] splentes schraggants & [thorns] in Grouesker [for] fagott. 1588-9: iij pownde & halfe of hempe to splente ye same howse vd...for ij hundered splentes with the caryage vs. 1607-8: for splent yarne iiijd. 1648: 12 bunches of splentes 6s. 1665: splented risered & daubed betweene the studs.*

splent small plate of armour to protect the inside of the arm. Palsgrave 1530: 'Splent, harnesse for the arme.' See STANDARD.

splentnail lath-nail, short nail for SPLENTS. See NAIL; SPIKING. *1274: xv spikings & c de splentenail iiijd. 1319: mˡvˣˣ de splentenayl [15d].*

splent yarn splinter, fibres of undressed hemp. See SPLENT.

split riven, cleft timber; 'sawing' in the 1654 quot. meant sawing into lengths for riving. See RIVE; BREAK. *1654: to ye Sawers for 224 foote of board cuttinge & 230 foot of splitt worke 11s. 3d. . . for sawing 600 & a halfe of splitt for Oxnet use and 1ᶜ ½ more for the Fulling mill at 2s. 6d. & 1 Breaking carfe of 12 foot 2s. 1 li. 2s. 1655: a hundred splitt worke for Tumbrills &c.*

splitter split willow, osier, ash, used for baskets, sieves, or where lightness is essential; basket or basketwork. *1537-8: jd. to John Mannyng for a pece of asche for splêtur paid ijd. a man ryvyng the same splêtur for the gyant. 1547: for a Splytter yt shadowed ye Gryffon iiijd. 1612: j save of splytter with lock & kei. 1619: 2 splitter buz skeepes, 6 Windles & A hand basket. 1664: Five little splitter basketts. 1665: a seive bottominge wth splitters 6d.*

splitting riving, cleaving timber along the grain. See BREAK. *1620: for splittinge Worke, sawne as square wise And 2 overwhart Cutts in toto vjˣˣ fotte. . . sawinge 2 stocks of Billetts to laie in to the newe walle in toto xjˣˣ fotte splittinge worke.*

splitting a split hide or splitting is one that has been split into two or more layers parallel

197

to the surface. *1592: One skine and spliting in the fattes xxvj and also x tanned splitings and xxj whole soales & vij heades & ij cheeles. 1594: xix splytinge hides.*

splitting carfe see BREAK; SPLIT

spoil from SPILE, pin or peg, plug, fit into socket. To insert spokes into wheel; dig holes. See FUR. *1663: for spoiling in the furrs...for a new spoake put into the cart wheele and spoiling in of spokes xijd.*

spoke see FURR; GONG

spong, spang ON *spang, spong,* narrow bridge; long narrow strip of land. *1665: the sponge by the old orchard.*

spoon up to the 18th century wood was the most common material for spoons, with pewter as a slightly more expensive alternative. Silver spoons were not uncommon, even in houses of craftsmen and yeomen, albeit in small numbers. See TOUCH. *1479: xx^{ti} spones on a bundell, weying xvj unc. j quarter...vj spones with acorns, weying v unc' & di. quarter. 1588: one doesen playne sylver spones. vj knopte spones. 1604: 20 pewter spoones and pewter latchspoone. 1637: [plate] 12 slipp spoones. 4 knopt spoones. j sugerbox with a spoone. one longe spoone wth a fork. j dozen a postell spoons caret 26 ounce ½ untutched.*

spoonbill see POPELER; SHOVELLER

spores spurs. *1522: pd for a payer of spores for hym viijd.*

sport L. *sporta,* basket; a very large basket. *1318: j sporta vd. 1407: ij sports [bought for carrying malt 6d.].*

sprag a salmon between one and two years old. *1593: a spragg ijs. vjd.*

spreed to spread, disperse. *1664: spreeding the molehills & cow dung.*

sprendle split length of wood. *1661: a bocke & sprendles & 2 peeces of barphew.*

sprenkill sprinkler for HOLY WATER in the unreformed church; usually a vessel with small perforations, on a handle or chain. *1459: [plate] j haly water stop, with j sprenkill and ij cruettes.*

sprig, prig small thin nail, either with a one-sided head,], or wedge-shaped and headless. *1321: iiij^{xx} durenayl. xxiiij prygges. 1738: Six pound of Spriggs.*

spring cutting, slip, SET, young shrub. *1665: for 560 Spring for the new orchard iiijs...for hedgeing and ditching in the New orchard there being about xvj rod & laying a double layer of spring xvjs.*

spruce Norway spruce, *Picea abies,* has been a source of timber since the Middle Ages. The best spruce, with a close grain and used for building, furniture, musical instruments etc. came from slow-growing mountain trees, which also provided masts for ships. The second-quality timber, from trees in fast-growing situations, has a wide grain and is the typical softwood DEAL. Confusingly, 'Spruce' was a corruption of Pruce, Prussia, so that 'spruce' timber could mean timber from Prussia, i.e. Baltic oak. Spruce leather and iron were imported from Prussia. *1474: j was spruys chyst with xxs. 1513: J oold spruce chest. 1562: viij ends of spruse iron. 1593: 1 little spruce chest. 1602: xij sprewes leathr skines xxijs. 1619-20: for 29 spruce deales 7 li. 19s. 6d...For 540 deales 28 li. 16s.*

spurkit see SPIRKET

spurling see SPIRLING

spyger ? spiker, that is, auger, boring tool. *1293: j spyger [bought 2d.].*

spynas, spynne, spynner pinnace, a small, light two-masted ship. *1450: ij shepes and a litel spynner. 1458: iij carvells, and iiij spynnes. 1466: a pompe, v polyves, and odre aparaylle for the spynas.*

square unit of one HUNDRED square feet, used for flooring, roofing, tiling, walling. *1620: [tilers] In the roofe over the range of building wch is the gallery & great chamber on the garden side is conteined 36 square of tile.*

square ⎾ -shaped tool of wood or metal or a combination of both, used by carpenters for measuring and setting a right-angle. *1597: iiij wimbles a squier & a souling yron.*
square measure multiplying one dimension by another e.g. length by breadth. *1620: The Architrave Freese and cornish about the Chapple conteineth by square measure 19 yards wch at 3s. 4d. the yard comes to 3 - 3 - 4. 1665: for planing 240 score and 6 deal planke for planchering in wch by square measure 6800 feet at six score to the hundred.* See also HUNDRED.
square windows flush with the wall. See CANT; CARROLL. *1621: principall muniall in the cant square and carroll windows.*
squewe variation of skiver, SKEWER; wooden stake - see HARTHIN. *1264: [collecting] harthing & squewes vjd. 1319: squewes & harth'.*
squier, squire see SQUARE
squinant, squynawnt schœnanth, a sweet-scented Asian grass, *Andropogon schœnanthus,* used medicinally; or squinancy wort (squinancy = quinsy) *Asperula cynanchica,* used to ease sore throats. *1465: an unce of squynawnt viijd.*
squirt, squort syringe; CLYSTER-PIPE for rectal irrigation. *1589: a latten squirt js. viijd. 1592: Fower brasen squorts.*
squirt wild CUCUMBER; the squirting cucumber *Cucumis agininus (Ecballium elaterium),* which expels its seeds with some force, may be a source for this pejorative term with perhaps a penile connotation; or it may be connected with 'squirt', looseness of the bowels. *1637-9: a younge squirtes.*
squob squab, cushion for chair; the chair itself; an ottoman or sofa. *1709: 1 cane squob.*
squob young pigeon or rabbit.
sraggyngs see SHRAG
s', st servant
staff, horseman's a long staff with a steel point, the horse-soldier's equivalent of a pike. A lavure staff was provided with a rest. *1590: iij horsemans staves, a lavure staff.*
staff, Spanish see SPANISH STAFF
stage, ale see ALESTOOL
stage, staging scaffolding, of wood up to the 19th century. Staging-line is cord for binding the staging. See ALDER; PUTLOG. *1386: [making] dil stages p le Chymene. 1433-4: [2 ash trees for] Stagyngtymber. 1647: 1 bunche of stageing lyne 1s. 1665: 10 deale staging poles. 1710: 30 pounds of staging-line at 5d. a pound.*
stained cloth up to the 17th century 'staining' in many cases meant 'painting', and the stained cloth was often a scene, figures, heraldry etc. Stained cloths of all descriptions, dimensions, and value were fairly common, although few have survived. The ground was usually canvas. See PAINTED CLOTH. *1519-20: Thomas Benet for le steynyng le clothys in the parlor. 1592: stayned cloth over ye table. 1592: the stayned clothes with pictures and tables of gentlemenes armes xs. 1595: a stayned cloth hanginge before the chymney.*
stained paper stained or painted paper was in use as a wall-covering from the late 17th century; before that 'stained' paper may have meant a picture. *1474: vj steyned paperis xijd.*
stake a small portable anvil on a stake or iron spike, for making nails.
stakeendez possibly = scales, but see STAKE. *1513:[bakehouse] j peyir stakeendez.*
stakyate stake-gate, gate of palings. *1302: [carpentering] le stakyate [and pales 4d.].*
stale a handle; side-piece, upright of ladder. *1588: payer of quernes wth the stale and the hutche.* See QUERN.
stale a decoy bird or animal.
stall 1. Market-stall, bench, table. 2. A stand for a cask - see alestool. 3. A QUERN stand.

4. Beehive, or stand for beehives. See p. 28. 5. A butcher's block. *1341: ij stalles [for meat 6d.]. 1592: viij stalles for butchers ij troughs & a cradle wt other smal bords xijs. 1599: a paier of quernes wth stalls. 1603: two Beere stals.*

stamin a narrow, coarsish worsted cloth, made in Norfolk from the end of the 15th century, used for clothes. *1507-8: xxx yerdes de stamyn viijs.*

stammel possibly a version of STAMIN: a coarse woollen cloth, usually dyed red; the colour red. *1593: one large cov'inge of Stammell.*

stammet glazed cloth made from worsted yarn that had been shrunk and smoothed by scouring; by the 17th century the cloth was called tammet and tammy. *c.1730: 41 yds of Tammy used to line the Window Curtains [mohair] and Valliens at 14d. £2 8s. 5d.*

stampel, stampele, stamper stamper or rammer for crushing apples. *1592: j cradle to straine crabbs iij stampers. 1593: ij drie tobe a fanne iiij stampeles a chese Racke. 1595: iiij stampeles for crabbes.*

stamping trough trough in which apples were crushed for VERJUICE or cider. *1597: stamping trough for crabbes vjd.*

stand a stack. *1584: In the middesteade 1 stand of Rye ixs. iiijd.*

standard, stander, stonderd large chest for storage. The derivation is uncertain. Association with 'stand' would point to a static rôle, but instances are known where standards were used to transport goods. *1513: One great standard callyd a chest. 1590: j old Stonderd chest [with weapons]. 1597: [sparver, trayne, quilt] in my mrs standard. . . 2 redd standerds bounde & barred wth yron. . . [sparver, trayne, quilte, cubbard cloth] thes things to be in the great stander in the Wardrupe. 1620: a lether Stondard. 1688: one old standard.*

standard 1. Pillar, post. *1664: pull downe the pticōn agt the wine siller & standards that supported the bricke & pavements in the great hall.* 2. A tall standing candlestick.

standard a collar of MAIL or plate armour. *1463: xij standardes of mayle xvjs.*

standard bow a long-bow for standard arrows, that is 36 inches long. OED: 1465: 'an English bow...with twelve shaftes of the length of three quarters of the Standard.' *1467: my master toke hym a standard bow...and it is worthe in mony vjs. viijd. 1482: he hath a peire brigandines keuered with purpil velvet, a salate, a standard, a cheef of arowes, a peir splents, and his jakete, and a gusset..* See ARROW; FLIGHT; YARD.

standell, stander stand, ALESTOOL. *1593: 1 soe 2 kelers 1 stander 2 old sowce tubbs. 1611: j hoggeshed ij standells.*

standish, standyche pen and ink stand, inkstand. *1587: v standyches at vjd a pece. 1595: a standyshe of peut'. 1634: two standishes.*

stang pole, bar, beam; cart-shaft, pole for carrying baskets or tubs.

stank L. stagnum, OFr. estanc, pool, pond. *1450: Sir John Bukk, Parson of Stratford, physshed my stankys at Dedham, and holp brake my damme.*

staple ∩-shaped piece of iron driven into doorpost or gatepost to house bolt, hasp, or hook. *1313: [nails], staples guggons [and other things of iron]. 1315: j barre & j stapel [for the south door 2d.]. 1319: [mending the lock of the lord's chamber with] staple haspes & snecke ijd. ob. 1335: [2 hanging locks with 2 keys] iij staples & j hespe vijd. 1360: j snekke [of iron with a] stapel [for the barn door]. 1374: iiij stapples [of iron bought for the said doors 3d.]. 1648: 1 hespes & staples 4d.*

starching pan, starcpanne pan for heating and preparing starch for ruffs, clothes. *1459: j lyttyll stercpanne of sylver. 1513: J starcpanne. 1597: a starchinge panne which is carryed wt them whereso they goe.*

start, stert handle, guiding handle, PLOUGH-start. *Prompt. Parv.:* 'Stert, of a plowe (or plowstert).' *1746: harrows with iron starts and hamble trees.*

startups see BRODKYNS

200

statute statute; grant, charter. *1597: A note of suche Statutes as remayne.*
statute book published book of laws. *1595: One byble & a Statute boocke xiijs. iiijd.*
statute lace see LACE
staves aker stavesacre, the seed of *Delphinium staphisagria*, used as an emetic and to destroy vermin. *1587: i box with Staues Aker & ye box iiijs.*
steathe staithe. *1588: For Bakers passage in a cock boote from the steathe to the meeles.*
steel to weld a steel edge to an iron tool. *1584-5: makyng of a Crowe & one pykex and for stelynge of ye same ijs.*
steelyard balance-type weighing mechanism in which a steel rod is balanced on a fulcrum, the short arm having the pan for the article and the longer arm having a counterweight that slides along the arm, which has a calibrated scale. Also called a Roman balance. See SCALES. *1459: j roste iron with vij staves and j foldyng stele of silver weiyng lxxiij unces. 1734: pair of Stillyards. 1748: One Ironning Box Stylyards and an old Gun 10s.*
steepinglead, -vat a large tub, CISTERN, LEAD or VAT, sometimes of considerable size and in a permanent emplacement, sometimes lined with lead, in which the barley was steeped in the process of BREWING. *1300: in j steping fat viijs. iiijd. 1300: [mending] del stepyngfat de souder* [solder] *iiijd. 1306: xv bord [of oak for] j stepingfat ijs. iiijd. ob. 1323: [carpentering wood about] del stepingled xiijd. [and 6 boards. Laying down and making] del stepingled vjs. viijd. [Lead for the same 4s. 2d. Tin for the same 12d. Carpentering] del gotere [of the same 4d. Lime bought for the plaster against the lead 7½d.]. 1587: one steepinge fatte xs. 1591: barleye in the stepe.*
steeple church tower; spire. *1539: for bordyng & latasyng of ij of ye stepyll wydows xijs.. 1593: in the steppell xxxx codge swells vj drage Rakes 3 barrels. 1619: Digginge downe Coxfurr Steple.*
steer young castrated ox. See STOTT. *1588: iiij cuntrie steres iiij li. xs. viij welche beasts x li. x smale cuntrie bestes x li.*
stent see STINT
stertwich, sterwich the element wych/wich may be the same as in wych-elm, from OE *wice, wic,* pliant, but the application to the medieval plough is not obvious, unless -wych/wick is 'wood'. See PLOUGH; START. *1306: [ploughs] in sulwych & stertwich [bought 2d.]. 1341: [plough] sterwich & sulwych jd.*
steward 1. The steward of the manor held the manorial court as representative of the lord of the manor. 2. The steward of the estate looked after the business of the estate, its farms etc. 3. The steward of the household was the chief official in a large household up to the 19th century, and usually kept the accounts. He had his own work-room, and in an aristocratic household might be of gentry status.
stews the fishpond, an important element in the supply of the household diet up to the 18th century. *1440: Your stewes do weel.*
stew yard area or yard of the STEWS. *1330: [one lock of the] stuyerd ob. 1544: mendynge the loke of the stewyards gate.*
stick a stick of eels was 25 eels, a number incorporated in the Assize of Weights and Measures 1302/3. The '26' eels to the stick of the quotation of 1481 perhaps records a deviation from the norm. Ten sticks made a bind. By 1615 a stick of herrings was a freshly-packed barrel. In the quotation of 1560, going by the price of 'duche herryngs', the stick = 1440 herrings, which is the capacity of a barrel, that is 12 long hundreds of 120, but the following item shows that they had settled as the barrel was filled up with 216 Dutch herring. *1481: to pay a pike man of Ippiswech for xx ellys ijs. vjd.; and for vj stekes of smale elle xxvj to the steke ijs. vjd. 1498-9: [for] xxxv stykkes [of eels 10s. 2½d.]. 1500-1: xxvj stykkes of browet eelys price viijs. viijd. and ij stykkes of kempys price iiijd and iiij stykkes of feedyng price iiijd. 1560: for one stycke of flemyshe herryngs xxs. paid to Geoge feld of laistofte for Ciiij^{xx} xvj duche herryngs*

201

at vj ₰ jd. to fylle up the barrell iijs. iiijd. for hopynge and spyllynge of that barell at the newe packyng xd.
stick a customary measure of Flemish cloth, varying according to the type of cloth. *1466: v stykes and di of fusteyn xviijd...the moste federbed conteyneth in lengthe iiij Flemishe stykes, iij quarters; and the brede of the same conteynethe in lengthe iij stykes, iij quarters and di, and in brede ij stykes...paid for a bordeclothe of Chawmpeyne clothe, conteynenge xiij Flemeshe stykkes, and v quarters brode, prise the styke, iiijd.* See TAPESTRY.

stifle bone the joint between the hind-leg and the body of a horse. *1665: cowelling the grey mare for a blow upon the styfle bone.*

stile vertical bar of a door, a window, or panelling. *1607-8: for fower peeces of tymber to make pillers and stoyles for the windowes ijs. ijd.*

still the simple still consisted of a vessel, the cucurbit, in which the liquid was heated, and a dome, the alembic, usually written LIMBECK, in which condensation of the vapour took place, with a spout to drain off the resultant liquid to a receiving vessel, usually a flask. The still was used for distilling concoctions of herbs for medicine, for spirits, and in the pursuit of alchemy. See p. 209. *1588: one Still vs. 1590: one Still of lead ijs. vjd. 1593: 1 Still upon a Copper of brasse. 1595: an olde topp of a styll. 1597: one Styll hanged...2 stylles wth their leaden pannes. 1637: a still a sisterne of pewter. 1709: a Still.* [note] *July ye 14: 1710 ye limback & all yt belonges to it my master lent to my lady Robinson.*

still deal possibly STILE. See BOARD; DEAL; FURRENDEAL. *1728: 12 Still Deals for Boarding ye well. 1729: 24 leaves of Still Deals.*

stilled distilled. *1562: For a glasse for stylled water iijd.*

still-house, still-room building or room for distilling and similar purposes.

stillion a stand for a barrel, an ALESTOOL. *1792: [Small Beer Cellar] A Quantity of Stillion... The Stillion in the old Ale Cellar. The Stillion in the Wine Cellar.*

stillyards see STEELYARD

stint the number of cattle a commoner was allowed to put on the common grazing; the amount of land allotted to each person for grazing. *1712: stent for the Comon.*

stint 'stints' were taken in large numbers on the coast in the 16th and 17th centuries. In 1593 at Stiffkey, 723 stints were bought Jan.-March, 35 in April, none May-July, 24 in August, and 1,512 in Sept.-Dec. This pattern, and the numbers, would fit the dunlin, *Calidris alpina*, one of whose alternative names is stint, better than the little stint, *Calidris minuta*, or Temminck's stint, *Calidris Temminckii*, not recorded in England until 1776 and 1832 respectively. 'Stint' has also been applied to *Calidris alba*, the sanderling, a name not occurring in the account of 1593, but the migratory pattern does not seem to fit. Sir Thomas Browne: 'A may chitt a small dark gray bird litle bigger then a stint of fatnesse beyond any. It comes in May into marshland and other parts and abides for aboue a moneth or 6 weekes. Another small bird somewhat larger than a stint called a churre and is commonly taken amongst them. Stints in great numbers about the seashore and marshes about Stifkey Burnham and other parts.' Cotgrave 1611 identifies the may-chit as the 'small meadow-lark', but Browne's description seems more like the sanderling. 'Churre' is supposed to be a Norfolk name for the dunlin, but this name has not been found in accounts. On the whole, it seems likely that 'stint' meant dunlin. *1593: [1-8 Jan] for ij dussen stintts to Battie viijd...for ij dussen stintts to Apleton & iij Redshanks xd.*

stirk young bullock or heifer, usually between one and two years old. *1592: iij Kyne vj styrkes of thage of ij yeres & ye vantage & j Budd x li.*

stirring staff, stirrer mashing OAR for stirring and beating the mash in BREWING. *1591: ij stirringe stafes & one scoope. 1692: storrer & sett.*

stirrups the support for a rider's feet. Several named types appear in the 16th and 17th

centuries. *1597: A bright Armor pcell guylt complete. A payer of styrrops guylt. . . one payer of scottish styrrops for my Mr his owne rydinge. 2 payer of ordinary styrrops. 2 payer of Morocco stirrops.*
stithe stithy, the anvil. *1582: a little broken styffe. 1592: one stythe and thre bonte hammers. 1595: A blome A Stythe & A beckhorne xxs.*
stoap a large bottle, possibly with a stopper; but see STOUP. *1734: three large stoop bottles 1s. 6d. five single stoap bottles 1s.*
stock 1. The trunk of a tree. 2. The trunk squared off into long rectangular balks. *1664: sawing one elming stocke 18 foot long 14 inch broad 21 foot in a board 15 boards 6 planke in the said stocke...sawing one pare tree stocke into halfe inch board 5½ foot long 12 inch broad 26 boards iijs. vjd. 1665: hewed a stock for ballasters...hewed one stocke of timber for the centers for the two arches to be made at the bridge. . . hewed two board stockes and 3 pale stockes.* See BOARD; DEAL; JOIST.
stock, stoke the funds and possessions of the PARISH or parish church.
stock the base of a tree on to which grafts are made. See PARADISE. *1664: To Tibenham of Eye for 7 crabtree stockes xiiijd.*
stock see BRICK
stock, fulling the trough in which the cloth was placed to be beaten by the mallet in the process of FULLING.
stockbedstead see BEDSTEAD
stock card large wool-card fixed to a stock or support, with the carding or combing action being performed with another, smaller, two-handed card - hence 'pair'. *1602: one payer of stockards. 1603: one payer of stock kards.*
stockfish cod, ling, or similar fish split open and air-dried without salt for preservation. *1415-16: in iiij stokfysshys [bought 2s. 4d.]. 1582: Stockffyshe iiij bo. pce ijs. 1591: xij stockfish iiijs.*
stock lock see LOCK
stocks stockings
stocks instrument of punishment for minor crimes, in which the offenders had to sit with their legs clamped in a wooden frame. *1312: [carpentered 1 pair] de stocks vijd.*
stole narrow strip of coloured cloth worn round the neck by deacon and priest in the unreformed church.
stole stool, stall. *1509: ij stolys lying upon stulpis.* See STOOL.
stolid see STOOL.
stolpe staple for gate or door-fastening. See STAPLE; STULP. *1648: 4 stolpes & hespes 6d.*
stomach rennet is curdled milk from the stomach of an unweaned calf, or is prepared from the membrane of a cow's stomach, and is used for curdling milk for making CHEESE. *1306: v stomach iiijd. ob.*
stomacher 1. A man's waistcoat. 2. In the 15th-17th centuries, a covering for the chest and front of women, worn under or between the lacing of the bodice. *1474: a stomaucher of a zerd of gode new hollond clothe xd...a stomaker of lenclothe viijd.*
stond stand, ALESTOOL. *1352: [3 barrels and] j stond.*
stondell, stondle a bearing-tub, carried with a pole through its ears between two men. See COWL; SOE. *1594: ij milking stondells...iiij stondles. 1603: one cowlle one stondle toube.*
stone unit of weight, the size ranging from 5 to 14 POUNDS, depending on the commodity and the period, with some regional variation. The stone of 14 lb., the statutory weight of a stone of wool (1340) was the most usual after *c.*1500. See R.D. Connor, *The Weights and Measures of England*, pp.130-1, 135-7, 335-6.
stone bow a CROSSBOW adapted for propelling stones or baked clay balls instead of bolts. *1591: two lutes & a stonebow. 1603: two longe bowes, one stone bowe. 1603: A paire of Playing tables and a Stone bowe vs. 1630: Two vyals one stonbowe & A watch vj li.*

stone sugar see SUGAR

stoned paved with stone or stones e.g. flint. *1664: the stond cort yard.*

stoned horse, stonde, stonn horse uncastrated, still in possession of its testicles or stones; a stallion. *1584: j stoned horse & vj ploughe geldings xij li. 1588: one stoned Horse x li. 1590: blacke stoned horse vij li. 1593: 1 great stonde horse liver colour xij li...1 darke sorrell stonde horse iij li. 1 old white stonde horse xxs.*

stoning made of stoneware, hard earthenware. *1590: stonynge pott tipt with silver.*

stood see STUD

stool as an item of seating furniture the stool reached its height of popularity and ubiquity in the 16th century. By 1600 it was being replaced by the CHAIR, but smaller households continued to use a variety of stools until the 19th or even 20th centuries. In one form the chair was a development of the stool, as the 'back chair' or 'chair stool' was a stool with a back or an armless chair. Constructionally, stools were of three main types: 1. The simple three-legged stool, a round or square top having legs, at a slight outward angle, let directly into the top and secured with an expanding wedge. 2. Rectangular-topped stool with solid ends, usually set outwards at a slight angle and divided into two feet by a central cut or opening, and connected by a stretcher. 3. Rectangular-topped stool with square or turned legs, mortised and tenoned with a deep frieze rail and stretchers connecting the legs near the bottom. These could be long enough to seat at least two people. The material was generally oak, though sweet chestnut, elm, and beech were also used. Spanish walnut was used from the 16th century, and mahogany from *c.* 1700. Better-quality stools had upholstered tops. The main categories of stool are:-

back stool with a back attached. See CHAIR, back. *1589: one chayer, two backe stoles & one forme xxijd. 1591: ij Backe Chayers xxd. one litle buffett stoole wth ij litle Chayers xvjd.*

buffet The OED denies any connection between buffet stools and 'buffet', a sideboard, side-table. *Prompt. Parv.* : 'Bofet, thre fotyd stole (boffet stole, p.) *Tripes.*' The learned editor of the *Promptorium* suggests that the buffet stool might have been placed under the buffet or 'court cupboard'. Forby describes it as a four-legged stool; 'it is the poor man's side-board, table, or stool, as occasion requires.' Cotgrave 1611, 'a Buffet, or ioyned, stoole to sit on' suggests that there was little difference between buffet, joined, and, by implication, framed stools. Although most inventories have only one of the three adjectives attached, the occurrence together of buffet and framed, buffet and joined, and framed and joined stools suggests that some contemporaries saw a difference. One must assume that buffet stools were single-seaters, although there are occasional references to 'long' buffet stools. The ordinary buffet stool was often associated with a table, and it is safe to assume that their primary use was seating for meals. Ralph Edwards, *Shorter Dict. of Eng. Furniture*, 1977, says that buffet stools were upholstered. Some were, but this was not invariable, and it is difficult to see upholstery being the defining characteristic. The OED defines buffet stool as a low stool, footstool, which seems even wider of the mark. *1444: [two long stools/benches [scanna] 1 stool/bench of medium length] ij scanna [called] buffet stoles ij bankar. 1587: viij hei buffetstools. 1588: vj Cushion buffett stooles of tapsterie vjs...vj ioyned stoles iijs. 1589: xij Buffyt Stooles xiijs. iiijd. 1592: on letyll table wt a bofot stole iiijd. 1595: ij buffett stoles...ij framed stoles. 1603: twoe longe buffet stooles two Lyttle Joyned Stooles. 1617: xj newe buffitt stooles. 1637: half a dozen buffett stooles covered wth red leather & twoe lowe leather stooles .* See BUFFET.

chair stool stool with a back but no arms. *1597: j chaier iiij smale chaier stolles and iij little formes ijs. vjd.*

children's small stool. *1604: vj stooles & ij childrens stooles.*

coffer stool the top lifted to reveal a small box. *1587: iij copher stooles to sitt on.*

<u>cushion stool</u> with permanent or semi-permanent upholstered top. *1593: 1 old Cushin stoole of nedleworke chequor wise xxd...6 Cushin stooles of Tapstry worke with Buckeram covers xxiiijs.*
<u>folding stool</u> X-shaped, more popular on the Continent, especially France, than in England. *1597: one fouldinge stoole.*
<u>framed stool</u> constructed with mortise-and-tenon frame; see <u>buffet</u>, <u>joint</u>. *1587: one framed longe table and a square table wt ix framed stooles xxxs. 1595: one Longe frame table...ij Framed stooles...vij Joyned stooles...one Cushynge stoole. 1595: ij buffett stoles...ij framed stoles.*
<u>high stool</u> *1595: a highe stole a lowe stole.*
<u>hog stool</u> ? hog-backed, slightly convex top. *1741 [dairy] a hogstool. 1806: one Hog's Stool.*
<u>joint stool</u> see <u>buffet</u>. Etymologically, it is a stool with mortise-and-tenon joints, but it is not entirely clear how it differed from a <u>framed stool</u>. *1588: ix greate ioyned stoles uncovered vjs. ij lowe ioyned stoles, the one covered wth nedell worke, and the other wth redde and grene valure ijs. 1595: iiij ioyned stooles ij longe stooles ioyned.*
<u>low stool</u> possibly a footstool. *1588: ij lowe stoles, the one covered wth chaungeable taffeta & imbrodered wth blacke vellet, and the other wth Nedleworke iiijs. 1637: 3 back chayers covered with silke dammaske & 2 lowe stooles covered wth the same 3 li.*
<u>plank stool</u> stool with solid board ends instead of separate legs. *1637: j plancke stoole.*
<u>rush stool</u> joint or framed stool with a rush instead of a solid seat. *1595: ij russing stoles.*
<u>woman's stool</u> slightly lower than normal. *1589: iiij womens stooles of tent worke xiijd.iiijd.*
<u>side stool</u> ? standing to the side of a table. *1602: One table wth a Fram and twoo side stoles.*
See also ALESTOOL.
stool stall, pew in church. *1649: for the natting of yor Worps stoole and Mr Eds. 2s. 8d. . . for new natts to the stoole wher Mr Wilcocks did sit at Church 1s. 4d. . . Matts for three stooles in the Church 1s. 6d. 1662-3: plainchering the Chancll stooles 2s. 3d. a gice* [joist] *for the stooles.*
stool, chopping a butcher's block. *1589: a stoole to chopp flesh on.*
stool, rabbeting see RABETTING STOOL
stool, smoothing a form of ironing-board. *1595: a stole to smothe lynnyng on.*
stool mill apparatus for spinning yarn. *1737: One Twistering mill and one Stool Mill £1.*
stop, stope, stoppe see STOUP
stopell a stopper. *1459: j litill botell, with j cheyne and j stopell, weiyng xxxvij unces.*
storrer see BREWING; OAR; STIRRING STAFF
story, storry, store as well as a book, a story could mean a picture or print. *1589: storry in a frame. 1602: j Store of tobyase iijs.*
stothes, stothys see STUD
stott although stott can mean a castrated ox, a STEER, Norfolk medieval manorial accounts make it clear that it usually meant a draught horse, probably castrated. *1307: [5 stotts remaining. And bought 1 stott. And 1 foal of the Snath mare. Sum 7. Of which sold 1 mare foal. Sum 1. And remains 6].*
stoup, stop a water-bucket, usually of wood, and often pertaining to a WELL. *1273: j stoppe. iij bollis. j basket & [1 great cup 6d.]. 1300: [dairy] j stoppe ijd. ob. 1374: [made] ij stopp [of old] boord vjd. 1552: one Stoppe of bell metyll to bere water wthin to ye founte...waynge x li. 1588: ye well ij stoppes on Great roppe & A pulling. 1591: the stoppe at the well wth the chaynes. 1593: Belonging to 2 wells 4 stopps 2 pullies & 2 roopes xjs. viijd.*
stove grate an open metal fire-grate. *1709: steel stove grate.*
stovell the wooden OAR to beat and stir the mash in BREWING. *1613: one stovell for the Mash fatt.*
stoyle see STILE
straights, streytes narrow rough woollen cloths, between 27 and 40 inches wide,

woven from the early 16th century. *1513-4: xlix yerdes of streytes, price of the yerde xjd.*

strail, strayll OE *strægl, stræl,* L. *stragula,* blanket, bed-covering. *1498-9: [for a pair of] strayll [for the novice 4s. 1d.].*

strake the iron rim or tyre of the wheel of a CART, wheelbarrow etc. *1592: two cart strakes. 1647: [smith] for 19 stone & halfe of Iron on the strake nayles hoopes & furrs at 4s. 4d. p̱ stone 4 li. 5s...for shooeinge the wheeles & puttinge in the furrs 4s. 1664: [smith] two cart strakes waite 10½ pound nayling them on & other strakes unto the cart wheeles...two strakes for a crudbarrow wheele xijd. 1665: for 60 five stroake nayles ijs.*

strake see PLOUGH

strangles, stranglings a horse disease, typified by swelling in the throat. *1665: dressing & cureing the sorrold horse of the water farine & stranglings ijs.*

strap dish see TRAP-DISH

straw engine ? mechanical chaff-cutter, for cutting straw into chaff for fodder. *1788: a straw engine.*

stre straw. *1417: a lode stre.*

strehous building for straw. *1318: [carpentering] j strehous [in the sheepyard 5s. 6d.]*

streyning see DISTRAIN

strice pole see TRICE

striggell, strigell a curry-comb, for grooming horses. *1319: j strigell [bought 1½d.].*

strik, stryk see PLOUGH

strike a dry measure of a BUSHEL, but sometimes half a bushel or 2 or 4 bushels.

strike the wood or metal striker used to strike across the top of e.g. a BUSHEL to give struck measure, level with the top of the container, rather than heaped measure.

string long beam; the upright of a LADDER; in a CART, horizontal main timber of the frame. *1595: payer of tumbrell stryngs.*

strope strap, leather band. *1631: tow payre of cart trace one cart sadle one payre of stropes iij collers ij halters.*

struollde see STOOL

stud, stoth, stuth, styth OE *studu, stuðu,* ON *stoð,* stud, upright post in timber-framed wall; substantial sawn building timber. *1294: j stuth & [6 old] raftr'. 1295: ix stuth [of oak bought 6d.]. 1298: ij styth iiij Bord iiijˣˣ x splent [bought for the house 13d.]. 1298: ix stuyes xijd. 1298: xxiij cuppl' j roftre iiij stuth ij Borfreyes ij Byer & iij Wyndbemes xjs. xjd. q'. 1302: iiij stothes [for the] stabul. 1401: les corbales sthoyes & scappeles. 1417: [carpenter putting] stothys [in the wall]. 1595: sawen studds for pillers for windowes. 1595: xviij stoodes iiijs. vjd. 1663: groundseele & stoods & booches & sparres & dogs...a studd for the old barne 10 foote long 3d. the foot. 1665: one studd stocke 36 peeces for lyninge for the chappell chamber & stable.*

stuff cloth of worsted or long wool. *1709: A Bed of strip'd stuff and Covering of the same...A Bed of blew stuff.*

stulp, stolp ON *stolpe,* post, pillar; main posts of a paling fence. *1509: ij stolys lying up on stulpis. 1588: certaine pale wth the stulpes p'ce xxs. 1619-20: Rivinge Stulpes, Rales, & Pales.*

stump see BEDSTEAD

sturgeon a large fish, *Acipenser sturio,* growing up to 11 feet in length. It visited the Norfolk coast, but occurs in accounts of the 16th and 17th centuries in kegs. The swim bladder supplied ISINGLASS, and the roe (eggs) was eaten as caviare. The beluga, *Huso huso,* also provided caviare. *1647: 1 cagg of sturgion 18s.*

stuyerd see STEW YARD

sty OE *stig,* path, way. *1553: Richard Hay inclosed with ditches the Mylstye leading from grynne Mille towards Woodforth.*

styffe see STITHE

s'tyfycat certificate

stylyards see STEELYARD

subbase the lowest part of the base in a building or architectural feature such as a pillar; a plinth. *1619: an addition to the sayd gate of 2 palosters For beautifying of it wch stand behinde the pillers with there bases pedistalls cronix subbase and capitalls.*

succade, succate, sucket, soket candied fruit, or fruit preserved in syrup. *1481: soket viij li. vj onces viijs. vjd.*

sudorific potion medicine that causes sweating. *1680: a Sudorifick potion 2s. 1800: Mixture a Pint 6s. Sudorific Pills 3s.*

sue see SOE

suet fat from the kidneys and loins of cattle, sheep, deer etc. Deer suet was used for greasing armour. *1593: 3 Cakes of deeres suytt. 1647: 6 li sewet 2s. 6d.*

sugar honey was the main sweetening agent in the Middle Ages, but some sugar from sugar-cane grown in the Middle East was imported. The juice was pressed out of the canes, boiled, and poured into a conical vessel to cool and harden. Two or three further boilings would refine and whiten it from the original dark-brown colour. From the 16th century sugar-cane was grown in South America and the West Indies. By the middle of the 17th century much sugar was bought as powder, although loaf sugar continued to be used. At Houghton in 1647 powder sugar averaged 1s. 6d. and loaf sugar just over 2s. a pound. *1530: sugar loffe weying iij li. at vijd. the li. 1533: ij loffs off sowgere aft' vjd. ob. a li. 1562: stone suger for thawks ijd. 1587: iiij li. & a halfe of suger vjs. ixd. Item v oz. of stone suger vjd. 1648: for 4 li. oz.ij Duble Refine Suger 9s. 8d. Item for 6 li. of the best pouder Suger 10s. 1649:1 loafe of Suger Wayeinge 3 li. oz.10 at 2s. 2d. - 7s. 10d. . . 1 Loafe of dubble Refine Suger Wayeinge 3 li. oz.10 at 2s. 4d. p li. 8s. 6d.*

sugar box for use at table. *1637: [silver] j Suger box with a spoone.*

sugar chest to transport sugar in bulk. *1588: for a sugar chest to pack in ye muskets ijs. vjd.*

sugar nipper scissor-shaped tool with flat, rounded ends to cut lumps off a sugar-loaf. *1764: nutmeg grate, sugar nipper.*

suitable matching; of the same colour and pattern. *1620: a drawing Table of wallnutt tree with his Carpett of greene Cloath fringed. a carving Table of wallnutt tree with his cloth suteable to thother...a chaier of greene Damaske fringed. lowe stooles of Damaske suteable vj, they all having Covers of greene Buckeram. one paier of Andyrons tipped with brasse with their fier shovell and tonges suteable...a Chaier & a high stoole suteable to ye bed.*

sultage, soultage a coarse, cheap cloth. J.O. Halliwell, *Dict. of Archaic Words*, gives 'Sultredge, a coarse apron worn by poor women in some parts of Wiltshire.' *1562: ij elles of Sultage to pack upp the stuf bought at Sturbridge xviijd. 1588: xliiij ells of soultage to make curteynes to hang before the armor at vijd. ob. the ellne.*

sulwych see STERTWYCH

summer OFr. *somier,* beam; the main horizontal beam of the wall of a timber-framed building. See DORMANT; BRESSUMER. *1622: Carpenters...in framinge of C ioyces to 3 Summers & ij Girders.*

summercorn spring-sown barley. *1602: [23 June] Corne on the ground Itm the wintercorne vj li. Itm the Somercorne iiij li.*

summerland, summerlay, -ley land uncropped, but not necessarily unploughed, in summer. *1664: [28 May] began to plowe the som'land in the parks.*

sumpter a pack, saddle-bag; the horse carrying it; a pack-horse driver. *1597: one Lether sumpter. . . one sumter of lether olde...one great Leather sumpter. 1603: one sumpter sadle. 1665: Ten* *new shoes 6 rem:* [removing] *on the sumpter horse & geldings iijs. xd.*

sumpter cloth cloth, sometimes decorative, on the back of the sumpter horse. *1597: [kitcheners chamber] one blewe sumpter Clothe for the Coverlet.*

suntable table of sunrise and sunset times. *1639: fower mapps & a suntable js.*

superaltar a portable altar used in the medieval church.

surcingle, sursingle girth for a horse, passing under the belly, to keep pack or saddle in place. *1591: j old sursingle.*

surplice long linen gown, worn under the alb in the unreformed church. In the Church of England from the middle of the 16th century the surplice was prescribed as necessary wear for all clergy taking services, but was rejected as a papistical garment by many of them. It was provided by the parish through the churchwardens.

surtout greatcoat, overcoat. *1753: One old Surtout Ratteen Coat 10s.*

surtout an epergne, centre-table dish with small vessels for sweets etc. on branches. *1751:* [plate] *a Surtout with four Branches & four Saucers.*

survaing, surveying place sideboard, hatch, serving room where food served under the care of the surveyor of the preparation and serving of food in a great household. *1620: For making a screene in the survainge place by the kitchin. . . a new bridge of timber strong and substantiall over the moat on the west side of the house coming to the kitchin & survaing place. 1622: That the boylinge Chimney in the Kitchen be sett neerest the surveyinge place.*

surveying table a plane-table: a circular plate marked with degrees mounted on a tripod or single pointed shaft, with an alidade or sighting instrument pivoting on the centre. *1756:* [Lumber room] *Some Glass Bottles, Surveying Table, & Chairs with some Lumber.*

sustarne see CISTERN

suwe a sow. *1352:* [2 boars] *iiij suwes [9 pigs 24 piglets].*

suytt see SUET

swaderake see RAKE; SWATHRAKE

swage piece of metal formed to a definite shape and used to shape other metal. *1665: [smith made] a swage.*

swanskin fine thick flannel. *1680: 6 yds Swans skyn 2s. 4d.* [per yard] *14s. 1753: One Small Swanskin Waistcoat 1s. 6d.*

swanirons S-shaped POTHOOKS. See ESS. *1584: potthookes and swannyrons.*

sware square. See Q. *1513: ij dosen sware trenchers. 1544: felling & swarynge timber.*

swath rake wide RAKE to collect corn or hay. *1592: v iron & v woden swath Rakes. 1666: one swaderake. 1734: four Swath Rakes 1 li. 1788: Two Iron Sweath Rakes, Three Wood D°.*

swather user of the SWATH RAKE. *1680: 2 swathers 2s. 9d.*

sweep see SWIPE

sweep, sweepage the crop of hay from a meadow. *1647: Of John Harwood of Cowlshall for ye grass of little Harper and the eatage till michãs 2 li. 15s. and ye sweepage of both Turfe meadows 3 li. 1681: the first sweep of the meadow.*

sweet sweet-scented herbs or dried flowers e.g. lavender, rosemary. *1647: for sweet paid to laye amongst lyninge 6d.*

sweet water perfume, perfumed water e.g. rosewater. *1588: iiij glasses wth sweete water.*

swegges, sweghes, swehes, sweth see SWEY

swelse see SWILL

swey, sway, swegge, wagh, wegh switch, pliable rod, laid horizontally across a thatched roof to secure the thatch. See BROACH. *1293: in xxx knoth de swehes & lxxv knoth de harthiñ [for the chamber]. 1313: in sweghes [and bindings 13½d.]. 1318: broches & sweyes xvjd. 1354: sweth & Byndyngs. 1362: Wagh & p'kkes [for thatching the house]. 1409: iiij^c virgar [called]*

sweyes xvjd. 1596: his master strake him with a swaye.
swift a light reel to receive spun silk or yarn. *1587: the swift & the perke. 1604: j reele and ij swyft wth their blocks. 1736: two pair of Wool Combs & a pair of Wrings skeeps & swifts 15s.*
swill a large shallow basket, a swell; according to Nall it contained 500 herrings and was made of unpeeled willow. *1591: j swill for bread. 1592: [in Fyshouse] xx swylles. 1592: iij oulde barrylse to put in swelse xijd. 1593: xxxx codge swelles.*
swine *Sus scrofa*, the domestic pig. A piglet is a new-born or very young pig. A SHOTT is a weaned pig under 12 months old. A BARROW is a castrated male pig. Boar and sow are uncastrated male and female adults.
swingle hemp and flax were beaten with a swingle against a swingletree, a flat board or stock. See HEMP.
swipe, swaipe a long pole pivoting on a post with a bucket at one end and counter balance at the other, for raising water from river, pond, or shallow well; a handle for a pump. *1666: a pumpe swaipe.*
swivel, swilve horse-harness coupling. *1319: iiij swyveles [bought for the horses 1½d.]. 1597: a pair of horse chaines a swilve ij new showels.*
sword the varieties of sword over the centuries are too numerous to appear in this glossary. See ARMING. Some examples from the 16th century are:- *1522: for makyng clene of my Mr armyng sworde ijd. 1588: one armyng sword & girdell iiij li. 1592: a towhande sworde. 1597: A brode arminge sworde pomell & hylt graven & gylt. a blacke Walkinge staffe wth a sworde blade in it.* Detailed works on the sword are E. Oakeshott, *European Weapons and Armour*, 1980, repr. 2000, and *The Sword in the Age of Chivalry* by the same author.
syes see SCYTHE
syllabub, sillabub milk curdled with cider or wine. *1836: sylabub voider & 20 glasses.*
syment cement. *1542: j li. of rosen for syment.*
synnamon see CINNAMON
synodals or PROXAGE, proxy, senage: annual payment from a benefice to the bishop on the occasion of a synod, or episcopal or archiadiaconal visitation. See also PROCURATIONS.
syntre centring, wooden support for an arch. *1510: [for] iiij popylbordes [bought in the market for] syntrees [for] j vice viijd.*
syrup 1. Sweet viscid medicine with various ingredients. 2. Unrefined sugar, molasses. *1587: v li. of serrop in a vessell xd. 1589: xiiij li. of syrope iijs. 1605: A good Purge. Take two ounces of syrrup of Damask roses, two ounces of syrrup of Ruberbe, and one ounce of syrrup Agrick mixt together, and a third part taken in possit ale will serve for a good purge.*
systne see CISTERN
syther cider; see CRAB.
sythern see CITTERN
syve see SIEVE

Still and limbeck 1566

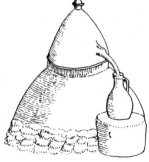

209

T

Taberet see TABOR

table the table had multiple uses and forms which led to a profusion of names and descriptions. In the Middle Ages most tables were simply boards placed on trestles, but even the tables used by servants and harvesters on the manor were covered with canvas cloths. The Prior of Norwich's manor-houses in 1352 had plenty of tables e.g. in the hall at Great Plumstead there were two great tables with trestles, two other tables with trestles and two benches, and the hall at Hemsby had 6 tables, five pair of trestles, and 4 benches. By contrast, not a single table is mentioned in the inventory of Caister Castle in 1459. An early form of a more permanent table was the 'table dormant', by which was usually meant boards fixed to posts sunk into the floor. This often accounts for the absence of tables in the hall in the inventories of the 16th and 17th centuries, as a *fixed* piece of furniture was outside the terms of reference of the inventory-makers. Such furnishings can only be picked up through other documents, e.g. an inventory made before letting the house, which would include all fittings. Until the 17th century tables were often covered with a CARPET, which was there all the time but usually removed for meals, when a cloth of linen was used. Before 1700 the type of wood is not usually stated unless it were something other than WAINSCOT or oak (and see below), but walnut and deal occur, and elm, ash, or beech may have been used. From the 17th century the table was often a decorative rather than simply a useful piece of furniture, and no attempt will be made here to analyse the 'fine furniture' type of table. Descriptions of tables in inventories usually take one or more of 4 main forms:- 1. Use e.g. brushing, dining, carving. 2. Form e.g. folding, framed, drawing. 3. Shape e.g. round, square. 4. Material e.g. wainscot, walnut.

brayden   OFr. *breie*, break; table for breaking HEMP. *1597: a brayden table & a pair of cannhookes xijd.*

brushing   for brushing clothes; dressing table. *1620: a brusshing Table with an ould Carpett.*

carved   figures or animals carved on the frame, legs or supports. *1589: [hall] a carved framed table with iiij lions. xxs.*

carving   side-table for carving meat. *1620: [parlour] a Carving Table wth a Carpett of greene cloth. . . [great chamber] a drawing Table of wallnutt tree with his Carpett of green Cloath fringed. Item a carving Table of wallnutt tree with his cloth suteable to thother.*

cupboard   probably a side-table, or at least not a table used for eating. *1588: one old Table wth a Cupborde xxd. 1589: table with ij cupbets ioyned into it. 1592: a lytle square table wth a Cubbord in ytt. 1620: a Foulding table wth Cupbords.*

deal   table of DEAL, that is softwood. *1637: one furindell table wth a frame iijs. iiijd.*

dicing   see TABLES

dining   the term 'dining table' did not come into general use until late in the 17th century, following the term 'DINING ROOM'.

with drawers   either with drawers or draw-leaves. *1589: a framed table with draws xxs.*

drawing   table with one or two leaves that could be drawn out to lengthen the table. In use by the early 16th century. See leaves. *1588: j square Table wth leves to drawe owte, & a carpet of brode grene cotton vs. 1589: one other framed table with leaves xxs. 1595: a table wth ye drawer wth ye bords thereon. 1618: one draweinge table wth eleaven old buffett stooles xviijs. 1620: a faier Drawing table of wallnutt tree a large Turkie Carpett. 1624: 1 drawing table with a tapestry cover. 1637: One large drawer table wth Twoe leaves.*

falt   see folding

fixed   on posts or legs permanently fixed in or to the floor. *1608: [hall] one foulte table...*
Fower other tables standinge upon turned posts fixed in the grounde.
folding   usually a small, portable table, either with X-legs or legs that fold inwards; a table
with folding leaves. *1509: a Falte tabyll. 1584: A Rounde Table to fowlde up and downe iijs.*
1588: one rounde fowlte Table wth vj ioyned stoles vjs. viijd. 1591: a foulded table vs. 1597: a square
folding table wth the frame thereto...a square table wth a foldinge frame...one lyv'y table on a folded
frame...one folded rounde table, wthout a frame. 1692: a clapping table. See above, cupboard.
framed   table with a top fixed to or lying upon a joined frame of legs and stretchers.   See
also drawing. *1588: a Table wth a frame ioyned vjs. 1591: table wt a frame. 1593: 1 longe framed*
table & 2 formes xs. 1597: one a Longe table wth the frame. 1637: j longe frame table and j old dornix
Carpit of Birdwork xiijs. iiijd...one litle old frame table broken a peecs wantinge the ledge & dustall for
thende therof js...one frame table wantinge a ledge before at the foot iiijd.
joined   with a joined frame of legs and stretchers; probably with the top fixed to the frame.
See framed. *1597: one ioyned table of walnuttree.*
with leaves see drawing; square. *1589: one litle old leaf table.*
livery   see LIVERY.   A common designation, originally meaning a side table from which to
serve or deliver food and drink, a meaning still current in the 17th century. *1592: a Lyvery*
table wth a carpett ijs. 1597: one lyv'y table: & thereon one brode square dycing table of spanishe Asshe.
1620: a litle Table to sett pott on.
marble   that is, marble-topped. *1709: 2 marble tables with wooden frames.*
pair   usually signifies playing-tables. See TABLES.
plank   probably planks on trestles. *1592: Too planketable xijd.*
round   before the late 17th century, small tables for setting by chairs etc. See folding.
side   See livery. *1595: one square syde table.*
square   as opposed to rectangular. See cupboard; drawing; folding. *1588: one square table*
wth turned posts and a Leafe to turne over iijs.
trestles   the basic form, still in use up to the present day. Medieval mss. show trestle tables,
with ornate trestles, being used for the greatest occasions. *1597: The Chappell nowe the*
folding house...a longe table to folde Clothes on...[inner chamber] one longe table: 2 trestells. [note] *now in*
the folding house.
wainscot   of oak board, see WAINSCOT. *1709: [great hall] 4 great Wainscot tables, one litle one.*
walnut   often imported from Spain, walnut was a popular wood for high-class furniture
from the late 16th century, although early on it seems to have been used for STOOLS,
CHAIRS, and BEDSTEADS rather than tables. By the late 17th century it was used for many
different types of furniture. See WALNUTTREE.
miscellaneous descriptions   *1590: a small table to sett by ye Fiere.   1590: a knyttynge table.*
1613-4: for a Table Plancke Inche board & halfe Inch board & quarters & Tables Feete for the
commi'ion table & seates for the Comysarie xxiijs. iiijd.
table   picture, print. Prized paintings were often protected by a curtain on a rail hung in
front of the picture. *1588: a Table of glasse wth Godsalves Armes xs. 1597: One table wth picture of*
K: H: 8 & a Curteyn of sylk to it. 1627: Two Tables conteininge the histories of the foundacōns &
Armes of all the Colleges in boath the Universityes xijd.
table, table plank   flat board, plank, or balk of timber, sometimes of considerable size.
1389: iiij tablis [bought for the repair] dil Speer [in the hall].   1416: [1 table [mensa]] de Waynskot
[bought for] les Flew.   1424: j mensa [for the kitchen window].   1620: Sawinge the greate Oke at
Coxford into iiij Tables, or Table Peice and ij Long Dressers, viz (in toto) the Table Peice vj^{xx} fotte at iiijd
fotte xls.   1620: helpinge to Lode the Table peice...Helpinge To Howse the Table peice and setting up
Bord. 1664-5: For breaking one table plank that came frō Sr Nich: Bacons 30 foot long 28 inch deepe.

table brick hard and impervious BRICK for the WATER-TABLE, the sloping top of a plinth. *1710: 3 hundred Table brick 12s.*

tables gaming boards, particularly of backgammon and related games. Usually referred to as a pair of tables. *1459: iij payre tablys of cipris, being in casys of lether. j payre tablys of G. enrayed withowght, and here men in baggys longyng thertoo. 1474: a payre of tabille of horne and box xvjd. 1531: playd att the tabylls. 1591: j pe of playinge tables wth their men xxd. 1597: one lyv'y table: & theron one brode square dycing table of spanish Asshe.. 1620: a paier of playing tables with their men...a paier of playing tables with their men of ivory. 1636: Two payre of Diceing tables.*

tabor, taboret tabor was the early name for a drum, and after the word 'drum' was introduced in the 16th century 'tabor' was used mainly for a small drum accompanying the pipe or trumpet. A taboret was a drummer, or the drum-horse. *1464: for a hedstalle for the taberet iiijd. . . corde for the taberettys taberete ijd.*

tafferill, tafferel Du. *tafeleel*, dim. of *tafel*, table. Panel, carved panel; upper part of the stern of a ship, often carved; the poop-rail (changed to taffrail in 19th cent.). *1618-20: For 12 tafferills within the little court and on the front at the coming in at 2 li. 10s. a peece.*

taffeta thin, plain-woven cloth, stiffened with extra weft threads. Of silk in the Middle Ages, later it incorporated linen and other materials, and was used for clothes and furnishing fabrics. Tuftaffeta had a nap or pile in tufts, and was often described as inferior to velvet. Changeable taffeta was given a lustre and 'changeable' appearance by watering and calendering. *1588: one framed chayer, the backe & seate of chaungeable taffeta imbrodered wth blacke vellet xiijs. iiijd...iij Wyndowe Cusshens, one of changeable taffata of blacke and redde imbrodered wth marie golds & Roses, and other flowers, and the other two of grene fygured silke xxvs. 1590: auncient of taffeta sarcenett. 1593: good gowne of tuft tavety v li. 1595: ij taffety Hatts. 1597: Tow wyndow curtayns of red and gren tafeta of eyght yarnes...5* [bed] *Curteyns of levant taffeta in 16 panes redd & blewe & yellow.*

tail tree shortened joist with one end tailed or tied into a frame, over a feature such as a fireplace. *1665: pulled up the plancher joyce tayle tree racke & manger in the strangers stable...made an end of framing tayle tree setting up the posts joyceing and began to planke & sett up manger posts in the strangers stable.*

tainter, taniter sharp nail for nailing matting. See TENTERHOOK. *1648: a C of Larg taniters 1s. 1649: yellow nayles 200 Tacks 200 & Taniters 100 1s. 4d.*

taithe see TATHE

tale, taylle, tally square rod with cuts or notches across it to represent payment, money etc., and split down the middle so that each party had one half. The word was transferred to a written account. *1456: And lyke yow to wete that y have a taylle with my cosyn Fenne of v^c marc and more, for to be chaunged uppon such places as a man myght have moste spedye payment. 1498: makyng of the tayll jd. and for wrytyng of them jd. and for joynyng of the taylle iiijd. and for the receyvyng of them into the courte of the Excheker ijd.*

tallow strictly, hard animal fat obtained from round the kidneys of ruminants and used for candles, soap etc. and processed in a tallowtrough. *1637: a tallowe trowe.*

tammy see STAMMET

tampon, tompion Fr. *tape*, piece of cloth used as plug; a plug, bung, stopper to seal the mouth of a gun. *1481: ij C tampons xvjd.*

tankard large open tub of wood; tall drinking vessel or jug. *1310: [making] j tankard [with hoops of iron 7½d.]. 1403: [1 new] tankard vijd. 1468: [wooden] iij gret tankerkes iijs vjd. xv galone tankarkes vijs. vjd. xv potelle tankerkes vs.*

tanning the process of making hides or skins into leather was quite complicated and varied according to the type of hide. <u>Butts</u> or backs were the thickest and heaviest oxhides.

212

Up to the 19th century butts were tanned by:-
1. Laying them in a smoke-house in which was a smouldering fire of wet tan (oak bark).
2. Scraping and scrubbing them to remove hair, grease etc.
3. Colouring: putting in a pit of ooze (ground bark infused in water).
4. Putting them into a pit, called a scowering, containing a solution of vitriol (sulphuric acid) or a vegetable acid made from rye or barley; this distended the pores of the butts to absorb the ooze, which combined with the gelatinous part of the skin and formed leather.
5. The butts were then placed in a water-pit called a binder, with ground bark between them, and left for 4-6 weeks.
6. They were then transferred to another pit filled with strong ooze and with ground bark between them for 10-11 months, during which time the ooze was changed twice.
7. They were then dried, compressed, and beaten smooth.
<u>Hides</u> were cowhides or light oxhides, and went through a similar process to the butts, except that they were treated in a lime-pit instead of a smoke-house, and the binder was called a layer, in which the hides were soaked from 4-6 months. <u>Skins</u> were the skins of calves, seals, swine, dogs etc. and were tanned by
1. Washing in water.
2. Putting them into a lime-pit to destroy the epidermis.
3. Scraping the hair off.
4. Putting them into a grainer or pit filled with water mixed with alkaline pigeon-dung to soak out the lime, grease, and soapy matter for 7-10 days, during which time they were scraped clean several times; this softened the skins and prepared them for the ooze.
5. They were then put into a pit of weak ooze, and transferred two or three times to pits of successively stronger ooze to finish in a pit of very strong ooze with fine-ground bark.
6. They were then taken out and hung on poles to dry.
7. Tanned skins could be made supple by currying, that is soaking them in water, scraping, beating, and flexing, and finally impregnating them with a mixture of fish-oil and tallow to make them both pliant and waterproof. See TEW.
Lighter hides, called dressing hides, and horse-hides were tanned in the same way as skins. The bark of other trees beside oak, e.g. horse chestnut, beech, willow, elder could be used.
tapestry woven textile with the design or picture in the weave, used for hanging on walls or in upholstery. 'Imagery' meant with figures, animals etc.; 'verdure' had flowers or foliage. See ARRAS; COSTER; HANGING; STICK. *1466-7: xij peces of curse tapstery, every pece conteynenge xx Flemyshe stykkes...for every stykke vijd. . . . x peces of counterfet tapstre, every pece conteynenge xx Flemyshe elles, pryse the pece xjs. 1588: one Coveringe of tapestrie...one Cusshen of Tapsterie xxd...ij Coverlets of Tapsterie, the one lyned with canvas, & the other unlyned...the hangings of the Chambre of olde Tappestrie wth scrowles. 1593: 5 peces of old hangings of Tapestrye worke wth Jelyflowers xxs. 1597: iij piecs of hangings ymagery of tapestry lyned wth Canvas wch bene in depth 3 yards qrter: in length one vj yards iij qrter, one other iij yards: & thother v yards di'...4 Cusshyons of tapestry verdure. . . 5 pecs of hangings tapestry: one of Imagery: 4 of forest work.*
tappetrow long shallow BREWING tub with a tap. *1352: [4 great] cuwe & ij kelers & j tappetrowe. . . iij keleres j tappetrou.*
tap scrue long tap screwed into a barrel. *1671: two tap scrues 1s. 6d.*
tapsell, tapseil an East Indian cotton material. *1680: 12 yds tapsell 18s.*
tar, tarras tar, distilled from wood, mainly coniferous, and later from coal, was used among other things for waterproofing buildings and, as it has antiseptic properties, for dressing the wounds of animals, particularly those sustained by sheep in being shorn. See PITCH. *1300: in xij li. picis & tar [for the boat]. 1498-9: [for] ij barell' of tarr vijs. iiijd. 1595: tarre,*

A pytch pan, brands. 1619-20: a bill of 40 barr' Tarras 15 li. 0s. 8d. 1647: [for greasing 143 hog sheep] for 8 li. sope to mix a monge their tarr.

tarcell, tercel, tersel see TERCEL

tares vetch; the cultivated vetch is *Vicia sativa*, used as a fodder crop. *1599: Tares j acr' di'. 1663: fetched the tares out of the parks.*

target 1. A light, round shield. 2. Shield-shaped ornament, often worn on the head. *1352: [2 benches] j target. 1459: j spice plate demi gilt, my maisters target enamyled in the myddes...ij galon pottes, gilt playn, enameled in the lyddes with my maisters target. 1588: a targett of proofe. 1592: Thre wooden Targetts. 1597: a headpeece & targat graven rytche. . . A Targett wth black vellet: fringed wth black sylk & gold.*

tarrice, tarris a terrace. *1619: ground table...in the tarrice walle towards the garden. 1665: pulling downe the old bridge over the moate betweene the best garden and tarris walle. . . They weeded the walkes in the best garden, kitchen garden tarris & the borders there sev'all times.* See p. 168.

tarrier an auger, for boring holes in wood.

tarriers tiring-irons, a puzzle consisting of 7 or 10 iron rings on an oblong closed wire, each also fastened to a wire within the oblong which passed through the next ring and had its other end attached to a strip of bone or metal nearly the same length as the oblong. The puzzle was to detach the rings. *1781: a pair of tarriers.*

tarris see TAR

tartryn rich silk fabric imported from China through Tartary.

tasel, teasel Fuller's teasel, *Dipsacus fullonum* ssp *fullonum* (now *D. sativus*) has hooked bracts on the flower head which were used for teasing wool and cloth; wild teasel, *D. fullonum* ssp *sylvestris* (*D. fullonum*) has straight bracts. *1339: teaseles [sold 12s.]...in plantis de Tasel [bought 18d]...[in seed] de Tasel [bought 6d.].*

task corn was often threshed by the task, that is by the quantity. *1649: 2 bushells of Taske Corne 5s.*

tasker 1. A valuer, taxer. 2. A thresher working by the TASK. *1706: and to avoyd further trouble & charge...wee agreed that the corne in the barn should be thrashed out & that one tasker be put in upon yr Ldships Accompt and the other by Dent & that each of them put a lock upon the barne doore.*

tassell see TERCEL

taster small flat silver or pewter cup for tasting drink. *1597: iij saultsellers iij vynyiers a pewter cupp and a taster ijs. 1636: [plate] one Taster with the cover. one Taster for strong waters.*

tathe sheep or cattle dung, spread as fertiliser by the producer. *1557: shall well & sufficiently tathe & compesture wth shepe in seasonable tyme of the yere according to the custome there used tenne Acres of land.*

tavety see TAFFETA

tea first known in England *c.*1650-55; a fashionable and expensive drink from 1660; common in the 18th century, together with its equipment. See SAUCER. *1709: a tea table, 16 Tea cups & saucers, a Tea Cup with a foot, a sugar dish with a cover, an Earthen Tea pot.*

tea kettle a kettle with a spout; kettle for brewing tea. *1738: A Tea kettle one Sauce Pan.*

tea kitchen an urn with its own burner for brewing tea. *1792: Three bronzed Tea kitchens.*

tearce, tearer see TERCE

tear sheet MDu., Low G. *teer*, from *teeder*, fine, delicate. The finest quality of flax or hemp. *1591: one paier of teare sheets vjs.*

teastare see BEDSTEAD, tester

tees Halliwell: 'Iron holdfasts in the shape of the top of the letter T, pendent on short chains from the seels of a horse's collar, or from the thilbells. They are thrust, one end first, through staples on the shafts'. Nall: 'Chains fixed to the *sales* of the thill horse'. *1731:*

214

2 payer of tees. 1743: a pair of Tees and Collars.

tems, temmes, tembes, temese a SIEVE, used in BREWING and preparing food. See BOLT. *1306: j temese [for the kitchen 2d.]. j temese [in the bakehouse]. 1507-8: a temse for ale xvjd. 1584: [dairy] one temmes & a theede. 1594: a worte temse.*

tenayl, tenaille pincers, forceps, tongs. *1318: in j vynding* [illeg.] *tenayl ad le spet & ad Le Foreyne vd.*

tene tin. *1474: a box of tene with sylver wire.*

tenell, tenile, teanel OE *tænil, tænel,* ON *teina,* wicker basket. *Prompt. Parv.:* 'Tenel, vessel. *Tenella.* Tenel, or crele. *Cartallus'. 1323: ij teniles ijd. 1433: In tenellys & hyrdelys [bought this year 11s.].*

tenement a holding, tenure; land, and/or a building which is held of another; the building or house itself; a portion of a house.

tening harrows tining is the teeth of a HARROW, so 'tening' is perhaps wooden-framed harrow with wooden as opposed to iron teeth. *1636: 2 tening harows one Eyorn Harow.*

tent tents used for the musters in the 16th and 17th centuries could be quite elaborate, with several compartments or rooms. *1597: [wardrobe] 2 Tents: & one pece of an old tent. . . A Tent, wth the chamber: & buttrye.*

tenterhook hook or sharp bent nail set on the edge of a frame (tenter) for stretching wet cloth so that it would not shrink while drying; any sharp hooks. See TAINTER. *1745: meat rack with tenter hooks.*

tent work embroidery in which the pattern was worked by stitches across the intersections of the threads of worsted cloth; also called petit-point. *1589: iiij womens stooles of tent worke xijjs iiijd...iiij other curtayns of tent worke and one of needell worke xxxs.*

terce, tearce, tierce OFr. *terce, tierce,* L. *tertium,* one third; wine-barrel containing 42 gallons or one third of a PIPE. *1603: a tearce of white wine. 1649: 1 Tearce of white wine 4 li. 5s. 1654: for 3 wine Hogsheads & 2 terces from Norwch. 1665: one terse of lynseed oyle cont' 39 gallons.*

tersel, tiercel, tassel male hawk; a tercel-gentle is a male peregrine. *1601: a tassell of a Goshauke. 1602: a tassell gentle.*

terrett a ring in horse harness, particularly on the SADDLE or the HAMES, through which the reins pass. *1310: j turetts [for the cords 1d.].*

term statue similar to that of the god Terminus, springing from a pillar or pedestal; a pedestal. *1745: Four Terms at Corners with Bust's on Each. 1751: Two Mahogany carved & gilt Thermes, with black & gold Marble Tops.*

terreen OFr. *therine, terrin,* of earth, earthen; a tureen, originally of earthenware. *1745: 1 Terreens, one Pewter Rim Dish.*

tester see BEDSTEAD

teuiron, tewiron the nozzle of a blacksmith's bellows. *1592: one whetstone two teuyrones one workinge yron.*

tew fishing gear nets, lines etc.; tools, working stuff. *1587: all his fysshyng tewe xs. 1588: all the fysshers tewe xs. 1591: the fishinge nette wth other tewe prized at xd.*

tew to dress leather, to make it supple by beating. See TANNING. *1499-1500: tewyng of an horskyn viijd. 1649: for the Teweinge of a horse hide 3s.*

tewke see TUKE

teys, tays, teise, taise OFr. *teise,* L. *tensa,* stretched; a fathom (six feet), the theoretical distance between the finger-tips of outstretched arms. *1296: j cord de xij teys [for the well 3½d.]. 1299: j lyne de xxx teys vd.*

thacbord, thackboard roofing BOARD. *1310: vjᶜ de thacbord [for roofing the chamber above the gate 24s. 6¼d. price per hundred 4s. 1d.] In mmcc de spykyng [for the said boards 9s. 2d.]. In*

215

ccc de splentenayl [for the same 7d. In wages of a carpenter laying the same boards for 11 days 7s. 4d.].
thack, thakk OE *þeccan, þeccean,* to thatch. Both reed and straw were used for thatch, straw being cheaper but reed much longer-lasting. *1417: to Cossey for a lode thak to ye Lathes. 1500-01: [for mowing] le thakke ijs. iiijd. 1591: c'ten thacke vs. 1625: strawe to thacke ijs. iiijd. 1675: new thack upon ye little barne...4 days of thacking ye head house on ye north side 2 days thacking on ye other side of ye head house. 1726: for Thakking done at Rising.* See THACKSTER.

thackster a thatcher. See THACK. *1639: John Wyne did lye wth a thacksters wife, and left his breeches behinde him and the thackster tooke them up & went up to ye toppe of the house and thacked in them.*

thackster's needle an iron rod about 2 feet long with a flattened spear-shaped end which was pierced to enable rope to be threaded through the thatch to secure it to the roof. *1593: One thaksters needle.*

thack tile, thakk tyle, thek tyle pegtile or PINTILE, FLAT TILES of brick material for roofing; possibly shingles or wooden tiles. *1532: ij m^l & di' thek Tyle xs. v^c bryk Tyle wt the caryage iiijs. iiijd. To Thoms Kett for m^l of breke tyle vjs. for m^l of thakk tyle vjs.*

thatcart a cart for reed or straw for thatching. *1352: [1 new] thatcarte [without wheels].*

thead, theed *Prompt. Parv::* 'Thede, bruarys instrument. *Qualus,* C.F. *vel calus,* Cath.' Forby: 'the tall wicker strainer placed in the mash tub over the hole in the bottom, that the wort may run off clear. It is perhaps more commonly called a *fead.*' See BREWING. *1584: one temmes & a theede. 1743: Two large stools one thead.*

therd, thread a very fine cloth ? *1474: ij kercher of therd xijd...a kerchey of therd and ther in was vjs. viijd. of gold...a kercher of thred viijd.* See THREAD; TICK.

therm see TERM

theswealle see THRESHOLD

thewe *Prompt. Parv.* : 'Thewe, or pylory. *Collistrigium.*' PILLORY; or an instrument for the punishment of women, probably an iron collar or scold's bridle. *1335: [carpentering] dil Cucstol & dil thewe [5½ days 22d. 2 hanging locks with 2 keys] iij staples & j hespe [for the same 7d.].*

thilbells, fillbells Halliwell: 'the chain-tugs to the collar of a cart-horse, by which he draws.' *1663: [knacker] three new seales xvijd. for his worke in mending one paire of thilbells making another paire & mending another cart trayse Dec 29th xijd. 1742: four dudfins a pr of Thilbells.*

thill, thiller, filler the pole or shaft of a cart, either a single shaft with the draught beasts harnessed on either side, or two shafts with the beasts in line between them. The thill-horse was the shaft or wheel-horse, next to the cart, and attached to it by the 'gear' or harness. See THILBELLS. *1417: a mendyng of ye carte Thyll a bonde of hyryn & nayle yer to iijd. 1587: Cart trayse furnisshed fore fowre horsses with the fyllers geere. 1593: iiij^{pr} payre of Carte trayce horse Collers ij payre of thillers harnes. 1779: 4 Pair of Harness with Fillers Geres...4 Pair Harness & Thillers Gears. 1836: Three pair Harness One pair Fillers ditto.*

thixel, thixhel, thiksel an adze, a carpenter's tool like a small axe but with the cutting edge at right-angles to the shaft; could be used with one hand. Adzes with convex edges were used to gouge out depressions in woodwork. *1352: j Wymbel j thixhel j chisel. 1588: j squier ij thixells ij hatchets. 1592: a thiksel & an hamer.*

thole-pin, tollpin *Prompt. Parv.*: 'Tholle, carte pynne (or tolpyn)'. A wooden or iron pin, particularly the pin passing through the axle to hold a wheel in place. *1619: 2 iron Tolpines for ye Cart 8d. 1649: [smith] for toll pins mendinge 1s. 6d.*

thornback the roker, *Raja clavata,* a ray measuring up to 24 inches across and weighing up to 38 lbs. *1560: paid for one Thornbacke viijd. 1593: a Thornbacke vjd.*

thrall a stand for a pail or barrel; ALESTOOL. *1590: j payer thralls.*

thread thread, usually of linen, was often sold in shops by weight, and was used not only for the usual purposes but also to make buttons. See THERD; TICK. *1587: ij grosse of tinn buttons at xiijd. - ijs. ijd...q' li. of blacke thrid vijd...ij grosse of thrid buttons at viijd. - js. iiijd...ij grosse of thred buttons at vijd. - xiiijd.*

threshold, threshel, thresweld, -wald, -wale, -weall horizontal timber connecting the feet of the doorposts and acting as a low barrier to water etc. The Norfolk pronunciation is 'troshel', following 'trosh' for thresh. *1302: j Theswealles [16 feet long and 4 studs for the stable 13d.]. 1313: [carpenter making doors anew and fitting] del threswald [of the great door 22½d.]. 1368: [fitting 1] thresshwale ad le post'ne [of the great gate]. 1665: a dorstal and a threshal.*

throff, through, throw see TROUGH

throms, thrums ends of waste wool or hemp yarn, used for making mops or rough brushes. *1466: for thrommes for pyche mapoltes ijd.*

throssyng threshing, following the Norfolk pronunciation (troshing). See THRESHOLD. *1546: Wylm Bykes xliij day in throssyng and iij day in ladyng of breke vijs. viijd.*

throughshoot, thorow shout wooden tine for HARROW. See TENING HARROW. *1636: 43 harrow backes and thorow shoutes.*

throughshot large long iron spike; bolt. *1663: drive two throughshotts into the posts at the end of the sponges that the gates might be kept shutt. . . throughshott for the ṗspect waite 1¾ lb for vijd.*

throw tool; ? small lathe. *1588: ij hattchetts - a throw of Iron iij philes ij wrests.*

thwart saw see SAW

tick 1. Case or covering for pillow, featherbed etc.; featherbed, pillow. 2. Linen cloth, for clothing as well as bed-linen. *1466: iij tylkes and bolsters to the same fore federbeddes xls. 1597: one olde torne ragged tyke whereof the feathers bene in a tubbe. 1618: one old Canvas tike. 1730: fine Ticken to line a Cushen and fine Feathers to fill it...For a large Bed for the Couch of fine Flanders Tick and filled it with fine sweet Feathers covering it with Damask silk thred.*

tiffany thin transparent silk, muslin or linen. *1665: One course hearinge seive at Norwich Aprill 29th and one tiffany bottome for a seive ijs.*

tight see TON TIGHT

tigurr, tugurr *Prompt. Parv.*: 'Tugurry, schudde. *Tugurrium.*' Cotgrave 1611: 'Tugure, a cottage, a shepheard's coat, shed or bullie'. L. *tugurium*, hut. *1363: [making] Tigurr [completely new 6s. 8d.] in xxxiiij bord de Waynskott [for the same] tigurr vijs. jd.*

tile in the Middle Ages and beyond roof-tiles were either brick tile or wooden tiles, that is shingles. 'Tile' also included paving-tile. See FLAT TILE; PIN TILE; PAMMENT; PANTILE; PATHING TILE; THACK TILE. *1466: for CC and di' of howse tyle prise xd...for xiij pathyng tyles, iiijd. 1519-20: le Breketyle vjs. viijd. 1609-10: for one thowsand of Tyle xiiijs...for iij thowsand of tile pynne xviijd. 1620: Tile iiij^{XX} vj M v^C att vjs M - xxv li. xixs. 1620: 19^{XX} foote & 10 sawinge of Popple Bord to be used for makeinge Tyle xjs. iiijd.*

tile nail NAIL to fix shingles or wooden tiles to the roof. *1665: 5000 tyling nayles 12s. 6d.*

tile pin wooden, usually oak, pegs or pins driven through the holes in a FLAT TILE to latch on the laths of the roof. *1620: makeinge xlviij^{ie} M v^C Tile pynnes wch he and his Cumpanie made in winter nights xvjs. ijd. c.1620: pd for 28 bush. tylepinnes 1 li. 6s. 8d. 1664: 10,000 tyle pin vs.*

tillet coarse cloth used for wrapping. *1466: xij yerdes of tyllete for the spynas.*

tilt covering, canopy of cloth or canvas. *1591: j stalle and a tylte vs.*

tilter mechanism for tilting a barrel, worked by lever. *1779: Tin Funnel and Tilter.*

timber a reckoning of furs, = 20 whole skins or 40 half-skins. *1465-6: xx tymbre of menever, prise the tymbre, xvjd; and for xiiij tymbre of odre menever, prise the tymbre, xviijd.*

timber drug long narrow four-wheeled cart for the carriage of long timber, particularly whole trunks. See GILL. *1752: 1 Timber drug 1 Timber gial 3 Timber Chains.*

tin valued from early times for its non-rusting property and as a constituent, with lead, of

217

soft SOLDER. See also THREAD. *1342: iij li. de tin [for repairing the lead cistern 1½d.]. 1584: A flaggon bottell of tyne defacyd xijd. 1648: Tyninge ware 2s. 6d. 1701: tinn lanthorn.*

tincescot possibly from OE *týn-an*, to hedge, enclose, with suffix -sl from ON, leading to *tinsel*, underwood, brushwood; customary payment for the right to hedge land, or to take brushwood. See TINING. *1313: in tincescot ob.*

tine a cask between a barrel and a vat in size, of uncertain capacity but possibly that of a wine HOGSHEAD (63 wine GALLONS, 52½ imperial gallons) or a FIRKIN (84 wine gallons). *1289: ij Cuue ij Tyn. 1352: [6 vats] iiij tines ij keleres.*

tine the prong of a FORK or a HARROW.

tinggelnayl, tyngelnayl see NAIL; TENAYL; TENELL

tining, tinynge, tyning see TINCESCOT. A hedge, particularly a dry hedge, one formed by cut brushwood, not planted. *1313: [making 12 ½ perches] j tyning [on the south side of the manor 2s. 7d.]. 1319: [making] j tynynge [on the foss of the manor].*

tinkler small bell, harness bell. *1788: Two Milk Casks & 7 Tinklers.*

tinkling halter halter with small bells. *1737: 4 Bell halters. 1747: the half part of 5 Tinkling halters 12s.*

tint, tynte Prompt. Parv.: 'Tynte, mesure. Satum.' Ibid.: 'Half a buschel, or eytendele (half or [sic] a bowndel, boshel, or ethyndel, s. or tynt, H.P.). Satum.' An *ey3tyndele* was one eighth of a COOMB, or half a BUSHEL.

tipe, tippe tipped. *1591: ij typped pottes wt sylver xvs. 1632: eleven silver spoones one tippe pott. 1636: one tipe pote vs.*

tipe a small dome or cupola. See VAUSE. *c.1619: [carpenters] Foure hollow Tipes within the little court: Two over the steare cases wch should have stood: but the old walles being rent: were forced to take them downe and make them new in lesse roome then they were beffore For the inlarging of the court: The third over the porch coming into the Hall: the Fourth over the Lobby or passage out of the hall to the great steares, Wch Tipes the curbs are made of timber: Inibeed [sic] in the manner of vauses with crock stones in the sayd curbs carved for the fastning of the Freise and architrave wch is to be made of stone: with compasse rafters and vinealls on the top: with bourding the rooffe with slitt deales: And making of a Floore all the whole bredth For the plasterer to seele to: with Dragon Joyce and all other carpentry worke: For the aforesayd tipes and sawing I valew at 5 li. a pees. 1619: [masons] For architrave and Frise of stone under the vause of the tipes in the little court with these Troclifies and garnish and under the cornish of the 3 great tipes.*

tippet 1. A long narrow strip of cloth attached to the hood. 2. From 1600, a cape reaching to or just below the waist, either outdoor garment or negligée. *1459: j typpet, halfe russet and halfe blacke felwet, with j jagge.*

tire cord used to hang TAPESTRY or HANGING. *1537: to Willes wiff for tyer for the plor hangyngs.*

tiring-irons see TARRIERS

tirrett a turret. *1665: two [wooden] moulds for great & small bowles for tirretts. . . boared & cutt some neckes & bowles at the kell for tirretts.*

tissue expensive, fine cloth woven on a draw loom with a weft figure, sometimes including gold or silver thread, on a satin ground. *1513: j Tyssue Gyrdyll wt long harnez. 1588: a tester of Tissue xiijs. iiijd. 1593: 1 posted beddstede wth a tester of wainscott & vallence of purple vellett & tissue. 1597: one olde Cusshing Case of clothe of tyssewe.*

tithe an ecclesiastical tax of a tenth of the produce of a parish, made compulsory in the 10th century, to support the priest, the church building, and the poor. Predial tithes were levied on produce such as grain, grass, hay, and increase of livestock; mixed tithes on the produce of stock, such as cheese, milk, wool; and personal tithes on the produce of labour,

218

trade, crafts etc. Another division of tithe was into <u>great tithes</u>, from corn, hay, and wood, and <u>small tithes</u>, from all other predial tithes plus mixed and personal tithes. Where a benefice (the living or office of parish priest with its income) had a priest with the title of RECTOR he received both great and small tithes; where, by APPROPRIATION, the rector was a monastery or bishop or, after the Dissolution, a layman, the great tithes went to the rector, whatever his status, while the vicar (in the Middle Ages the deputy who did the actual work of the benefice for the rector and after the Reformation the incumbent of the vicarage) received all the small tithes. This could mean that the great tithes no longer directly supported the church and the incumbent. Tithes were collected by the rector or vicar in kind, that is each tenth sheaf of corn, lamb born, etc., although from early times an agreement to pay a fixed annual sum of money in lieu of tithes in kind might be established. The Tithe Commutation Act of 1836 established that rent-charges for all tithable land could be substituted by agreement for payment in kind, and led to the production of tithe maps and written schedules, mapping and describing all tithable land within the parish. The Tithe Act of 1925 vested all tithe rent-charges in Queen Anne's Bounty, established in 1704 to supplement the incomes of poor clergy from the revenues confiscated by Henry VIII from the Church; 4.5% of rent-charges was to go into a sinking fund to discharge land from rent-charges, 5% was to go to the Inland Revenue for rates, and the balance, less a few very small charges, to go to the incumbent of the parish. The Tithe Act of 1936 finally extinguished tithe rent-charges and provided for the issue by the Treasury of tithe redemption stock, the interest on which would compensate the incumbent for the loss of the rent-charge; this was funded by an annuity on tithable land collected by the Inland Revenue.

tithe barn   the barn in which tithe corn or hay was stored. The term is often wrongly applied to any large old barn.

titters   a corn-weed, probably of the vetch species, either hairy tare, *Vicia hirsuta*, also called tine or tine-grass, or tufted vetch, *V. cracca*, or both. Thomas Tusser: 'From wheat go and rake out the titters or tine,/ If eare be not foorth it will rise againe fine.' According to Hillman (1710) the best way of dealing with titters in wheat and rye was to rake it to break it off at the root and leave it in the standing corn. The common vetch, *Vicia sativa*, was grown for forage and the seed was fed to doves. See TARES. *1664: 1 co. 3 bu. ij pec. of titters for the Dowes. 1746: one Titter rake.*

tobacco press   a small press for pressing tobacco into a cube. Tobacco was grown in England on a small scale from the late 16th to the 18th centuries. It was valued for its medicinal and antiseptic as well as its recreational properties.   The clay tobacco-pipes were bought in large numbers - in the twelve months from 19th April 1647 Robert Walpole of Houghton bought 11½ gross, that is 1,656 pipes. No tobacco occurs in his accounts.   *1647: for halfe a groose of Tobacco pipes 1s. 6d.   1700: Tobacko Press Two Choping Knives one Ingen one press.*

tobacco tongs   small tongs for picking up tobacco to press into the bowl of a pipe, and for conveying a coal from the fire to light it. *1688: Twoe paire of Tobacco Tonges 1s.*

tod   a weight of wool, usually 28 lbs. but with local variations. *1736: ten tod of Wool 5 li.*

toeryd   two-eared, that is with 2 lugs. *1513: J great toeryd panne.*

tolpin, tollpin   see THOLE-PIN.

tomb   OE *tóm*, ON *tómr*, empty, leading to toom, teem; to scrape, hollow out joint in stone preparatory to pointing. *1732-3: Tombing and pointing ye Cornish &c one house. Tombing and pointing ye Cornish and Balisteraide.*

ton   a weight of 2240 lbs. (POUND), or 20 HUNDREDWEIGHTS, or 160 STONES.

tonale a book containing the tones or notes for singing the psalms and canticles in the unreformed church.

tongs an indispensible part of the furniture of the hearth; in great houses the tongs were often part of a suite. See ANDIRONS.

ton tight a ton tight was a way of expressing the burthen of a ship by means of the number of TUNS it could carry. Applied e.g. to stone, a ton tight was roughly the weight of a tun of wine, 2,000 lbs. *1425: every pece of the stoon be iij foote longe, and that xv tunne tyght of the stoon be every stoon weel bedded into the walle...I wold have swiche stoan a xxᵗⁱ tunne tight caried to Moneslee in Norffolk.*

topnet, top, tapnet, toppet a rush-basket to contain fruit. *1483: for a topet of fyggs codes ijs. 1530: a topenett of fyggs cods.*

topping fork see FORK

tonnecle see TUNICLE

torcayn to bring old panelling up to date by bevelling the edges of the larger panels to leave a 'table' in the middle, a practice current in the mid to late 17th century. *1665: began to torcayne the wainscott in the great plours...They finished torcayning wainscott in the great plour & setting the same up all but the doors & windowes.*

torel a ring, circle; the iron ring at the end of the VIROLE that fitted over the GUDGEON in a HINGE. *1391: in plat' Gogins verolys & torelys [for] le Wodehosgate xvjd.*

tornback see THORNBACK

tornbroche see TURN BROCHE

toster, tost a toaster. *1591: an yron tostt at the back of the Chymney ijs.*

touch silver or gold marked with a standard mark of purity. *1459: vj chacyd pecys gilte bi the bordurys, with the towche of Paryce. 1479: iiij Parys cuppis with a cover. with a rose in the botom, weyeng lvj unces j quarter. 1637: 12 slipp spoones 4 knopt spoones Cont 49 ounces at 4s. 8d. ye ounce tutcht...1 Wine Cupp 1 Crewet untucht...6 trencher plats 2 Candlesticks Cont 85 ounce at 4s. 8d. the ounce tutchet.*

touch box box for carrying priming or touch powder for firearms. *1592: Two steele flasks wth touchboxes. Eleven other Flasks of woode with touchboxes.*

tour a tower

tow, toughe fibrous stems of flax and HEMP, either raw or prepared. Strictly, tow was the short stems. *1595: A flaskett wth towe & lynnyng.*

tow comb a tow comb or HECKLE was a piece of wood set with several rows of sharp teeth, through which the beaten HEMP or flax would be drawn to remove unwanted, short, or useless fibres and pieces of stem. Combs were made in several different degrees of fineness. *1592: ij towe Combes. 1592: one Riplinge combe for flax.*

towels, towles tools. *1592: all his towells belonging to a ioyner.*

town up to at least the 18th century, a village having its own separate identity, that is having boundaries and its own basic government (churchwardens, overseers of the poor, etc.) was known as a town, and its possessions (buildings, rents, miscellaneous income etc.) as the town stock. There is no implication of urbanisation in the term. See PARISH.

towne see TUN

toy apparently derived from Netherlandish *tooi*, meaning clothing, finery, the cloths called toys were woven in Norwich. Originally of silk, worsted toys were being woven from the mid-17th century, and were small-pattern twills. *1763: a banyan of Norwich toy.*

trace the rope or leather straps connecting a draught beast to the object it pulls. Often referred to as a pair of trace. See CART; PLOUGH; THILL. *1593: 10 Cart Collers wth traice wherof 3 paire pinn traice. 1595: the furnyture belonging to a payer of tryse. 1648: one payer of pinn trayce &*

4 payer of shacktrace 12s.
trafell, trafle dish see TRAP DISH
train, trayn see BEDSTEAD
trammel a long narrow fowling or fishing NET. *1595: an old tramell wth ye staves.*
trammel chimney iron to hang pots on.
trammel a horse-hobble; device for teaching horse to move the legs on the same side together.
trammel the hopper of a mill.
trane oil, train oil oil from the boiled blubber of whales (especially right whale), seals, and fish. Used in soap and for treating cloths, leather etc. *1602: Certaine Trane Oyle ixs.*
transom a cross-beam, window bar; the horizontal member of a mullioned and transomed window ⊞ . See MULLION.
transom a bolster. *1484: a Fetherbedde and a traunsom. 1591: j posted bedstead wth a fetherbed a transome one pillow one donge. 1603: two transumes thone of Fethers the other of flocke.*
trap dish, trafell dish, strapdish a perforated dish through which new milk was strained to remove the hairs. *1593: One chume and three trafell dishes xd. 1665: two tropping dishes. 1788: a strapdish.*
trapper, trappars trappings, furnishings; covering for horses, of metal or leather, for protection; horse-cloth. *1459: j canope of greene silke, borderyd with rede. Item, iij trapuris, with iij clothis of the same sute...j pece of skarlot for trappars for horsys, with rede crossis and rosys.*
trash worthless items. *1601: olde Iron and other trash in the shopp xijd. . . an olde sworde a peece of whitt leather an olde skepp and other olde trash ijs. vjd.*
traverse a curtain or screen across a room; a TRANSOM. *1685: a payre of traverses. 1737: [bed] Two Pair of Travers.*
travess, travis a frame for holding an unruly horse when being shod, and from that the shoeing shed. *Prompt. Parv.* : 'Trawe, of a smythe'. Catholicon 1483: 'A trave for to scho horse in'. The carpenter's wife, in Chaucer's the Miller's Tale, when grabbed by the lecherous clerk, 'sprong as a colt doth in the trave.' Nall: 'Travvis. A smith's shoeing shed.' See p. 226. *1517: the howse at the travesse. 1673: sawing of stuf for ye travis 2s.*
tray a hurdle. See CLEY.
tray OE *trieg, trig,* ON *troy,* measure of a definite quantity. In early 15th century Norfolk this seems to be 8 bushels. *1410: iij treys iiij bz [of lime bought for a stone wall 4s. 10½d.].*
tray a flat, open vessel used in the dairy and buttery. *1513: j oold laver of laten j treye. 1589: ij beare stooles & a trey. 1595: a pair of trays a sholve & twoe stampells. 1688: one Milk Ledde and one salting traie. 1743: One Milk Lead one Milk Tray.*
treacle, triacle, treakell a medicinal compound, often containing portions of the animal, particularly adders, to whose venomous bite it was an antidote. Also a general remedy. Treacle of Genoa was the most highly valued. London treacle contained cummin seed, bay-berries, germander, snakeroot, cloves and honey. *1451: that ye woll send me a potte with treacle in hast. 1479: I pray yow send me by the next man that cometh fro London ij pottys of tryacle of Jenne, - they shall cost xvjd. - for I have spent ought that I had with my yong wyf, and my yong folkys, and my sylff. 1530: for a boxe of treacle xd. 1587: treakell in a vessell viijd.*
treavet see TRIVET
trebuchet 1. A large mechanical catapult consisting of a pivoted lever weighted at one end and with the missile, generally a rock, at the other. 2. An apparatus for ducking common scolds, a CUCKING STOOL, resembling the military trebuchet in basic construction. 3. A trap for small birds. 4. A small pair of scales. *1274: [carpentering 1 ladder] & j trebuchet iijd. 1312: [mending] del trebuchet ijd.*

trecle see BEDSTEAD

tree a large timber, e.g. an AXLE-TREE. *1647: for treeinge of a Carte 1s. 1663: a tree for the water Cart & treeing & staving 2s. 1673: one tree for ye courch 1s. 6d.*

treen, treing, tryin wooden, made of a tree. The cheapest material for tableware up to the 18th century. *1499-1500: treen plateres et dysshes et cyppuys iiijs. iiijd. 1593: all the treen platters dishes spones and trenchers wth a salte boxe xxd. 1595: ij wooden ladelles...treane dishes fassets & tappes treane spoones...treene dyshes, spones, A table knyfe of woode...treane dyshes and platters...A treane cuppe. 1597: syx tryin disshes syx tryin tranchers six spones & a triin drynckyn cupe.*

trefoote see TRIVET

trench see BIT

trench, trenchar a ditch. *1293: [made] j Trenchar [in the meadow 22d.].*

trencher Fr. *trancher*, to cut; a flat or slightly dished wooden slab, round or square, on which to cut and serve meat, fruit, and other food. By the 17th century 'trencher' might mean plates of pottery or metal. *1511-2: a gross of trenchours xvjd. 1587: ij dozin thick flanders trenchers xiiijd...ij rounde trencher boxes ijd...i grosse of trenchers iijs. v dozin Flander trenchers iijs...i grosse and a halfe of thyck threnchers xs. vjd. 1589: j dozen of whight trenchers. 1590: xviij fruite trenchers of wood...xij Case trenchers. 1591: One dozen rounde trenchers with a cou' iiijd. 1593: 1 dozen & 6 frute trenchers wth boxes & 1 voider knife iijs. iiijd. 1593: j dozen bankettinge trenchers with a boxe. 1637: [silver] 6 trencher plats. 1647: 2 duszen of the best Maple Trenchers 4s.*

trencher salt a small salt-cellar placed near a diner's TRENCHER; open dish for SALT. *1588: one silver Trencher Salte. 1597: a trencher salt gylt wth a Cover. a litle trencher salt gylt.*

trendle a wheel, mill-wheel. *1313: [binding] de trendles ad Suthmille vijd.*

trendle see BEDSTEAD

trental thirty-days' mass for the dead in the unreformed church.

tresenz, tresaunts covered passage. *1345: [carpentering new doors for] le tresenz [towards the kitchen]. 1367: [1 roofer making and repairing] le tresaunts [of the kitchen]. 1482: for ij lanternes, the xxix day of Octobre, on for the tresaunce, and a nother for the porters loge ijs. 1557: the tresense fro the chawmbur dore to the halle dore, the whiche chawmber and tresense cost xl marc.*

trestall a table-trestle, an A-frame support for a TABLE-board or indeed anything else. *1371: [carpenter making] trestall [for the cistern with repairing the well].*

trestle tripod, three-legged STOOL.

trevede, trewet, trewt see TRIVET

trice, tryse, strice MDu. *trîse, trijs*, windlass, pulley, hoisting block; sheer-legs, a mobile crane consisting of a pair of long poles joined at the top with a pulley and winding-gear, often used for lifting and moving timber. *1500-1: a gabyll roop for the stryces xvjd. 1595: boorde bricks tryse sparrs. 1647: Blake for his helpe wth tryces one day at Siderston wood. . . For 1 new topnayle for ye Tryces Wayinge 6 li. & qtr 2s. 1d. 1648: 1 new hausrope & Lop rope for the Tryces. 1664: carryed home strice poles borrowed of John Scase...To John Scase for th'use of his strice poles they receiving hurt at the loading of the said timber vjs. To John Brooke of Dickleburgh for the use of his strice poles Oct 10th paid vs. 1711: for strice poles and the things belonging to them at 1 li.*

trickle tricle, trindle see BEDSTEAD

triglyph a projecting grooved tablet alternating with metopes in a frieze of the Doric order. *1619: [masons] the Freise with carving in the litle court with letters Roses and troclifies after the order of dorick.*

tripod small iron platform or ring with three feet to stand in or in front of the fire to support cooking pots. *1319: [mending] j tripod ob. 1335: j tripode vijd.*

tristram, tristrum a support for fireside pots or a kettle consisting of three rods joined at the centre so that each is at right angles to the other two - however it was dropped it always landed on its feet. See CATCHERS. *1771: Tristrum, sugar nippers, brush & mahogany waiter 5s. 6d. 1791: for an Iron-Cat, alias Trisram, 3s. 6d. The Ends and middle bright, the other parts painted black.*

trivet three-footed stand for pots in front of an open hearth. *1506-7: for a trevede xviijd. 1592: ij trewetese xxd.*

troclifies see TRIGLYPH

tromepere see TRUMPERY

tristram

tropping dish see TRAP DISH

trostelles TRESTLES, for a TABLE. *1444: j par de trostelles.*

trough, through, troe, troue, troff, trow, troyve a trough, usually pronounced 'trow' in Norfolk and often spelt phonetically, was a long, narrow vessel with a section either ∪ ⊔ or half-hexagonal, often on a stand or legs, with a variety of uses:-

making dough - mixing or minging trough. See p. 72. *1444: [1 great] trow [for flour]. 1588: a mynggyn trowe. 1602: minging troyve. 1738: minking trow...a yeast Throw 8s.*

salting or powdering meat *1588: a salltyn trowe. 1592: one Saultynge trowgh ijs. 1595: a Powdering Troffe. 1636: one pouderin trowe one pouderin vesell.*

for BREWING *1352: ij Troues...j tappetrow. 1536: makyng of a throff to the bruhousse. 1591: a seething trowe.*

for VERJUICE *1595: a vergys troffe. 1597: a stamping trough for crabbes.*

for processing TALLOW *1637: a tallowe trowe.*

for feeding animals *1595: treane dyshes & platters & henne's troffes. 1618: ij hogges trowes.*

trousers originally trews, close-fitting divided drawers or breeches covering the buttocks and thighs, with stockings attached to the lower parts. See TRUNK HOSE. *1602: for an old wastecoate & a truser ijs.*

truck see TRUNK

truckle see BEDSTEAD, trendle

trug, drug shallow basket of wood, thin laths, or wickerwork, about two feet long by 1 foot wide, with a central handle, used in the garden. *1621-2: making barrows & Druggs for ye Gardiner.*

truggell, trukle see BEDSTEAD, trendle.

trumpery things of little value. *1584: ij Bolles ij Chernes wyth other Trumperye iiijs. 1592: other tromepere there vs.*

trunk a tube for darts or a pea-shooter; a long-barrelled gun. *1634: one gunn one short sword two ould rapiers wherof one is broke and a pocket dager wth a trunck to shote birds 13s. 4d.*

trunk, truck 1. A primitive boat, originally a hollowed-out tree-trunk. 2. A low trolley for launching boats. 3. A perforated box to keep fish alive under water. *1591: ij old boats ij old trunckes in the Fenn. 1592: iiij small trunckes. 1602: ij whashen botes j skefe v trouckes xxxxs.*

trunk large CHEST, usually with a rounded or coffered lid, for storing linen etc. and for travelling. *1604: j trunke covered wth seales skinnes vjs. viijd. 1620: one large new Trunke couered wth Blacke leather. 1636: one great round trunke. 1637: Two trunckes one wth diaper & a nother wth damaske 40 li...one great truncke wth iron barrs...one great truncke wth household linnen (viz) 30 p of sheets whereof 3 pe of holland sheets, tenn pe of pillowbears 13 dozen of napkins eight board cloaths 4 cubboard cloaths 8 towells six side boards cloaths wth other old wearinge linnen.*

trunk horse horse for carrying TRUNKS, baskets etc.; pack horse. *1590: one bayed balde truncke horse iij li vjs. viijd.*

trunk hose up to *c.*1650, 'hose' was used for stockings of both sexes. Trunk hose were padded breeches sewn to NETHERSTOCKS.

trunk saddle for carrying a trunk or pack on horseback. *1463: Mendyng of a tronke sadylle. 1466: a new tronke sadylle xs. 1636: one trunke saddle.*

truser see TROUSERS

truss a carved bracket, often in the form of a scroll, to support a statue or the cornice of a door, etc. *1745: Eight Trusses with Bust's on D° and festoons over.*

trussel a TRESTLE

trussing, trust see BEDSTEAD

try to sift, strain, separate, purify. *1531: for trying of the waxe of my Mr Candyll and my ladys ijd. 1588: for ij daies in tryinge of the corrupcion from the first oyle...for viij smale vesselles at the last tr'inge of the oyle. 1592: tried tallow xxviij stonne v li. iiijs. iiijd. a bagge to trye with all ijd. 1654: a Firken of Hoggs suett tryed up & sold by Nan Fishman 17s.*

tryenge, tryin see TREEN

tuched, tutcht see TOUCH

tuck OFr *étoc*, Fr. *estoc*, thrust; slim, pointed sword for thrusting; a rapier. *1592: a horsemans tucke wth a rest in the ende xxd.*

tuftaffeta woollen velours or TAFFETA with tufts of silk or silk mixed with the yarn. *1588: stole covered wth tuftafyta. 1592: A Gowne of Tufftafatye vj li. 1597: A Cannopie paned wth tufftaffeta white & black.*

tuft mockadow see MOCKADOE

tugurr' see TIGURR

tuke, tewke 1. Canvas. 2. A fine cloth. *1481: iiij yardes di' of tewke rossett, price vjs. viijd... viij yardes tewke whight, at xvjd.* [a yard].

tumbrel, -il, tumberill, tumbler two-wheeled CART, usually horse-drawn, that can be tipped backwards to shed its load; a dung cart or muck-cart. *1278: ccc & dim' [nails for] tumerell [and other things in the court 9d.]. 1283: [carpentering] j tumerell [1 carpenter for 3 days 9d.]. 1301: v bord [bought for] tumbrell iijd ob. 1482: v dayes with a tomberel. 1588: iiij tumbrelles. 1595: one payer of tumbrell stryngs. 1597: j shodd cart & too ould tumbrells xxs. 1603: i Shood carte & i tumberill ij li. 1636: one tumbrell wth shod whels.*

tun a measure of capacity for liquid; the vessel itself; to put the liquid into barrels. A tun of ale: 256 gallons, or 210 Imperial gallons. A tun of wine: before the 14th century 256 gallons, afterwards 252; 210 Imperial gallons. See TON. *1463: For ij tonns off Spanyshe wyne... xvj marc. 1466: for a tonne to cary ynne feder beddes xxiijd. 1536: for a last of barrells to tun bere in, that is to sey a dosen barrells xjs. 1591: In the Meale Chamber tow Boultinge townes tow Seyves.*

tune a small drinking-cup, holding about ⅔ of a pint. *1592: a neaste of tunes of pewter. 1636: 3 peuter tunes 12d. one Chamber potte 12d.*

tuner see TUNNER

tunic, tunicle, tunacle, tunekell pre-Reformation clerical garment with narrow sleeves, similar to the DALMATIC. *1459: j vestement of [? &] tunekell. 1518: a tunycle to a vestment. 1552: ij tynniclis of whit damaske.*

tunnel, tunner 1. A funnel. 2. Funnel-shaped bird-net. *1354: j tunnor. 1593: 2 wort tubbs 1 tunnell 1 berestoole. 1606: a tuner wth an ale stolle. 1663: mended the tunnell, staved the jett. 1743: one Wooden Tunnell.*

turf block of peat for firing. *1654: for 20000 Turfs cuttinge and Rigginge twice at 18d. ₱ 1000.*

turfspade turfing-iron, spade for cutting turf or peat, often ♣ or △ shaped. *1312: [1 iron bought for] j turfspade jd. ob.*

turett see TERETT

turkey brought from Mexico soon after 1518, the turkey, *Mealagris gallopavo*, was confused in the 16th century with the guinea-fowl, *Numida meleagris*, an African bird known to antiquity and brought from Guinea via the Turkish dominions in Africa. 'Turkey' before *c.* 1600 could therefore mean either turkey or guinea-fowl.

turkey bean   possibly the scarlet runner, *Phaseolus multiflorus*, although this originated in America; but there was turkomania in the 17th century, when the runner bean was introduced. See TURKEY. *1654: Turky Beanes 6d.*

turkey carpet   see CARPET; TURKEY WORK

turkey stone   the turquoise. *1595: iiij golde ryngs wherof one wth A Turkeye stone.*

turkey work   true Turkish carpets were imported from Turkey or other Levantine countries, and turkey yarn (camel-hair or MOHAIR) was also imported. Table carpets, cushion covers etc., hand-knotted and of richly-coloured wools, made in England by the middle of the 16th century, were called turkey-work. *1597: one Carpet turkyworke ij yards j qrter longe: an ell brode. 2 old turkye Carpetts hanging in the Chamber...One wyndowe cloth Turky worke: Long 2 yards lat: one ell. one large Cusshyen turkye-Work. 1709: six turkeywork stools.*

turk's head broom   broom with a long handle and a round head, also called pope's head. *1792: a turks head broom.*

turm   a body of horsemen, 30 or 32; ? an alternative for CORSLET.

turn broche, tornbroche   a turnspit, the person (usually a boy) who turned the SPIT. *1593: to Sparke a turne broche for xiiij^e dayes ijs. iiijd.*

turn button   a small metal rectangle, pivoting in the middle, for keeping doors shut. *1819: brass buts & screws & turn button.*

turned   furniture of components made on a lathe by a turner. *1584: A turnyd chayer vjd. ij old square turnyd stolles viijd.* See CHAIR; FRAMED; JOINED; STOOL; TABLE.

turnip   although known as a vegetable throughout the Middle Ages, the turnip became popular as a field crop only from the middle of the 17th century. By the early 18th century it had become an important component of the Norfolk four-course rotation system of cropping. Fields of turnips were often grazed by cattle and sheep, and the stubs removed by hand for winter fodder. *1602: a Remånts of turnupp in Mr hasels Close iijs. iiijd.*

turnip hoe   a draw-HOE, for singling (spacing out) field-TURNIPS. *1692: One turnib-hough.*

turnip pick   small pick for removing the stumps of turnips from the ground after the tops had been grazed off. *1752: 3 turnip picks.*

turnip womb   a large basket or skep.

turnsole   violet-blue colouring from the small turnsole, *Crozophoria tinctoria*, a Mediterranean plant, used for jellies, cakes, and as a pigment in painting. The great turnsole or heliotrope, *Heliotropium Europaeum*, was used as a purge, for the stone, menstruation, childbirth, gout, joints, warts etc. *1648: oz 1 of Saffron 2s.6d. for Turnsole 6d.*

twibill, twybil   OE *twibil, twibile*; axe with two cutting edges, often used for cutting mortises. See p. 242; AXE. *1306: [mending] ij Twibill jd. 1588: one twyble.*

twilt   a QUILT. *1597: one large Twylt of Caffa damask changeable grene & orenge tawney...one twylt of yellowe sylk saye...one twylt of crimson Carrell sylk.*

twister, twisterer   one who spins or twists thread or cord. *1589: In the twisterers chamber.*

twistering mill   a machine for spinning. *1736: One twistering mill and one stool mill 1 li.*

two meal cheese   cheese made from the milk of two milkings, one of new milk and the other of old skimmed milk. See CHEESE. *1655: a q^t of old 2 Meal Cheese 1 li. 15s. . . 1 weigh and Halfe of 2 Meale Cheese 2 li. 2s.*

ty-   for words beginning ty- see TI-.

tylke   see TICK

225

U

U interchangeable with v in Latin, and in English up to the 17th century, e.g. covering is often written couering, the abbreviation for cover for is cou' as well as cov', while unkempt might well be written vnkempt. This interchangeability did not extend to Roman numerals: 5 is always written v, 8 is viij, and so on.

uffer a variant of juffer, from Du. *juffer*, spar or beam; long timber, 4 or 5 inches square. *1729: 4 20' Uffers. 9 pieces of uffers 10'. 17 Deals & Uffers.*

umber a brown earth used as a pigment. Raw umber is light brown, almost buff; burnt umber is darker and redder. The pigment could be bought dry and hard, and was ground and mixed with oil to make paint. *1664: Umber 3 pound & yellowe oker 3 pound xviijd.*

uncut oysters see OYSTER

underback, -beck, -deck low flat tub placed under the mash tub to receive the wort in BREWING. *1591: j underbacke xxd. 1647: in the Brewhouse One Copper, Twoo Large Fats, One underbeck A doble Cooler and One Dandy. 1738: A Cover for the Underdeck. 1779: a small under Back.*

underpin, underset to provide support or foundations of a building, often in the sense of an addition or a temporary support. *1572-3: brick or els stone for the under pynnyng. 1665: halfe a day underseting the hous.*

unpeld, unpilled, unpillid see HEMP

untucht see TOUCH

urinal glass or pewter bottle for a sample of urine or for use when travelling. *1595: an urynall wth ye case.*

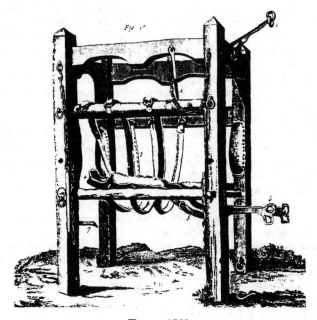

Travess 1760s

226

V

V the Roman numeral for 5, and used in combination e.g. vij = 7, xviij = 18, v^{xx} = 100. See C; D; I; J; L; M; U; X. As a letter, interchangeable with U.

vair OFr. *vair, veir,* L. *varium,* parti-coloured; fur obtained from a squirrel with a white belly and a grey back (perhaps the Siberian squirrel *Pteromys volans*), used to trim garments; an heraldic fur, usually shown as interlocking bell-shapes coloured alternately azure and argent, the shape derived from the skin. See p. 230; CALABAR.

valence 1. An awning over a shop-front. *1587: the vallars for the shopp. 1590: the valence that longe to the shop.* 2. The deep fringe or side panels of the ceiling or canopy of a curtained bed. See BEDSTEAD. *1593: 1 close posted beddsteade wth a heade of wainscott ingraven wth tester & vallence of redd cloth. 1637: one guilt bedstead the valines of cloath of gould & taffety curtaines 6 li. 13s. 4d.*

vallans almons see ALMONDS

valuer, valure see VELOUR

vambrace piece of armour worn on the forearm. *1459: v payre vambras. 1464: a payr of smale curas wyth gardys and vumbarde.*

vamp the upper part of a shoe; short stocking, sock, reaching up to the ankle; lower part of stockings or hose; the front part of a boot or shoe covering the toes; to repair with patches. *1459: j payre of blake hosyn, vampayed with lether. 1464: for vawnpeyinge of a peyr botys xijd. 1753: One Pair of old Shoes & 1 Pair of Old vamps 1s.*

vamplate funnel-shaped plate of iron or steel to guard the hand on a LANCE.

van see FAN

vance roof, vansroffe, vauncerufe, fannce roof, false roof. Possibly from Fr. *vanner,* to ventilate. Garret, attic, loft, space under the rafters. Used for storage of grain, linen, wool etc., and for servants' beds - perhaps a contraction of 'servants'. The form 'false roof', unless simply a phonetic misspelling, suggests an inserted ceiling. *1593: ye vannc Roofe ou' ye plor chambr [barley, fetches]. 1593: on the fansse roffe* [5 beds]. *1593: on vance ruff* [wool, 2 spinning wheels]. *1616: in the highe lofte or vannc roffe* [wool]. *1626: vansruffe ov' the chamber* [3 beds]. *1629: vance roofe...vance roofe chamber. 1664: planchered pte of the vance ruff at the dayery fearme it being decayed. 1665: began to take tyle shodds & rubish of the vance ruff towards the kitchen yard. 1731: One the vance Rufe one Bed as it stand 1 li. 5s.*

vardell see VERTIVELL

vargis see VERJUICE

vas a small vessell or pot. *1352: j vas [for butter]. . . j vas [for keeping necessaries].*

vat, fat large barrel, cask, tub used for storing liquid and in BREWING. See p. 72. *1597: ij dry fattes & other ould tubbes. 1665: one banbury fatt.*

vault 1. Attic, garret. 2. Cellar. *1590: straw & Tyles in the Vaute.*

vause as an architectural term, a vase, basket or bell is the top of a Corinthian column, around which the foliage of the capital is arranged. 1563: 'The Abacus, the which lieth on the vasse or basket.' According to an authority of 1688, 'vausing' is 'to make the Jaumes or sides of Stone Windows and Doors...to over sail the other part of the wall they are set in', in other words, to project. See CROCKSTONE; TIPE. *1618-20: [carpenter] For sawing framing and rearing 4 hollow tipes upon the stearcases in the little court with their vauses & crockstones. 1622: the vawse under the type be wth a gutter of lead to carry the water.*

veil 1. A curtain hung between the altar and the choir and congregation during Lent in the pre-Reformation church; Lenten veil. 2. A covering for crucifix or statue in the pre-Reformation church. *1554: payd for ye staynyng of ye vayll to sextyn xs. payd for the Lyne Ryngs ye hookes for ye vayll...payde for a pece of tymber for to hang ye Lyne for the vayll and for ye lace for ye Ryngs vjd. 1557: the veyl of the chirche.*

vellet, velvet a fabric, originally of silk, with a dense, smooth, short-piled surface, used for clothes and furnishing. *1552: j westment red wellett. 1588: one other framed Chayer sometyme sett wth bone, the backe and seate of crymsen Velvett vjs. . . one framed chayer, the backe & seate of chaungeable taffeta imbrodered wth blacke vellet xiijs. iiijd. 1593: tester & vallance of black figured vellett & russett satten ymbroydered wth yellowe. . . 1 Canapie of black vellett pincked. 1597: A Targett wth black vellet: fringed wth black sylk & gold.*

velour, valuer, valure 1. Velvet, see above. 2. Woollen material with a velvet-like pile. *1588: ij lowe ioyned stoles, the one covered wth nedell worke, and the other wth redde and grene valure ijs. 1589: iij qzters of valuer ijs.*

venegar see VINEGAR

venetians wide knee-breeches, gathered at the waist and shaped to button or tie below the knee. *1584: A payer of vynicōns of brode clothe...A payer of vynicōns of lether vs. 1588: payre of venisyons of Russet Cloth. 1590: a payer of venisions of violet culler & a payer of yellow stockings. 1590: ij paire of venesians & ij paire of knitt Stokynges xs.*

ventaylett see AVENTAIL

verdews see VERDURE

verdigris green or greenish-blue substance, copper carbonate, formed by the action of dilute acetic acid on copper, and also occurring naturally as rust on copper and brass. Used as a pigment and as a constituent of medicine. *1562: for verdegreace...grene copres turpentine bremestone to dresse the balde colts fots xijd.*

verdoll see VERTIVELL

verdure vegetative decoration. See TAPESTRY. *1597: 4 cusshyens of tapestry verdure.*

verjuice, vargis, verges, vergys the juice of unripe fruit such as apples and grapes, fermented into a sharp VINEGAR for use in cooking. See CRADLE. *1513: j barell wt vertiuse... j veriuse presse. 1588: a vergs cradle. 1593: 2 hoggsheades with verges. 1595: a vergys creadell...a vergys troffe.*

verole see VIROLE

vertivell, vardell, verdell, vervell doorbands, long hinges with an eye to receive the hook on the post of door or gate; a ring for a HINGE. See GUNFIS; VIROLE. *1256: in vertivell ijd. 1320: In gnfis & vertivell [for the window of the dairy house 1½d.]. 1344: vj cletis [of iron for] vertivell [of the doors of the barn]. 1526: hengells, verdolls & hoks. 1647: hookes & vardells wayinge 6 li & halfe 2s. 2d. 1648: hookes & hingells & vardell. A new snack. 1649: [smith] a vervell 4d.*

vest a sleeveless, loose garment, buttoned and tied with a sash, worn underneath the coat and introduced 1663-4. *1708: 12 Lades vests at 1 li. 4s. 7 menes vests at 1 li. 1s.*

vetch the leguminous or common vetch *Vicia sativa* was introduced from Asia Minor and grown from the Middle Ages for forage; the seed was fed to pigeons. *1533: ij combe of fetchys bought for seed the xxjst daye of February iiijs. 1587: ij hurreyes of fitches. 1593: one golfsted wt Rye, pease, feaches, & barleye. 1594: a golfstead of Fytches in the Coddes. 1654: For 8 Coome Fetches bare at 9s. & 5 Coom more at 9s. 6d.* See TARE; TITTERS.

veveri ivory. *1474: a combe of veveri vjd.*

viall see VIOL

vicar, vicarage see RECTOR; TITHE

vice OFr. *vis*, from L. *vitis*, vine with reference to its spiral; a newel stair turning around a central post. *Prompt. Parv.* : 'Vyce, rounde grece or steyer'. *1510: [for] iiij popylbordes [bought in the market for] syntrees pro j vice viijd. 1588-9: ij payer of gemowes for ye vyce dore viijd.*

vice board a bench with a vice on it. *1709: a Piersing board & a vice Board 3s.*
vill settlement, township, village; the word 'village', although used from late in the 14th century, was uncommon until the 18th. See TOWN.
villein an unfree tenant of a manor, obliged to perform services such as ploughing, harvest etc. in return for his landholding, and subject to fines or customary payments such as merchet (permission for his daughter to marry) and heriot (his best beast, later commuted to a fine paid by his heirs to succeed to the holding).
vineall finial, ornament, usually of pointed shape, on top of a roof, gable, buttress etc. *1619: [wall] of stone...with pedistalls in rustick: with a handsome garnishe of vinealls upon the sayd pedystalls.*
vinegar dilute acetic acid produced by the fermentation of wine and other liquids; the pot or vessel containing vinegar for cooking or table use. *1513: j veneg' pott. 1584: saucers porrengers pewter pottes & salts also twoe vyngers. 1593: glasses botles & 1 vinger. 1597: iij sault sellers iij vynyiers.* See VERJUICE.
vinehaye a hedge. See HAY. *1313: [making] j vinehaye [on the east part of the manor for 6 days 12d.].*
viol, vial, vyal musical instrument with 5-7 strings and a fretted finger-board, played with a bow, and held downwards between the knees, or in the case of the bass viol, often called the viol da gamba, between the legs. Viols were common in inventories of the 15th-17th centuries. A set of viols was often listed as a chest of viols.
violente, vyollen a violin. *1589: j violente to playe on vjs. viijd. 1597: One olde Chest: wth 2 vyollens & 2 Shalmes.*
virginals a small keyboard instrument of the harpsichord family, in which the single string to each note is plucked when the key is depressed. Virginals usually took the form of an oblong box on a table, though occasionally the instrument had its own stand. The instrument was usually described as 'a pair of virginals'; quite common in inventories of the 16th and 17th centuries, virginals went out of use in the 18th century. *1593: paire of Virginalls xvs. 1593: One table with a payer of virginalls thereon xs. 1603: A ioyned Presse with a paire of Virginalls uppon it xls.*
virgins' chamber chamber for the maidens of the family. *1665: The Virgens chamber.*
virgin's wax fresh, unused beeswax, produced by the first swarm; purified or white wax, used for candles. *1647: 12 oz Virgins Wax 3s.*
virole, verole OFr. *virole, virelle*, ring, band, ferrule; a metal eye on the end of a HINGE; socket for the axle-pins of a wheelbarrow. *1387: gogones plates viroles staples & hespes. 1391: in plat gogins verolys & torelys [for] le Wodehosgat. 1655: 2 new sithes...wth Rubbs virolls & hanging. 1665: virrells gudgirons & plates for a crudbarrowe.* See GUDGEON; VERTIVELL.
visitation made by the bishop at intervals, usually soon after his installation and thereafter every 6-7 years. Visitation articles, consisting of questions on the administration of the parish, the religious and moral behaviour of the clergy and parishioners, and the furnishing and repair of the parish church, were issued to each parish and the answers delivered at the visitation, which took place at a set location e.g. Swaffham, North Walsham. The archdeacons of the diocese also had visitations, which often concentrated on the fabric and furnishings of the churches. Complaints against individuals in response to the articles could either be dealt with summarily at the visitation or referred to the archdeacon's court or the court of the bishop, the consistory court.
vivar, vivary L. *vivarium*, enclosure for live animals, fishpond. *1352: De vivarie in le ker [this year 7s.].*
vnce ounce

229

voider 1. table vessel for sweetmeats etc. 2. basket or vessel for plates or cutlery. 3. container for used cutlery, plates, and food remains. 4. from mid-18th century, a tea-tray. A voider knife was for scraping dishes etc. *c.1530: pd for a payer of voyder yt my Mr gaffe ye seid Sir John, xd. 1592: A Voyder knife xviijd. 1637: a bason & voider of pewter. 1688: one wicker voider 3s. 1751: Six Voiders. 1779: a neat Mahogany Voider. 1836: Sylabub voider & 20 glasses.*

voult a vault, usually in the sense of cellar.

voyce blacksmith's or carpenter's vice.

vumbarde see VAMBRACE

vy- see vi-

vynyier see VINEGAR

Types of heraldic vair, and the shape of the fur from which it was derived

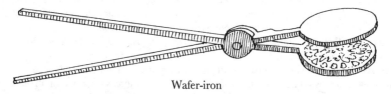

Wafer-iron

Wheelwrights 1760s

230

W

W the old Norfolk practice of pronouncing v as w, particularly in the first letter of a word, e.g. wicar (vicar), wet (vet), wery (very) is occasionally found in documents. *1552: j westment red wellet.*

wafer iron wrought-iron tongs with jaws in the form of a flat discs 4-5 inches in diameter, with a pattern embossed or impressed on the inside face. The tongs were heated, and a batter or biscuit mixture placed between the jaws to produce flat wafers or biscuits. See p. 230. *1588: one iron to make wafer kakes xijd. 1606: payer of wafer iornes.*

wagh see SWEY

wainscot originally good quality oak board and plank from the Baltic countries - Russia, Germany, and Scandinavia, often imported into Britain through Holland. Used particularly for furniture and for panelling - hence the transfer of the word to any type of panelling. See BEDSTEAD; CEIL; CHEST; TABLE. *1363: bord de Waynskot [for] tigurr vijs. jd. 1416: [1 table of] Waynskot [for] les Flew. 1468: fore iiij^{xx}chefe waneskottes, prise the pece vd..fore xxxviij othere smallere waneskottes, price the pece iiid. ob. 1584: a pece of waynscott seelyng for the chimey. 1588: a shorte settle of Waynscotte ijs. vjd. . . a trussinge bedsteade of Waynscot ijs. 1588: The Waynscott chambre. 1592: a new box of Waynescote. . . A carved box of Wainscote wth loose papers in yt iijs. . . a lytle fowldinge bedsted of waynescotte vjs. viijd. 1593: 1 posted bedsteede of wainscott. 1620: In the Parlor Imprimis the same wainscotted. . . In the Gallery the same wainscotted and matted... wainscot fourmes twoe one plaine wainscott table...three wainscott Chests and one furrendeale Chest. 1665: began to torcayne the wainscott in the great plours. . . began to wainscott the great dining room. 1709: In the Drawing room to the dineing room Japan Wainscot. [great hall] 4 great Wainscot tables.*

waiter, dumb waiter an English invention in use from just before 1730, a waiter was a piece of furniture consisting of 3 or 4 trays of diminishing size revolving on a central stem on a stand or castors, for serving drink, cakes, or dessert. Also a single tray. *1753: 1 Range of Peggs, Pail, & 1 Broken Waiter 1s. 9d. 1779: one small Japan Waiter. 1787: a small Mahogany Waiter.*

Wakefield board ? board from Wakefield, Yorks. See BOARD. *1296: ij^c de Wakefeld bord [for roofing the chancel 13s. 0¼d.]. 1319: xlv bord de Wakefeld [bought for repairing] del bay [of the great bridge 2s. 8¼d.]. . . In iiij^{xx} viij bord de Wakefeld [for the windows and the pentice 4s. 10d.]. 1319: in cccxxxiiij bord de Wakefeld xvjs. vd. ob. 1319: [for sheephouse] xx bord de Wakefeld xijd.*

walking staff walking-stick. *1593: one Mapp and one Walking Staff vjd. 1597: A blacke Walkinge staffe wth a sword blade in it.*

wallet a bag, of leather or cloth, for carrying food, fine clothes etc. *1444: j walet [for harvest]. 1625: j lynne wallett. 1649: 1 new meale wallett 3s. 4d. 1709: 1 Meal Wallet.*

wallplate the horizontal beam running along the top of a wall to form the base of the roof structure. See PLATE; p. 175. *1344: Clx de Greetspykyngs [for] Walplates [and other things].*

walnuttree walnut was the preferred timber for fine furniture from the later 16th century to the early 18th century. The common walnut, *Juglans regia*, grew in England, but the demand for walnut from c.1660 onwards was such that supplies of it were imported from Europe, and of the black walnut, *J. nigra*, from eastern North America. See BEDSTEAD. *1597: 2 longe formes of walnuttree. 2 ioyned stooles of walnuttree...one Chayer of Walnuttree. . . a payer of tables of Walnuttree. . . one ioyned table of walnuttree. . . one bedsted of wallnut tree. 1633: A long draw Table of walnut tree. c.1730: For 12 Walnuttree Chair Frames with Compass seates a carved shell on the feet a fine Compass India back vener'd with the finest Grenople Walnuttree. 1764: Two walnuttree settees.*

wan see FAN

wanton, wanty rope or band for fastening the pack or PEDS on the back of a packhorse; belly-band. *1592: iiij pr pedds iiij pr wantons.*

warden several varieties of red and white wardens, a baking pear, were grown from the Middle Ages onwards. See PEARMAIN for derivation. *1415-16: in cc de Wardon' [pears 9d.].1603: a maunde of Wardens. 1649: Wardens brought by John Benwell 6d.*

wardnap, gardnap table mat or thick cloth, put under dishes to protect the fine tablecloth. See SAVENAP. *1513: xvj Wardnappys.*

wardrobe, wardrape OFr. *warderobe,* variation of *garderobe.* Room for storing clothes, dressing-room, often containing a PRIVY. See GARDEROBE. Up to the 18th century 'wardrobe' meant a room rather than a piece of furniture; the latter meaning only became general in the 19th century. *1296: [1 man for 12½ days thatching the chapel and passage] & j Warderobe [& 1 chamber 2s. 1d.]. 1343: [1 pair of hinges for the door of the] Werderobe [over the south] solar iijd. ob. 1363: [2 locks with 2 keys for the door of the granary and the door of the] Warderob [of the bailiff's chamber 21d.]. 1597: the warderrobe* [bed, pieces of bedsteads, bedding, cloth, curtains, furniture, tents, close stools].

ware brace, ware brasse guard of leather worn on the bracing arm by a bowman. See GARBRASSE; VAMBRACE. *1592: one arminge bowe wth a ware brasse & shooting glove.*

warp a set of four, but sometimes two or three, usually of fish. *1533: ij warpe of lynge & a warpe of codd. 1593: in Codd fish v^{xx} & viij - iiij li. in Linge fish 3 warpe xijs.*

warp lengthwise threads in weaving, set in a frame (the stage); the traverse held the bobbins of yarn; the warping mill was for winding the warp. See HEDDLE. *1602: [dornix weaver] iij close warpe wth ij dussz yarne xvs. . . A warping stage, a travice and hornings* [awnings] *ov' them wth the warpe iijs. 1603: one warping mill at vs. . . one silke warpe at xxxs.*

warrope corruption of warp, a rope, hawser. *1584: tenne hearring flewes & nyne nynestores hearing nettes, with warropes.*

washing block, stock, stool a block or stool on which clothes being washed were beaten with a bat or BEETLE. *1587: a wasshing Blocke. 1592: a washing stoole a washing stocke. 1593: In the washing howse Itm 1 boylinge Leade 1 keler 1 paile 3 washing tubbs 1 washing stoole xs.*

washing engine tub with beaters activated by turning a handle. *1756: a Washing Engine, two washing Killers.*

washpit the pit or channel in which sheep were dipped. *1648: [10th July, sheep-shearing] to Glover & Goulty for their helpe at the wash pitt 1s.*

wash sand see SAND

wassyng washing. *1535: ij^c whete strawe for to wassyng fuell*

watch candle, candlestick see CANDLESTICK

watchet light blue colour; cloth of this colour; also green. See SUITABLE. *1597: one ioyned table of walnuttree one Cloth Carpet brode Watchet: 5 yards. Itm 2 lyv'y Cupbords 2 Carpetts brode Cloth: Watchett Lo: 3 yards qrtr. Itm 8 Joyned stoolesd cou'ed wth dark grene clothe sutable to the Carpetts 2 lowe stooles cou'ed wth watchett...Itm one great Chayer cou'ed wth blewe Watchet velvet wth armes & fringed wth changeable...3 Wyndowe Cusshions cou'ed with watchet velvet fringed wth gold.*

watching bill, staff a BILL or staff carried by a watchman. *1591: one Sworde & one watchin bill xijd. 1595: ij watching bills one bowe & iij arrowes. 1597: j watching Staffe viijd. 1717: One Chest, one old trunk a spinning wheel and two old watch-bills 6s.*

water barrow, water cart a hand-cart consisting of a tub or barrel mounted on gimbals on a wheeled frame, for transporting water. *1663: a tree for the water cart & treeing & staving 2s. 1738: A Water Barrow 4s.*

232

waterboard 1. Weatherboard, horizontal cladding board with a wedge-shaped section, the thin upper edge being overlapped by the thicker lower edge of the board above. 2. Board to throw off water, for example EAVESBOARD, under the lower edge, or BARGEBOARD, on the gable-end, of a thatched roof. The quotations from 1296-1419 are probably all eavesboards or bargeboards. The *clav'* of 1296 and 1363 are probably the same as the *middelspykys* of 1339. *1296: x clav' ad waterbord q'. 1323: [2 boards for] waterbords [of the hall 4d.]. 1339: xl middelspykys p̱ Wat'bordes [of the barn 1d.]. 1361: vij sparres p̱ le Wat'bordes [of the vicar's house 7d.]. 1363: in clav' [bought to attach] Wat'bordes ijd. 1419: in longe clav' [bought for] le Watbord [of the same stable 1d.]. 1541: bord, steppyng & waterbord agen the stepyll.*

water closet the medieval PRIVY was flushed out by bucket from time to time, and a closet flushed from a cistern was built in London in 1449. A mechanism for flushing a privy from a cistern was invented by Sir John Harrington in 1596, and flushable water-closets were in use by the middle of the 18th century, though there are few traces of them in inventories as the rooms normally contained little or no furniture. See CLOSE STOOL. *c.1830: Water Closet. A painted deal shade outside window. A spring holland blind in box. A small Mahogany box. A brass bolt on door. A Mahogany chair for child with convenience. Two painted jars for scent. The brussels carpet as fitted.*

water facine see FARCY

waterfurrow furrow to conduct water away from the ridges of the open field at right angles to and/or between the ridges; a temporary drain channel. See EARTH; GRUPP.

watergong watercourse, mill-leat. *1321: Joyberdes watergongs xiiijd.*

water-hen the moorhen, *Gallinula chloropus*. Edible, but tough and fishy. *1533: a watter hen kylled wt the gun.*

watering bridle a bridle with a snaffle-bit, used for taking horses to watering. *1738: Four Bridles Three Watering Bridles.*

water plate a plate with a cavity underneath for hot water to keep the food warm. *1738: Half a dozen Water Plates 1 li. 1s. 1779: six water Plates Two Water Dishes.*

watertable the top course of the plinth of a wall, sloping to throw off the rain. See TABLE BRICK. *1620: [brick] to the height of the water table on both sides the building is contained 725 foot 3 brick. From the height of the water table to the roofe on both sides and the p̱tisions and stearcases to the roofe windows and dores deducted is contained 2965 foote 1½ brick. 1665: water table bricke & skewes.*

water wowe see WOWE

waur, were weir, dam; pit. *1325: [cleaning out] j Waure in Le Launde iiijd. 1325: [cleaning out] Waure [at the gate 2d.]. 1326: [making] del Waur vd. 1336: [fishing] dil Were xs.*

waxpunde see POUND

way, weigh, wey OTeut *weg*, to move, journey, carry; unit of weight. In 1302/3 it was 175 lb. (14 stone of 12½ lb. each) for LEAD, wool, tallow and CHEESE, but in 1430 it was declared to be 224 lb. or two hundredweight, and it continued at that figure into the 19th century, although in Suffolk the way of cheese was 256 lb. and in Essex it was 336 lb. The way of wool in 1638 was 182 POUNDS, and in 1674 a way of SALT was 40 bushels. See R.D. Connor, *The Weights and Measures of England*, 130-1, 170. *1498-9: a weye of cheese xs. 1562: a Waye of chese being xxij cheeses xxijs. vjd...for di' a waye of cheses beinge xxiiij cheeses. . .To Hicks of Tyvetsall for xv cheeses beinge j weye besides viij cheeses beinge di' a weye given by Ricks of the same towne xxiiijs. 1594: Lxxiij cheses beinge in weighte a waye and a quarter xls. 1595: one waye & a halfe of chese iij li. 1655: 1 weigh and Halfe of 2 meale cheese 2 li. 2s.*

weasel ling a marine fish. See SANDLING. OED suggests a rockling, but the price in the quotation suggests the weasel ling was bigger than even the largest of the rocklings, the three-bearded rockling *Gaidropsarus vulgaris*, which averages about 16 inches in length and

233

under 2 lb. in weight. Sir Thomas Browne: 'Mustela marina called by some a wesell ling which salted and dryed becomes a good Lenten dish.' Perhaps Browne meant the smooth hound, *Mustelus mustelus*, a small shark, which can reach over 5 feet in length, but it is more likely to have been the lamprey, *Petromyzon marinus*, identified by Nall: 'Weasel Ling. The lamprey, *gadus mustela*, grows up to 3 ft and weighs over 5 lb. At one time considered a delicacy, its flesh is rich and oily.' *1654: 9 Sandlins & one weasell Linge 6s.*

weaver's board perhaps the weaver's beam, used in setting up the warp on the loom. *1596: j payer weavers bords.*

web webbing, a band of strong material used for girths on horses, to support beds etc. *1655: for girt webb 2s. 6d.*

web a sheet of lead. *1588: x webbes of leades & ij peacis price xls*

web the measurements of cloth are very complicated: see R.D. Connor, *The Weights and Measures of England*, pp 87-95. In the 15th century the statute width of broadcloth was supposed to be 63-72 inches. This would make sheets of 3 webs (see 1484 quot.) between 15 feet 9 inches and 18 feet, which seems rather too large. Even if the web were the same as the ell, 45 inches, three webs would produce a measurement of 11 feet 3 inches. A bed 6 feet wide would require sheets of a minimum width of 9 to 10 feet, making the web 36-40 inches. *1459: j payre of schetys, every schete iiij schete iiij webbes*[sic]...*ij fustian blanketts, every of hem vj webbys. 1484: ij peir of my fynest shetes, ich of iij Webbes, a fine Hedshete of ij Webbes. 1501-2: for a webbe of heyr iiijs. viijd. & for a webbe of sekken iiijs. viijd.*

webbing woven cloth, linen. *1590: xxⁱ payer of Shetes of Webbin of div's sorted v li.* [and 12 pillowberes, 8 hand towels, 3 dozen napkins, 8 table cloths, 1 cupboard cloth, and 4 shirts, all of 'webbing'].

wedderys see WETHER

wedehoc see WEEDING HOOK

wedge for splitting logs, hammered in with a sledge hammer. *1631: one Ieren wegh. 1649: a new wedge wayeinge 8 li. & a halfe 1s. 4d.*

weeding hook 1. A draw-hoe, the normal type of garden or field HOE. 2. A pair of elongated pincers, which grasped the stem of the weed between the jaws and enabled it to be pulled out without the operator having to bend his back and dive into the standing corn. 3. A stick about 3 feet long with a forked end, the weed being jammed in the fork with the curved end of another stick and pulled out. See p. 242. 4. A draw-hoe with a V-shaped blade, the inner edges sharpened to cut through the stem of the weed. *1352: [1 new] Wedehoc. 1592: viij weedinge hooks. 1592: a syeth & a sickle & a pease pik & 2 weding hooks ijs. 1595: on drafte howke on payer Chenes with a Fetterloke & iiij weadynge howkes.*

wegh see WEDGE

weghe see SWEY

weigh of cheese see WAY

weilbarugh see WHEELBARROW

weld, weilde dyer's rocket or weld, *Reseda luteola*, which gives a brilliant, pure, fast yellow dye. *1590: fyve acres of weilde ls.*

well there were two basic types of well: 1. Deep, from which water was drawn by (a) a bucket on the end of a rope or chain wound around a horizontal capstan, or (b) buckets on hooks attached to an endless rope or chain running on a pulley and operated directly by hand. 2. Shallow, from which the water was drawn either (a) by scooping it up with a bucket held in the hand or on a short rope or (b) by a bucket on the end of a counterbalanced and swinging pole, the SWIPE. Lined wells were built from the top downwards, the shaft being gradually deepened and a cylinder of brick, flint, or wood

234

built up to the lower edge of the cylinder above it. If a surface spring were available the water would often be contained within a large tank or cistern. By the 17th century at the latest water could be drawn up by a PUMP. See p. 242; BUCKET; FATHOM; SNEAP; STOUP. *1323: j axe [for the well 11d...1 rope of 14 fathoms for the well 5d.]. 1352: j stoppe & j Wellerop. 1361: j Wellerop [containing 4½ fathoms 3d.]...[making] ij lynkes [for the chain of the well 2d. digging the well 10d.]. 1382: [thatching] dil Wellhos. 1664: Md that Rich: Shuckforth of Disse plummer hath altered the force of the well pumpe.*

wellett see VELVET

werenet fishnet for use at the weir or dam. *1296: [mending] le Werenet xd.*

wereyren, wereiron see CART

wesontyd Whitsuntide. *1466: And at thes nexte wesontyd.*

westfaleham Westphalia ham. *1648: 1 westfaleham 3s. 6d.*

westment a vestment. *1552: j westment red wellet.*

wet larder the LARDER where drink and moist, liquid food was stored. *1589: In the weet Larder one Saltinge trow 3 stooles 2 cheesefatts & one shelfe. 1665: the inward wett larder towards the kitchen yard.*

weteston a whetstone, sharpening stone. See RUB. *1310: j weteston jd. ob.*

wether adult male sheep, usually castrated. *1484: iij good fatt wedderys. 1588: in Sheape, viz, Ewes, Wethers & hogges, fyvescore and seaventen xx li.*

wey see WAY

wharle see WHORL

wheel wooden wheels, either spoked or solid, turned on wooden NAVES and were lubricated with tallow or animal grease. See CART; PLOUGH. *1620: 5 furres in ye wheles & 5 li. pith & ½ li. tallow for ye nafes.*

wheel, spinning the spinning wheel reached Europe in the 13th century, and was in general use by the 15th, although the spindle, which could spin more tightly and finely than the wheel, remained in use throughout the 16th and 17th centuries.

wheelbarrow the wheelbarrow was developed from the hand-barrow, a stretcher-like construction carried by two men, and seems to have come into general use by the 13th century. Medieval illustrations usually show it without legs. See p. 242; BARROW; CRUDBARROW. *1537: a weilbarugh xd.*

wheelstool a stool on wheels or casters.

whey butter buttermilk, the acidulous milk left after the butter is made. *1655: a firkin of whey butter 9s. 6d.*

whins, quinnis gorse or FURZE, *Ulex europæus*, was cut and used for fuel, particularly for brewing, baking, and brick-burning. 'Whins' might also cover broom (*Cytisus scoparius*) and heather (*Calluna vulgaris*) - see 1319 quotation. Whins were also dug and cut for dead hedges. *1318: quinnis [sold 2s. 6d.]. 1319: [mowing] de quynnes xjd. 1321: j acra de quynnes [sold 5s. 6d.]. 1362: De Whynnes [sold this year nothing]. 1363: in whinnes [bought against harvest 2s.]. 1396: [wage of 3 men working 1 day in cutting heather] & whinnes [against harvest 16d.]. 1648: for the digin of 2 loade of whins 2s...for the digin of 2 loade to fence in the hempland 2s.*

whin gloves leather gloves to protect the hands of those handling WHINS. *1537: a payer of whynne gloves.*

whin hew a billhook for cutting WHINS. *1587: one Ravens bill...A whyn hewe.*

whirdle a hurdle. *1621: wheels wheel barrowe whirdles & other lombardie.*

whisk a fly, a simple winnowing implement for separating the corn from the chaff. See also FAN. *1685: one whisk & forkes & rakes 10s. 1730: a whisk 2 ridles A bushell & Fan & windle 18s. 1742: One Whisk &c to Dress corn.*

235

whisk, whisker a brush, duster of hair or feathers. *1649: 1 mope brought by Chamberlyn 9d. 1 longe Whisker 8d. 1654: markum broom & 4 whisks.*
whisk hand implement for beating eggs, mixing drink etc. *1655: glasses, potts, whiskes, Pottspoones &c...Glasses, whiskes, Pipes &c.*
whitecharrell see CARRELL
white lead lead carbonate or lead hydroxycarbonate, a basic pigment of paint. *1664: white lead...3 qrters of a hundred 13 pound and an halfe xxxiijs. xjd. ob...white lead one hundred & fourteen pound at 34s. p̱ cent xxxviijs. iijd...one firkin for lead viijd.*
white leather leather of a natural or light colour. See TANNING.
white money silver coins. *1594: gowlde iij li. xixs. iiijd. in white mony iij li.*
white pea a small-seeded variety of pea, cultivated as a garden or field crop. *1594: ij acres & qr whight peas.*
whitester a cloth-bleacher. *Prompt. Parv.* : 'Bleystare, or wytstare'. *1718: James Mendham, whitester, Pulham St Mary...the whiteing House.*
whitethorn the hawthorn, *Crataegus monogyna*, or the Midland hawthorn *C. oxyacantha* (less common) used for hedging. *1619-20: ij longe Whitethorne setts ijs. 1654: white Thorne Laire to 4 Rodd 2s.* See LAIR; QUICKSETT.
whorl, wharl the leaden or stone weight at the end of the SPINDLE that maintains the momentum. *1595: spyndelles & wharles & other tryfles.*
wicket 1. A small door, gate, often of thin uprights. 2. A grill, loophole, opening. *1320: [making pales before the hall 12d. In gunphis and vertivells for] j Wyket [of the same 2d.]. 1449: have made wykets on every quarter of the hwse to schote owte atte, bothe with bowys and with hand gunnys.*
wifle OE *wifel*, to wave, swing, shake; a weapon or symbolic weapon, the precise form of which may have varied. A whiffler was a man carrying a LATTEN or wooden sword who marched in front to clear the way for the procession of the Norwich corporation. Until the 15th century at least it seems to have been a serious weapon, either a sword or a spear. *1449: Gonore spaketo my maisteresse that she shuld make here men to leve here wyfeles and here jackis. 1459: Item, j borespere Item, vj wifles Item, j rede pavys.*
wild man see WODEWOSE
wilderness the informal, or wilder, part of a renaissance or formal garden of the 16th-18th centuries, usually consisting of shrubs and groves of trees planted in geometrical patterns, or a grove cut by straight and curving walks with occasional openings. *1709: plants for the Quarters of the Willdernes.*
wimble Anglo-Fr. *wimble*, a variant form of *guimble*, yielding the diminutive *gimlet*. A gimlet, auger, PIERCER; a brace to hold bits, often of considerable size. See p. 242; TERRIER. *Prompt. Parv.* : 'Wymbyl, or persowre. *Terebellum.*' *1319: j martell ij Wymbles & ij p̱ceurs. 1352: j Wymbel j thixhel j chisel. 1588:[plouwright] x wimbles. 1590: [joiner] iij wimbles xviijd. 1590: ij tap wimbles. 1595: ix planyngs A palinge wimble and other smale tooles & tryflyng things in the Inner Shope ijs. viijd. 1665: lengthened a wimble for the boaring of a hole in the plugg to let the Wast water out of the moate.*
windac a winch, windlass; iron apparatus for drawing the cord of a CROSSBOW. *1449: I... prey zw to gete som crosse bowis, and wyndacs to bynd them with, and quarrels; for zour hwsis ben so low that ther may non man schet owt with no long bowe.*
windbe•m, winebeam, wyndbeme 1. Cross-beam, collar tying together the principal rafters in a roof. 2. A windbrace, a brace from the principal rafter to the PURLIN, to counter longitudinal movement in a roof. See p. 175. *1298: xxiij cuppļ j roftre iiij stuch ij Barfreys ij Byer' & iij Wyndbemes. 1661: 2 winebeames at the end of the stable.*
winding narrow strip of cloth or linen, used for dress, bandage, wrapping a baby or a

corpse. etc. *1680: 1 doz winding 1s. 6d...2 yd winding 3d.*

winding band iron tyres, or iron bands to repair or strengthen cartwheels. *1310: In Wyndyngbondes [for 1 wheel bought 2d.]. 1649: 2 windeinge bands for the cart wheeles 1s. 8d.*

windle OE *windel*, from *winden*, to plait; a basket, skep; sometimes a FAN. *1306: ij Wyndel jd. ob. 1306: [mending] iiij cophines viij wyndel [and 1 seedleap 4d.]. 1592: Two fans one Wynle one Corne Skreene. 1593: 2 riddles 2 windles 2 bushells. 1619: 2 splitter buz skeepes, 6 windles & A hand basket iijs...A Cator Basket & iiij windles iijs. iiijd...xij windles or Skeppes iijs...Lyne to fyx togethir xij windles. 1648: 2 windleskeps 10d.*

windle capstan, windlass. *1738: Ship Wreck Timber...The windle and Sixteen Oak pieces 1 li. 3s.*

window cloth a window CURTAIN. Curtains came into use in the 16th century, but until the 18th century most small and medium-sized houses relied on external or internal shutters. *1588: Two wyndowe clothes of Fustyan of Naples striped vjd. one other wyndowe Clothe of grene Cotton iiijd. 1597: one wyndowe cloth Turky Worke Long 2 yards: lat: one ell.*

window cushion a CUSHION for a seat on the sill or recess of a window. *1588: a carpett of grene brode cotten...j longe windowe Cusshinge of like grene and redde furgured...a Wyndowe Cusshinge of olde peces of clothe bodkyn iijs. iiijd.*

windownail a small NAIL. *1343: m^{l}c de windowenayl ijs. ob. qu.*

window shade see SHADE

window stick stick to draw curtains and blinds. *1751: two Mahogany Window sticks.*

wind stove stove or fireplace with damper or register to restrict the flue aperture. *1751: a Wind Stove compleat.*

winnow cloth, winecloth cloth or canvas used to catch the chaff when corn is winnowed with a FAN, i.e. cast in the air to separate the heavy grain from the light chaff. *1352: j Wynewecloth & ij Rydeles. 1591: wineclothes with six Sakes.*

winter corn corn, usually wheat or rye, sown in the autumn and therefore growing through the winter. SUMMER CORN, usually barley, was sown in the spring. *1587: in the wintercorne bearne in wheat and Rye not threshed by estimatio' 20 combes 6 li. 13s. 4d. In the barlie barne. 1602:[June] Corne on the ground Itm the wintercorne vj li. Itm the Somer corne iiij li. 1674: [15 August] eight & twenty acres of Wynter Corne 40 li. three & Forty acres of sumer Corne 50 li.*

winterfare a set of sails for use on a fishing boat in winter. *1584: Sea ware...two towes, 2 bollances for the winterfare.*

withdraught private chamber, closet, privy. See DRAWT, and following entry. *1459: My maister is Chambre and the withedraughte withe the Stable.*

withdrawing chamber room to which the family could withdraw from the great HALL or great CHAMBER for more privacy. It became the DRAWING-ROOM in the 18th century. *1621: carpenters worke For the bracketing of the gallery round about & the great chamber & withdrawing chamber.*

wode, wood OE *wód*, possessed, mad, lunatic. *1455: Howard was as wode as a wilde bullok.*

wodewose, woodwose, woodhouse OE *wudewása*, wild man of the woods, faun, satyr, green man. A favourite subject in medieval and 16th-century art, usually shown with vegetation springing from all parts of his body. One of the origins of the surname Woodhouse. *1459: j clothe of arras for the dese in the same halle, with j wodewuse and j chylde in his armys. 1537-8: paid ijd. to a man gadderyng moss to aray a woodhouse. 1597: a tester paned wth black velvet & watchet sylk: wth the goate & the wylde man ymbrodered thereon.*

wolding line MLG *wolen*, Flem. *woeln*, to bind, wind cord around e.g. mast or scaffolding. *Prompt. Parv.* : 'Wolynge, or stronge byyndynge (woldynge, K.)' *1619-20: for 21 li. woulding line 7s.*

wolhous the woolhouse, the building or room where wool was kept.

womb 1. Belly for making into soft leather. 2. The stomach, supplying rennet used in the process of making cheese. *1513: for wombys vjs.*

womb, turnip ? a belly-shaped skep, for collecting turnips in the field. *1752: 4 Seed Laps 6 Turnip wombs 3 Turnip Picks.*

womb rope belly-rope or girth for a horse. *1417: for lyne for womberopys ijd. 1663: for a new wombe rope and a redgewith 5½ li. - ijs. iijd.*

wong OE *wang, wong* field. A field, part of the open field; meadow. Does not seem to mean a specific type of soil, area, or shape. *1328: stondwong.*

woodhouse see WODEWOSE

wood knife see SKEYNE

wood leg a wooden leg for preserving the shape of stockings while drying. *1764: 4 Wood Legs for stockings.*

wool cards two oblong pieces of wood set with metal teeth, one fixed to a bench and the other held in the hand, for carding or combing wool. *1595: A payer of wooll cards.*

wool chapman trader or merchant in wool. *1648: for the Wooll Chapmens dynners at Siderstone 4s. 2d. More spent uppon their men at there Suppers and the next day morneinge at there Breckfast 5s. 9d.*

workhouse 1. A workshop. *1592: Lumberment in the workehowse. 1620: ye Building...wher the Old Bearn is ther agayne to be builded for a Workehouse.* 2. A poorhouse.

wormseed dried head of certain plants e.g. hog's fennel or sulphurwort, *Peucedanum officinalis*; treacle (mustard) or English wormseed, *Erysimum cheiranthoides*; and various species of artemesia, used as a treatment for parasitic worms - flatworm, roundworm, tapeworm - in the human body. *1587: oz & a halfe of wormseed & more xiijd. 1680: a plaster against wormes 6d. wormseed i oz 1s.*

wormwood the bitter leaves of wormwood, *Artemesia absinthium*, were used as a tonic and a treatment for worms, for protecting clothes and bed-clothes from moths, and in flavouring. Roman wormwood is *A. pontica. 1642: 1 pot wth Conserve of roman Wormewood 2s. 9d.*

wort sieve, temse, tub, vat wort is the infusion of malt which, fermented, becomes beer. See BREWING; TEMSE; VAT. *1591: j wort tubb. 1594: a worte temse. 1636: Two sweet woorte fattes. 1664: one woort seive.*

wowe, wough OE *wág, wah*, wall. *Prompt. Parv.* : 'Wowe, wal (wowe or wall, K.P.). *Paries, murus.*' *1498-9: [For the repair] of the Wheell at the Bysshopys Mylle and for the makyng of bothe Water Wowes xxiiijs.*

wrest tool for turning bolts or screws; screwdriver, spanner. *1590: ij fils wt a wrest & gong.*

wrestyrin see PLOUGH

wrethyn with twisted or twining decoration. *1459: potte of silver wrethyn.*

wrong ON *wronge, rong*, rib of ship, from *wrangr*, bent; bent timber for boat-building; bent branch. *1415-16: [received of Henry Bakon for] Wrongges [of boats].*

wudehock woodhook, for splitting or chopping wood. *1313: j wudehocke iiijd. ob.*

wy- see wi-

wycher wicker

wyllyng woollen. *1592: iiij pownd of wyllyng yearne xvjd.*

wynd possibly WINDLE. *1306: in vj Wynd [bought 2½d.].*

wyndas a windlass. *1410: [grease for the] wyndas.*

wyndfork ? sheaf-fork, pitchfork. See FORK. *1352: iiij Wyndforks.*

wynew see WINNOW

wynle, wynler see WINDLE

X

X as a Roman numeral x = 10; therefore xx = 20, xxx = 30, lxx = 70, etc. Used above the line as a multiplier, e.g. v^{xx} = 5 x 20 = 100. Used before another figure, 10 is subtracted from that figure e.g. xl = 40. See C; D; I; J; L; M; V.

x in the 14th-16th centuries x was used, particularly in East Anglian mss., for some words beginning sc-, sh, sch-. *1448: Kateryn Walsam xal be weddyd on the Munday nexst after Trinyte Sonday, as it is told me, to the galaunte with the grete chene.* See also Z.

Y

Y often used as an alternative to i, in the middle of a word or as an initial letter e.g. hangyng, whynns, ymagery. And see Z.

yard OE *geard*, fence, house, enclosed area. The second element in courtyard, orchard, vineyard. Used on its own for courtyard, backyard, enclosed field adjacent to house or farm; farmyard. *1591: [and the garden called] the yarde.*

yard OE *gieard, gyrd, gird*, stick, rod, staff. A measure of length, established by the early 12th century, to make 5½ yards = 1 ROD, a land measure already existing. Traditionally said to be the distance from Henry I's nose to the tip of his outstretched finger, the standard yard of 3 feet or 36 inches was established by *c.*1100, and was formalised by iron bars of a yard in length *c.*1196. The cloth yard added an inch (about the breadth of a thumb) to make 37 inches, but by the early 15th century some merchants added a hand's breadth (about four inches) to each yard of cloth. A statute of 1439 allowed the yard + inch and prohibited the yard + hand, but in spite of this the latter continued in use until the 16th century. See R.D. Connor, *The Weights and Measures of England*, 1987, 83-5. In some contexts a yard was an area of land, varying locally from a ROOD i.e. a quarter of an acre, to 30 acres.

yard the penis, a sarcastic reference to length. *1637-9: Shewinge his yarde & privie member.*

yard-pole horizontal timber of a fence. *1718: 74 yard-poles wth their Bearᵣˢ and crutches 1 li. 5s.*

yarn, yearne, yern, yorne see IRON

yatch a yacht. *1709: a case for glasses, from the yatch.*

yate a gate. *1424: the yates of the Priorie of the Trinite chirche of Norwiche.*

yearday annual commemoration of the death of a benefactor, celebrated in the unreformed church by a mass. *1484: which yerday I wille myn heire kepe in the same Cherch for me, my seid Husband, and myn Auncetes, yerly, during the t'me of xij yeres aft' my decese.*

yeere an ear. *1590: pann wth Two yeeres.*

yegys eggs.

yelfate see BREWING; GYLE

yellows jaundice. *1664: drinching & dressing the blacke gelding called Symonds supposing he had the yellowes xxd.*

yeoman from youngman, a medieval term for a servant or attendant in a great household; by the 16th century applied to a freeholder of land below the rank of gentleman. A mark of status rather than a term based strictly on economics, it was sometimes used by the maker of a will when his neighbours, making his inventory, would term him tanner, brewer, or even HUSBANDMAN.

yeomans see BREAD

239

yew *Taxus baccata*, the best wood for the long-BOW, although other wood, notably elm, was also used. *1588: one Ewghe bowe & some shafftes ijs. vjd. 1590: one bagg wt yugh bowes. c'teine yugh bowestaves.*

yewere see EWERY

ymagerie see IMAGERY

ynne an inn; eating place, lodgings. *1597: Footemans ynne vizt the Chamber next the lytle plor: ye est Chambr on the south syde of the howse.*

yoke, yok 1. A wooden yoke fitted to the shoulders of oxen for traction. 2. A piece of wood fitting over human shoulders to support a bucket at each end. 3. A frame put round a pig's neck to stop it getting through hedges. *1621: 2 pitchforke shafts 1s. & 10 hogs yoks 18d.*

youery see EWERY

ypocras hippocras, spiced wine. *1464: a potelle of ypocrasse xxd. 1588: ij gallons of ypocras.*

yugh see YEW

Z

Z in later ME scripts the letter y, particularly as the initial letter of a word, was often written as *ʒ*, a loose form of OE ʒ, and in manuscripts was often identical with the letter z and is so printed in many transcriptions. In this glossary, where this form occurs in quotations, either from ms. or printed sources, a z is used, e.g. *c.1449: I pray zw that ze wyl vowche save to don bye for me j li. of almands and j li. of sugyr, and that ze wille do byen sume frese to maken of zour child is gunys. 1513: vj zards iij qrters murrey.*

Medieval hall

1. Bench 2. Table dormant on daïs 3. Canvas tablecloth 4. Sanap or savenap 5. Dish or doubler
6. Perch or perk 7. Laver 8. Chest 9. Saucer 10. Gotch 11. Andiron 12. Candlestick 13. Salt

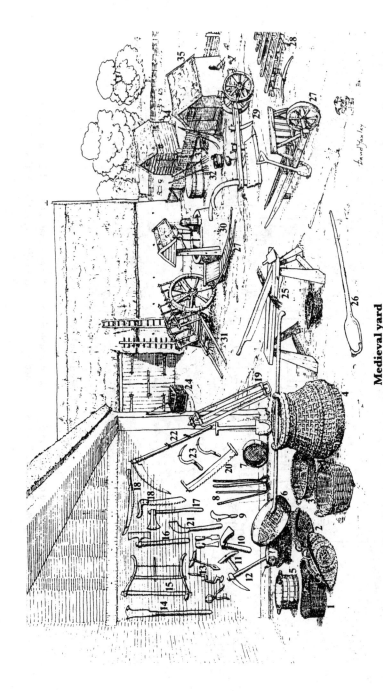

Medieval yard

1. Pannier 2. Fans 3. Skeps 4. Bearing-skep 5. Bushel 6. Riddle 7. Sieve 8. Weedhooks 9. Hook 10. Adze 11. Twybill
12. Pick 13. Wimbles 14. Bill 15. Bow-saw 16. Side-axe 17. Belt 18. Handsaw 19. Pit saw 20. Overthwart saw 21. Axe
22. Scythe 23. Sickles 24. Seedleap 25. Hemp cutter and beater 26. Shovel 27. Wheelbarrow 28. Harrow 29. Plough
30. Well and stoup 31. Cart 32. Muckhook 33. Muck fork 34. Foldcote 35. Fowlhouse

APPENDIX

The following are some of the terms to be found in collections of deeds. For a full explanation see Julian Cornwall, *How to Read Old Title Deeds* (1970)

Bargain and sale an agreement by INDENTURE between two persons to convey the use of a property in the ownership of the grantor A to the grantee B, while the SEISIN remained with A. By the 17th century the Bargain and Sale could include specific ENFEOFFMENT or transfer of ownership with livery of seisin.

demise to transfer property or estate to another.

fee farm the result of a demise to a tenant. See below, lease.

fee simple an heritable estate held from a lord by the performance of services.

enfeoffment, feoffment act or document (charter of feoffment) conveying the fee simple or ownership under the Crown of property, land etc. with its rights, duties, and services.

fine and recovery a fictitious action at law to register the title to property and to bar the entail. In the medieval fine A (plaintiff) began the action in a royal court against B (deforceant) for possession of the property and with leave of the court made a 'final agreement' (the fine) conceding the plaintiff's title, 3 copies of which were written on an INDENTURE, in Latin until 1733. Details of acreage of land were conventional and generally larger than reality. The fine was used in a MORTGAGE to convey the fee simple. A recovery, in use by the reign of Edward IV, was a fictitious lawsuit in which A (plaintiff) claimed property from B (respondent) alleged to possess it by a wrongful disseisin by C. B pleads that he had the property from D, whom he summons to vouch for his title. D fails to appear in court, is held in contempt, and the court awards the case to the plaintiff A, who 'recovers' his property, thus assuring his title to it. The recovery was published as an Exemplification in the form of a royal writ. Fines and recoveries were abolished in 1833.

indenture a deed and its counterpart(s) written on a single piece of vellum and separated by an indented cut so that the parts could be matched in the event of a dispute.

lease a document conveying the use of a property, similar to BARGAIN AND SALE but using the phrase 'demise grant and to farm let', for a term of years or lives and for a substantial rent, often with conditions.

lease and release from *c.* 1614, a form of bargain in which A leases his property to B for a year for a nominal consideration, followed immediately by a release of the freehold reversion from A to B for a substantial sum, in effect selling the property to B.

mortgage a document pledging property as security for a loan, with a DEMISE for a long term e.g. 500 years, which is void on repayment of the loan. A mortgage sometimes took the form of a FEOFFMENT or a LEASE AND RELEASE.

seisin actual possession, as opposed to ownership, of property.